"This book offers a timely and comprehensive selection of topics for anyone who cares about making progress on societal challenges. The carefully curated chapters offer deep insights into how to organize for and around sustainable development. A must read for students and researchers!"

– **Johanna Mair**, PhD, Professor of Organization, Strategy and Leadership, Hertie School of Governance, Berlin, Distinguished Fellow at the Stanford Center on Philanthropy and Civil Society, Co-Director of the Global Innovation for Impact Lab

"Achieving the Sustainable Development Goals requires a collective human effort with a key role for all kinds of different organizations, each playing their part. This book provides a unique insight into how various forms of for-profit and non-profit ways of organizing have emerged to help address grand challenges such as global poverty and climate change. It brings together so far disconnected theoretical perspectives and applies their insights to insightful cases related to sustainable development. The book forms a great starting point for much-needed, more impactful management and organization research."

– **Jonatan Pinkse**, PhD, Professor of Strategy, Innovation, and Entrepreneurship, Executive Director of the Manchester Institute of Innovation Research (MIoIR), Alliance Manchester Business School, University of Manchester

"It is high time to go back to the fundamental question of purpose for today's organizations: are they truly working towards a more sustainable future? This volume does just that by discussing topics such as the future of NGO management, the dynamics of inter-sectoral collaborations, and the continuous struggle of appropriately measuring social impact, to name just a few. The book brings academic research closer to overarching societal questions and highlights the need for more integrated work between research and practice in tackling grand challenges. It serves as an opportunity to reflect on our individual roles and that of our organizations to truly shape a more just and sustainable world."

– **Alexandra Ioan**, PhD, Head of the Ashoka Learning and Action Center

"This book brilliantly discusses organizational solutions for sustainability challenges. More than other books on grand challenges and sustainability, this one explicitly focuses on organizational, supra-organizational and intra-organizational practices and structures – from corporate social responsibility, hybrid organizing and base-of-the-pyramid innovation, to impact investing, multi-stakeholder arrangements and inter-organizational networks. I congratulate the authors on a very timely, relevant and well-developed contribution to our understanding of the organizational challenges and opportunities in shaping a more sustainable future."
– **Stephan Manning**, PhD, Professor of Strategy and Innovation, Co-Chair of Responsible Business Research Group, University of Sussex Business School

"This book builds on a strong assumption: Norms and values give shape to our organisations and to how we organise. New types of organisation and new ways of organising have emerged with the aim to create value for various stakeholders; important to study, but also to question. The authors in this book offer fresh views on hybridization, networks, and organising for positive impact. Insightful!"
– **Florian Lüdeke-Freund**, PhD, Chair for Corporate Sustainability, ESCP Business School, Berlin, Germany

"Organising for Sustainable Development: Addressing the Grand Challenges is exactly the book we need right now. With clarity and care, it sets out a compelling case for organisational change and how business can contribute to a just transition to inclusive growth. This is a powerful vision of a better way of doing things, and it shows us how we can organise to achieve it."
– **Kate E Pickett**, PhD, FRSA, FFPH, Professor of Epidemiology, Deputy Director of the Centre for Future Health, Associate Director at Leverhulme Centre for Anthropocene Biodiversity, University of York

Organizing for Sustainable Development

The Sustainable Development Goals (SDGs) recognize the increasingly complex, interdependent nature of societal and environmental issues for governments and business. Tackling such "grand challenges" requires the concerted action of a multitude of organizations and multiple stakeholders at different levels in the public, private, and non-profit sector.

Organizing for Sustainable Development provides an integrated and comparative overview of the successes and failures of organizational efforts to tackle global societal issues and achieve sustainable development. Summarizing years of study by an interdisciplinary board of authors and contributors, this book provides readers with an in-depth understanding of how existing businesses and new hybrid organizations can achieve sustainable development to bring about an improved society, marking a key contribution to the literature in this field.

Combining theoretical views with empirical approaches, the chapters in this book are highly relevant to graduate and undergraduate (multidisciplinary) programs in sustainable development, organization studies, development economics, development studies, international management, and social entrepreneurship.

Federica Angeli is Chair in Management at the York Management School, University of York, UK. She has held positions at Tilburg University and Maastricht University, The Netherlands, and was Visiting Scholar at the Indian Institute of Management, Bangalore, India.

Ashley Metz is Assistant Professor of Organization Studies at Tilburg University, The Netherlands, and serves as a Fellow at Human Futures Institute, a think tank focused on sustainable long-term strategy for organizations across sectors.

Jörg Raab is Associate Professor of Policy and Organization Studies at the Department of Organization Studies and Academic Director of the International Bachelor Global Management of Social Issues at Tilburg University, The Netherlands.

Organizing for Sustainable Development

Addressing the Grand Challenges

Federica Angeli, Ashley Metz
and Jörg Raab

Image Credit: © Getty Images / Ivan Bajic

First published 2022
by Routledge
2 Park Square, Milton Park, Abingdon, Oxon OX14 4RN

and by Routledge
605 Third Avenue, New York, NY 10158

Routledge is an imprint of the Taylor & Francis Group, an informa business

© 2022 Federica Angeli, Ashley Metz and Jörg Raab

The right of Federica Angeli, Ashley Metz and Jörg Raab to be identified as
authors of this work has been asserted in accordance with sections 77 and
78 of the Copyright, Designs and Patents Act 1988.

The Open Access version of this book, available at www.taylorfrancis.com,
has been made available under a Creative Commons Attribution-Non
Commercial (CC-BY-NC) 4.0 International license.

Trademark notice: Product or corporate names may be trademarks or registered
trademarks, and are used only for identification and explanation without intent
to infringe.

British Library Cataloguing-in-Publication Data
A catalogue record for this book is available from the British Library

Library of Congress Cataloging-in-Publication Data
Names: Angeli, Federica, author. | Metz, Ashley, author. | Raab, Jörg, author.
Title: Organizing for sustainable development : addressing the grand challenges /
    Federica Angeli, Ashley Metz and Jörg Raab.
Description: 1 Edition. | New York, NY : Routledge, 2022. | Includes
    bibliographical references and index.
Identifiers: LCCN 2021051828 (print) | LCCN 2021051829 (ebook) | ISBN
    9780367197681 (hardback) | ISBN 9780367197698 (paperback) | ISBN
    9780429243165 (ebook)
Subjects: LCSH: Organizational change. | Industrial management. | Social
    responsibility of business. | Sustainable development.
Classification: LCC HD58.8 .A724 2022 (print) | LCC HD58.8 (ebook) | DDC
    658.4/06—dc23/eng/20211210
LC record available at https://lccn.loc.gov/2021051828
LC ebook record available at https://lccn.loc.gov/2021051829

ISBN: 978-0-367-19768-1 (hbk)
ISBN: 978-0-367-19769-8 (pbk)
ISBN: 978-0-429-24316-5 (ebk)

DOI: 10.4324/9780429243165

The Open Access version of this book was funded by Tilburg University Library.

Contents

Editors	ix
Contributors	xi
Acknowledgments	xiv
List of Figures, Tables and Boxes	xv

Introduction: A Compelling Call to Address the Grand Challenges through New Forms of Organising   1
FEDERICA ANGELI, ASHLEY METZ AND JÖRG RAAB

1   **Corporate Responsibility: An Overview**   15
JULIA BARTOSCH AND JÖRG RAAB

2   **Responsible innovation: The Role of Organizational Practices and Structures**   31
ASHLEY METZ AND NIKOLAS RATHERT

3   **Understanding the Evolution of BOP Narratives: A Systematic Literature Review and Topic Modeling Analysis**   46
FEDERICA ANGELI

4   **Learning in Hybrid Organizations: A Systematic Literature Review**   73
KRISTIAN MARINOV, ASHLEY METZ, KELLY ALEXANDER, AND FEDERICA ANGELI

5   **On NGOs and Development Management: What Do Critical Management Studies Have to Offer?**   100
EMANUELA GIREI, FEDERICA ANGELI AND ARUN KUMAR

6   **Organizational Networks for Sustainable Development**   117
JÖRG RAAB

7   **Impact Investing and New Social Funding: History, Actors and Promise**   141
LAURA TOSCHI AND ASHLEY METZ

viii *Contents*

8 Social Impact Evaluation: Moving From Method to Realist Strategy   168
GORGI KRLEV AND FEDERICA ANGELI

9 Fix Forward – Building Experts: An exemplary case of a
hybrid organization and its quest for financial independence   191
KELLY ALEXANDER AND JÖRG RAAB

10 Value Co-Creation Through Multi-Stakeholder Collaborations for
Health in Fragile Settings: The Case of the High-Risk Pregnancy
Referral Tool   212
SIMONA ROCCHI, ZAHRA SULTANY, FEDERICA ANGELI, PATRAY LUI,
STEPHANIE SARASWATI CRISTIN AND KOEN JOOSSE

11 Medical Device Innovation at the Base of the Pyramid: General
Electrics' India Strategy to Make Healthcare Affordable   236
ANAND KUMAR JAISWAL AND FEDERICA ANGELI

12 Moving Beyond Fragmented Traditions: Toward an Integrated View
of Organizing for Sustainable Development   261
ASHLEY METZ, FEDERICA ANGELI AND JÖRG RAAB

Index   270

Editors

Federica Angeli

Federica Angeli is Chair in Management at the York Management School, University of York. She obtained her PhD in Management and a *Laurea* in Industrial Engineering *(summa cum laude)* from the University of Bologna. She has held positions at Tilburg University and Maastricht University and was a visiting scholar at the Indian Institute of Management, Bangalore. Her interdisciplinary research investigates how organizational forms and policymaking practices adapt and learn to address complex societal issues, with a particular focus on inclusive healthcare delivery and poverty alleviation. Her work has been published in Social Science & Medicine, Sociology of Health and Illness, Regional Studies, Research in the Sociology of Organizations, Organization & Environment, *PLOS One*, World Development and Long Range Planning among other international outlets. She serves as Academic Editor for *PLOS One* and is Fellow of The Royal Society for Arts, Manufactures and Commerce.

Ashley Metz

Ashley Metz is Assistant Professor of Organization Studies at Tilburg University and serves as Research Fellow at Human Futures Institute, a think tank focused on applied insight and foresight practices. She has conducted research to support progress on social challenges such as sustainability and health via two linked research lines: (1) Social innovation, including social enterprises and impact investing, and (2) Technology adoption for grand challenges, and institutional change involved, particularly in healthcare settings. She is inspired by practice and prior industry experience with technology firms, bringing a first-hand understanding of technology adoption challenges, social innovation and unintended outcomes. She holds degrees from Northwestern University (BA), IESE Business School (MBA) and the Hertie School (PhD). Her work has appeared in the Academy of Management Journal and Technological Forecasting & Social Change, as well as in articles for practitioners.

Jörg Raab

Jörg Raab is Associate Professor of Policy and Organization Studies at the Department of Organization Studies and Academic Director of the International Bachelor Global Management of Social Issues at Tilburg University, The Netherlands. He received his PhD in Public Policy and Management in 2000 at the University

x *Editors*

of Konstanz, Germany. He has conducted research in the fields of (temporary) organizations, inter- and intra-organizational relationships, policy networks and the governance, and effectiveness of purpose-oriented networks. He has published in journals such as the Journal of Public Administration Research and Theory, Public Administration Review, Research Policy, Organization Studies and the Journal of Management Inquiry.

Contributors

Kelly Alexander is a PhD candidate at the School of Social and Behavioral Sciences at Tilburg University, and is currently researching Social Entrepreneurship in Sub-Saharan Africa. Her research interests include social entrepreneurship, hybrid organizations, and the influence of the institutional environment – specifically in the SSA context. Kelly has a Masters in Development Sociology and, in a former life, worked in research and consulting roles focused on a number of African economies and other emerging markets.

Julia Bartosch is a postdoctoral researcher at the Freie Universität Berlin. She received her PhD in Management from Freie Universität Berlin. Her research centers around the topic of corporate responsibility and corporate irresponsibility, examining this social phenomenon from a multi-actor perspective, including management, labor and ownership. She utilizes organization and management theories, often inspired by cross-national comparisons. Moreover, she is interested in diverse methodological frameworks, including Qualitative Comparative Analysis (QCA).

Stephanie Saraswati Cristin has been leading the health innovation and partnerships agenda at the International Committee of the Red Cross (ICRC), which includes among other responsibilities navigating and mobilizing key stakeholders across sectors with the objective to better meet the health needs of people and communities affected by armed-conflict. She has worked on a full range of humanitarian and development public health efforts at both the local and global levels, from the first years of her career based in a rural clinic in Burkina Faso with the United States Peace Corps to mobilizing c-suite and executive stakeholders at the World Economic Forum at Davos.

Emanuela Girei is Lecturer in Organisation Studies at the Sheffield University Management School. Her research agenda lies at the intersection of management and organization studies and development studies. It develops through two intertwined lines of inquiry, one focusing on non-profit management and social transformation and the other on decolonizing management education and research practices. Both lines of inquiry are underpinned by a key interest and commitment toward research that can contribute to progressive social transformation and social justice. Her research has been published in Human Relations, Organizations Studies and Management Learning.

Koen Joosse has been a program manager at the Philips Foundation since its inception in 2014. He is responsible for the cooperation program with international

xii *Contributors*

and local NGOs, where besides funding they seek to add unique value through the application of innovation, talent and resources available in Philips. Since the forming of the Philips Foundation they have initiated over 250 projects in more than 40 countries, touching the lives of millions of people and striving for sustainable and scalable impact. Koen Joosse has spent 25 years at Philips, first in industrial R&D and engineering, followed by roles in corporate communications and government and public affairs. He holds a PhD degree in applied physics from the University of Twente in the Netherlands.

Gorgi Krlev is a senior researcher at the Centre for Social Investment (CSI) of the University of Heidelberg, Germany. Currently his main research interests are organizational hybridity, social innovation, entrepreneurship and impact. Gorgi holds a PhD degree in Business and Management with a focus on measuring social impact from the University of Oxford (Kellogg College). His dissertation won the first prize of the Roman Herzog Institute's 2020 "Social Market Economy" competition. Social Innovation: Comparative Perspectives, which he co-wrote and edited, won the 2019 Best Book Award of the Academy of Management's Public and Nonprofit Division.

Arun Kumar is Lecturer at the University of York, UK. He researches the role of businesses and management, broadly defined, in global development, with a particular specialism in philanthropic foundations. His research monograph on Indian business elites' philanthropy and development is currently in press with the Oxford University Press. His interdisciplinary research has been published in Academy of Management Learning and Education, Development and Change, Economy and Society, Enterprise and Society, and Journal of Business Ethics.

Kristian Marinov is a Bachelor's degree graduate from the University of Tilburg. He is broadly interested in the managerial, psychological and sociological factors causing and influencing global social issues. Currently he is an aspiring consultant and changemaker for fields focusing on sustainable development.

Patray Lui is a design strategist at Philips Experience Design. She is responsible to design several strategic healthcare interventions and tools to improve healthcare access, especially in underserved communities. She often works closely with medical experts and NGO partners to facilitate design co-creation. Her work at Philips has been recognized internationally and won multiple prestigious design awards. She is also an inventor of several patents in area of healthcare design. Patray received her design education in Interaction Design Institute Ivrea Italy and BA in Environmental Design in the Hong Kong Polytechnic University.

Nikolas Rathert is Assistant Professor in the Department of Organization Studies, Tilburg University, the Netherlands. His research examines how corporations and other market-based forms of organizing, for example social enterprises, address a range of complex challenges facing societies today. Current research interests include the factors that enable corporations to develop substantive responses to stakeholder demands, the organizational dynamics that underpin such responses, and the extent of novelty in alternative forms of market-based organizing for social issues. His research has been published in the Journal of International Business Studies, Socio-Economic Review, Research in the Sociology of Organizations, and the Oxford Handbook of Corporate Social Responsibility. He received his PhD in Management and Organization Theory from the Freie Universitaet Berlin.

Simona Rocchi is Senior Research Director of Design for Sustainability & Innovation at Philips Experience Design, responsible for the global creative direction of various strategic design initiatives that shape solutions on complex health and well-being challenges, which require system changes. Simona also oversees the development of transformative design practice and tools that enable access to care via more inclusive business models in low-resource settings, and she consults the Philips Foundation on the topic of social innovation and collaborative design for shared value creation. Results of her activities have been widely recognized via publications, conference speeches, Ips and prestigious international design awards. She is frequently invited to lecture at design and business schools around the world.

Simona holds a PhD degree in Cleaner Production, Cleaner Products and Sustainability from Erasmus University, an MSc in Architecture from the Politecnico di Milano and an MSc in Environmental Management and Policy from Lund University.

Zahra Sultany is a Bachelor's and Master's degree graduate from the University of Tilburg. She is interested in the social and economic factors influencing global social challenges particularly in fragile settings. She has worked with the humanitarian and non-profit sector focusing on projects that are devoted to achieving social justice and promoting the rule of law to advance sustainable development. Currently she is working within the department international office of the division Academic services of Tilburg University.

Laura Toschi is Associate Professor in Entrepreneurship and Innovation Management at the University of Bologna (UNIBO), Department of Management, and she serves as Deputy Director of the Executive Master in Technology and Innovation Management at Bologna Business School. At UNIBO, she received her PhD in Management in 2009 and a *Laurea* in Industrial Engineering in 2004 (100/100 cum Laude). She has been a visiting scholar at Boston University (2008), SPRU (2011), University of Queensland (2017) and Queensland University of Technology (2020). Her main research interests are environmental and social entrepreneurship, entrepreneurial finance and impact investing, sustainability transitions, innovation management, and technology transfer. Her research outputs include publications in journals such as Research Policy, Ecological Economics, Journal of Business Venturing, Industrial and Corporate Change, Journal of Technology Transfer, International Small Business Journal and Technological Forecasting and Social Change.

Acknowledgments

The authors thank Naana Kumah and Eda Çeker for their assistance in completing the manuscript and the Department of Organization Studies at Tilburg University for supporting the research.

Figures, Tables and Boxes

Introduction

o   Figure 0.1   4
o   Figure 0.2   5
o   Figure 0.3   6
o   Figure 0.4   7
o   Figure 0.5   7
o   Figure 0.6   8
o   Figure 0.7   9
o   Figure 0.8   9
o   Figure 0.9   10
o   Figure 0.10   11
o   Figure 0.11   11

Chapter 1

o   Table 1.1   25
o   Table 1.2   26

Chapter 2

o   Table 2.1   32
o   Table 2.2   41

Chapter 3

o   Figure 3.1   54
o   Figure 3.2   55
o   Figure 3.3   56
o   Figure 3.4   60
o   Figure 3.5   60
o   Figure 3.6   61
o   Figure 3.7   61
o   Figure 3.8   62
o   Figure 3.9   63

xvi   *Figures, Tables and Boxes*

o   Table 3.1   51
o   Table 3.2   53
o   Table 3.3   58

Chapter 4

o   Figure 4.1   78
o   Figure 4.2   79
o   Figure 4.3   82
o   Figure 4.4   84
o   Figure 4.5   85
o   Figure 4.6   88
o   Figure 4.7   90
o   Figure 4.8   93
o   Figure 4.9   94

Chapter 5

o   Figure 5.1   103
o   Figure 5.2   107
o   Table 5.1   111

Chapter 6

o   Figure 6.1   126

Chapter 7

o   Box 7.1   146
o   Box 7.2   152
o   Box 7.3   154
o   Figure 7.1   143
o   Figure 7.2   148
o   Figure 7.3   150

Chapter 8

o   Figure 8.1   175
o   Figure 8.2   177
o   Figure 8.3   178

Chapter 9

o   Box 9.1   196
o   Box 9.2   197
o   Box 9.3   208
o   Figure 9.1   192
o   Figure 9.2   192

Figures, Tables and Boxes   xvii

o	Figure 9.3	194
o	Figure 9.4	199
o	Figure 9.5	205
o	Figure 9.6	207
o	Table 9.1	193
o	Table 9.2	196

Chapter 10

o	Box 10.1	217
o	Box 10.2	233
o	Figure 10.1	213
o	Figure 10.2	215
o	Figure 10.3	221
o	Figure 10.4	231
o	Table 10.1	216
o	Table 10.2	220

Chapter 11

o	Box 11.1	257
o	Figure 11.1	237
o	Figure 11.2	247
o	Figure 11.3	248
o	Figure 11.4	249
o	Figure 11.5	250
o	Figure 11.6	253
o	Table 11.1	238
o	Table 11.2	238
o	Table 11.3	238
o	Table 11.4	239

Chapter 12

o	Figure 12.1	263

Introduction

A Compelling Call to Address the Grand Challenges through New Forms of Organising

Federica Angeli, Ashley Metz and Jörg Raab

The ambition of this book is to consolidate and advance the contribution of Organisation and Management Studies towards the pursuit of Sustainable Development. In doing so, this book responds to a compelling call to develop a finer-grained understanding of novel forms of organising that can more efficiently and effectively channel resources whilst developing new norms and values towards a more sustainable future.

Although much progress in several development areas has been achieved through the Millennium Development Goals between 2000 and 2015, inequalities nowadays are rising, in all domains, between and within countries. While average poverty levels have dropped from 42% of the worldwide population living below 1.90$ a day (purchase power parity 2011) in 1981 to 9.3% in 2017 (World Bank, 2021a), as of today, 1% of the world's population owns as much as 6.9 billion people, and half of the world's population lives with less than 5.50$ a day (Oxfam International, 2021). Socio-economic disparities lead to inequalities of access to health, education, water and sanitation, and pass on to the next generation. A child born in the Central African Republic has a life expectancy of 53 years, against a child born in Japan who could live on average 84 years (World Bank, 2021a). In 2017, 94% of mothers dying during childbirth lived in low-middle-income countries, with 2 maternal deaths every 100,000 live births in Italy against 1,150 in South Sudan (World Bank, 2018). Today, 258 million children, 1 in 5, will not be allowed to go to school, and every year 100 million people are pushed into poverty because of unaffordable healthcare costs (Oxfam International, 2021). Even with such stark differences, however, between-country inequality has improved while within-country inequalities have worsened (United Nations, 2020a). Socio-economic disparities within the same country are inequalities that people experience every day, and that lead again to dramatic differences in education and health outcomes (United Nations, 2020a). During the seven-stop train trip south-east from Jordanhill to Bridgeton in Glasgow, the average male life expectancy decreases from 75.8 years to 61.9 years (Campbell, 2017), the same level as Burkina Faso or Niger (World Bank, 2021a); similarly, the poorest neighbourhoods of Baltimore in the U.S. have the same life expectancy as Iraq. The COVID-19 pandemic has further exacerbated deeply rooted inequalities, determining setbacks on gender equity and social cohesion, with minorities and women disproportionately affected by the virus morbidity and mortality and/or by the economic and social repercussion of policy containment measures (Angeli & Kumar, 2020; Institute for Fiscal Studies, 2020). In addition to issues of social cohesion and rising interdependent inequalities, the depletion of natural resources, the shrinking of biodiversity and the degradation of the natural environment is progressing at an alarming pace. Carbon dioxide produced

DOI: 10.4324/9780429243165-1

This chapter has been made available under a CC-BY-NC 4.0 license.

by human activities is increasing more than 250 times faster than it did from natural sources after the last Ice Age (NASA, 2021). This is causing a very rapid climate change, with warming oceans, shrinking ice sheets, rising sea levels, shifting precipitation patterns and progressing ocean acidification. These phenomena are leading to more extreme weather conditions (Giordono et al., 2020; Linnenluecke et al., 2012), and to widespread damages to both natural and built environments, with linkages to increasing risks of pandemics and negative mental health repercussions (Marazziti et al., 2021; Perera et al., 2020, Tosepu et al., 2020). Such rapid changes will leave the next generations with a significantly impoverished and more unpredictable pool of natural resources. Ethical issues of intragenerational and intergenerational justice are therefore stronger than ever and seem inextricably linked to the nature of our social and economic systems (Piketty & Saez, 2014; Raworth, 2017).

Shifting the discourse towards addressing development inequalities, the United Nations Sustainable Development Framework and its 17 Sustainable Development Goals (SDGs) have marked an important step forward in recognizing the increasingly complex and interdependent nature of societal and environmental issues (United Nations, 2015). In fact, most of the current 'grand challenges' can be understood through the lens of wicked problems. These value-laden, complex issues, often paired with uncertainty about future developments and the effects of interventions, engender polarisation of views and subsequent conflict among stakeholders around both the definition and the potential solutions to these problems (Alford & Head, 2017; Head & Alford, 2015; Reinecke & Ansari, 2016). An illuminating example is the COVID-19 pandemic, which has created a context in which multiple urgent, interdependent but sometimes also contradictory societal goals simultaneously exist (Angeli et al., 2021; Camporesi & Mori, 2020). Societies facing the public health emergency need to pursue short-term reduction of the virus morbidity and mortality, whilst curbing long-term social repercussions of containment policies (rising social inequalities, mental health issues due to social isolation, intergenerational conflicts) and the risk of severe economic recessions, with subsequent rise in unemployment, poverty levels and social tensions (Angeli & Montefusco, 2020; Camporesi, 2020). In the second phase of the COVID-19 pandemic, after the vaccine had been hailed as an undisputed solution, problems have instead arisen around the ethical and equitable distribution of scarce vaccine doses, both within and across countries (Emanuel et al., 2020; WHO, 2021). How policymakers and expert advisors establish trade-offs and prioritise choices across different societal goals generate conflicting stakeholder views about what the problem actually is (e.g. catastrophic death toll versus potential economic meltdown) and the related solutions (e.g. lockdown measures versus looser mechanisms of virus control versus strong investments to enhance healthcare systems' capacity, secure vaccine supplies and prompt, equitable vaccine rollout).

At the same time, as a dramatic, sudden, global, systemic shock, the COVID-19 pandemic has underlined the deep and complex interconnections between individuals, communities, social and natural systems, across political borders and generations (United Nations, 2020b). We now know that interdependences that are not adequately understood and leveraged create fragile systems, where interventions – whether promulgated by policies, civil society initiatives, or organisational actions – will lead to unexpected consequences that might further complicate issues. Tackling such grand challenges and their underlying interdependencies from a management and organisation studies perspective requires a concerted action of multiple stakeholders at different levels, including the private sector (George et al., 2016; Howard-Grenville et al., 2019). It also requires rethinking current organisational models to leave space to new forms of organising. In a span of 50 years since Friedman (1970) claimed that "the only social responsibility of business is to increase its profits", nowadays very few would argue the independence of business from society. The fact that organisational forms and societal outcomes influence each other and co-evolve is clear by now. The complex dynamics of co-evolution extend much beyond the private sector to encompass any organisational entity or arrangement, from public organisations, civil society and the third sector, to forms of (cross-sector) partnerships for development. Interdependencies are also intersectional, and span across levels of analysis. It is therefore critical to embed organisation studies in policy and socio-cultural contexts, with a much wider and deeper appreciation of the co-evolution between individual behaviour and systemic outcomes. A socio-ecological, complexity-oriented perspective is increasingly necessary to appreciate the influence of factors at individual, community, organisational and policy levels, embedded in the natural environment (Bansal et al., 2020; Dentoni et al., 2020).

Even though transformative changes will have to be initiated and accompanied by global agreements between nation states as well as through regulation on the continental and national levels, the necessary changes manifest themselves in and through organisations (see also Howard-Grenville et al., 2019). Since we live in a society of organisations and increasingly in a society of networks (Perrow, 1991; Raab & Kenis, 2009), much of the necessary transformation to more sustainable economies and societies has to be invented and implemented in and through organisations with very likely new forms of organisations and organising. As a consequence, our thinking about organisations and organising also has to be revised in light of these challenges (Howard-Grenville et al., 2019). A wide range of literatures have, largely independently, discussed various ways organisations work towards a more sustainable world. However, organisation theories still fall short in understanding, explaining and harnessing interdependencies between organisational practices and sustainable development (George et al., 2016, 2012). Organisation and management studies fall way short of presenting an integrated framework even though they are in principle very well suited to make a major contribution to the transformation due to their multi-disciplinary background and multi-level perspective (Howard-Grenville et al., 2019).

In this book, we argue that fragmentation of research traditions has hindered effective progress towards understanding, implementing and evaluating (innovative) management practices geared towards people, profit and planet. We therefore develop what is to our knowledge the first combined overview of the several fragmented perspectives that have emerged over time to explain the role of formal organisations and other forms of organising in tackling grand challenges and contributing to improve civil society. Theoretical views are combined with empirical approaches, thus enabling an in-depth understanding on how different organisational forms such as existing businesses, NGOs or hybrid organisations can be an active tool to achieving sustainable development, and can at the same time mitigate the socially detrimental effects that unregulated and unethical business practices may cause. Part 1 reviews existing theoretical perspectives, such as base-of-the-pyramid approaches, hybrid organisations, responsible innovation, corporate social responsibility, network governance, the frameworks underpinning the work of NGOs and third sector organisations, along with aspects of impact investing and social impact evaluation. Part 2 presents in-depth case-based chapters from various contexts with a clear connection to the SDGs, to illustrate how specific organizational endeavours can contribute to improve socio-economic indicators and complement policy interventions in several areas.

Chapter 1 by Julia Bartosch and Jörg Raab gives an overview on the concept of corporate responsibility, which is a highly important but disputed idea. Similar to other concepts like corporate sustainability or corporate citizenship, it has become a crucial cornerstone in the discussion about how to transform our current societies and economic model into more sustainable ones. The central question is what framework for business activity should be applied once profit maximisation within legal boundaries is not sufficient and acceptable anymore. In addition, research shows that the business world has to date achieved only little in this regard. The chapter shows the many ambiguities of the concept "corporate responsibility" once we move beyond profit maximisation, the different rationales underpinning the discourse and the adoption of the concept in practice in different countries and issue areas. The authors show that the discussion on corporate responsibility cannot be conducted in isolation but is intricately connected to the role of the state, international regimes and legal frameworks. However, despite the conceptual ambiguities, the authors underline the value of a multifaceted nature of the concept to develop a common understanding over time that can ultimately enable business, political and societal solutions for a more sustainable economy and society. Figure 0.1 visually represents the chapter through a Wordcloud derived from its text.

Chapter 2 by Ashley Metz and Nikolas Rathert introduces an overview of the responsible innovation research stream. The term 'responsible innovation' has traditionally referred to the process of developing scientific innovations that increase societal welfare and avoid harm, for example by considering the unintended consequences of new technologies like healthcare robotics. In existing research, facilitating responsible innovation has largely been associated with regulators and oversight bodies. In this chapter, the authors extend this discussion and more specifically focus on the role that organisational practices and structures, including accounting methods and legal forms, play in enabling responsible innovation in relation to both technological and

Figure 0.1 Wordcloud representing the main concepts addressed in Chapter 1.

social innovations. They posit that ensuring responsible innovations requires attention to the ways an organisation is designed and how it operates, rather than focusing on the individual efforts of researchers, engineers, designers and others working to develop innovations. Broadening their discussion of responsible innovation to the organisational level carries important implications for how organisations, including corporations and other market-based forms of organising, can better serve society as a whole. Figure 0.2 gives a snapshot of the main topics covered by the chapter.

Chapter 3 by Federica Angeli offers a discourse analysis of the literature addressing the base-of-the-pyramid (BOP) business approach, almost 20 years after the concept was first formulated by Prahalad and Hart in 2002 (Prahalad & Hart, 2002). The author argues how BOP discourse reflect a process of deliberate or undeliberate framing within management research, and are encapsulated in both the topics addressed and in the wording choices of the related academic literature. This chapter therefore develops a longitudinal text analysis of all BOP-related scientific studies, through a systematic literature review methodology, followed by a topic modelling analysis. The findings highlight a salient evolution of the BOP discourse, from a focus on BOP strategies and related business model innovation of the initial days to a much stronger emphasis on mutual social value creation, and to the ethics and inequalities implications of the approach. This evolution reveals how scholars and practitioners adjusted their discourse to mitigate criticism and adapt to the claims of various stakeholders over time. Because the BOP field has generated both hype and strong controversies, that author underlines that understanding how framing is used to appease stakeholders' concerns is important, as it highlights the often hidden 'institutional work' that shapes the evolution of any field of literature and related practices. Figure 0.3 represents the Wordcloud derived from the chapter and highlights the main concepts at the core of the piece.

Chapter 4 by Kristian Marinov, Ashley Metz, Kelly Alexander and Federica Angeli explores how learning occurs in hybrid organisations, such as social enterprises with dual financial and social goals. Learning is particularly important for hybrid organisations which experience unique pressures and have multiple goals and where

Figure 0.2 Wordcloud representing the main concepts addressed in Chapter 2.

Figure 0.3 Wordcloud representing the main concepts addressed in Chapter 3.

organisational learning has potential implications for social and financial goal attainment. Social enterprises are impacted by logic tensions in terms of scalability, sustainability, stakeholder accountability, talent retention and reputation management. This chapter brings the literatures on learning and hybrid organising in conversation through an integrated review, which categorises the types of organisational learning by types of logic tensions (Smith & Lewis, 2011) – namely organising, belonging, performing, and learning tensions. These logic tensions are discussed in light of the learning literature, highlighting the emergence, significance and resolution of tensions for organisations and individuals. Adaptation to logic tensions can unfold through multiple, sometimes overlapping and complementary, pathways. Feedback loops that form and drive organisational learning need to be monitored to minimise mission drift and tensions need to be managed and resolved. The informed management and thorough theoretical understanding of hybrids are therefore a necessity if hybrids are to be nodes of progress in societal systems seeking to address wicked problems. Figure 0.4 represents the chapter wordcloud.

Chapter 5 by Emanuela Girei, Federica Angeli and Arun Kumar explores the role of NGOs within international development, focusing in particular on how they structure and manage their roles, relationships, and responsibilities. Starting from acknowledging that NGOs' progressive involvement in the aid sector has not brought the promised and expected transformation in development thinking and practice, the authors critically explore to what extent the dominant understandings of NGO management might have contributed to the current state of affairs. More specifically, drawing on insights from critical management studies, the authors problematize the progressive adoption of managerialism in international development and the NGO sector. They argue that the pervasive faith in supposedly scientific, rational management approaches is problematic and might hinder the same purposes for which they are adopted. In this sense, they think it is crucial to re-think what kind(s) of management knowledge and practice might support NGOs to strengthen their engagement with social change agenda, driven by a commitment to social justice and self-determination. The authors

Figure 0.4 Wordcloud representing the main concepts addressed in Chapter 4.

Figure 0.5 Wordcloud representing the main concepts addressed in Chapter 5.

suggest that this requires an appreciation of the political role of NGOs and civil society organizations (CSOs) more broadly, and the acknowledgement that management is not only about 'how to do' but also, and often especially, about 'what to do', thus making choices among different agendas, interests and priorities. Figure 0.5 provides a visual representation of the chapter through its wordcloud.

Chapter 6 by Jörg Raab discusses organisational networks as an important organisational form to foster sustainable development. Current academic literature sees such networks for example in the form of cross-sector partnerships or collaborations as one of the most promising organisational forms to tackle wicked problems as they also manifest themselves in the SDGs. This is also expressed by the fact that setting up functioning networks has received its own goal status in the SDG 17 'partnerships for the goals'. The chapter discusses, from a structural governance perspective, why such organisational networks in the area of sustainability exist, what types of networks we can distinguish and how they evolve. In addition, the chapter sheds light on how they can be governed, how they function and how they can be evaluated. Even though there is some evidence for the hope that networks form a suitable answer to complex sustainability issues, they are no panacea and are a complex organisational form in itself. The chapter concludes with some lessons for forming, governing and managing such organisational networks for sustainable development. Figure 0.6 portrays the chapter through its semantic wordcloud.

Chapter 7 by Laura Toschi and Ashley Metz analyses impact investing as a new financial practice to support the development of companies combining social and economic goals in their activities. The development of the impact investing phenomenon is shown as being part of a general rethinking of existing financial models in order to create a more sustainable economic system from a social and environmental perspective. In this chapter, the authors first discuss the history of the field and review the main academic works, highlighting a strong ambiguity in defining impact investing. Second, the authors introduce the organisational actors involved, showing the importance to adopt an ecosystem approach with heterogeneous, coherent and coordinated players, to guarantee the effectiveness of the field. Third, they present the main instruments used, suggesting a broad range of options, from social investment funds, to guarantees, green and social bonds, mission and programme related investments. They conclude with a discussion of the next trajectories of impact investing to capture where the field is going and suggesting topics for future research. The chapter wordcloud can be viewed in Figure 0.7.

Chapter 8 by Gorgi Krlev and Federica Angeli turns to the measurement of social impact. The number of available tools for measuring social impact is manifold, and yet both researchers and practitioners continue to struggle with the question of how to best assess and analyse which social impact organisations are achieving. The chapter first discusses persistent problems in the measurement of social impact and where they come from. Subsequently, it is proposed that analysts of social impact should turn away from tools and linear evaluation models and instead think strategically

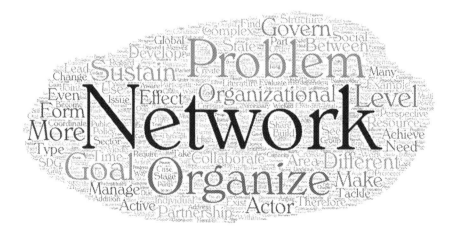

Figure 0.6 Wordcloud representing the main concepts addressed in Chapter 6.

Introduction 9

Figure 0.7 Wordcloud representing the main concepts addressed in Chapter 7.

Figure 0.8 Wordcloud representing the main concepts addressed in Chapter 8.

about what it takes to perform a solid impact measurement. In particular, the chapter develops a realist perspective to measurement that takes into account the complexity of social realities and systems. It outlines an analytic strategy for how to decide on appropriate research designs and methods as well as how to gather data and analyse them in order to make an informed decision about which impacts have been achieved and how they could be improved. Chapter 8 can be visualised through its wordcloud in Figure 0.8.

Chapter 9 by Kelly Alexander and Jörg Raab addresses the role of social enterprises in an empirical case. The Fix Forward case examines a South African social enterprise operating in the building and construction sector. The goals and activities of the social enterprise address especially the Sustainable Development Goals Quality Education (#4) and Decent Work and Economic Growth (#8). Based on empirical

10 *Federica Angeli, Ashley Metz and Jörg Raab*

Figure 0.9 Wordcloud representing the main concepts addressed in Chapter 9.

research, the case examines the unique emerging market context in which Fix Forward operates. The authors examine a number of areas in which hybridity manifests in the social enterprise, including the mission, legal form and revenue generation strategy. The case briefly examines the growth of Fix Forward, the social enterprise's plans for scaling and then turns to the challenges facing the organisation. These challenges result from the hybrid nature of Fix Forward, as well as the institutional environment in which it operates – dealing with a number of wicked problems and grappling with the legacy of Apartheid. The authors position Fix Forward in the relevant theoretical framework of hybrid organising literature. Finally, they develop a seven-stage theoretical model of funding based on the steps taken by Fix Forward, to assist hybrid organisations in reaching financial sustainability. Figure 0.9 depicts Chapter 9 in a Wordcloud.

Chapter 10 by Simona Rocchi, Zahra Sultany, Federica Angeli, Patray Lui, Stephanie Saraswati Cristin and Koen Joosse outlines the case of an organisational intervention aimed at tackling the ongoing, highly complex challenge of improving antenatal care in Sub-Saharan Africa. Increasing antenatal care access and effective delivery are recognised to be salient aspects to reduce maternal mortality, which is still unacceptably high in SSA settings. The chapter proposes a description and analysis of a multi-stakeholder partnership between the International Committee of the Red Cross, Philips Foundation and Philips Experience Design, aimed at developing a high-risk pregnancy (HRP) detection tool. The chapter describes the co-creation process that led to the design and implementation in SSA settings of HRP Referral Cards, a low-tech, low-cost checklist to support the identification and communication of symptoms that can lead to risky pregnancies, before they become life-threatening. The theoretical analysis highlights the importance of trust formation among the partners, and the co-evolution between trust and a blended organisational culture that is specific to the partnership. Pursuing flexibility and emphasising a co-creation approach emerge as crucial to the partnership success. The wordcloud in Figure 0.10 offers a visual representation of the chapter.

Chapter 11 by Anand Kumar Jaiswal and Federica Angeli highlights the experience of General Electric (GE) in India. GE successfully developed more than 25

Figure 0.10 Wordcloud representing the main concepts addressed in Chapter 10.

Figure 0.11 Wordcloud representing the main concepts addressed in Chapter 11.

low-cost medical devices for the Indian market. This was part of its aim to reduce the cost of healthcare, increase access and improve quality of healthcare delivery in developing countries. This chapter first discusses the development of MAC 400, a low-cost, portable ECG machine developed by GE in India. This particular device was designed keeping in mind the unique characteristics of a rural environment and the needs of physicians working there. Thereafter, the chapter develops a theoretical framework on how GE's innovation strategies in India have evolved in four key stages from defeaturing to clean slate approach and then to local innovation and finally to reverse innovation. The framework outlines the antecedents of GE's strategy at each stage. The development of MAC 400 and other low-cost devices exemplifies GE's approach of creating both social and economic value in the base of the pyramid markets. Figure 0.11 represents the chapter and its core concepts through a wordcloud.

12 *Federica Angeli, Ashley Metz and Jörg Raab*

The concluding chapter 12 by Ashley Metz, Federica Angeli and Jörg Raab provides an overview of the heterogeneous literature streams addressed in the book, whilst emphasising the need to move beyond the current disciplinary silos towards a more integrated approach. Based on the concepts and perspectives addressed in the book, the chapter proposes a conceptual framework that highlights how an interdisciplinary, intersectional effort is necessary to strengthen and sharpen the contribution of organisation and management studies to sustainable development and grand societal challenges. The proposed framework is designed to consolidate existing research into an integrated model that can inform future research and enable knowledge accumulation in a field that has been so far highly fragmented.

References

Alford, J., & Head, B. W. (2017). Wicked and less wicked problems: A typology and a contingency framework. *Policy and Society, 36*(3), 397–413. https://doi.org/10.1080/14494035.2 017.1361634

Angeli, F., Camporesi, S., & Del Fabbro, G. (2021). The COVID-19 wicked problem in public health ethics: Conflicting evidence, or incommensurable values? *Humanities and Social Sciences Communications, 8*(1), forthcoming.

Angeli, F., & Kumar, A. (2020). *Covid-19 pandemic and global inequalities*. University of York.

Angeli, F., & Montefusco, A. (2020). Sensemaking and learning during the Covid-19 pandemic: A complex adaptive systems perspective on policy decision-making. *World Development, 136*, 1–4.

Bansal, P., Grewatsch, S., & Sharma, G. (2020). How COVID-19 informs business sustainability research: It's time for a systems perspective. *Journal of Management Studies*. https://doi.org/10.1111/joms.12669

Campbell, D. (2017). The growing gulf in life expectancy shows how austerity has deepened inequalities: Health policy. *The Guardian*. Retrieved June 7, 2021, from www.theguardian.com/politics/2017/aug/12/growing-gulf-life-expectancy-shows-austerity-deepened-inequalities

Camporesi, S. (2020). It didn't have to be this way: Reflections on the ethical justification of the running ban in Northern Italy in response to the 2020 covid-19 outbreak. *Journal of Bioethical Inquiry, 17*(4), in press.

Camporesi, S., & Mori, M. (2020). Ethicists, doctors and triage decisions: Who should decide? And on what basis? *Journal of Medical Ethics, Medethics-2020*, 106499. https://doi.org/10.1136/medethics-2020-106499

Dentoni, D., Pinkse, J., & Lubberink, R. (2020). Linking sustainable business models to socioecological resilience through cross-sector partnerships: A complex adaptive systems view. *Business & Society*. https://doi.org/10.1177/0007650320935015

Emanuel, E. J., Persad, G., Kern, A., Buchanan, A., Fabre, C., Halliday, D., Heath, J., Herzog, L., Leland, R. J., Lemango, E. T., Luna, F., McCoy, M. S., Norheim, O. F., Ottersen, T., Schaefer, G. O., Tan, K. C., Wellman, C. H., Wolff, J., Richardson, H. S., & Richardson, H. S. (2020, September 1). An ethical framework for global vaccine allocation. *Science*. American Association for the Advancement of Science. https://doi.org/10.1126/SCIENCE.ABE2803

Friedman, M. (1970, September 13). The social responsibility of business is to increase its profits. *The New York Time Magazine*. https://doi.org/10.1007/978-3-540-70818-6_14

George, G., Howard-Grenville, J., Joshi, A., & Tihanyi, L. (2016). Understanding and tackling societal grand challenges through management research. *Academy of Management Journal, 59*(6), 1880–1895. https://doi.org/10.5465/amj.2016.4007

George, G., McGahan, A. M., & Prabhu, J. (2012). Innovation for inclusive growth: Towards a theoretical framework and research agenda. *Journal of Management Studies, 49*(4), 661–683. https://doi.org/10.1111/j.1467-6486.2012.01048.x

Giordono, L., Boudet, H., & Gard-Murray, A. (2020). Local adaptation policy responses to extreme weather events. *Policy Sciences*, *53*(4), 609–636. https://doi.org/10.1007/s11077-020-09401-3

Head, B. W., & Alford, J. (2015). Wicked problems: Implications for public policy and management. *Administration & Society*, *47*(6), 711–739. https://doi.org/10.1177/0095399713481601

Howard-Grenville, J., Davis, G. F., Dyllick, T., Miller, C. C., Thau, S., & Tsui, A. S. (2019). Sustainable development for a better world: Contributions of leadership, management, and organizations. *Academy of Management Discoveries*, *5*(4), 355–366. https://doi.org/10.5465/amd.2019.0275

Institute for Fiscal Studies. (2020). COVID-19 and inequalities. *Inequality: The IFS Deaton Review*. www.ifs.org.uk/inequality/covid-19-and-inequalities/

Linnenluecke, M. K., Griffiths, A., & Winn, M. (2012). Extreme weather events and the critical importance of anticipatory adaptation and organizational resilience in responding to impacts. *Business Strategy and the Environment*, *21*(1), 17–32. https://doi.org/10.1002/bse.708

Marazziti, D., Cianconi, P., Mucci, F., Foresi, L., Chiarantini, I., & Della Vecchia, A. (2021, June 15). Climate change, environment pollution, COVID-19 pandemic and mental health. *Science of the Total Environment*. Elsevier B.V. https://doi.org/10.1016/j.scitotenv.2021.145182

NASA. (2021). *Evidence | facts – climate change: Vital signs of the planet*. Retrieved June 7, 2021, from https://climate.nasa.gov/evidence/

Oxfam International. (2021). *5 shocking facts about extreme global inequality and how to even it up*. Oxfam International. Retrieved June 7, 2021, from www.oxfam.org/en/5-shocking-facts-about-extreme-global-inequality-and-how-even-it

Perera, A. T. D., Nik, V. M., Chen, D., Scartezzini, J. L., & Hong, T. (2020). Quantifying the impacts of climate change and extreme climate events on energy systems. *Nature Energy*, *5*(2), 150–159. https://doi.org/10.1038/s41560-020-0558-0

Perrow, C. (1991). A society of organizations. *Theory and Society*, *20*, 725–762.

Piketty, T., & Saez, E. (2014). Income inequality in Europe and the United States. *Science*, *344*(6186), 838–843. https://doi.org/10.1126/science.1251936

Prahalad, C., & Hart, S. L. (2002). The fortune at the bottom of the pyramid. *Strategy+Business Magazine*, *26*, 1–14. https://doi.org/10.2139/ssrn.914518

Raab, J., & Kenis, P. (2009). Heading toward a society of networks: Empirical developments and theoretical challenges. *Journal of Management Inquiry*, *18*(3), 198–210. https://doi.org/10.1177/1056492609337493

Raworth, K. (2017). *Doughnut economics: Seven ways to think like a 21st-century economist*. Random House Business Books.

Reinecke, J., & Ansari, S. (2016). Taming wicked problems: The role of framing in the construction of corporate social responsibility. *Journal of Management Studies*, *53*(3), 299–329. https://doi.org/10.1111/joms.12137

Smith, W., & Lewis, M. (2011). Toward a theory of paradox: A dynamic equilibrium model of organizing. *Academy of Management Review*, *36*(2), 381–403. https://doi.org/10.5465/amr.2009.0223

Tosepu, R., Gunawan, J., Effendy, D. S., Ahmad, L. O. A. I., Lestari, H., Bahar, H., & Asfian, P. (2020). Correlation between weather and Covid-19 pandemic in Jakarta, Indonesia. *Science of the Total Environment*, *725*, 138436. https://doi.org/10.1016/j.scitotenv.2020.138436

United Nations. (2015). *Transforming our world: The 2030 agenda for sustainable development*. United Nations. https://doi.org/10.1007/s13398-014-0173-7.2

United Nations. (2020a). *Inequality – bridging the divide | United Nations*. Retrieved June 7, 2021, from www.un.org/en/un75/inequality-bridging-divide

United Nations. (2020b). *UN research roadmap for the COVID-19 recovery | United Nations*. Retrieved March 31, 2021, from www.un.org/en/coronavirus/communication-resources/un-research-roadmap-covid-19-recovery

WHO. (2021). *Access and allocation: How will there be fair and equitable allocation of limited supplies?* Retrieved June 7, 2021, from www.who.int/news-room/feature-stories/detail/access-and-allocation-how-will-there-be-fair-and-equitable-allocation-of-limited-supplies

World Bank. (2018). *The World Bank data: Health*. https://data.worldbank.org/topic/health

World Bank. (2021a). *Life expectancy at birth, total (years) | Data*. Retrieved June 7, 2021, from https://data.worldbank.org/indicator/SP.DYN.LE00.IN?most_recent_value_desc=true

World Bank. (2021b). *Poverty headcount ratio at $1.90 a day (2011 PPP) (% of population) | Data*. Retrieved June 1, 2021, from https://data.worldbank.org/indicator/SI.POV.DDAY?end=2015&start=1981&view=chart

1 Corporate Responsibility
An Overview

Julia Bartosch and Jörg Raab

Why Should We Deal with the Question of Corporate Responsibility?

Corporate Responsibility refers to corporate policies, practices and outcomes related to issues including employee well-being, climate change, human rights or diversity. It can include changes in the production process to reduce greenhouse gas emissions, changes in labour relations to secure and improve working conditions both within the firm and its supply chain or contributions to the local community such as infrastructure or philanthropy (Aguilera et al., 2007) Therefore, corporate responsibility tackles issues relevant for human day-to-day life and the constitution of the natural environment.

Why should we address and deal with the question of the responsibility of corporations? In light of the sheer extent of ecological and social challenges, the urgency to fundamentally change the way our economy operates is apparent (Klein, 2014; Wright & Nyberg, 2015) The aim for this development is stated in the definition of sustainable development, defined as meeting "the needs of the present without compromising the ability of future generations to meet their own needs" (Brundtland Commission, 1987, p. 24). For corporations, this has been translated into the so-called triple-bottom line. The core idea states that business firms should address sustainable development via integrating economic, social and environmental goals at the same time (Elkington, 1998). Therefore, corporate responsibility in principle connects to all 17 Sustainable Development Goals. While governments are essential in setting the legal frameworks to create a more sustainable economic system and societies, it is corporations that have to implement the necessary changes in production, transportation, and consumption as well as (co-) develop and deploy new technologies in this process. In addition, it is impossible to regulate everything in detail. Therefore, addressing the responsibility of corporations also implies that they should not try to find the potential loopholes but act in the spirit of the regulation. Given the enormous social and environmental challenges and the role that especially big corporations both play in causing them but also their crucial role in tackling them, we use the term "corporate responsibility" instead of corporate social responsibility. With this terminological choice, we indicate that corporations have a broad responsibility towards society with regard to economic prosperity, social equity and environmental integrity (Montiel, 2008). They must go beyond treating these issues as just one part of their activities or even only for the sake of appearances (Roberts, 2003). Rather, in the understanding of corporate responsibility, corporations have to integrate economic prosperity, social equity and environmental integrity in all their structures and processes, i.e. in their strategic thinking as

DOI: 10.4324/9780429243165-2

This chapter has been made available under a CC-BY-NC 4.0 license.

16   Julia Bartosch and Jörg Raab

well as their daily operations. However, we do not deny that there can be real tensions between financial and ethical imperatives and that engagement in corporate social responsibility activities can serve different functions (see also Roberts, 2003).

However, and despite a growing urgency for change towards more sustainability (e.g. Rockström et al., 2009; United Nations Environment Program, 2018), scientific results demonstrate that the business world has achieved only little in this regard to date (Whiteman et al., 2013; Wright & Nyberg, 2015). Yet, the current pandemic shows how relevant it is that the business world is taking its responsibility, e.g. towards its workers:

> **The Companies Putting Profits Ahead of Public Health** – *Most American restaurants do not offer paid sick leave. Workers who fall sick face a simple choice: Work and get paid or stay home and get stiffed. As the new coronavirus spreads across the United States, the time has come for restaurants, retailers and other industries that rely on low-wage labor to abandon their parsimonious resistance to paid sick leave. Companies that do not pay sick workers to stay home are endangering their workers, their customers and the health of the broader public. Studies show that paying for sick employees to stay home significantly reduces the spread of the seasonal flu. There's every reason to think it would help to check the new coronavirus, too. A federal law mandating paid sick leave is necessary because the coronavirus is just an instance of a broader problem. Norovirus, a major cause of food poisoning cases, sickens some 20 million Americans each year, and kills several hundred. Outbreaks often are traced back to sick food service workers, prompting the C.D.C. to recommend paid leave as a corrective. The spread of seasonal flu and other diseases is also greatly exacerbated by sick workers. If we work sick, then you get sick, Chipotle workers chanted during a recent protest.*
>
> (The New York Times, March 14, 2020).

> **Covid outbreak exposes dire conditions at Guatemala factory making US brands** – *A garment factory supplying Gap, American Eagle and Amazon was at the centre of one of the worst Covid-19 outbreaks in Guatemala, the Guardian can reveal. When all 900 workers were tested, 201 positive cases were reported. The virus outbreak went on to cause the death of at least one KP Textile garment worker. In statements to the Guardian, Gap, American Eagle and Amazon said their suppliers had been issued with detailed guidance on Covid-19 preparedness and mitigation and they are committed to rigorous labour standards. Despite the billions of dollars generated in the zones, Guatemala's garment workers have been left particularly vulnerable to coronavirus, and are unable to save for times of sickness or unemployment. The minimum wage for the sector is 2,831 Quetzales (£330) a month, although unions report that some workers are paid as little as £181. The living wage in Guatemala is £680. Only two maquilas in the country have trade unions as attempts to organise have been met with violence and dismissal. The pandemic has exposed the brutal conditions workers have to endure.*
>
> (The Guardian, August 6, 2020)

These two examples demonstrate the urgency and relevance to engage in discussions about corporate responsibility – within the scientific community, among management practitioners, politicians and students.

This is a timely discussion given that "not only government officials and social activists but also millennials (Deloitte, 2019), global investors (Mudaliar & Dithrich, 2019), and even CEOs of corporate giants (Business Roundtable, 2019) are calling upon companies to account for their effects on people and planet and to take actions that positively impact society in addition to serving their shareholders" (Battilana et al., 2020, p. 3). The topic is also gaining more and more relevance for the scientific community of organization studies and the management literature more generally. Whereas the topic has long been discussed in specific sub-communities in their respective journals (such as "Journal of Business Ethics", "Business and Society"), it has become a mainstream topic with publications in highly ranked journals, encompassing areas such as strategic management, accounting, or entrepreneurship. Moreover, the annual meetings of the large scientific associations in that field put the topic prominently on their agenda. For instance, already in 2009, the Annual Meeting of The Academy of Management was held under the theme of "Green Management Matters". Similarly, the European Group of Organization Studies put the topic on the agenda and, for instance, held its annual colloquium in 2020 under the general theme "Organizing for a Sustainable Future". Despite these important changes, the topic of corporate responsibility is not yet belonging to the key topics in management and organization research and is in many places still a niche when it comes to student education.

To Whom and for What Are Corporations Responsible?

For looking at the phenomenon of corporate responsibility, a central starting point is to understand that "corporations receive a social sanction from society that requires that they, in return, contribute to the growth and development of that society" (Devinney, 2009, p. 44). But what is a "social sanction"? Within the last two centuries, corporate law has developed in many countries around the world and the corporation has become the dominant economic institution. For this development it was crucial that jurisdictions guaranteed business initiatives a license to operate, including the privilege of limited liability and rights as a "legal person" (Bakan, 2004). If the corporation is granted these conditions to run its business, make profit and accumulate wealth for itself, its leadership and shareholders, the question arises what responsibilities it has towards society.

This matter is hotly debated among academics, politicians and the general public. The question is whether corporations deliver their part by "creating and delivering products and services consumers want, providing employment and career opportunities for employees, developing markets for suppliers, and paying taxes to governments and returns to shareholders and other claimants on the rents generated by the corporation" (Devinney, 2009, p. 44). A prominent advocate of such a very narrow view about corporate responsibility is Milton Friedman with his popular statement that "there is one and only one social responsibility of business – to use its resources and engage in activities designed to increase its profits so long as it stays within the rules of the game, which is to say, engages in open and free competition without deception or fraud" (Friedman, 1962). In this view, the responsibility to the shareholders and with that profit-maximization is central (for a recent critique, see Battilana et al., 2020)). This model has been the dominant model in management practice during the last 50 years. It has become an almost "natural" expectation for

18 *Julia Bartosch and Jörg Raab*

companies to put maximizing the share price above any other organizational goal (Battilana et al., 2020, p. 3).

Opponents to Friedman argue that corporations should serve the whole society and should superordinate ecological and social concerns over profit seeking. These scholars, often inspired by ethics (Ulrich, 2008; van der Byl et al., 2020), argue that firms that normatively subscribe to the idea of profit maximization cannot contribute to a life-serving economy, which includes social as well as ecological aspects. In addition, large corporations undeniably exert significant political influence on legislation and policymaking to further their profit interests and sometimes engage in rent-seeking. This clearly extends their sphere of influence beyond producing shareholders wealth and in that respect violates Friedman's postulate of free competition.

In this view, the economic vitality of the firm is only possible if it does not cause problems for or even harm the environment or any social groups. In other words, making profits at the expense of the environment or any social groups is strictly rejected. In the last decades, such a view has been secondary in management practice. Yet, more and more company leaders show sympathy with perspectives not exclusively focusing on shareholder value maximization. Although, how far they deviate from this ideal differs [see, for example, Grant Reid, CEO of MARS, or former Unilever CEO Paul Pohlmann, who envisioned their companies becoming more sustainable and tried to fundamentally change their corporation's strategy (Reid, 2020; Gelles, 2018)].

These two views mirror the ends of a continuum and stand in clear opposition to each other. Yet, the debate shows how difficult it is to find a way to define "responsibility" within the phenomenon of corporate responsibility. In addition, one can argue that it is extremely difficult for managers to reconcile the different and often contradicting imperatives, if they move away from the current standard model of making profit within the legal frameworks. Moreover, as Raghunandan and Rajgopal (2020) have demonstrated, socially responsible firms and funds do not appear to follow through on proclamations of concerns for stakeholders and social responsibility. Therefore, these two views represent not only the academic discussion. Instead, they are connected to a general debate about the role of corporations in society which can be found also in political debates, newspaper articles or in discussions with friends.

Beyond the question whether a firm has responsibility towards society, a second question addresses the particular kind and extent of these responsibilities. Carroll (1991, 2016), for example, suggests that companies have economic, legal, ethical and philanthropic responsibilities. As described in the beginning of this chapter, corporate responsibility refers to a very broad set of corporate policies and outcomes related to manifold issues including employee well-being, climate change, human rights or diversity. However, the nature of corporate responsibility remains "essentially contested" (Okoye, 2009) because different stakeholders may place different expectations and a different focus with regard to the various SDGs on companies.

Different issues may compete for public attention, and societal expectations around different issues are likely to emerge and change over time. This becomes clear with the example of the following two questions: Is a company responsible for the workers employed at its factories only or also for the working conditions in the whole supply chain? Is the company responsible for greenhouse gas emissions during its production process (so-called primary and secondary emissions) only or also for the emissions produced while using the company's products (so-called tertiary emissions – imagine a car, for instance)? Different people may answer these questions differently. Whether or not corporate actions are considered appropriate remains a matter of the social and political context. Especially, since we need to understand that "corporations do not operate in a singular clear society with unambiguous and uncontested norms" (Devinney, 2009).

Finally, corporations themselves play an important role in defining the meaning of corporate responsibility: "A potentially naive assumption underlying CSR is that firms are guided by society and do not deliberately manipulate that society for their own benefit" (Devinney). One of the most prominent and extreme examples in this process is the financing of "alternative research" by the oil and gas industry that has successfully sawed doubts in parts of the population in the scientific mainstream as expressed by the Intergovernmental Panel on Climate Change (IPCC) on global climate change and given some legitimacy to climate change deniers with decision-making power as the Trump government in the U.S. (The Guardian, 2015).

Defining Corporate Responsibility

A single definition of corporate responsibility is difficult. Against the backdrop of the questions discussed earlier, such a definition differs depending on how to answer those questions. In particular, the questions "To whom are corporations responsible?" and "For what are corporations responsible?" are highly disputed and controversial. Depending on the answer, the definition of corporate responsibility is significantly different.

Despite these ambiguities, corporate responsibility has become increasingly relevant for modern corporations over the last decades (Shabana et al., 2017) and has induced a major new strand of literature, in which the term Corporate Social Responsibility (CSR) is prevalent. Importantly, the term CSR, which is widely used in academic literature, newspaper articles or political discussions, is only one term to describe the phenomenon of corporate responsibility. Related concepts include the terms "corporate sustainability", "corporate citizenship" or concepts from the field of business ethics such as "ethical leadership".

The term CSR is particularly linked to the development of corporate responsibility in the approximately last 20 years, when corporate activities towards issues like employee well-being, climate change or human rights became more prominently discussed in the business world. Other terms like "moral obligations" have historically been more prominently used. For instance, Lohmeyer (Lohmeyer, 2017; Lohmeyer & Jackson, 2018) illustrates for the German case that while in the last 20 years instrumental motives are central or even dominate, the earlier discourse about corporate responsibility (in the 1970s and 1980s) was focused on moral motives of "an ethos of the entrepreneur and his or her ethical obligation". That illustrates again that corporations may have a variety of instrumental, moral or relational motives for adopting corporate responsibility policies (Aguilera et al., 2007).

In addition, defining corporate responsibility needs to account for variations across business systems and countries. Corporate responsibility is a culturally embedded phenomenon (Aguilera et al., 2007; Campbell, 2007; Matten & Moon, 2020). For instance, several definitions limit the scope towards those activities that corporations do "voluntarily" or limit corporate responsibility to policies and practices which go "beyond legal requirements" (most prominently, see McWilliams & Siegel, 2001). Looking at corporate responsibility from a cross-national perspective, it becomes clear

20 Julia Bartosch and Jörg Raab

that the legal context differs from one country to another and the same action may be considered voluntary in one context, but not so in another. This is for instance true for health insurance or paid sick leave, where corporate participation is mandated in many European countries but remains voluntary in the U.S. except in the minority of states and cities where it is required by law. Understanding these differences is very important when engaging with corporate responsibility within an international context, where, for instance, the headquarters might be located in a context very different to those of the subsidiaries.

To acknowledge the variability and contestedness of corporate responsibility, this chapter focuses on the phenomenon instead of sticking to one particular concept dogmatically.

Research Foci

In the following, we will discuss three relevant and promising research foci in the field of corporate responsibility research.

Business Case

Going back to the beginning of this chapter and the question about the role of corporations in society, one particular strand of research is very important. This strand aims to show that corporate efforts in contributing towards the social good also pay off financially at least in the long run. In this argumentation, corporate activities related to issues including employee well-being, climate change, human rights or diversity not only cost money (despite all the other positive effects for communities, workers, the environment etc.), but have a financial benefit as well, presenting an answer to the ethical dilemma outlined earlier. One prominent example of this approach, which is also often addressed in the business press and by business leaders, is the idea by Porter and Kramer called "shared value" (Porter & Kramer, 2011), arguing that financial and social goals can become synergistic.

To illustrate this perspective, let's take the example of a garment retailer. In this firm, putting financial resources in activities that eliminate child labour in the production chain and shifting towards suppliers that secure fair trade conditions in terms of labour rights, a ban on child labour and high environmental standards would definitely be cost-intensive. However, such efforts could pay off financially through better supplier relations, reduction of problems in the production process, higher prices paid by the consumer etc. In a business case framework, the relationship between financial costs and financial benefits is addressed.

This perspective is often summarized with the expression "doing well by doing good". However, it has often been criticized for its one-sided normative orientation on profit maximization (Battilana et al., 2020; Meyer & Höllerer, 2010). Although social or environmental considerations are included in business decisions, they are only relevant as long as they generate profit in some regard. Instead, corporate sustainability research has argued that business needs to balance economic, ecological and social demands to achieve these competing sustainability objectives simultaneously (Gao & Bansal, 2013; Hahn et al., 2014, 2015, 2018, p. 235; van der Byl et al., 2020).

A recent and very prominent critique of this perspective is articulated by Sarah Kaplan in her article "Beyond the Business Case for Social Responsibility" (Gao &

Bansal, 2013). This article beautifully summarizes the academic critique of the "business case on CSR" by raising three points. First, it appears that the business case may not provoke corporate action. Second, those who are the subject of the business case – for example, women or racial minorities who are the supposed beneficiaries of the "business case for diversity," or environmental activists who should feel support from the "business case for sustainability" – may actually experience negative consequences. Third, advocates for social change both within and outside organizations may feel diminished by the experience of having to make the business case for the social issues they support.

Kaplan argues that there are oftentimes real trade-offs that simply cannot be resolved through a win-win business case, and using a "business case" framework keeps us from addressing those trade-offs. In order to overcome this problem, she suggests three interrelated solutions: (1) Find legal and moral justifications that provoke real commitment to change, where the business case – if it is needed at all – can be constructed ex post to fit the desired course of action; (2) develop better measures that capture the interests of a diverse set of stakeholders so that companies are not trapped into focusing on the shareholder's bottom line; and (3) construct alternative governance models that would allow stakeholders to cocreate value in a collaborative process.

Stakeholder Perspective

Another important perspective on the phenomenon of corporate responsibility is the stakeholder perspective. It was developed in the 1980s and prominently introduced by Edward Freeman in 1984 with his book "Strategic Management: A Stakeholder Approach." The approach can be read as an attempt to overcome the dogmatic focus on shareholders as the only relevant group managers should be held accountable for.

The underlying idea of stakeholder approaches to strategic management suggests that

> managers must formulate and implement processes which satisfy all and only those groups who have a stake in the business. The central task in this process is to manage and integrate the relationships and interests of shareholders, employees, customers, suppliers, communities and other groups in a way that ensures the long-term success of the firm. A stakeholder approach emphasizes active management of the business environment, relationships and the promotion of shared interests.
>
> (Freeman & McVea, 2001)

It is thereby a strategic approach to ensure long-term success of a company.

A core effort for scholars in the field of stakeholder management has been to develop methods to identify the relevant stakeholders of particular firms. By definition, stakeholders are "any group or individual who is affected by or can affect the achievement of an organization's objectives" (Freeman & McVea, 2001). By this definition, groups, neighbourhoods, organizations, institutions, societies, the natural environment are generally thought to qualify as actual or potential stakeholders (Mitchell et al., 1997). One prominent approach to identify the most relevant stakeholders for a single firm was suggested by Mitchell et al. (1997). They suggest classifying stakeholders as more

22 *Julia Bartosch and Jörg Raab*

or less salient, based on their power, legitimacy, and urgency (Mitchell et al., 1997). The more of the three attributes a single stakeholder combines, the higher its salience for the managers of a single firm. This approach is deliberately a descriptive theory of stakeholder salience, aiming to "explain the conditions under which managers do consider certain classes of entities as stakeholders" and which "can reliably separate stakeholders from nonstakeholders" (Mitchell et al., 1997)

Although many diverse sub-interpretations of the stakeholder perspective exist, a common critique of this perspective concerns the scope of it. For instance, taking the idea seriously that particularly those stakeholders are relevant which have power, legitimacy, and urgency, this could melt down the range of diverse stakeholders to finally only include shareholders. Similarly, critics have cast doubt about the harmonist view inherent in the stakeholder perspective. They cast doubt whether corporations can actually follow goals which are not reducible to the interests of shareholders, especially since the basic moral framework of capitalism is widely accepted across the stakeholder perspective (Mansell, 2013).

Corporate Wrongdoing

Examples of corporate irresponsibility and misconduct abound. Recent events, just to name a few examples, are the Volkswagen emissions scandal, the Wirecard accounting (and possibility also governance) scandal, the Rana Plaza disaster or tax avoidance practices of many large corporations. Interestingly, but not surprisingly, monitoring of the responsibility of German companies in their supply chains since 2018 showed that not even 20% of the companies with more than 500 employees voluntarily fully complied with responsibility standards (Auswärtiges Amt, 2020) even though this was formally not illegal behaviour at that time.

Like the phenomenon of corporate responsibility, a clear definition is difficult due to the several reasons already outlined related to the phenomenon of corporate responsibility. For instance, it is an ongoing political dispute if tax avoidance practices are irresponsible or not (e.g. the case of Ireland in the European Union). Moreover, it is an ongoing discussion if corporations are responsible for activities not occurring within their direct discretion but for instance within their supply chain (e.g. the initiative "Konzernverantwortung" in Switzerland or the Supply Chain law initiative by the governing coalition in Germany that would require German companies to abide by German legal standards also in their supply chains). This directly effects if we call a corporation irresponsible for its activities or not.

Rana Plaza is an example where corporate irresponsibility is striking and the consequences on life and peoples' well-being are shockingly clear. In 2013, the Rana Plaza disaster happened in Bangladesh. An eight-story commercial building collapsed, with a death toll of 1,134 people and approximately 2,500 injured. The press called it the deadliest structural failure accident in modern human history and the deadliest garment-factory disaster in history. Whereas the local building's owner did not take his responsibility to evacuate the building after cracks had appeared the day before, the responsibility of several globally known garment chains was discussed too. Especially their extraordinary power in global supply chains and with that their pressure to complete orders on time was criticized, all linked to the system of the fast fashion industry (https://en.wikipedia.org/wiki/Fast_fashion). However, also the other events like the Volkswagen emissions scandal or the Wirecard accounting scandal had and have severe consequences for diverse corporate stakeholders and are illustrative of the significance of corporate irresponsibility.

Irresponsible activities include corporate fraud, corruption, various forms of misconduct or "grey areas" (like tax avoidance) and have detrimental effects on environmental sustainability, basic human rights, social inequality and well-being. Excluding such negative performance outcomes leads to an incomplete understanding of corporate responsibility. To investigate these effects, it is important to acknowledge that the empirical phenomenon of corporate irresponsibility and corporate misconduct is more than just an antipode to corporate responsibility.

However, for several years, research has been biased towards explaining corporate responsibility and sustainability, thus potentially neglecting it as a joint phenomenon. Taking both phenomena under study enables us to also better access the quality and effectiveness of corporate responsibility measures. For instance, an important question is not only if corporate responsibility measures increase some stakeholders' well-being, but also if it reduces other stakeholder's harm. Since quite some time scholars doubting the effectiveness of corporate responsibility measures have labeled it a form of symbolic management decoupled from any substantial change (Delmas & Burbano, 2011). These scholars argue that corporate responsibility measures have little to no effect on outcomes which directly affect stakeholders' well-being. Others have criticized corporate responsibility measures even more severely and labelled them as a form of "greenwashing" (Jackson et al., 2014; Marquis et al., 2016; Strike et al., 2006). They argue that corporate responsibility measures are often aimed to deflect attention from corporate irresponsibility. Authors show how corporate responsibility is often correlated with irresponsible practices of corporations (Jackson et al., 2014; Kotchen & Moon, 2012).

Corporate Responsibility in Practice

Since several years, the role of corporate responsibility in practices is gaining increasing relevance. This is the case at the regulatory level, at the level of an infrastructure around companies (such as consultancy, rankings) and, most importantly, at the corporate level itself.

At the regulatory level, more and more national governments started to initiate respective laws, which encompass both strict regulation and softer approaches. An example for strict regulation is the "Child Labour Due Diligence Law" in the Netherlands which requires companies selling goods and services to Dutch end-users to determine whether child labour occurs in their supply chains (Business & Human Rights Resource Center, 2019). Softer approaches often used a so-called 'comply and explain method' which mandates companies to report or to explain why they are not reporting and leave large leeway for 'what' exactly to report on. One example is the non-financial reporting directive in the European Unions (European Commission, 2020; Jackson et al., 2020). This directive mandates large companies in the European Union to report (or to explain why they are not reporting) on issues like child labour, environmental topics etc., all summarized as non-financial issues in terms of going beyond information typically listed in financial reports. Moreover, and in addition to national law, multi-actor initiatives such as the UN Global Compact or the Roundtable on Sustainable Palm Oil were founded. These frameworks, jointly supported by companies, NGOs, governments and other civil society and international organizations, are meant to guide companies to enhance their responsibilities and work as a signal to diverse stakeholders (e.g., to consumers). Beyond their guiding role, they have no binding character, however.

Another area that reflects the increasing relevance of corporate responsibility in practice is the growing infrastructure around this topic. This infrastructure includes consulting firms helping firms to address their responsibilities (Gond & Brès, 2019), data providers that collect data from firms' webpages and reports in order to create large-scale datasets (e.g., Thomson Reuters environmental, social, and governance (ESG) data), ESG ratings benchmarking company's performance (Averisyan & Gond, 2013) or stock indices that are oriented towards firms' responsible activities (e.g. FTSE4Good Index, Dow Jones Sustainability Index or MSCI Climate Change ESG Index). That all mirrors an increasing interest at firms to engage in corporate responsibility, or at least to please their stakeholders.

Finally, looking at the role of corporate responsibility in practice, we can observe an increasing effort at the company level to demonstrate companies' responsibilities. Recent academic literature has pointed to the diverse set of drivers leading companies to adopt corporate responsibility in practice, including legislative requirements (Jackson et al., 2020; Matten & Moon, 2008, 2020), CEOs' political ideologies and values (Chin et al., 2013) or the potential business case (Hafenbradl & Waeger, 2017). Here, CSR reports by companies are particularly important. Although they often do not report about the company's activities in detail, they provide a good overview about what companies are (not) doing and what they wish others to know about their activities. To get a good impression about the diffusion of corporate responsibility practices worldwide, looking at these reports or company websites is therefore particularly helpful. Whereas most companies published a separate CSR report in the beginning, more and more firms turn to integrated reporting now – they have one report that includes both financial and non-financial information. The reports, no matter how the report is structured, often include information about adopted policies, targets, or adopted standards such as the UN Global Compact.

The following table shows a selection of relevant CSR practices and their adoption. The table illustrates the adoption worldwide. However, and since countries all have a very different CSR culture, history and also regulatory framework (Matten & Moon, 2008, 2020), the Table 1.1 shows the adoption rate in selected countries, too. As discussed earlier in terms of defining CSR, what counts as responsible business practices highly diverges between contexts. Particularly when it comes to comparing countries or regions, however, it is central to acknowledge differences in terms of diverse policy frameworks across countries. Therefore, it is important to remember from the discussion earlier that corporate responsibility is not limited to policies and practices adopted voluntarily by corporations or which go "beyond legal requirements." Since the legal context differs from one country to another, the same action may be considered voluntary in one context, but not so in another.

That is particularly important as the data set used for this illustration mirrors large stock indices worldwide. This yields important insights about the worldwide trend of CSR adoption. Moreover, looking at different countries or regions is important, too. First, it is important to acknowledge the differences in institutional context just discussed. Second, and as the concept of CSR is becoming more and more relevant not only in 'Western' countries but worldwide, the data set used for this illustration is still evolving – as the firms listed at "S&P 500" or "FTSE 250" or DAX" are included since

Corporate Responsibility   25

Table 1.1 CSR Adoption Rate (in %) Worldwide and Separately for Regions/Countries, 2019.

	Whole Sample	China	Emerging Markets	France	Germany	Great Britain	Japan	North America
Global Compact	11	5	7	43	24	10	30	4
Board Diversity Policy	56	29	16	69	69	65	39	65
Human Rights Policy	46	39	24	78	71	60	63	33
Resource Reduction Policy	54	78	42	79	76	57	74	40
Emission Reduction Policy	44	69	22	77	66	51	68	28
Energy Efficiency Policy	47	70	36	78	70	52	71	32
Environmental Supply Chain Selection Management	33	37	22	69	57	33	53	21
Emission Reduction Targets	24	7	8	54	43	29	55	14
Energy Efficiency Targets	17	5	7	44	29	18	36	10
Environmental Supply Chain Monitoring	24	24	9	58	47	22	38	15

*Thomson Reuters Refinitiv ESG Dataset (Download January 2021); 2019 as the most recent year as in early 2021, many data points for the year 2020 were still missing.

several years, firms belonging for example to the "MSCI Emerging markets-China" were added only recently. That mirrors an uneven distribution across countries, which is also reflected in the numbers reported here. Combining all these data into one large "average" therefore omits significant differences between countries and regions.

First, it is striking how the adoption rates differ between the different issue areas. Looking at the whole sample, it is striking how the adoption rates for some environmental policies such as resource reduction (54%) are higher than having a human rights policy (46%). Interestingly, the adoption rate of the Global Compact across the whole worldwide sample is only 11%.

Beyond the insights about policy adoption, it is important to investigate if firms formulate specific objectives, too. For instance, the rate of an emission reduction policy is about 44% whereas the rate of companies that formulate specific objectives is only about 24%. This is similar for energy efficiency and the environmental supply chain. Whereas 47% of companies have a policy for energy efficiency, only 17% have specific targets. Similarly, 33% of companies have a policy for environmental supply chain selection management, whereas only 24% have an active monitoring installed.

Second, the adoption rate differs quite heavily between the different countries or world regions. Speaking about board diversity, two-thirds of the companies in Great Britain (65%) have a respective policy compared to only 39% in Japan. In contrast, Japanese companies have a high adoption rate of energy efficiency (71%) or resource reduction policies (74%). It is interesting since companies in emerging markets, which score quite low in many areas, have a comparable high adoption rate in these domains, too.

Third, and looking at the adoption rate over time (Table 1.2), it becomes quite clear that the adoption rate in all countries is increasing. For instance, looking at the adoption rate of the UN Global Compact, 2% of companies have signed the compact

26 Julia Bartosch and Jörg Raab

Table 1.2 CSR Adoption Rate (in %) Over Time (2005, 2010, 2015 and 2019), Worldwide Development*

	2005	2010	2015	2019
Global Compact	2	6	10	11
Board Diversity Policy	1	6	31	56
Human Rights Policy	3	13	25	46
Resource Reduction Policy	8	29	38	54
Emission Reduction Policy	5	23	30	44
Energy Efficiency Policy	5	24	33	47
Environmental Supply Chain Selection Management	3	16	23	33
Emission Reduction Targets	4	15	16	24
Energy Efficiency Targets	3	10	13	17
Environmental Supply Chain Monitoring	0	5	14	24

* Thomson Reuters Refinitiv ESG Dataset (Downloaded on 10 January 2021); 2019 as the most recent year as in early 2021, many data points for the year 2020 were still missing.

in 2005, 6% in 2010, 10% in 2015 and 11% in 2019. This development is similar for companies that adopt a board diversity policy: 1% in 2005, 6% in 2010, 31% in 2015 and 56% in 2019. Similarly, the increase happened for policies on human rights. Interestingly, we can observe that the increase of firms having a respective policy happened earlier for environmental topics: Here, also in 2010, 29% of companies had a policy on resource reduction (8% in 2005 and 38% in 2015). This is similar for emissions reduction or energy efficiency policies.

Conclusion

Corporate responsibility is a highly important but disputed concept. Similar to other concepts like corporate sustainability or corporate citizenship, it became a crucial cornerstone in the discussion about how to transform our current societies and economic model into more sustainable ones. This is important against the backdrop of the sheer extent of ecological and social challenges and the urgency to fundamentally change the way our economy operates (Klein, 2014; Wright & Nyberg, 2015). Yet, and despite the growing urgency, scientific results show that the business world has to date achieved only little in that regard (Whiteman et al., 2013; Wright & Nyberg, 2015). This demonstrates the urgency and relevance to address questions of corporate responsibility within business practices, political discussions, in discussions with friends, in university seminars and in research on business, management and organizations.

This chapter has highlighted the many questions internal to the phenomenon. But instead of closing the chapter by arguing that the phenomenon is complicated, too many different perspectives exist, normative views would never collide – we would like to underline the value of such a multifaceted understanding of the phenomenon. First, taking one of the perspectives only would hide the plurality of perspectives that exist (Rasche & Scherer, 2014). Thinking and arguing about the different perspectives instead helps to develop our own understanding of the topic, facilitates the discussion with others as we better understand their (likely diverging) views and it finally enables business, political and societal solutions. Only through such a discussion will we be able to make progress in the transformation of our societies to a more sustainable future that is ahead of us. As we have shown, this discussion cannot be conducted in isolation but is intricately connected to the role of the state, international regimes and legal frameworks. However, no matter what the legal, managerial and governance solutions will be that will be developed to make progress towards a more sustainable future, there will always be areas that will be contested and where the concept of corporate responsibility will have to play an important role.

References

Aguilera, R. V., Rupp, D. E., Williams, C. A., & Ganapathi, J. (2007). Putting the S back in corporate social responsibility: A multilevel theory of social change in organizations. *Academy of Management Review*, 32(3), 836–863. https://doi.org/10.5465/AMR.2007.25275678

Auswärtiges Amt. (2020). *Monitoring zum Nationalen Aktionsplan Wirtschaft und Menschenrechte*. Retrieved December 21, 2021, from https://www.auswaertiges-amt.de/de/aussenpolitik/themen/aussenwirtschaft/wirtschaft-und-menschenrechte/monitoring-nap/2124010

Avetisyan, E., & Gond, J. P. (2013). Institutional dynamics of CSR standardization: A multilevel perspective in the field of ESG rating. *Academy of Management Proceedings*, 1, 15122–15122. https://doi.org/10.5465/ambpp.2013.15122abstract

Bakan, J. (2004). *The corporation*. Constable.

Battilana, J., Obloj, T., Pache, A. C., & Sengul, M. (2020). Beyond shareholder value maximization: Accounting for financial/social tradeoffs in dual-purpose companies. *Academy of Management Review*. https://doi.org/10.5465/amr.2019.0386

Brundtland Commission. (1987). *Report of the world commission on environment and development*. Brundtland Commission.

Business & Human Rights Resource Center. (2019). *Dutch senate votes to adopt child labour due diligence law*. Business & Human Rights Resource Centre. www.business-humanrights.org/en/latest-news/dutch-senate-votes-to-adopt-child-labour-due-diligence-law/

Business Roundtable. (2019). *Our commitment*. Business Roundtable.

Campbell, J. L. (2007). Why would corporations behave in socially responsible ways? An institutional theory of corporate social responsibility. *Academy of Management Review*, 32(3), 946–967. https://doi.org/10.5465/AMR.2007.25275684

Carroll, A. B. (1991). The pyramid of corporate social responsibility: Toward the moral management of organizational stakeholders. *Business Horizons*, 34(4), 39–48. https://doi.org/10.1016/0007-6813(91)90005-G

Carroll, A. B. (2016). Carroll's pyramid of CSR: Taking another look. *International Journal of Corporate Social Responsibility*, 1(1), 1–8. https://doi.org/10.1186/s40991-016-0004-6

Chin, M. K., Hambrick, D. C., & Treviño, L. K. (2013). Political ideologies of CEOs: The influence of executives' values on corporate social responsibility. *Administrative Science Quarterly*, 58(2), 197–232. https://doi.org/10.1177/0001839213486984

Delmas, M. A., & Burbano, V. C. (2011). The drivers of greenwashing. *California Management Review*, 54(1), 64–87. Sage Publications. https://doi.org/10.1525/cmr.2011.54.1.64

Deloitte. (2019). *The Deloitte global millennial survey 2019: Societal discord and technological transformation create a "generation disrupted"*. https://www2.deloitte.com/global/en/pages/about-deloitte/articles/millennialsurvey

Devinney, T. M. (2009). Is the socially responsible corporation a myth? The good, the bad, and the ugly of corporate social responsibility. *Academy of Management Perspectives*, 23(2), 44–56. https://doi.org/10.5465/AMP.2009.39985540

Elkington, J. (1998). Partnerships from cannibals with forks: The triple bottom line of 21st-century business. *Environmental Quality Management*, 8(1), 37–51. https://doi.org/10.1002/tqem.3310080106

European Commission. (2020). *Corporate sustainability reporting.* https://ec.europa.eu/info/business-economy-euro/company-reporting-and-auditing/company-reporting/corporate-sustainability-reporting_en

Freeman, R. E., & McVea, J. (2001). A stakeholder approach to strategic management. In *The Blackwell handbook of strategic management* (pp. 189–207). Blackwell.

Friedman, M. (1962). *Capitalism and freedom.* The University of Chicago Press.

Gao, J., & Bansal, P. (2013). Instrumental and integrative logics in business sustainability. *Journal of Business Ethics, 112*(2), 241–255. https://doi.org/10.1007/s10551-012-1245-2

Gelles, D. (2018). Paul Polman, a "crucial voice" for corporate responsibility, steps down as Unilever C.E.O. *The New York Times.* www.nytimes.com/2018/11/29/business/unilever-ceo-paul-polman.html

Gond, J. P., & Brès, L. (2019). Designing the tools of the trade: How corporate social responsibility consultants and their tool-based practices created market shifts. *Organization Studies, 41*(5), 703–726. https://doi.org/10.1177/0170840619867360

The Guardian. (2015). Work of prominent climate change denier was funded by energy industry: Climate change. *The Guardian.*

The Guardian. (2020). Covid outbreak exposes dire conditions at Guatemala factory making US brands. *The Guardian.* www.theguardian.com/global-development/2020/aug/06/covid-outbreak-exposes-dire-conditions-at-guatemala-factory-making-us-brands

Hafenbradl, S., & Waeger, D. (2017). Ideology and the micro-foundations of CSR: Why executives believe in the business case for CSR and how this affects their CSR engagements. *Academy of Management Journal, 60*(4), 1582–1606. https://doi.org/10.5465/amj.2014.0691

Hahn, T., Figge, F., Pinkse, J., & Preuss, L. (2018). A paradox perspective on corporate sustainability: Descriptive, instrumental, and normative aspects. *Journal of Business Ethics, 148*(2), 235–248. https://doi.org/10.1007/s10551-017-3587-2

Hahn, T., Pinkse, J., Preuss, L., & Figge, F. (2015). Tensions in corporate sustainability: Towards an integrative framework. *Journal of Business Ethics, 127*(2), 297–316. https://doi.org/10.1007/s10551-014-2047-5

Hahn, T., Preuss, L., Pinkse, J., & Figge, F. (2014). Cognitive frames in corporate sustainability: Managerial sensemaking with paradoxical and business case frames. *Academy of Management Review, 39*(4), 463–487. https://doi.org/10.5465/amr.2012.0341

Jackson, G., Bartosch, J., Avetisyan, E., Kinderman, D., & Knudsen, J. S. (2020). Mandatory non-financial disclosure and its influence on CSR: An international comparison. *Journal of Business Ethics, 162*(2), 323–342. https://doi.org/10.1007/s10551-019-04200-0

Jackson, G., Brammer, S., Karpoff, J. M., Lange, D., Zavyalova, A., Harrington, B., Partnoy, F., King, B. G., & Deephouse, D. L. (2014). Grey areas: Irresponsible corporations and reputational dynamics. *Socio-Economic Review, 12*(1), 153–218. https://doi.org/10.1093/ser/mwt021

Klein, N. (2014). *This changes everything: Capitalism vs. the climate.* Simon & Schuster.

Kotchen, M., & Moon, J. J. (2012). Corporate social responsibility for irresponsibility. *B.E. Journal of Economic Analysis and Policy, 12*(1). https://doi.org/10.1515/1935-1682.3308

Lohmeyer, N. (2017). *Instrumentalisierte Verantwortung?: Entstehung und Motive des »Business Case for CSR« im deutschen Diskurs unternehmerischer Verantwortung.* Bielefeld: Transcript Verlag.

Lohmeyer, N., & Jackson, G. (2018). The business case as new vocabulary of motive: Discourse coalitions around CSR in Germany, 1970–2014. *Academy of Management Proceedings, 2018*(1), 14169.

Mansell, S. F. (2013). *Capitalism, corporations and the social contract: A critique of stakeholder theory.* Cambridge University Press.

Marquis, C., Toffel, M. W., & Zhou, Y. (2016). Scrutiny, norms, and selective disclosure: A global study of greenwashing. *Organization Science, 27*(2), 483–504. https://doi.org/10.1287/orsc.2015.1039

Matten, D., & Moon, J. (2008). "Implicit" and "explicit" CSR: A conceptual framework for a comparative understanding of corporate social responsibility. *Academy of Management Review*, 33(2), 404–424. https://doi.org/10.5465/AMR.2008.31193458

Matten, D., & Moon, J. (2020). Reflections on the 2018 decade award: The meaning and dynamics of corporate social responsibility. *Academy of Management Review*, 45(1), 7–28. https://doi.org/10.5465/amr.2019.0348

McWilliams, A., & Siegel, D. (2001). Corporate social responsibility: A theory of the firm perspective. *Academy of Management Review*, 26(1), 117–127. https://doi.org/10.5465/AMR.2001.4011987

Meyer, R. E., & Höllerer, M. A. (2010). Meaning structures in a contested issue field: A topographic map of shareholder value in Austria. *Academy of Management Journal*, 53(6), 1241–1262. https://doi.org/10.5465/amj.2010.57317829

Mitchell, R. K., Agle, B. R., & Wood, D. J. (1997). Toward a theory of stakeholder identification and salience: Defining the principle of who and what really counts. *Academy of Management Review*, 22(4), 853–886. https://doi.org/10.5465/AMR.1997.9711022105

Montiel, I. (2008). Corporate social responsibility and corporate sustainability: Separate pasts, common futures. *Organization and Environment*, 21(3), 245–269. https://doi.org/10.1177/1086026608321329

Mudaliar, A., & Dithrich, H. (2019). *Sizing the impact investing market acknowledgments.* Global Impact Investing Network.

The New York Times. (2020, March 14). The companies putting profits ahead of public health. *The New York Times.* www.nytimes.com/2020/03/14/opinion/sunday/coronavirus-paid-sick-leave.html

Okoye, A. (2009). Theorising corporate social responsibility as an essentially contested concept: Is a definition necessary? *Journal of Business Ethics*, 89(4), 613–627. https://doi.org/10.1007/s10551-008-0021-9

Porter, M. E., & Kramer, M. R. (2011). Creating shared value: How to reinvent capitalism and unleash a wave of innovation and growth. *Harvard Business Review*, 89(1–2), 62–77.

Raghunandan, A., & Rajgopal, S. (2020). Do the socially responsible walk the talk? *SSRN Electronic Journal.* https://doi.org/10.2139/ssrn.3609056

Rasche, A., & Scherer, A. (2014). Jürgen Habermas and organization studies – contributions and future prospects. In P. Adler, P. Du Gay, G. Morgan, & M. Reed (Eds.), *The Oxford handbook of sociology, social theory, and organization studies* (pp. 158–181). Oxford University Press.

Reid, G. (2020). *Mars sustainability in a generation plan\mars incorporated.* www.mars.com/sustainability-plan

Roberts, J. (2003). The manufacture of corporate social responsibility: Constructing corporate sensibility. *Organization*, 10(2), 249–265. https://doi.org/10.1177/13505084030100 02004

Rockström, J., Steffen, W., Noone, K., Persson, Å., Chapin, F. S., Lambin, E., Lenton, T. M., Scheffer, M., Folke, C., Schellnhuber, H. J., Nykvist, B., Wit, C. A. de, Hughes, T., Leeuw, S. van der, Rodhe, H., Sörlin, S., Snyder, P. K., Costanza, R., Svedin, U., . . . Foley, J. (2009). Planetary boundaries exploring the safe operating space for humanity. *Ecology and Society*, 14, 472–475.

Shabana, K. M., Buchholtz, A. K., & Carroll, A. B. (2017). The institutionalization of corporate social responsibility reporting. *Business and Society*, 56(8), 1107–1135. https://doi.org/10.1177/0007650316628177

Strike, V. M., Gao, J., & Bansal, P. (2006). Being good while being bad: Social responsibility and the international diversification of US firms. *Journal of International Business Studies*, 37(6), 850–862. https://doi.org/10.1057/palgrave.jibs.8400226

Ulrich, P. (2008). *Integrative economic ethics: Foundations of a civilized market economy.* Cambridge University Press.

United Nations Environment Program. (2018). *Emissions gap report 2018*. http://wedocs.unep.org/bitstream/handle/20.500.11822/26895/EGR2018_FullReport_EN.pdf?sequence=1&isAllowed=y

van der Byl, C. A., Slawinski, N., & Hahn, T. (2020). Responsible management of sustainability tensions: A paradoxical approach to grand challenges. In O. Laasch, R. Suddaby, R. E. Freeman, & D. Jamali (Eds.), *Research handbooks in business and management series.* (pp. 438–452). Edward Elgar Publishing Limited.

Whiteman, G., Walker, B., & Perego, P. (2013). Planetary boundaries: Ecological foundations for corporate sustainability. *Journal of Management Studies, 50*(2), 307–336. https://doi.org/10.1111/j.1467-6486.2012.01073.x

Wright, C., & Nyberg, D. (2015). *Climate change, capitalism, and corporations.* Cambridge University Press. https://doi.org/10.1017/CBO9781139939676

2 Responsible innovation

The Role of Organizational Practices and Structures

Ashley Metz and Nikolas Rathert

Introduction

Generally speaking, innovation is the process of recombining existing elements (raw materials, social practices, ideas, etc.) in ways that are new to a given context, such as in an organization or a country (Criscuolo et al., 2017; Fleming, 2001). For example, the iPhone brought together mobile calling, a camera, and internet capabilities largely accessed through mobile applications. The iPhone was the first smartphone to be successful on a large scale and it precipitated the rise of two dominant ecosystems, Apple and Google's Android, and their respective app stores, which revolutionized the idea and functionalities of a phone. Yet, the iPhone production process has resulted in serious negative social and environmental consequences. Apple has perpetrated detrimental labor practices such as hostility, excessive overtime and violence through supplier Foxconn (Chan et al., 2020) and its production has a high environmental impact (Aayan, 2020). Considering the extensive harm involved in its production, the 'net' value produced by an iPhone could be debated. In comparison, by organizing sourcing, production, and post-use recycling differently, phone company Fairphone (a social enterprise and B-corporation)[1] is able to offer a smartphone with more fair labor practices and a smaller environmental impact. The ambiguous nature of innovation poses an important question: How can innovation processes be organized to benefit society and the environment, but also avoid harm?

In the literature on the governance of innovation and technology, the term 'responsible innovation' (RI) has been introduced to refer to evaluating science and technological innovations based on their potential for harm, their potential for positive impact on the planet and on people, and how the innovation process can be governed for desirable outcomes (Stilgoe et al., 2013). At the core of this debate so far is the notion that policy-makers and the broader public need to ensure that innovations avoid unintended consequences and harm to society. In its original conception, the term 'responsible innovation' revolved around processes of developing and governing the use of new technologies, such as geoengineering (Stilgoe et al., 2013), healthcare robotics (Stahl & Coeckelberg, 2016) or nanotechnology (Fisher et al., 2012). These debates focused on how the governance of scientific research and innovation could be facilitated at the sectoral and societal levels, such that innovation would benefit society and prevent negative consequences (Burget et al., 2017; Stilgoe et al., 2013). Ultimately, this kind of governance would lead to "a proper embedding of scientific and technological advances in our society" (von Schomberg, 2012). It involves four main dimensions, or principles, summarized in Table 2.1: *anticipation* to consider potential

DOI: 10.4324/9780429243165-3

This chapter has been made available under a CC-BY-NC 4.0 license.

32 Ashley Metz and Nikolas Rathert

Table 2.1 Four Principles of Responsible Innovation (Based on Stilgoe et al., 2013)

Anticipatory of potential intended and unintended consequences
Reflective about underlying motivations and assumptions
Inclusive and deliberative about ideas, plans, issues with stakeholders
Responsive and adaptable

implications of unintended consequences; *inclusion* and *deliberation* involving stakeholders; *reflexivity* to critically assess one's own role as an innovator; *responsiveness* to shift in response to new information (Lubberink et al., 2017a). For example, in developing health care robotics, scientists and managers could *anticipate* how usage could cause unrest or job loss with medical staff; *include and engage* physicians and patients in the development process; *reflexively consider* biases built into how they operate; and be *responsive* as unexpected issues are experienced.

These scholars were focused on scientific innovations, and thus considered the governance of responsible innovation to mainly lie with oversight bodies such as research councils, or field-level regulators typically included in scientific developments. Focusing on governance at this level, however, neglects the many elements at play in *organizations* as key sites of the development process of innovation. While the scientists and managers working on the development of specific products have some say over how product development happens, and external regulators can set scope conditions for development, these individuals are also working in organizational contexts. In organizations, other goals coexist alongside responsible innovation, for example, financial goals, that can interact with behavior stipulated by responsible innovation principles. As such, expanding the concept of responsible innovation to the organizational level can shed light on how to organize for RI in practice.

Recently, organization scholars have begun to consider how organizations and corporations in particular – as sites where many innovations are developed and scaled – can facilitate responsible innovation. This research has put forward various *governance* principles, for example stakeholder participation or accountability, which may enable responsible innovation to become institutionalized at the organizational level (Scherer & Voegtlin, 2020). It has also expanded the *types* of innovation under consideration, and examined how organizations may embed the four principles in their innovation processes. Specifically, the debate on innovation has highlighted the relevance of organizations in developing social innovations (besides technical ones) for addressing a host of societal problems (Luo & Kaul, 2019), i.e. innovations whose primary focus is changes in behavior and of institutionalized norms and rules that are detrimental to societal groups (Cajaiba-Santana, 2014). In such cases, embedding and applying the principles of responsible innovation may be even more relevant, as social innovations typically involve altering social processes and cultural elements, such as gender norms (Mair & Marti, 2009). In this chapter, we build on this nascent debate to further develop our understanding of organizational governance structures and processes that can facilitate responsible innovation. We do so because although the application of responsible innovation at the organizational level implies a range of possible structures and processes that may facilitate RI, our understanding of *what* these structures and practices are and *how* they in turn enable organizations to contribute to more sustainable forms of organizing, remains underdeveloped. It is important because responsible innovation has the potential to facilitate sustainable development by reducing harm or 'doing good' and emphasizes the role and importance of organizations in sustainable development.

To address this gap, we provide an overview of how corporations and other market organizations integrate RI into their organizing models, employing a perspective that focuses on (a) governance *structures* and (b) organizational *practices* as manifestations of RI on the organizational level. Building on this perspective, our chapter uses illustrative examples from corporations and social enterprises to highlight the diverse structures and practices to embed RI at the organizational level, for both technical and social innovations. We seek to open up a future research agenda to examine the outcomes of these structures and practices with respect to embedding anticipatory, reflective, deliberative, and participatory mindsets in innovation, and what this may mean for the emergence of a new organizational form that has RI at its core.

From Irresponsible to Responsible Innovation in Market Organizations

Across different sectors and societies, there is considerable consensus that commercial objectives are no longer sufficient as the sole focus of corporations in the face of many pressing global challenges (Barnett et al., 2020; Segrestin et al., 2020). As a result, shareholder value maximization[2] as the central objective of commercial organizations is increasingly criticized. The detrimental and/or unintended consequences of corporate innovations have, in particular, been linked to the primacy of shareholder value and economic goals. These consequences include sweatshop labor, cuts to employee benefits, environmental mistreatment, among other issues. Indeed, management scholars have shown how corporations perpetuate many of society's most pressing problems ranging from climate change, gender inequality, racial relations, and others (Amis et al., 2020; Bapuji et al., 2020). While the literature on corporate social responsibility (CSR) has sought to map out and understand the different ways in which corporations take on societal issues and possibly address the consequences of their innovations (Haack et al., 2012; Halme et al., 2020; Wickert & de Bakker, 2018; see also chapter by Bartosch and Raab on CSR in this volume), the literature on RI documents how many of these initiatives remain decoupled from detrimental commercial activities and, as a result, do not address their harmful consequences (Crilly et al., 2012; Mair & Rathert, 2019a).

In this regard, the textile industry is illustrative to understand how the RI principles are often not embedded in innovations. Innovations that have facilitated, for example, the widespread and rapid availability of affordable garments, such as IT systems that enable the flow of information and finances, simultaneously imply harm to a range of stakeholders. In fact, supply chains in the textile industry are characterized by unsafe working conditions (Schuessler et al., 2019), negating firms' various CSR efforts meant to address issues such as lack of employee health and safety, or child labor (Rathert, 2016). In the pharmaceutical industry, where corporations create innovations in the form of medicines, these products are often not available uniformly across geographies and societal groups. Likewise, many diseases, especially in developing countries, remain neglected as pharmaceutical corporations devote less attention and priorities to developing and making available medicines targeting these diseases (Roemer-Mahler, 2015). The lack of embeddedness of responsibility principles in innovations has led to a lack of access to medicine for billions of people that perpetuate health inequality. In this case, innovations fail to meet and respond to the needs of stakeholders.

How, then, can market organizations enable and institutionalize RI as a key organizational objective? Given their tremendous expertise, geographical reach, and resources, corporations are crucial actors in addressing pressing problems and may become sites where solutions of these problems can be developed. This question has taken on additional relevance in light of the growing need for social innovations and the role that market actors may play in their design and implementation (Mair & Rathert, 2019a). These organizations, including social enterprises and various other organizational forms (Haigh & Hoffman, 2014; Mair & Marti, 2006; discussed in the chapter on hybrid organizations), leverage market strategies to make progress on social issues (Mair & Marti, 2006; Mair, 2020). To understand how organizational governance structures and practices may facilitate the embedding of responsibility principles in innovation, we now discuss various examples of such structures and practices and how these link to the principles.

Governance Structures for Responsible Innovation

In this section, we consider two illustrative governance structures – legal forms and participatory structures – and discuss how they can enable responsible innovation in organizations. While the literature conceives of governance structures in various ways, among others as means to distribute power and control among stakeholders, or to determine how returns are distributed among them (Aguilera et al., 2015), for our purposes we interrogate governance structures to the extent to which they are instrumental in facilitating *anticipatory, reflective, deliberative*, and *responsive* innovation processes. In practice, legal forms and participatory structures can overlap as certain legal forms incorporate or allow for greater or lesser participation.

Legal Forms

Broadly speaking, legal forms affect not only various aspects of the organization, including taxation, liability, and accountability, but also the goals that organizations can legitimately pursue (Mitchell et al., 2016; Mair, 2020). Recently, a range of new legal forms have emerged as a governance structure of market-oriented organizations that allows for embedding anticipatory, reflective, deliberative, and participatory mindsets in innovation activities, by extending the range of objectives organizations can pursue (Levillain et al., 2019). These forms are often referred to as 'social businesses' (Yunus et al., 2010), though their specific manifestations differ across contexts. In the UK, the Community Interest Company (CIC) has become a widespread legal form to allow commercial organizations to use commercial activity toward a social purpose. Within the CIC form, dividends are capped and an 'asset lock' limits disbursements to community benefit purposes. In the United States, the low-profit limited liability company (L3C) allows organizations to pursue non-financial purposes alongside financial ones. These multiple objectives are safeguarded by an operating agreement that states the social purpose of the organization. As another example, the Benefit Corporation is a legal form with an even stronger focus on social goals and value. Organizations using this legal form must publish a publicly available report measuring social performance against a third-party standard. Investors of Benefit Corporations may receive unlimited midstream and residual returns, but statutes explicitly reject wealth maximization (Reiser & Dean, 2013).

We argue that legal forms can enable responsible innovation activities through their explicit focus on multiple goals, compared to the more limited range of goals in traditional for-profit legal forms. A key mechanism through which the inclusion of social alongside economic goals affects responsible innovation is knowledge sourcing. To develop new products, processes, or services that generate benefit and avoid harm to stakeholders, these organizations need to engage in knowledge sourcing practices that involve external stakeholders (Stephan et al., 2019). To gain knowledge about the feasibility of innovations that are primarily meant to enable social and institutional change, this form of external knowledge sourcing enables anticipatory, inclusive, and/or deliberative practices. For example, French company Le Slip Français, a 'société a mission' that has explicit social and environmental goals in its by-laws (Segrestin et al., 2020), has developed a supply chain model for textiles that uses entirely localized production in France. To make this model feasible, the company relies on local producers for knowledge on how to design and implement the production process, but also to assess the feasibility of innovations such as automation of production processes when these take place in small, family-owned suppliers (Hadjadji, 2019).

These recently emerging legal forms with a wider range of organizational goals can enable responsible innovation in many issue domains, for example public health (Vickers et al., 2017). This effect is not limited to newly emerging forms, but can also be observed in older forms such as cooperatives, that have recently seen a resurgence (Mair & Rathert, 2019b). For example, cooperative companies in France (société coopérative; a legal form for commercially focused organizations that prohibits the transfer of shares to third parties) have sought to develop innovations to address shortages in social housing. A key problem with regard to innovations in this area is that previous efforts (i.e. development of new housing solutions) did not match the housing needs of people, in that these housing solutions were either too scarce or too expensive.[3] Several social businesses operating in this space have reversed the innovation process to include target populations in the design of housing solutions that entail deliberation with these populations over their needs, but also the anticipation of constraints by other stakeholders (e.g. landlords, local authorities) via collaborative steering tools.

Participatory Structures

Another example of governance structures that can enable responsible innovation is organizational participatory structures that allow for regular engagement with stakeholders, review firm-stakeholder interactions, and assess the impact of innovations on the stakeholder environment. In many corporations, board-level stakeholder committees have become prevalent to fulfill these purposes (Burke et al., 2019). Research has shown that such structures make corporations more responsive to stakeholder concerns and, once introduced, also make them more receptive to future stakeholder issues (McDonnell et al., 2015). Once these participatory structures are put in place, they have the incidental effect of enabling the actors who staff them to further institutionalize awareness of societal implications of organizational actions. This is because these actors tend to interact directly with outside stakeholders and experience negative consequences of existing business practices more directly (Soderstrom & Weber, 2020;

Wickert & de Bakker, 2018). In social enterprises and other social businesses, such structures often take the form of governing or advisory boards that can include target populations and beneficiaries (Mair et al., 2020).

Our argument regarding the role of these participatory structures for responsible innovations is that they can embed anticipatory and reflective mindset in organizational innovation processes, as well as offer spaces for deliberation over the legitimacy and effectiveness of innovations. The role of these structures for enabling deliberation and reflexivity has been well established in studies on how social enterprises use them to create downward accountability for their innovations with target populations (Spear et al., 2009). These functions are thus especially important for organizations that seek to design and implement social innovations, but also hold potential for traditional commercial organizations. These innovations, perhaps more than purely technical innovations, involve creating awareness among future beneficiaries and potentially overcoming resistance to adopting such innovations. Where awareness and acceptance are lacking, social innovations have a reduced impact or generate unintended consequences (such as reinforcing detrimental institutional arrangements; Mair & Marti, 2009; Zhao & Lounsbury, 2016). For example, organizations seeking to improve sanitary practices (i.e. access to clean water, toilets) and associated health outcomes in India, where almost half of the population has no access to toilet facilities (Ramani et al., 2017), established participatory structures to enable acceptance of social innovations among beneficiaries. These governance structures, such as 'village committees' (Mair et al., 2016), create spaces for deliberation over a specific innovation such as creating access to sanitation and offer regular opportunities for reflecting on whether a specific innovation is effective and legitimate by involving various groups affected by it. This is relevant given that such innovations entail changing social norms that create resistance or rejection among both beneficiaries and those that benefit from existing arrangements, such as elites.

In the corporate setting, the food company Barilla offers an example of how participatory structures can embed reflection and inclusiveness in organizational innovation processes such as hiring programs. By establishing a diversity and inclusion advisory board that includes external experts and advocates for diversity matters, the company was able to consider how changes to its internal programs and policies (i.e. internally focused innovations) affected LGBTQ employees, which in turn led to the adoption of new policies that were more effective in increasing gender diversity and inclusiveness and have garnered praise from activists (BarillaGroup, 2021; BEQPride Magazine, 2018).

Taken together, we argue that participatory structures constitute a governance structure, much like the legal form that a company operates under, that can facilitate the adoption of responsible innovation as an inherent feature of the innovation process. As shown, the principles associated with responsible innovation can affect both externally focused innovations, such as social innovations, as well as more internally oriented ones, such as new hiring and employment quality policies.

Organizational Practices for Responsible Innovation

Apart from governance structures, a range of organizational practices have emerged across a variety of settings that enable responsible innovation through their daily enactment in organizations. These practices are an important level of analysis for considering how re-orienting organizational innovation processes toward the responsible innovation principles can be facilitated through everyday activities (e.g. Metz & Hartley, 2020; Pollock & D'Adderio, 2012). In the following sections, we discuss two such sets of practices – social accounting and procedures to conceptualize problems.

Social Accounting

Accounting practices influence what is considered important at organizations, or 'counting what counts' in terms of how goods and services are valued in and by organizations. Practices, and in this example, the accounting of value, play an important role in responsible innovation. Work in the accounting field highlights and raises questions about how by *anticipating* the way in which goods, services, inputs and outputs are counted and appraised, organizations may lead to more responsible outcomes. Accounting for multiple types of value could, for example, support managers to count pollution and fair labor wages as outputs, facilitating the avoidance of harm and the creation of positive impact. On the contrary, if organizational actors are considering the four dimensions of RI as they work to develop a new product or service, they may neglect to count all salient impacts if the accounting practices employed focus purely on economic value.

Traditional accounting tracks and counts economic value alone. Much research in critical accounting and sociology discusses that accounting is not a neutral process (e.g. Hines, 1988). Double-entry bookkeeping, the precursor to modern accounting, enabled rational business decision-making that focused on accumulating capital (Sombart, 1967; Weber, 1927). For example, in a study of city strategies, Kornberger and Carter (2010) identify that calculative practices inform city league tables that compare and encourage competition among cities, which thus influences cities to create strategies. Critical views on accounting emerged in the mid-1980s when accounting scholars raised the issue of accounting practices' social consequences and the need to account for environmental regulations in or potential liability from incompliance (Tinker, 1985). Tinker's book is said to have sparked awareness of the social consequences of accounting practices, stimulating a new field of critical management and accounting study. The way accounting constructs what it measures has been discussed: "Until we recognize [revenues in financial accounting], they are, for just about all intents and purposes, not real" (Hines, 1988). Around this time, there was a turning point in accounting research with an investigation into non-technical aspects (Englund et al., 2011).

In order to count other types of outcomes, social and environmental impact reporting of innovation has been discussed by academics for several decades in various respects. However, rather than reporting achievements for goals like legitimacy and decision making, as seen in the social sector, such reporting originating with for-profit firms tends to relate to avoiding problems. The field of social impact assessment as a prospective tool emerged in the 1970s as a response to the National Environmental Policy Act of 1969, which requires Federal agencies to "make integrated use of the natural and social sciences in decision making which may have an impact on man's environment" (see Freudenburg, 1986 for a review). Such analysis, typically applied to large construction projects, covers both technical and political approaches; this practice aims to limit harm rather than measure good performance.

38 *Ashley Metz and Nikolas Rathert*

Social accounting is a branch of social impact measurement for the mainstream business world. Though some scholars claim that social accounting is now "approaching mainstream" (Mook, 2013), social accounting project scholars (Gray, 1992, 2002; Spence, 2009) note that businesses "capture the sustainability agenda and rearticulate it into a discourse that does not challenge the fundamental pillars of business-as-usual" (Spence, 2009). Likewise, the need to return shareholder value provides structural basis for ignoring other agendas (Bakan, 1997). Integrated reporting (IR) is a relatively new practice that aims to facilitate more responsible organizations. IR was developed by the International Integrated Reporting Council and standardized in 2013 to combine traditional accounting with CSR or sustainability reports to create a more comprehensive picture of firm activities (Rowbottom & Locke, 2013). Integrated reporting aims to encourage broader and longer-term thinking (de Villiers et al., 2014; Adams, 2015). However, research so far is mostly normative and has not begun to critically assess the new practice (Dumay et al., 2016).

Problem Conceptualization

Another practice that enables organizations to embed RI principles in innovation activities and processes relates to conceptualizing, acting on, and changing the explicit or implicit set of problems that the organization purports to solve through an innovation. A problem can be understood as a gap between the current reality and a future goal situation (Battilana et al., 2019; Senge, 2009). Every organization works to solve one or more problems. For example, a bank solves the problem of financing for people wishing to buy houses or start small businesses, while solving others' problems around where to keep or invest their money. A large consumer goods store solves problems about peoples' daily needs like washing their hair or procuring machines to make coffee. Other types of organizations exist specifically to solve a societal or environmental issue – financing for the poor who are left out by organizations that focus on wealthier clients, for example. Arguably, the basic idea of defining a problem is viewed differently by different types of organizations – traditional businesses think of problems from their perspective as organizations – Is there a large enough market of people who have a certain problem? Is an organizational concern identified really the problem a solution should be designed for (Astor et al., 2016)? In contrast, social innovators may instead start from an environmental or social problem and from the perspective of beneficiaries (Mair & Rathert, 2019a).

The problem an organization aims to solve – and for whom – can clarify and help define the meaning of responsible innovation. When designing a novel product, service or other organizational output, limiting harm and/or creating positive impact can be perhaps best achieved when the "problem" defined articulates an issue that, if solved, has the most positive outcome potential. In leadership studies, scholars have distinguished between technical and adaptive problems (Heifetz & Laurie, 1997). Technical problems are easy to identify and lend themselves to clear solutions, such as administering a drug or implementing a new system, whereas adaptive problems are more difficult to identify and require amendments to values, beliefs, relations, and typically require work across organizations (ibid). These authors argue that leaders fail when they treat adaptive challenges like technical problems, and design and implement innovations accordingly. In the social enterprise literature these adaptive problems are referred to as relational problems (Seelos & Mair, 2020). Innovations may address technical and/or relational problems and often need to address or incorporate both. For example, seemingly technical problems such as a lack of vaccines may only be addressed by devising innovations that address relational problems aspects such as asymmetric power dynamics (Seelos & Mair, 2017). Understanding and reflecting upon these problem distinctions can be helpful across perspectives and organizations – whether for leaders, social innovators, or anyone else in organizations to anticipate potential consequences of innovations.

The way a problem is defined affects how organizations approach an innovation, how it may be designed and implemented, and whether they should pursue it in the first place (Battilana et al., 2019). For example, in a popular business school case study, a dilemma about whether or not Fair Trade coffee should go mainstream (selling more fair trade coffee in larger stores) or stay niche (maintaining a small operation with a limited set of farmers), is debated from the perspective of FLO, a certifier (Locke et al., 2010). Students are asked to analyze the trade-off between expanding the label to sell more Fair Trade coffee, or preserving the integrity and small scale it has at the time. Yet by simply shifting the starting point/problem definition, the question changes significantly. Is the problem that FLO wants more market share in comparison to other coffee products, a question implied by the idea of confronting the mainstream versus niche question in the first place? Or is the problem that farmers are not paid a living wage? By analyzing an innovation from a certain perspective, we may miss to see the option that reduces the most harm or has the potential to do the most good. The innovation of Fair Trade coffee is actually about helping farmers. Focusing on a problem definition that is tightly defined around creating positive impact raises questions about what the best organizational approach to solving the identified or decided upon problem is. If organizations working on CSR initiatives or other approaches to social or environmental value were to critically assess the problem they wanted to address, they may arrive at very different routes. For example, in the World Wildlife Fund's Market Transformation Initiative, the NGO sought to identify the greatest leverage points on commodity sustainability. Rather than trying to persuade 7 billion consumers or 1.5 billion producers to change how they produced or consumed items like coffee, palm oil, soy or tuna, they focused their efforts on the 500 companies that control 70% of choice in the supply chain.[4] It was easier to get a smaller number of stakeholders with high collective market power to discuss ideas around sustainable sourcing and agree to change practices and protocols, than to approach consumers with marketing messages. By conceptualizing the problem around impact, they became less concerned about encouraging more consumers to buy fair trade products, and focused instead on producers – the innovation was a simple shift in focus on a different stakeholder group.

Further research may investigate how to assess the importance of a problem and help organizations critically think about the relationship between problem definition and innovations. When problem conceptualizations are not directly related to social or environmental issues, structures and other processes may inhibit the embedding of RI principles in innovation processes. For example, a fashion brand solves problems associated with basic warmth, dignity, as well as self-expression, identity and status. Yet the fast fashion processes employed at some fashion houses create a large amount of waste and may exploit workers, creating both environmental and social harm. In order to embed RI principles, shifting the problem conceptualization could help, so that sustainable fashion brands include sustainability in their view of the 'problem' they are aiming to solve. Debating and defining a problem in such a way can help *anticipate* issues associated with specific innovations in, for example, supply chain management. Even considering questioning and debating 'the problem' demonstrates *reflexivity* and *deliberative thinking*. These four principles alone will not be enough to ensure an organization working on a problem with little environmental or social impact will be a strong responsible innovator.

Discussion

Ranging from access to medicine, environmental impact, or disregard for local needs, the detrimental effects of corporate innovations have been established across different sectors and societies. Moving beyond a focus on external governance structures, organizational research on RI can help further the conversation about the role of market organizations in embedding the principles of RI in innovation processes (Voegtlin & Scherer, 2019). In this chapter, we discuss how the dimensions associated with responsible innovation can be facilitated by organizational governance structures and practices. We summarize our illustrative examples discussed in this chapter as well as related emerging research questions in Table 2.2.

We may conceive of these organizational governance structures and practices as enablers of responsible innovation, and there are surely more organizational elements that future research can investigate in this regard. Thus, we see organizations as assemblies of elements (Meyer & Rowan, 1977), wherein RI can be enabled in different ways. In some industries, it may not be possible to adopt a certain legal form – for example, current norms held by certain types of investors, but also regulation may limit choices. Some firms may struggle to shift their problem definition from one that involves polluting the environment to one that does not. We can also critically question taken-for-granted assumptions – certain investors may also enable the choice of different forms; firms that choose a given form and are rewarded in the market may encourage others to follow suit. The plurality of forms associated with RI that emerges in our discussion of governance structures and practices indicates potential for supporting RI from the organizational level. Overall, we can see organizing for RI for its component parts – in some contexts, it will be easier and more fruitful to apply new accounting frameworks than to shift an organizational form – and result in improvements to the extent to which RI principles are embedded. The constellation of RI-related organizing elements will thus necessarily be idiosyncratic of context. One implication of increasing the number of structures and practices that embed RI principles in innovation, however, might be that RI can eventually become part and parcel of an organization's form. Organizational forms can be understood as a set of structures and processes underpinned by ideas about an organization's raison d'être, its appropriate principles for organizing, and criteria for evaluation (Greenwood & Hinings, 1988). In organizations in which RI has been institutionalized, RI principles may thus pervade the organization's very identity and mission, its organizing elements and its evaluation criteria.

In conclusion, to become more responsible innovators, organizations need to strive for innovation processes that are anticipatory, reflective, inclusive, deliberative, and responsive. These principles are realized within organizational structures and practices. Considering the structures and practices at work, and how they enable or hinder organizational efforts for responsible innovation can help organizations ensure that all aspects of their activities support one another in concert toward their ultimate goals. Further work could also investigate the emphasis organizations place on these

Responsible innovation 41

Table 2.2 Structures and Practices Enable Innovation to Integrate Dimensions of RI

	Examples discussed in this chapter	*Examples of open questions and potential future research*
Legal forms	• Legal forms can help firms anticipate conflicts by considering how innovation impacts non-financial goals	• To what extent do legal forms result in more inclusion of stakeholders in the innovation process?
Participatory structures	• Deliberative board-level committees or teams that enable regular engagement with stakeholders and review of firm-stakeholder interactions; possibly enabling anticipatory and reflective behavior as well	• How can governance structures be further adjusted to reduce and avoid harm as a distinct function of responsible innovation? • Are there structures that enable RI in lower levels of organizational hierarchies?
Social Accounting	• Anticipating 'what counts' for organizations and employing new types of accounting may enable more responsible outcomes	• Domain-specific accounting scholars, as well as organizational scholars, are investigating many dimensions of social accounting, and their antecedents and consequences.
Problem conceptualization/ definition practices	• Reflecting on and possibly altering the problem type an organization approaches (technical and adaptive/ relational) and its specific nature may help organizations anticipate potential consequences • Deliberative involvement of multiple stakeholders in problem-definition discussions and adaptations may help organizations steer better toward responsible outcomes	• What factors can enable or hinder organizations to adapt their problem definitions? • If organizations re-think the problem, they are trying to solve, can it result in more responsible outcomes?

different dimensions throughout organizational structures and practices; for example, arguably anticipation may yield higher impact, but may be difficult to embed. Working toward responsible innovation does not occur only in R&D labs but is enabled or hindered across the different practice domains of an organization. Organizations can take even small steps to change structures and practices to ensure innovation processes are anticipatory, reflective, inclusive and responsive.

Notes

1 The B Corp certification is not a distinct legal form, unlike the Benefit Corporations. Similar to fair trade certification, it is a way for firms to signal their commitment to sustainable business and is a certification available for multiple legal forms. The B Corp is different from the legal form of Benefit Corporation, though a Benefit Corporation is the best way for corporations to meet the requirements for B Corp certification. It does not require an explicit social or environmental mission. To become a B Corp, firms must get at least 80 out of 200 points on a test that assesses practices about governance, workers, community and the environment.

They must thereafter pass an impact assessment every two years. B Corp certifications started in the United States but are in use globally.

2 Since the 1970s, the predominant perception of fiduciary duty – which refers to the requirement that those who manage others' money do so responsibly – was that boards and executives had a responsibility to maximize profits and returns to shareholders – also known as shareholder primacy. This understanding was popularized in the 1970s by economist Milton Friedman, who believed that focusing on profit-generation would lead to more efficient allocation of capital and labor through the market Friedman, M. (1970). The Social Responsibility of Business Is to Increase Its Profits. New York Times Magazine, September 13. It was expected that customers, society, the environment or other stakeholders benefited indirectly, rather than through direct company efforts (ibid). Many managers, investors and journalists perpetuate the idea that this is enforceable by law and that managers who do not do so may be held legally liable, which is not the case. However, though there is no legal requirement for fiduciaries to maximize profits, this concept became deeply embedded in business thinking since the 1970s. The rise in adherence to this theory coincided with a tumultuous macroeconomic environment characterized by inflation and increased competition, primarily from Japan. New tools for measuring firm value The Economist. (2016). Shareholder Value: Analyze this: The enduring power of the biggest idea in business. *The Economist*, April 2, 2016. and an enabling environment of financial deregulation drove takeovers, layoffs and the sale of physical assets Krippner, G.R., (2011). Capitalizing on Crisis: The Political Origins of the Rise of Finance. Harvard University Press Dobbin, F. & Zorn, D., (2005). Corporate Malfeasance and the myth of shareholder value. Political Power and Social Theory.Ed. Diane E. Davis. Elsevier Ltd as companies were restructured throughout the 1980s and 1990s to increase value. Managers were incentivized accordingly, and these circumstances converged into a prevailing way of thinking – this was 'business as usual'.

3 www.at-entreprise-pauvrete.org/en/projet/construction-of-affordable-housing/#146460250 8312-f487b476-68f0

4 World Wildlife Fund Fact Sheet 2015. Market Transformation Initiative.

References

Aayan. (2020). *The life of an iPhone*. https://storymaps.arcgis.com/stories/08b8f73b70b2478a 8da1c518d7440b7c

Adams, C. A. (2015). The international integrated reporting council: A call to action. *Critical Perspectives on Accounting*, 27, 23–28.

Aguilera, R. V., Desender, K., Bednar, M. K., & Lee, J. H. (2015). Connecting the dots: Bringing external corporate governance into the corporate governance puzzle. *Academy of Management Annals*, 9(1), 483–573.

Amis, J. M., Mair, J., & Munir, K. A. (2020). The organizational reproduction of inequality. *Academy of Management Annals*, 14(1), 195–230.

Astor, T., Morales, M., Kieffer, D., & Repenning, N. (2016). *What problem are you trying to solve: An introduction to structured problem solving*. MITSloan School of Management.

Bakan, J. (1997). *The corporation: The pathological pursuit of profit and power*. Constable.

Bapuji, H., Ertug, G., & Shaw, J. D. (2020). Organizations and societal economic inequality: A review and way forward. *Academy of Management Annals*, 14(1), 60–91.

BarillaGroup. (2021). *Diversity Inclusion*. www.barillagroup.com/en/diversity-inclusion

Barnett, M. L., Henriques, I., & Husted, B. W. (2020). Beyond good intentions: Designing CSR initiatives for greater social impact. *Journal of Management*, 46(6), 937–964.

Battilana, J., Butler, B., Kimsey, M., Mair, J., Marquis, C., & Seelos, C. (2019). Problem, person and pathway: A framework for social innovators. In *Handbook of inclusive innovation: The role of organizations, markets and communities in social*. Edward Elgar Publishing.

BEQPride Magazine. (2018). *The Barilla group: Leading the way with its commitment to the LGBTQ community worldwide*. https://businessequalitymagazine.com/barilla-group-commit ment-lgbtq-community-worldwide/

Burget, M., Bardone, E., & Pedaste, M. (2017). Definitions and conceptual dimensions of responsible research and innovation: A literature review. *Science and Engineering Ethics*, *23*(1), 1–19.

Burke, J. J., Hoitash, R., & Hoitash, U. (2019). The heterogeneity of board-level sustainability committees and corporate social performance. *Journal of Business Ethics*, *154*(4), 1161–1186.

Cajaiba-Santana, G. (2014). Social innovation: Moving the field forward. A conceptual framework. *Technological Forecasting and Social Change*, *82*, 42–51.

Chan, J., Selden, M., & Pun, N. (2020). *Dying for an IPhone: Apple, Foxconn, and the lives of China's workers*. Haymarket Books.

Crilly, D., Zollo, M., & Hansen, M. T. (2012). Faking it or muddling through? Understanding decoupling in response to stakeholder pressures. *Academy of Management Journal*, *55*(6), 1429–1448.

Criscuolo, P., Dahlander, L., Grohsjean, T., & Salter, A. (2017). Evaluating novelty: The role of panels in the selection of R&D projects. *Academy of Management Journal*, *60*(2), 433–460.

De Villiers, C., Rinaldi, L., & Unerman, J. (2014). Integrated reporting: Insights, gaps and an agenda for future research. *Accounting, Auditing & Accountability Journal*, *27*.

Dumay, J., Bernardi, C., Guthrie, J., & Demartini, P. (2016). *Integrated reporting: A structured literature review*. Paper presented at the Accounting Forum.

Englund, H., Gerdin, J., & Burns, J. (2011). 25 years of Giddens in accounting research: Achievements, limitations and the future. *Accounting, Organizations and Society*, *36*(8), 494–513.

Fisher, E., Boenink, M., Van Der Burg, S., & Woodbury, N. (2012). Responsible healthcare innovation: Anticipatory governance of nanodiagnostics for theranostics medicine. *Expert Review of Molecular Diagnostics*, *12*(8), 857–870.

Fleming, L. (2001). Recombinant uncertainty in technological search. *Management Science*, *47*(1), 117–132.

Freudenburg, W. R. (1986). Social impact assessment. *Annual Review of Sociology*, 451–478.

Gray, R. (1992). Accounting and environmentalism: An exploration of the challenge of gently accounting for accountability, transparency and sustainability. *Accounting, Organizations and Society*, *17*(5), 399–425.

Gray, R. (2002). The social accounting project and accounting organizations and society privileging engagement, imaginings, new accountings and pragmatism over critique? *Accounting, Organizations and Society*, *27*(7), 687–708.

Greenwood, R., & Hinings, C. R. (1988). Organizational design types, tracks and the dynamics of strategic change. *Organization Studies*, *9*(3), 293–316.

Haack, P., Schoeneborn, D., & Wickert, C. (2012). Talking the talk, moral entrapment, creeping commitment? Exploring narrative dynamics in corporate responsibility standardization. *Organization Studies*, *33*(5–6), 815–845.

Hadjadji, N. (2019). *Produire en France, est-ce si compliqué? Le cas du Slip Français*. www.ladn.eu/entreprises-innovantes/produire-en-france-le-slip-francais/

Haigh, N., & Hoffman, A. J. (2014). The new heretics: Hybrid organizations and the challenges they present to corporate sustainability. *Organization & Environment*, *27*(3), 223–241.

Halme, M., Rintamäki, J., Knudsen, J. S., Lankoski, L., & Kuisma, M. (2020). When is there a sustainability case for CSR? Pathways to environmental and social performance improvements. *Business & Society*, *59*(6), 1181–1227.

Heifetz, R. A., & Laurie, D. L. (1997). The work of leadership. *Harvard Business Review*, *75*, 124–134.

Hines, R. D. (1988). Financial accounting: In communicating reality, we construct reality. *Accounting, Organizations and Society*, *13*(3), 251–261.

Kornberger, M., & Carter, C. (2010). Manufacturing competition: How accounting practices shape strategy making in cities. *Accounting, Auditing & Accountability Journal*, *23*(3), 325–349.

Levillain, K., Segrestin, B., & Hatchuel, A. (2019). *Profit-with-purpose corporations an innovation in corporate law to meet contemporary corporate social responsibility challenges.* Oxford University Press.

Locke, R. M., Reavis, C., & Cameron, D. (2010). *Fair trade coffee: The mainstream debate.* MIT.

Lubberink, R., Blok, V., van Ophem, J., & Omta, O. (2017a). A framework for responsible innovation in the business context: Lessons from responsible-, social-and sustainable innovation. In *Responsible innovation* (Vol. 3, pp. 181–207). Springer.

Lubberink, R., Blok, V., Van Ophem, J., & Omta, O. (2017b). Lessons for responsible innovation in the business context: A systematic literature review of responsible, social and sustainable innovation practices. *Sustainability, 9*(5), 721.

Luo, J., & Kaul, A. (2019). Private action in public interest: The comparative governance of social issues. *Strategic Management Journal, 40*(4), 476–502.

Mair, J. (2020). Social entrepreneurship: Research as disciplined exploration. In W. W. Powell & P. Bromley (Eds.). *The nonprofit sector: A research handbook* (pp. 333–357). Stanford University Press.

Mair, J., & Marti, I. (2006). Social entrepreneurship research: A source of explanation, prediction, and delight. *Journal of World Business, 41*(1), 36–44.

Mair, J., & Marti, I. (2009). Entrepreneurship in and around institutional voids: A case study from Bangladesh. *Journal of Business Venturing, 24*(5), 419–435.

Mair, J., & Rathert, N. (2019a). Social entrepreneurship: Prospects for the study of market based activity and social change. In *The Oxford handbook of corporate social responsibility: Psychological and organizational perspectives* (pp. 359–373). Oxford University Press.

Mair, J., & Rathert, N. (2019b). Alternative organizing with social purpose: Revisiting institutional analysis of market-based activity. *Socio-Economic Review.* https://doi.org/10.1093/ser/mwz031

Mair, J., Wolf, M., & Ioan, A. (2020). Governance in social enterprises. In H. K. Anheier & T. Baums (Eds.), *Advances in corporate governance* (pp. 180–202). Oxford University Press.

Mair, J., Wolf, M., & Seelos, C. (2016). Scaffolding: A process of transforming patterns of inequality in small-scale societies. *Academy of Management Journal, 59*(6), 2021–2044.

McDonnell, M. H., King, B. G., & Soule, S. A. (2015). A dynamic process model of private politics: Activist targeting and corporate receptivity to social challenges. *American Sociological Review, 80*(3), 654–678.

Metz, A., & Hartley, P. (2020). Scenario development as valuation: Opportunities for reflexivity. *Technological Forecasting and Social Change, 155*, 120027.

Meyer, J. W., & Rowan, B. (1977). Institutionalized organizations: Formal structure as myth and ceremony. *American Journal of Sociology, 83*(2), 340–363.

Mitchell, R. K., Weaver, G. R., Agle, B. R., Bailey, A. D., & Carlson, J. (2016). Stakeholder agency and social welfare: Pluralism and decision making in the multi-objective corporation. *Academy of Management Review, 41*(2), 252–275.

Mook, L. (2013). Social accounting for the social economy. *Accounting for Social Value,* 5–28.

Pollock, N., & D'Adderio, L. (2012). Give me a two-by-two matrix and I will create the market: Rankings, graphic visualisations and sociomateriality. *Accounting, Organizations and Society, 37*(8), 565–586.

Ramani, S. V., SadreGhazi, S., & Gupta, S. (2017). Catalysing innovation for social impact: The role of social enterprises in the Indian sanitation sector. *Technological Forecasting and Social Change, 121,* 216–227.

Rathert, N. (2016). Strategies of legitimation: MNEs and the adoption of CSR in response to host-country institutions. *Journal of International Business Studies, 47*(7), 858–879.

Reiser, D. B., & Dean, S. A. (2013). Hunting stag with fly paper: A hybrid financial instrument for social enterprise. *Boston College Law Review, 54,* 1495.

Roemer-Mahler, A. (2015). The pharmaceutical industry as a global institution: The tension between private mandate and public function. In K. Brennan (Ed.), *Making global institutions work: Power, accountability and change.* Routledge.

Rowbottom, N., & Locke, J. (2013). *The emergence of integrated reporting*. Paper presented at the 7th Asia-Pacific Interdisciplinary Research in Accounting Conference, Kobe.

Scherer, A. G., & Voegtlin, C. (2020). Corporate governance for responsible innovation: Approaches to corporate governance and their implications for sustainable development. *Academy of Management Perspectives, 34*(2), 182–208.

Schuessler, E., Frenkel, S. J., & Wright, C. F. (2019). Governance of labor standards in Australian and German garment supply chains: The impact of Rana Plaza. *ILR Review, 72*(3), 552–579.

Seelos, C., & Mair, J. (2017). *Innovation and scaling for impact: How effective social entrepreneurs do it*. Stanford University Press.

Seelos, C., & Mair, J. (2020). 5. Innovation and scaling for transformative impact. In *Innovation and scaling for impact* (pp. 117–150). Stanford University Press.

Segrestin, B., Hatchuel, A., & Levillain, K. (2020). When the law distinguishes between the enterprise and the corporation: The case of the new French law on corporate purpose. *Journal of Business Ethics*, 1–13.

Senge, P. M. (2009). The leader's new work: Building learning organizations. In G. Robinson Hickman (Ed.), *Leading organization: Perspectives for a new era*. Sage Publications.

Soderstrom, S. B., & Weber, K. (2020). Organizational structure from interaction: Evidence from corporate sustainability efforts. *Administrative Science Quarterly, 65*(1), 226–271.

Sombart, W. (1967). *Luxury and capitalism* (Vol. 4). University of Michigan Press.

Spear, R., Cornforth, C., & Aiken, M. (2009). The governance challenges of social enterprises: Evidence from a UK empirical study. *Annals of Public and Cooperative Economics, 80*(2), 247–273.

Spence, C. (2009). Social accounting's emancipatory potential: A Gramscian critique. *Critical Perspectives on Accounting, 20*(2), 205–227.

Stahl, B. C., & Coeckelbergh, M. (2016). Ethics of healthcare robotics: Towards responsible research and innovation. *Robotics and Autonomous Systems, 86*, 152–161.

Stephan, U., Andries, P., & Daou, A. (2019). Goal multiplicity and innovation: How social and economic goals affect open innovation and innovation performance. *Journal of Product Innovation Management, 36*(6), 721–743.

Stilgoe, J., Owen, R., & Macnaghten, P. (2013). Developing a framework for responsible innovation. *Research Policy, 42*(9), 1568–1580.

Tinker, T. (1985). *Paper prophets: A social critique of accounting*. Greenwood.

Vickers, I., Lyon, F., Sepulveda, L., & McMullin, C. (2017). Public service innovation and multiple institutional logics: The case of hybrid social enterprise providers of health and wellbeing. *Research Policy, 46*(10), 1755–1768.

Voegtlin, C., & Scherer, A. G. (2019). New roles for business: Responsible innovators for a sustainable future. In A. McWilliams, D. E. Rupp, D. S. Siegel, G. K. Stahl, & D. A. Waldman (Eds.), *The Oxford handbook of corporate social responsibility: Psychological and organizational perspectives* (2nd ed., pp. 337–358). Oxford University Press.

Von Schomberg, R. (2012). *The quest for the "right" impacts of science and technology: An outlook towards a framework for responsible research and innovation*. Paper presented at the Les Nanotechnologies/Nanotechnologies, Vers un Changement D'échelle Éthique? Colloque: Université Libre de Bruxelles, 4 et 5 avril 2011/towards a Shift in the Scale of Ethics? Conference: Université Libre de Bruxelles on the 4th and the 5th of April 2011.

Weber, M. (1927). *General economic history* (F. H. Knight, Trans.). Transaction.

Wickert, C., & De Bakker, F. G. (2018). Pitching for social change: Toward a relational approach to selling and buying social issues. *Academy of Management Discoveries, 4*(1), 50–73.

Yunus, M., Moingeon, B., & Lehmann-Ortega, L. (2010). Building social business models: Lessons from the Grameen experience. *Long Range Planning, 43*(2–3), 308–325.

Zhao, E. Y., & Lounsbury, M. (2016). An institutional logics approach to social entrepreneurship: Market logic, religious diversity, and resource acquisition by microfinance organizations. *Journal of Business Venturing, 31*(6), 643–662.

3 Understanding the Evolution of BOP Narratives

A Systematic Literature Review and Topic Modeling Analysis

Federica Angeli

Introduction

The bottom/base-of-the-pyramid business (BOP) approach, as coined by Prahalad and Hart in their seminal 2002 article (Prahalad & Hart, 2002), can be considered as the first line of thought bringing social concerns to the core of business strategy and practices. Corporate social responsibility promoters acknowledged the wider impact of business on society beyond the creation of wealth and jobs (Carroll, 1999; Doh & Guay, 2006), and accordingly encouraged businesses to adopt a responsible and ethical behavior in order to reduce their potentially negative social and ecological impact. With a shift in focus, the BOP proponents instead championed the possibility for businesses not just to mitigate harm, but also to do good by combining business prowess with a logic of poverty alleviation for the large populations of disadvantaged individuals across the world. The 'fortune at the bottom-of-the-pyramid' discourse relied on the simple reasoning that product and process innovation could lead to the design of products and services affordable to the poor, thereby unleashing new unchartered and profitable market opportunities whilst providing disadvantaged communities with a wide new range of products offered that could enhance their standards of living (Prahalad, 2004, 2006). In this sense, profit-oriented entities were envisioned to engage with BOP customers in a win-win situation yielding both profits and social impact.

Widely studied examples in the BOP field come from the healthcare sector in India (Angeli & Jaiswal, 2016; Govindarajan & Ramamurti, 2013; Prahalad, 2012). Indian government healthcare spending is nowadays still very limited and amounts to around 1% of the national GDP against total healthcare expenditures in India of 3.5% GDP and an average public national spending of 5.86% GDP worldwide (World Bank, 2018). The limited government investments in healthcare leads to 70% of the health diagnostics and treatment costs paid out-of-pocket by massive segments of the population to private healthcare providers. In 2011, India reported a 22.5% population living below the poverty line (World Bank, 2018) – hence at least 307 million people cannot afford healthcare and are forced to forgo treatments because of financial constraints. Tapping into this widely underserved markets, Narayana Health – a health hospital specialized on cardiovascular diseases and heart surgeries – and Aravind Eye Hospital, specialized in ophthalmological treatments and cataract surgeries became worldwide famous examples of successful BOP strategies (Govindarajan & Ramamurti, 2013). Their innovative business models center around patient needs, with promotion and delivery strategies that cater to the lifestyle of very low-income patients,

DOI: 10.4324/9780429243165-4

This chapter has been made available under a CC-BY-NC 4.0 license.

and financial formulas – coupled with operational excellence – that render very expensive treatments affordable or completely free to the poor (Angeli & Jaiswal, 2016), while ensuring the possibility for organizational scale-up.

Understandably, the BOP approach has been welcomed with great enthusiasm and hype by business scholars and practitioners alike, as a viable, financially sustainable alternative to corporate philanthropy and international aid to promote development in resource-constrained, disadvantaged settings (Cooney & Shanks, 2010; Fitch & Sorensen, 2007; Gollakota et al., 2010). However, early BOP ventures led to high-profile business failures, such as Nike's World Shoe project, Procter & Gamble water purification powder, DuPont Solae and its soy-fortified snack food, Essilor International and its mobile eye clinics or SC Johnson and its home-cleaning services (Prahalad & Hart, 2002; Simanis, 2012). Coupled with lack of evident success of initial ventures, the ethical discomfort toward the new colonialist tones and implications of the initial BOP formulas (Jaiswal, 2008; Karnani, 2006) has prompted various revisions of the BOP approach over time (Dembek et al., 2019; Simanis & Hart, 2008). Three main literature reviews have been conducted to shed light on the evolution of the field, which provided a much needed overview of the factors underpinning BOP strategies, and related outcomes and challenges (Dembek et al., 2019; Follman, 2012; Kolk et al., 2014). However, we know little about the evolution of the discourse surrounding BOP approaches as embedded in its *narratives*. Narratives are "grammatically structured (discursive) constructions that actors use to shape their own and to impact others' understandings" (Logemann et al., 2019; Sonenshein, 2010, p. 480). The formation of managerial narratives can be seen as connected to a process of 'framing', namely the 'packaging and organization of information, which can be a powerful tool for shaping others' understandings and behaviors because it brings attention to a few stylized dimensions of reality, while hiding others' (Giorgi, 2017; Raffaelli et al., 2019). I argue here that the BOP narratives reflect a process of deliberate or undeliberate framing enacted by related management research. Narratives particularly emerge through the analysis of the topics addressed and of the wording used to describe the approach and delineate its expected benefits. In a field that has sparked both strong controversies and enthusiasms, understanding the evolution of such framing processes and related narratives are crucial, as an indication of how scholars adjusted their discourse to mitigate criticism and adapt to the claims of various stakeholders over time.

Through a powerful intuition and a compelling discourse, Prahalad and Hart (2002) invented and popularized the BOP approach. Beyond providing an overview of the field since its early beginnings, this chapter advances knowledge by investigating the evolution of the BOP narratives over time. To do so, this chapter develops a longitudinal text analysis of all BOP-related scientific studies conducted over the past 15 years (2004–2018). A systematic literature review methodology has been applied to select all the relevant articles in the period of interest, followed by a topic modeling analysis performed on the resulting 72 articles. Topic modeling is a relatively new technique used to analyze large texts (Moro et al., 2019). Based on an iterative procedure that analyses the recurrence of words across documents, this technique – based on the Latent Dirichlet Allocation (LDA) model developed by Blei and colleagues (2003) – allows for clustering words into larger topics of similar content (Schwarz, 2018).

48   *Federica Angeli*

Theoretical Background

In its initial formulation, the Bottom of the Pyramid approach, also known as BOP 1.0, advocated the unprecedented possibility for business firms in general and multinational corporations (MNCs) in particular to be agents for social change, not through charitable initiatives but by means of profit-driven business ventures. The 'fortune at the bottom of the pyramid' identified in half of the world's population living below the poverty line new untapped markets which could be profitably targeted through highly efficient operations and large volumes, against low product margins (Dembek et al., 2019; Prahalad & Hammond, 2002; Prahalad & Hart, 2002). Importantly, the BOP represented a shift in perspective with respect to other approaches such as CSR or microfinance and social entrepreneurship in that it envisioned a business-oriented entity from outside the BOP getting involved with the target communities to sell products or services (Dembek et al., 2015; London, 2008). Notable examples include Unilever selling shampoo and detergent in BOP markets (Angeli & Jaiswal, 2015), Nike's World Shoe initiatives (Hart & London, 2005; Prahalad & Hart, 2002), Procter & Gamble with its water-purification powder called PUR and DuPont's Solae unit, aimed to address malnutrition by selling soy-fortified snack foods (Simanis, 2012). Multinational corporations were considered best placed to take on the challenge, because of their resource munificence and the opportunities to more easily transfer products and business models across locations. Moreover, at the time of the BOP 1.0 MNCs were facing intense competition on increasingly saturated Western markets. Disenfranchised communities could constitute new, much needed market opportunities for MNCs while at the same time offering a testing ground for new technologies that could then deliver a competitive edge in traditional, top-of-the-pyramid markets (Anderson & Markides, 2007; Hart & Christensen, 2002; Prahalad, 2006, 2012). This point was further reiterated through the lens of disruptive innovation developed by Christensen and colleagues (BOP) (Christensen et al., 2016, 2015), who argued how innovations developed for low-end markets had the potential to disrupt and push a radical rethink of traditional offers for high-income segments. More recently, the concept of reverse innovation – hence innovation developed for low-income markets that was successfully introduced also in high-income settings – has highlighted the potential benefits of BOP strategies (Ahmed et al., 2017; Malodia et al., 2019).

Despite its promises of initiating a new form of inclusive capitalism by proposing a concrete, sustainable alternative to international aid and corporate philanthropy, BOP 1.0 encountered strong opposition. The perspective was criticized for embodying an imperialistic attitude, with the ultimate goal of ensuring legitimacy to MNCs' quest for new markets and hence fostering a neo-liberal agenda (Arora & Romijn, 2012; Montgomery et al., 2012). Importantly, BOP 1.0 held simplistic assumptions around the needs and values of BOP communities and their resulting purchasing behavior. Disenfranchised individuals were perceived as a wide, homogenous, un-served pool of potential consumers who are unquestionably assumed to desire and benefit from goods and services designed for Western markets (Arora & Romijn, 2012; Jaiswal, 2008; Karnani, 2007). BOP opponents identified three main lines of criticism, along which BOP 1.0's failure to deliver on its promise of lifting poverty through a sound business proposition. First, no attention had been paid to whether and how the increased supply of new goods and services would succeed at promoting long-lasting improvement of BOP consumers' socio-economic outcomes (Jaiswal & Gupta, 2015).

Understanding the Evolution of BOP Narratives 49

While for example new products/services aimed at enhancing access to education and health (such as Narayana Health, Aravind Eye Care or DuPont attempts to commercialize fortified snacks to combat malnutrition) might arguably benefit BOP communities by increasing chances of stable employment and income, other consumer products such as computers (commercialized by Simputer), World Shoes (proposed by Nike) or shampoo distributed in small affordable quantities (sachets) (distributed by Unilever) present a weaker link to durable socio-economic change. In some cases, it has been argued that the exposure to wealthier, Western-like lifestyles farther from BOP's own customs and norms, might instead create dangerous aspirational demand that could further deplete the BOP already scarce financial resources by favoring the purchase of unnecessary aspirational goods (Karnani, 2006). Second, BOP 1.0 efforts viewed BOP communities only as passive consumers instead of building local capacity and new income opportunities by involving the BOP as producers, distributors, suppliers, or entrepreneurs. Therefore, beyond the immediate (and already controversial) benefit that BOP products and services could generate, no positive externalities have been considered that could foster community development, by stimulating local economy or altering the dynamics leading to social exclusion. Therefore, early BOP approaches were felt to fall fundamentally short in promoting real poverty alleviation by fostering individual empowerment and systemic change (Arora & Romijn, 2012). As a third point of criticism, which also met with high-profile failures of many initial BOP products, multinational corporations emerged as inadequate to serve BOP markets, despite the early emphasis on multinationals as BOP ambassadors and change-makers (Geradts et al., 2018; Gooderham et al., 2016; London & Hart, 2004). MNCs' attempts to access the BOP were mostly unsuccessful because serving disadvantaged customers required a radical business model redesign not only to address affordability challenges, but also to take into account aspects of distribution (product availability), marketing (product awareness) and product acceptability. The socio-cultural and socio-economic circumstances of BOP consumers are highly heterogeneous and are likely to substantially vary not only across but also within countries (Angeli & Jaiswal, 2015). Serving an urban slum as opposed to a rural village presents an entirely different set of challenges, and even urban slums may be present large differences due their unique cultural, religious, ethnic, socio-economic makeup and spatial layout (Angeli et al., 2018; Das et al., 2018). These considerations require a level of organizational flexibility to customize the offer according to local needs that multinational corporations struggle to achieve, as opposed to grassroots enterprises or born-BOP businesses (Chmielewski et al., 2020). Moreover, market heterogeneity hinders economies of scales, as products and services needs to be tailor-made to the specific needs of many market niches, hence reducing the profit potential initially attached to BOP ventures (Angeli & Jaiswal, 2015).

The recognized weaknesses surrounding the initial formulation of the BOP approach stimulated its revision into a BOP protocol 2.0 (Simanis & Hart, 2008; Simanis et al., 2008). Based on a view of development closer to Amartya Sen's capability approach and the idea of 'empowerment as freedom' (Sen, 1999) – which theorizes underdevelopment as a state of powerlessness and inability for individuals to convert personal and public resources into capabilities and functioning and ultimately well-being – this new BOP perspective advocated deeper and longer-term engagement with BOP communities (Ansari et al., 2012; Rivera-Santos et al., 2012). The new BOP thinking aimed at involving the BOP as partners, rather than consumers, with a view to

50   Federica Angeli

stimulating local development through dialogue, trusted-based relationships, and a focus on capability development and mutual commitment (Hall et al., 2012; Webb & Morris, 2013). Disenfranchised individuals became embedded into new BOP models as distribution agents, input suppliers and entrepreneurs (McMullen, 2011; Mezias & Fakhreddin, 2015; Mohr et al., 2012). Examples of this approach are the Philips low-cost, improved cooking stove (Bloomberg BusinessWeek, 2008), GE's innovation in the field of low-cost medical devices (General Electric, 2015), or d.light, which sells solar-power product to the BOP (Gunther, 2014), which all promoted engagement and dialogue with the target communities from the product design stage. Although this approach has resolved some of the ethical discomfort provoked by the BOP 1.0, and proved much more effective in guiding business attempts to stimulate development and reduce poverty, it was still tainted by a Western-centered perspective, which provided the yardstick against which needs and empowerment were conceptualized. According to many observers, this perspective lacked an in-depth understanding of poverty, in its multifaceted meanings and in its underpinning power dynamics, deeply entrenched in the social fabric (Simanis et al., 2008).

BOP 3.0 was introduced to meet such shortcomings and renew once again the BOP discourse and practice, and was particularly encapsulated in the work of Caneque and Hart (2017). This new iteration of theoretical reflection proffers a more holistic, encompassing view of poverty alleviation, in which organizational efforts strive to trigger development as a process of systemic change and transformation, rather than just economic growth (Caneque & Hart, 2017; London & Fay, 2016; Roxas & Ungson, 2011). From a development perspective, BOP 3.0 can be considered close to the 'new commons' school of thought, which views development as a long-term dialogical process between innovators and target communities. This perspective is close to Yunus' Grameen microfinance initiatives and his conceptualization of social business models (Simanis et al., 2008; Yunus et al., 2010). This approach has also been implemented by, for example, SAB Miller, which supports small businesses by embedding them in their business models as suppliers, distributors and retailers. In Mozambique, SAB Miller produces and sells beer made from cassava, while in Uganda its beer is brewed with sorghum, to adapt to local tastes and crops availability. In South Africa, SAB Miller has supported former bottling plant employees in starting their transportation business (Gunther, 2014). Importantly, this approach recognizes the complexity of poverty as a concept and as a phenomenon that varies across settings, and aims at targeting the underlying, multifaceted and interacting causes rather and not only its manifest symptoms. As such, an income-focused definition of poverty was felt too limited (Yurdakul et al., 2017) and unable to represent the complex social, cultural, political and emotional aspects linked to an underprivileged status (Angeli et al., 2018; Caneque & Hart, 2017; Undp, 2014). This broader focus on poverty as a multifaceted, context-dependent, socially constructed concept translates into the need for companies to seek for a deeper understanding of local communities, through long-term engagement and collaborative practices and models (Chmielewski et al., 2020). Moreover, poverty alleviation achievements should be regarded against the increase of communities' well-being and the development of individual capabilities (Khavul & Bruton, 2013; Nussbaum, 2001; Sen, 1999), rather than looking at the average rise of income levels. BOP 3.0 emphasizes the importance of local BOP ventures, which benefit from a privileged vantage point toward recognizing local needs and tailor locally grown solutions (Angeli & Jaiswal, 2015; Chmielewski

Understanding the Evolution of BOP Narratives 51

et al., 2020; Dasgupta & Hart, 2015). Finally, BOP 3.0 re-integrates the environmental sustainability discourse much overlooked in the previous iterations of BOP thinking, mostly focused on poverty alleviation/eradication. In this sense, BOP 3.0 explicitly connects the BOP perspective to triple-bottom-line thinking underpinning sustainability and sustainable development framework (Elkington, 1997; Glavas & Mish, 2015), as well as ethical concerns of inter-generational justice, in addition to intra-generational concerns of social inclusion (Arnold & Williams, 2012; Hahn, 2009; Heuer & Landrum, 2016). Table 3.1 illustrates the three waves of BOP theoretical evolution.

BOP 2.0 and BOP 3.0 also sparked emphasis on co-creation approaches, aimed at value discovery and mutual value creation through early involvement of BOP users and consumers at an early stage of product development (George et al., 2012; Nahi, 2016). Co-creation have since gained increasing recognition as crucial aspects of BOP business modeling, in healthcare (Angeli et al., 2018; Angeli & Jaiswal, 2016) and across sectors (Alexy & George, 2013). However, such business models are still relatively rare (Kolk et al., 2014), because of the time-consuming, research-intensive process of understanding consumer needs (Nahi, 2016) and because of the inherent difficulty of capturing unbiased BOP voices and product preferences, given within-community power dynamics (Arora & Romijn, 2012). These difficulties led to the use of a loosely defined view of co-creation, mainly focused on the inclusion of local NGOs and organizational partners as representatives sufficiently close to the communities to be able to interpret their views (Dahan et al., 2010).

Table 3.1 Evolution of BOP Approaches

	BOP 1.0	*BOP 2.0*	*BOP 3.0*
Perception toward the BOP	BOP as consumers	BOP as partners	BOP as small producer (self-management)
Mode of engagement	Deep listening	Deep dialogue	Ad hoc process, cross-sector partnerships, networks
Value creation	Reduce price-points	Innovative, highly customized end-to-end solutions	Immediate value appropriation by BOP small producers for products and services
Innovation focus	Redesign packaging, extend distribution	Understand socio-cultural factors, marry capabilities, build shared commitment	Shared skills and knowledge appropriated by small producers
Partnership model	Arm's length relationship mediated by NGOs	Direct, personal relationships facilitated by NGOs	Direct relationship with stakeholders and BOP producers
Development view	Basic Needs	Development as Freedom	New Commons
Vision	Selling to the poor	Business co-venturing	Sustainable development, bottom-up model

Source: Adapted from Dembek et al. (2019)

Methods

The methodology adopted for this chapter combines a systematic literature review technique of data collection with a topic modeling technique of data analysis. Systematic literature reviews are a widely popular methodology used to develop a comprehensive, rigorous overview of a field of study. From being a fundamental tool for knowledge accumulation in the medical discipline, systematic literature reviews have been increasingly adopted in multidisciplinary work (Goel et al. 2018; Latten et al., 2018) and in management studies (Maier et al., 2016; Ritz et al., 2016; Savolainen et al., 2012). Topic modeling is a statistical technique able to cluster large volumes of texts into a finite number of topics, based on the word frequency and co-occurrence. Such machine learning applications for data mining have rarely been used so far in management studies, although attention is increasing as promising tools to handle big volumes of qualitative data (e.g. Moro et al., 2019). The combined use of systematic literature review and topic modeling represent a methodological innovation, designed to ensure rigor and replicability in both phases of data collection and data analysis of this literature review.

Search Strategy

The EBSCO host (Business source Elite and EconLit), Web of Science and ABI global database were searched for peer-reviewed articles written in English that employed either qualitative or quantitative designs, a combination of both (mixed-methods), or that proposed a conceptual framework. The intended publication timespan ranged between 2004 and 2018. The databases were searched through a combination of the following keywords: (Bottom of the pyramid) OR (BOP) OR (Business AND poverty alleviation) OR (Multinational corporation AND poverty alleviation) OR (MNC AND poverty alleviation) OR (BOP AND sustainable development). Table 3.2 reports the keyword combination used for each database as reflected into the search syntax, and the resulting number of hints.

Study Selection

From the total of 2,739 articles initially identified, 804 articles were removed as duplicates. The initial sample of 1,935 unique articles was screened for suitability, based on titles and abstract. Only articles in English, published on peer-reviewed journals, were retained for further processing. The selected articles had to report an empirical study, whether quantitative or qualitative, or a conceptual piece. The articles included in the sample were also required to address the base-of-the-pyramid business approach, and hence to have a managerial/organizational focus, which led to the exclusion of policy documents and commentaries. An important selection criterion for study inclusion was also the explicit acknowledgement of the BOP lens or approach, as a distinct poverty alleviation effort rather than for example corporate philanthropy or social entrepreneurship. This was deemed as crucial to ensure that all selected studies had deliberately positioned themselves within the BOP discourse and hence recognized each other's contribution towards knowledge accumulation in the field. This thorough screening procedure led to the exclusion of 1,828 articles. The full text of the 107 remaining articles was then assessed, leading to select out another 35 contributions, because they were

Understanding the Evolution of BOP Narratives   53

Table 3.2 Keyword Combination by Search Database

Database	Keyword combination/Search syntax	Number of results
EBSCO host (Business source Elite and EconLit)	(TI = ((Base of the pyramid) OR (Bottom of the pyramid) OR (Business AND poverty alleviation) OR ((Multinational corporation) AND (poverty alleviation)) OR (MNC AND poverty alleviation) OR (BOP AND sustainable development))) OR (AB = ((Base of the pyramid) OR (Bottom of the pyramid) OR (Business AND poverty alleviation) OR ((Multinational corporation) AND (poverty alleviation)) OR (MNC AND poverty alleviation) OR (BOP AND sustainable development)))	1098, of which 921 from Business Source Ultimate;
Web of Science	TI = ((Base of the pyramid) OR (Bottom of the pyramid) OR (Business AND poverty alleviation) OR (Multinational corporation AND poverty alleviation) OR (MNC AND poverty alleviation) OR (BOP AND sustainable development))	296
ABI global	TI=((Base of the pyramid) OR (Bottom of the pyramid) OR (Business AND poverty alleviation) OR ((Multinational AND corporation) AND poverty alleviation) OR (MNC AND poverty alleviation) OR (BOP AND sustainable development)) OR ((Base of the pyramid) OR (Bottom of the pyramid) OR (Business AND poverty alleviation) OR ((Multinational AND corporation) AND poverty alleviation) OR (MNC AND poverty alleviation) OR (BOP AND sustainable development))	1345

either not peer-reviewed, or not published in international journals (but only available as conference proceedings), or they were review articles. The flowchart highlighting the selection process as recommended by PRISMA (Preferred Reporting Items for Systematic Reviews and Meta-Analyses) is represented in Figure 3.1.

Data Analysis

The 72 articles included in the qualitative synthesis were analyzed through a topic modeling procedure, a text mining technique that allows automated parsing on unstructured data, unlike the more common data mining tools (Moro et al., 2019). Topic modeling is based on Latent Dirichlet Allocation (LDA) model developed by Blei et al. (2003), an iterative algorithm that allows for developing clusters of meaning based on words' co-occurrence. Unlike other techniques, the LDA procedure relies on the assumption that words can be associated to different topics, as well as to different documents. Likewise, documents are associated to different topics and words. This approach translates into a tri-dimensional space characterized by associations between words, documents and topics, where any word is related to any topic or document (Moro et al., 2019) through a beta distribution.

The practical implementation of the technique has followed the procedure described by Schwartz using the ldagibbs command in STATA 14.0 (Schwarz, 2018). After a

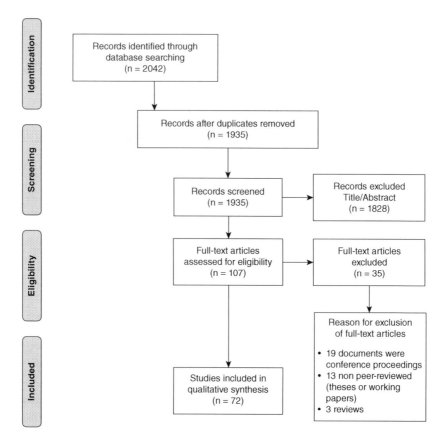

Figure 3.1 PRISMA flow diagram.

standard data-cleaning procedure – which included exclusion of common words – all abstracts of the 72 sample articles constituted the input for the lda algorithm. The analysis focused on abstracts as opposed to full texts for two reasons. First, abstracts have a similar word count and therefore are more comparable than full texts', the length of which varies considerably depending on the journal. Analyzing abstracts therefore avoids the potential overrepresentation bias of longer articles. Moreover, full texts might vary considerably in their emphasis on methodological details versus theory development, while abstracts offer a more concise, balanced account of the various scientific aspects of a peer-reviewed article.

The analysis conducted with STATA allowed for developing the topics and map the evolution of their average share over time. Moreover, word-clouds were used to visually represent the narratives pertaining to each topic, through the beta coefficients of the word-topic matrix. A narrative refers to a grammatically structured discourse

(Logemann et al., 2019), in which the set of words used and their relations construct meaning. Although unable to reflect the grammatical structure of narratives, the word-clouds represent their wording choices, and are hence able to highlight similarities and differences across narratives in their fundamental lexical and semantic aspects. To appreciate the value of topic modeling, word-clouds were also produced for full-text documents clustered on the basis of publication years (as opposed to the topic clustering offered by the topic modeling procedure). MaxQDA and an online tool available on wordart.com were used to create full-text word-clouds and beta-distribution word-clouds respectively.

Results and Discussion

Descriptive Analyses

Figure 3.2 shows the trend line related the number of articles published over time. A peak has been reached in 2013, with eight articles published. The publications are spread over 60 journals across disciplines and locations, from the more widely circulated *Journal of Cleaner Production*, or *Organization and Environment*, to *African Studies Review* or *South Asia Journal of Management*. The most targeted journals are within the international management and business ethics disciplinary fields, with *Greener Management International, Journal of Business Strategy, Journal of Business Ethics, International Business Review, Stanford Social Innovation Review, World Development* and *Journal of Marketing Management* being on top of the list for most contributions hosted.

Figure 3.3 shows the word clouds derived from clustering the articles by years of publication, therefore representing a chronological trend of BOP narratives evolution.

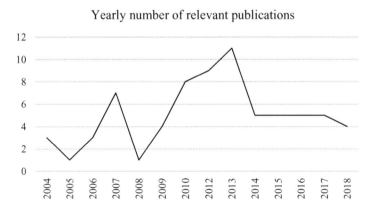

Figure 3.2 Number of BOP articles published per year.

56 Federica Angeli

Figure 3.3 Chronological evolution of BOP narratives.

To ensure a fairly comparable number of articles, the first cluster stretches over 6 years (2004–2009), while the last two are five year long (2009–2013 and 2014–2018). The figure also marks the introduction BOP 2.0 (2008) and BOP 3.0 (2015). Although the words within the clouds vary in color to ease readability, only their size is indicative of the relative importance (frequency) in the documents used to generate the clouds.

The chronological word clouds do show some variation of the narrative foci over time. The first cluster emphasizes the business opportunities associated with the BOP approach and the role of MNCs as leaders in experimenting with this new business opportunity, in line with the earlier formulation of the BOP perspective. The first cloud also presents the key concepts associated with the early BOP narrative, such as 'poverty', 'poor', 'corporations', 'market' and 'development'. Corporations, in particular those already globally oriented, are called to promote development and poverty alleviation through business propositions, where the BOP communities are mainly seen as potentially very profitable markets.

The second cluster reveals a narrative transition from considerations about the internal business strategy toward the needs of external stakeholders. We see for example the prominence of 'markets', 'social', 'value' and 'constraints', on the same level as 'business', 'companies and 'strategies'. In line with the introduction of BOP 2.0, the prominence of MNCs almost disappears, to instead leave room for 'companies', 'strategies', 'ventures' and 'firms'. The narrative emerging in this cluster appears richer, and more distributed across a variety of conceptualization efforts.

The third cluster reflects a deepening of the trend appreciating the challenges facing the disenfranchised communities, in line with a co-creation, bottom-up design of BOP ventures. On this line, we see the rise to prominence of concepts such as 'communities', 'social', 'capabilities' and 'stakeholders'. At the same time, business strategies become more loosely identified as 'models' or 'approach'. It seems also that over time, new attention has been devoted to measuring the 'implications' of BOP efforts, in terms of generating 'value'. In line with that, there is an effort also to take stock of the findings available in the scientific scholarship 'literature' and 'research'). In its increasing emphasis on communities and co-creation efforts, the third cluster does incorporate the conceptual advancements proposed by the BOP 3.0 formulation, although no mention about environmental sustainability or triple bottom line is apparent yet.

Topic Modeling Analysis

Whereas the word clusters represented in Figure 1.3 illustrate the frequent use of terms in articles from three different periods (and grouped according to publication date), the topic modeling analysis instead clusters the articles by semantic similarity, regardless of the publication date. As such, the LDA procedure iteratively isolates topics of relevance based on words' co-occurrence, where documents, topics and words constitute three axes of a tri-dimensional space. The procedure has been launched with a varying user-inputted number of topics, ranging from 3 to 10. Five topics (Topic 1 through 5) guaranteed the best face validity, in terms of distinctiveness of narratives being represented. Based on the titles of the papers that presented the largest topic share (Table 1.3), the following titles have been chosen: Topic 1 – Co-creation and bottom-up approaches; Topic 2 – Ethics and inequalities at the BOP; Topic 3 – Innovation and the BOP; Topic 4 – Mutual and social value creation; and Topic 5 – Business strategies for BOP markets. To visualize the distinctive features of

58   Federica Angeli

Table 3.3 Topics Emerging from the Topic Modeling Analysis. Under Each Topic, the Titles of the Five Papers that Reported the Largest Topic Share Are Listed.

Authors	Year	Title	Journal
Topic 1 – Co-creation and bottom-up approaches			
J. N. M. Muthuri, Jeremy: Idemudia, Uwafiokun	2012	Corporate Innovation and Sustainable Community Development in Developing Countries.	Business & Society
B. H. Paton, Minna	2007	Bringing the needs of the poor into the BOP debate.	Business Strategy & the Environment
N. C. Nguyen	2013	Examination of existing arguments on business oriented towards poverty reduction with the case of people with disabilities in Vietnam	Asian Journal of Business Ethics
M. S. Viswanathan, Srinivas	2009	From subsistence marketplaces to sustainable marketplaces: a bottom-up perspective on the role of business in poverty alleviation	Ivey Business Journal
B. S. Fitch, Leif	2007	The case for accelerating profit-making at the base of the pyramid: what could and should the donor community be seeking to do, and what results should it expect?	Journal of International Development
Topic 2 – Ethics and inequalities at the BOP			
H. D. Darwish, L Van	2018	Bottom of Pyramid 4.0: Modularising and Assimilating Industrial Revolution Cognition into a 4-Tiered Social Entrepreneurship Upliftment Model for Previously Disconnected Communities	Journal of Industrial Integration and Management
M. R. Rivera-Santos, Carlos	2010	Global village versus small town: Understanding networks at the Base of the Pyramid	International Business Review
R. Diaz-Pichardo R, P.S. Sanchez-Medina, C. Garcia de la Torre	2017	Explaining inequalities within the BOP: urban vs rural	Journal of Developmental Entrepreneurship
F. B. Filardi, Filippe Delarissa: Fischmann, Adalberto A	2018	Business strategies for the bottom of the pyramid: multiple case studies of large companies in the pacified communities of Rio de Janeiro	Revista de Administração
R. Hahn	2009	The Ethical Rational of Business for the Poor – Integrating the Concepts Bottom of the Pyramid, Sustainable Development, and Corporate Citizenship.	Journal of Business Ethics

Understanding the Evolution of BOP Narratives   59

Authors	Year	Title	Journal
Topic 3 – Innovation and the BOP			
J. B. Anderson, Niels	2007	Serving the world's poor: innovation at the base of the economic pyramid.	Journal of Business Strategy
K. G. Gollakota, Vipin: Bork, James T	2010	Reaching customers at the base of the pyramid – a two-stage business strategy.	Thunderbird International Business Review
A. Agnihotri	2013	Doing good and doing business at the bottom of the pyramid.	Business Horizons
M. Z. Habib, Leon	2010	The Bottom Of The Pyramid: Key Roles For Businesses	Journal of Business & Economics Research
V. B. Panapanaan, Tytti: Virkki-Hatakka, Terhi: Linnanen, Lassi	2016	Analysis of Shared and Sustainable Value Creation of Companies Providing Energy Solutions at the Base of the Pyramid (BoP)	Business Strategy and the Environment
Topic 4 – Mutual and social value creation			
T. Chikweche	2013	Revisiting the Business Environment at the Bottom of the Pyramid (BOP) – From Theoretical Considerations to Practical Realities.	Journal of Global Marketing
T. A. London, Ravi: Sheth, Sateen	2010	Creating mutual value: Lessons learned from ventures serving base of the pyramid producers	Journal of Business Research
H. S. Gebauer, Caroline Jennings: Haldimann, Mirella	2017	Business model innovation in base of the pyramid markets.	Journal of Business Strategy
N. S. Sinkovics, Rudolf R: Yamin, Mo	2014	The role of social value creation in business model formulation at the bottom of the pyramid – Implications for MNEs?	International Business Review
H. Sugawara	2010	Japanese business and poverty reduction	Society and Business Review
Topic 5 – Business strategies for BOP markets			
P. N. U. Gooderham, Svein: Elter, Frank	2016	Beyond local responsiveness – multi-domestic multinationals at the bottom-of-the-pyramid	Perspectives on Headquarters-subsidiary Relationships in the Contemporary MNC
S. L. L. Hart, Ted	2005	Developing Native Capability	Stanford Social Innovation Review
M. M. M. Alam, Rafiqul Islam	2012	The Limitations of Microcredit for Promoting Microenterprises in Bangladesh	Economic Annals
J. V. Hillemann, Alain	2014	An internationalization theory perspective on the bottom of the pyramid	Progress in International Business Research
A. T. R. Rashid, Mizan	2009	Making profit to solve development problems: the case of Telenor AS and the Village Phone Programme in Bangladesh.	Journal of Marketing Management

60 *Federica Angeli*

Figure 3.4 Word-cloud for Topic 1 emerging from the topic modeling analysis.

Figure 3.5 Word-cloud for Topic 2 emerging from the topic modeling analysis.

each topic, five word-clouds have been created (Figure 3.4 to Figure 3.8). Following the methodology proposed by Schwarz (2018), the chronological evolution of the five topics has been plotted in a trend line based on the average topic share per document over time (Figure 3.9).

It is interesting to note how topics span across the whole timeline under observation, as the five most representative articles for each topic (reported in Table 3.3) contain both older (<2011) and newer contributions. The word-clouds also present striking differences in terms of their semantic emphases. The 'Innovation at the BOP' topic clearly focuses on the challenges and opportunities related to 'design' product innovation that BOP consumers can 'afford'. This finding is in line with the initial BOP-efforts of MNCs to serve BOP markets by implementing strategies such as de-featuring, while ignoring other important aspects of product innovation such as product availability,

Understanding the Evolution of BOP Narratives 61

Figure 3.6 Word-cloud for Topic 3 emerging from the topic modeling analysis.

Figure 3.7 Word-cloud for Topic 4 emerging from the topic modeling analysis.

acceptability and awareness (Anderson & Markides, 2007; Angeli & Jaiswal, 2015). The chronological evolution pictured in Figure 3.9 in fact reveals that this topic has decreased in importance over time, to instead favor approaches to product design that involve consumers through bottom-up, co-creation strategies.

Another theme that has known initial prominence and progressively slid in the background relates to 'Business strategies at the BOP'. This word-cloud reveals that the topic theme focuses on ways to access BOP markets, still defined at the 'bottom' of the pyramid (rather than the later 'base'). BOP communities are here perceived mainly as 'consumers' and the emphasis is on ways to develop successful business proposition through appropriate 'strategy' choices along an 'economic' rationale. Unsurprisingly, this topic is strongly attached to the initial formulation of BOP 1.0, and its main narrative has been over time replaced by more socially-oriented,

Figure 3.8 Word-cloud for Topic 5 emerging from the topic modeling analysis.

community-focused models that promoted empowerment – rather than consumption – in line with BOP 2.0.

The 'co-creation and bottom-up approaches' topic average share is fluctuating around a rather stable level over time. The 'business' concept is very prominent in its narrative. This semantic feature of the theme reveals that co-creation and bottom-up product design have a strong profit-driven character, where user involvement in product and service innovation is conceived to deliver more successful business-models that are effectively tailor-made to user needs, and hence more profitable. At the same time, concepts such as 'implications' and 'context' – albeit not the most prominent in the narratives – reveal new appreciation of the contextual idiosyncrasies of BOP communities which might mediate the implications of new products introduction on the BOP communities' well-being and socio-economic outcomes. Therefore, dedicated product design strategies through deep involvement of final users are emphasized here, as the only viable way to achieve the intended outcomes. The co-creation approach is very much recognizable in contributions of BOP 2.0 (Ansari et al., 2012; Mohr et al., 2012; Nahi, 2016; Simanis et al., 2008; Webb & Morris, 2013) and in a view of development that emphasizes empowerment (Nussbaum, 2001; Sen, 1999). A reduced distance between innovators and innovation recipients is sought for, as in the business case promoted by Yunus (Rashid & Rahman, 2009; Yunus et al., 2010).

Steeply rising in semantic prominence is the topic of 'mutual and social value creation'. Possibly incorporating the influence of Porter's shared value concept, it first appeared on Harvard Business Review in 2011 (Porter & Kramer, 2011), this topic revisits the BOP narrative by strongly de-emphasizing 'profit' logics to instead introducing the concept of mutual 'value'. Creating mutual value points to advancing both companies' and communities' goals. This innovative perspective implies navigating the complexity of different goals while focusing on the synergies that can be established between business propositions and the communities' needs. As a consequence, the narrative evidenced in the word-cloud reveals a markedly different wording than other topics, with a strong focus on 'community development', 'social', 'inclusive'

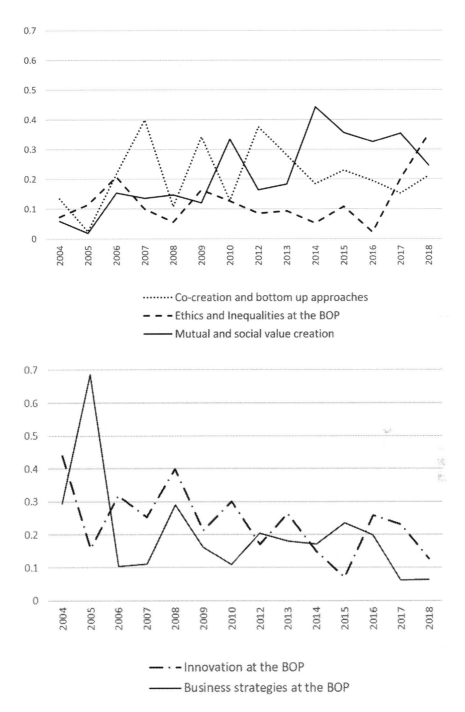

Figure 3.9 Evolution of average topic share per topic over time.

64   *Federica Angeli*

and 'sustainable' 'models' and 'initiatives'. Interestingly, sustainability starts entering the conversation, although it is difficult to discern the meaning that has been attached to it. This topic probably embeds the most the 'new commons' development model inspired by Yunus (Simanis et al., 2008; Yunus et al., 2010), where co-creation efforts go beyond simply delivering a more successful business proposition, but produce value defined in more encompassing, multifaceted terms. By favoring corporates' deeper understanding of communities' needs, this approach advocates a less instrumental and more ethical engagement with disenfranchised populations (Hahn, 2009). This view recognizes the potential conflict between market and non-market goals – most notably the juxtaposition of short-term financial results versus organizational actions' long-term outcomes and impact for individuals and communities' development (Arnold & Williams, 2012; Hahn et al., 2018).

The last topic on 'ethics and inequalities' has strongly emerged in the very recent past and proposes a deeper conversation about the rationale for BOP ventures and the inequalities persisting at the BOP. Concepts such as 'ideologies' point at the necessity to take a moral stance toward BOP ventures and to 'validate' their actions through evidence-based models and approaches. In this sense, business models should be seen as 'enablers' to reduce socio-economic inequalities among the disenfranchised communities. This perspective, focused on income differentials rather than on average poverty levels, can be considered as a recent development within the BOP discourse. The traditional perspective has focused on poverty alleviation in low-income settings, however without a more complex and critical appreciation of the fact that some BOP interventions might be reducing average poverty levels while exacerbating inequalities within target communities and countries (Caneque & Hart, 2017; Dasgupta & Hart, 2015). The first recognizable antecedent to this new discourse is the recognition that any development intervention is inherently political and has to carefully consider the power dynamics within communities and between communities and operators delivering the intervention, it being a product or a service aimed at enhancing living conditions (Arora & Romijn, 2012). Simplistic approaches may run the risk to involve or meet the requirements of only the most powerful community representatives, thereby isolating and leaving unserved the neediest, marginalized individuals (Arora & Romijn, 2012; Hall et al., 2012; Montgomery et al., 2012). Another important antecedent relates to the ethical rooting of BOP efforts. The instrumental rationale – justifying the BOP possibility in view of profit opportunities – has gone uncontested for most BOP historical evolution. Instead, the more recent concept of corporate citizenship has suggested an inherent ethical responsibility of corporates to participate to the development challenge, given their more than significant influence in worlds' politics and in the wealth concentration. The concept of corporate citizenship (Hahn, 2009) points in fact to the necessity to go beyond instrumentality to trigger a deeper, more political and ethical recognition of corporates' role in reducing socio-economic inequalities that they often contribute to generating. Ethical and political considerations of BOP ventures have for example problematized the BOP approach as potentially instrumental to further the neoliberal agenda (Arora & Romijn, 2012; Montgomery et al., 2012).

Theoretical and Methodological Contributions

The chapter advances the current BOP literature along two main lines. Theoretically, this study sheds new light on the semantic choices reflecting both the natural evolution of BOP narrative and the 'significant work' put in by both scholars and practitioners to re-establish and maintain legitimacy of BOP scholarship and practice. On the one side, the BOP discourse had to naturally mutate over time because of the conceptual criticism it received as well as the failure of MNCs' empirical efforts to develop solid BOP-oriented business models. On the other side, stakeholders – in the form of scholars and practitioners – have devoted significant efforts to redefine the BOP logic, starting from the wording and semantic choices. A vivid example is the shift from 'bottom' to the less denigrator (or perceptually so) 'base' (Simanis & Hart, 2008) and the effort of revisiting the concepts of poverty or community engagement through BOP 2.0 and BOP 3.0. In this sense, 'significant work' can be recognized, which refers to the framing efforts deliberately carried out by stakeholders to mold perceptions and divert efforts in a new direction (Reinecke & Ansari, 2016; Sharma & Jaiswal, 2018). Here a natural link to theories of framing occurs, widely applied in social movements (Benford & Snow, 2000; Snow, 2004) but also relevant to organizations' activities. Organizational decision-makers employ framing tools and narratives as part of sensemaking and sensegiving processes around innovation (Raffaelli et al., 2019), organizational change (Logemann et al., 2019), or to crystallize a strategic vision (Kaplan, 2008) or around sustainability challenges (Sharma & Jaiswal, 2018). This chapter empirically documents how narratives around a conceptual approach factually evolve over time. In doing so, it provides an original lens that constitutes what could be called 'second-order' framing, which points to how researchers and academics make sense of organizational practices, which in turn use framing and narrative techniques to gain and maintain legitimacy whilst evoking both emotional and cognitive resonance (Giorgi, 2017). In this sense, this article provides insights into how the academic community's narratives about BOP practices morphed over time (Sharma & Jaiswal, 2018), which likely reflects actual changes in organizations' BOP strategies and models but also the researchers' shifting focus of theoretical attention, which returns shifting interpretations. This changing perspective exemplifies a co-evolution between BOP practices and theories, and highlights how theories and concepts co-evolve with phenomena and are situated in time and space.

A second line of contribution is methodological. This study shows how a semantic analysis solely based on chronological clustering provides only a limited picture of the evolution of a narrative over time. The topic modeling methodology critically allowed for discerning other invisible sub-narratives, describe their own specific discourse, and detect their evolution in time. This resulted in a much more fine-grained understanding of the field and how it morphed during the period of observation, and how different views within this literature have sprouted and evolved independently and from very different starting points. Examples are the 'Innovation and the BOP', which clearly emphasized design challenges to profitable business modeling, and the co-creation approach, which again seems to be embedding a profit rationale, as opposed to 'ethics and inequalities', which instead problematizes the profit goal to promote a broader, more complex view of poverty and growth. Importantly, by automating the identification of topics, the methodology improves the accuracy and reduces the weight of the researcher's subjective understanding of the literature. Thereby, it improves reliability and validity of the methods used for topic isolation, while enhancing the researcher's room for interpretation and identification of relevant patterns.

66 _Federica Angeli_

Lessons for Policy and Practice

The study presented in this chapter has underlined the changing nature of the BOP business approach and of the related academic narrative, both of which were required to significantly morph over time to meet the ethical and pragmatic expectations of various stakeholders. Two relevant lessons can be derived for managerial practice. Beyond adopting substantially new approaches over time, devoting attention to renovating the related narrative and to ensuring appropriate dissemination channels to emerge as crucially important to maintain legitimacy. From this point of view, careful semantic choices allow for crafting socially acceptable messages, which in turn activate the proper contextual conditions for business initiatives to be understood and accepted. In complex contexts such as the BOP, any successful business endeavor needs to establish and maintain legitimacy within the target communities, in the network of suppliers, in partner organizations such as NGOs and grassroots enterprises, at the level of local government, all with plausibly different claims and interests. A 'significant work' of framing (Reinecke & Ansari, 2016; Sharma & Jaiswal, 2018), which emphasizes the crucial benefits of the organizational initiative and makes them understandable and acceptable for the various constituents if of paramount relevance. This work has also highlighted a new way to gain a deeper understanding for the evolution of narratives and discourses, which can generate a wide array of managerial uses. Topic modeling and the related visualization techniques can be used to develop a fine-grained understanding of users' feedback, to understand stakeholders' positions on relevant issues, to screen press releases and public opinion's views on organizations' actions.

From a policy perspective, the overview presented in this chapter offers an exhaustive compendium of the use and evolution of business approaches to reduce poverty. As such, it is aimed to provide policymakers with actionable points on how to leverage BOP approaches, narratives and sub-narratives for joint poverty alleviation efforts. By understanding the evolution of the concept over time, and the conceptual pillars of the current BOP thinking, policies could be designed to favor business BOP endeavors, both locally – in the regions where the target communities are located – as well as internationally – where the business firms are headquartered. Moreover, given the emphasis and advantages associated to local, grassroots enterprises in development and poverty alleviation efforts, devoted policies should be formulated to support locally grown enterprises and embed them into the broader governmental efforts. In this sense, the cross-sector partnerships and generally the collaboration, network-based approach advocated by BOP 3.0 and emphasized in the 2015–2030 Sustainable Development Framework Agenda should become integral part of new development policies, not only from donors' countries but most importantly at the level of local governments.

The BOP approach has been adopted at various degrees and in many different forms over the years, and has often provided an alternative to CSR that has been perceived more valuable and effective. The stronger emphasis on co-creation approaches, mutual value and ethics and inequalities of recent studies reveal an increasing awareness that BOP practices cannot operate in a vacuum but need to be harmonized and coordinate within the specific target settings, to avoid unwanted adverse consequences. Multi-dimensional interdependences among social and environmental challenges, and their systemic nature, require efforts at multiple levels of analysis and in several interconnected domains leading to social exclusion. It remains however challenging to evaluate the true systemic benefits of BOP initiatives. While some success stories are known for their long-lasting achievements (e.g. Narayana Health, Aravind Eye Care, GE, SAB Miller, d.light) these tend to remain geographically bounded and fall short in spurring true systemic change. Many BOP ventures still struggle to scale-up, because of the often unachievable high market penetration, the very low price points, the need for a radical rethink of promotion and distribution channels, the challenge to design products and services in deep connection with the target communities, the high heterogeneity of BOP practices (Angeli & Jaiswal, 2015, 2016; Simanis, 2012). In light of this, two caveats should be highlighted in observing the evolution of BOP frames and narratives. First, the semantic changes over time – rather than reflect substantial adaptation of practices on the ground – might conceal a mere re-branding efforts of what are actually cosmetic approaches, which might only go to benefit multinational corporations' reputation and legitimize their neo-liberal practices and market expansions (Arora & Romijn, 2012). Second, the semantic evolution of frames and narratives used in academic literature might reflect the adaptation of researchers' sensemaking and theorization processes, rather than again an actual change in practices. Erik Simanis, one of BOP main thinkers, in 2013 insightfully considered that *We (include myself here) got too caught up with our own beautiful theories and abstract concepts (like mutual value creation, inclusive business) and lost sight of the pressure on managers to meet next quarter's sales and earnings forecast. We theorized ourselves out of being relevant.* (Gunther, 2014) When understanding the complex BOP phenomenon, it is therefore important to consider the potential disconnect between theories, recollection of empirical experiences and actual practices.

In light of the aforementioned considerations, decision-makers – at both organization and policy levels – will have to carefully consider risks and benefits of base-of-the pyramid approaches and design incentives at different levels to stir such efforts in light of a systemic perspective to poverty alleviation and social inclusion, and with in-depth considerations and understanding of the complex interdependencies between organizations, communities, policies and individual behavior.

References

Ahmed, F., Ahmed, N. E., Briggs, T. W., Pronovost, P. J., Shetty, D. P., Jha, A. K., & Govindarajan, V. (2017). Can reverse innovation catalyse better value health care? *The Lancet Global Health, 5*(10), e967–e968.

Alexy, O., & George, G. (2013). Category divergence, straddling, and currency: Open innovation and the legitimation of illegitimate categories. *Journal of Management Studies, 50*(2), 173–203. https://doi.org/10.1111/joms.12000

Anderson, J., & Markides, C. (2007, August). Strategic innovation at the base of the pyramid. *Sloan Management Review, 49,* 83–88. https://doi.org/10.1108/02756660710732611

Angeli, F., Ishwardat, S. T., Jaiswal, A. K., Capaldo, A., Angeli, F., Ishwardat, S. T., & Capaldo, A. (2018). Socio-cultural sustainability of private healthcare providers in an Indian slum setting: A bottom-of-the-pyramid perspective. *Sustainability, 10*(12), 4702. https://doi.org/10.3390/su10124702

Angeli, F., & Jaiswal, A. K. (2015). Competitive dynamics between MNCs and domestic companies at the base of the pyramid: An institutional perspective. *Long Range Planning, 48*(3),

182–199. http://10.0.3.248/j.lrp.2013.08.010; http://search.ebscohost.com/login.aspx?direct=true&db=bsh&AN=102464811&site=ehost-live

Angeli, F., & Jaiswal, A. K. (2016). Business model innovation for inclusive health care delivery at the bottom of the pyramid. *Organization and Environment*, 29(4), 486–507. https://doi.org/10.1177/1086026616647174

Ansari, S., Munir, K., & Gregg, T. (2012). Impact at the "bottom of the pyramid": The role of social capital in capability development and community empowerment. *Journal of Management Studies*, 49(4), 813–842. http://10.0.4.87/j.1467-6486.2012.01042.x; http://search.ebscohost.com/login.aspx?direct=true&db=bsh&AN=75009169&site=ehost-live

Arnold, D. G., & Williams, L. H. D. (2012). The paradox at the base of the pyramid: Environmental sustainability and market-based poverty alleviation. *International Journal of Technology Management*, 60(1–2), 44. https://doi.org/10.1504/IJTM.2012.049105

Arora, S., & Romijn, H. (2012). The empty rhetoric of poverty reduction at the base of the pyramid. *Organization*, 19(4), 481–505. http://10.0.4.153/1350508411414294; http://search.ebscohost.com/login.aspx?direct=true&db=bsh&AN=78072243&site=ehost-live

Benford, R. D., & Snow, D. A. (2000). Framing processes and social movements: An overview and assessment. *Annual Review of Sociology*, 26(1), 611–639.

Blei, D. M., Ng, A. Y., & Jordan, M. I. (2003, January). Latent dirichlet allocation. *Journal of Machine Learning Research*, 3, 993–1022.

Bloomberg BusinessWeek. (2008). *Philips: Philanthropy by design*. www.bloomberg.com/news/articles/2008-09-10/philips-philanthropy-by-design

Caneque, F. C., & Hart, S. L. (2017). *Base of the pyramid 3.0: Sustainable development through innovation and entrepreneurship*. Routledge.

Carroll, A. B. (1999). Corporate social responsibility: Evolution of a definitional construct. *Business & Society*, 38(3), 268–295.

Chmielewski, D. A., Dembek, K., & Beckett, J. R. (2020). "Business unusual": Building BoP 3.0. *Journal of Business Ethics*, 161(1), 211–229.

Christensen, C. M., McDonald, R., Altman, E. J., & Palmer, J. (2016). *Disruptive innovation: Intellectual history and future paths*. Harvard Business School.

Christensen, C. M., Raynor, M. E., & McDonald, R. (2015). What is disruptive innovation. *Harvard Business Review*, 93(12), 44–53.

Cooney, K., & Shanks, T. R. W. (2010). New approaches to old problems: Market-based strategies for poverty alleviation. *Social Service Review*, 84(1), 29–55. www.journals.uchicago.edu/toc/ssr/current; http://search.ebscohost.com/login.aspx?direct=true&db=ecn&AN=1113441&site=ehost-live

Dahan, N. M., Doh, J. P., Oetzel, J., & Yaziji, M. (2010). Corporate-NGO collaboration: Co-creating new business models for developing markets. *Long Range Planning*, 43(2–3), 326–342. https://doi.org/10.1016/J.LRP.2009.11.003

Das, M., Angeli, F., Krumeich, A. J. S. M., & Van Schayck, O. C. P. (2018). Patterns of illness disclosure among Indian slum dwellers: A qualitative study. *BMC International Health and Human Rights*, 18(3), 1–17. https://doi.org/10.1186/s12914-018-0142-x

Dasgupta, P., & Hart, S. L. (2015). Creating an innovation ecosystem for inclusive and sustainable business. In F. C. Cañeque & S. L. Hart (Eds.), *Base of the pyramid 3.0: Sustainable development through innovation and entrepreneurship*. Greenleaf Publishing Limited.

Dembek, K., Neville, B. A., & York, J. (2015). Creating value at the base of the pyramid: A business model's perspective. *Academy of Management Annual Meeting Proceedings*, 1. http://10.0.21.89/AMBPP.2015.16956abstract; http://search.ebscohost.com/login.aspx?direct=true&db=bsh&AN=116913260&site=ehost-live

Dembek, K., Sivasubramaniam, N., & Chmielewski, D. A. (2019). A systematic review of the bottom/base of the pyramid literature: Cumulative evidence and future directions. *Journal of Business Ethics*, 1–18. http://doi.org/10.1007/s10551-019-04105-y

Doh, J. P., & Guay, T. R. (2006). Corporate social responsibility, public policy, and NGO activism in Europe and the United States: An institutional-stakeholder perspective. *Journal of Management Studies, 43*(1), 47–74. https://doi.org/10.1111/j.1467-6486.2006.00582.x

Elkington, J. (1997). *Cannibals with forks, the triple bottom line of 21 century business.* Capstone.

Fitch, B., & Sorensen, L. (2007). The case for accelerating profit-making at the base of the pyramid: What could and should the donor community be seeking to do, and what results should it expect? *Journal of International Development, 19*(6), 781–792. http://10.0.3.234/jid.1398; http://search.ebscohost.com/login.aspx?direct=true&db=bsh&AN=26041607&site=ehost-live

Follman, J. (2012). BoP at ten: Evolution and a new lens. *South Asian Journal of Global Business Research, 1.*

General Electric. (2015). *GE healthcare strengthens "make in India" capability for accessible, affordable healthcare.* www.ge.com/news/press-releases/ge-healthcare-strengthens-make-india-capability-accessible-affordable-healthcare

George, G., McGahan, A. M., & Prabhu, J. (2012). Innovation for inclusive growth: Towards a theoretical framework and research agenda. *Journal of Management Studies, 49*(4), 661–683. https://doi.org/10.1111/j.1467-6486.2012.01048.x

Geradts, T., Battilana, J., & Kimsey, M. (2018). Inside a multinational corporation combining commercial and social objectives. *Academy of Management Annual Meeting Proceedings, 1*(1). http://10.0.21.89/AMBPP.2018.17931abstract; http://search.ebscohost.com/login.aspx?direct=true&db=bsh&AN=131019676&site=ehost-live

Giorgi, S. (2017). The mind and heart of resonance: The role of cognition and emotions in frame effectiveness. *Journal of Management Studies, 54*(5), 711–738.

Glavas, A., & Mish, J. (2015). Resources and capabilities of triple bottom line firms: Going over old or breaking new ground? *Journal of Business Ethics, 127*(3), 623–642. https://doi.org/10.1007/s10551-014-2067-1

Goel, S., Angeli, F., Dhirar, N., Singla, N., & Ruwaard, D. (2018). What motivates medical students to select medical studies: A systematic literature review. *BMC Medical Education, 18.*

Gollakota, K., Gupta, V., & Bork, J. T. (2010). Reaching customers at the base of the pyramid – a two-stage business strategy. *Thunderbird International Business Review, 52*(5), 355–367. http://10.0.3.234/tie.20361; http://search.ebscohost.com/login.aspx?direct=true&db=bsh&AN=53022764&site=ehost-live

Gooderham, P. N., Ulset, S., & Elter, F. (2016). Beyond local responsiveness – multi-domestic multinationals at the bottom-of-the-pyramid. In B. Ambos & J. T. C. Birkinshaw (Eds.), *Perspectives on headquarters-subsidiary relationships in the contemporary MNC* (Vol. 17, pp. 3–26). Emerald Group Publishing Limited.

Govindarajan, V., & Ramamurti, R. (2013). Delivering world-class health care, affordably. *Harvard Business Review, 91*(11), 117–122.

Gunther, M. (2014). The base of the pyramid: Will selling to the poor pay off? *The Guardian.* www.theguardian.com/sustainable-business/prahalad-base-bottom-pyramid-profit-poor

Hahn, R. (2009). The ethical rational of business for the poor – integrating the concepts bottom of the pyramid, sustainable development, and corporate citizenship. *Journal of Business Ethics, 84*(3), 313–324. http://10.0.3.239/s10551-008-9711-6; http://search.ebscohost.com/login.aspx?direct=true&db=bsh&AN=36608940&site=ehost-live

Hahn, T., Figge, F., Pinkse, J., & Preuss, L. (2018). A paradox perspective on corporate sustainability: Descriptive, instrumental, and normative aspects. *Journal of Business Ethics, 148*(2), 235–248. https://doi.org/10.1007/s10551-017-3587-2

Hall, J., Matos, S., Sheehan, L., & Silvestre, B. (2012). Entrepreneurship and innovation at the base of the pyramid: A recipe for inclusive growth or social exclusion? *Journal of Management Studies, 49*(4), 785–812. https://doi.org/10.1111/j.1467-6486.2012.01044.x

Hart, S. L., & Christensen, C. M. (2002). The great leap: Driving innovation from the base of the pyramid. *MIT Sloan Management Review*, 44(1), 51–56.

Hart, S. L., & London, T. (2005). Developing native capability. *Stanford Social Innovation Review*, 3(2), 28–33.

Heuer, M., & Landrum, N. E. (2016). In search of environmental sustainability at the base of the pyramid. *Journal of Corporate Citizenship*, 61, 94–106. http://10.0.38.46/GLEAF.4700.2016.ma.00007; http://search.ebscohost.com/login.aspx?direct=true&db=bsh&AN=114710825&site=ehost-live; https://search.proquest.com/docview/1818716770?accountid=14338; https://tilburguniversity.on.worldcat.org/atoztitles/link?genr

Jaiswal, A. K. (2008). The fortune at the bottom or the middle of the pyramid? *Innovations: Technology, Governance, Globalization*, 3(1), 85–100. https://doi.org/10.1162/itgg.2008.3.1.85

Jaiswal, A. K., & Gupta, S. (2015). The influence of marketing on consumption behavior at the bottom of the pyramid. *Journal of Consumer Marketing*, 32.

Kaplan, S. (2008). Framing contests: Strategy making under uncertainty. *Organization Science*, 19(5), 729–752.

Karnani, A. (2006). Misfortune at the bottom of the pyramid. *Greener Management International*, 51, 99–110. http://search.ebscohost.com/login.aspx?direct=true&db=bsh&AN=25290811&site=ehost-live

Karnani, A. (2007). The mirage of marketing to the bottom of the pyramid. *California Management Review*. https://doi.org/10.2139/ssrn.914518

Khavul, S., & Bruton, G. D. (2013). Harnessing innovation for change: Sustainability and poverty in developing countries. *Journal of Management Studies*, 50(2), 285–306.

Kolk, A., Rivera-Santos, M., & Rufin, C. (2014). Reviewing a decade of research on the "base/bottom of the pyramid" (BOP) concept. *Business & Society*, 53(3), 338–377. https://doi.org/10.1177/0007650312474928; http://search.ebscohost.com/login.aspx?direct=true&db=bsh&AN=95432793&site=ehost-live

Latten, T., Westra, D., Angeli, F., Paulus, A., Struss, M., & Ruwaard, D. (2018). Pharmaceutical companies and healthcare providers: Going beyond the gift – An explorative review. *PLoS One*, 13, e0191856.

Logemann, M., Piekkari, R., & Cornelissen, J. (2019). The sense of it all: Framing and narratives in sensegiving about a strategic change. *Long Range Planning*, 52(5), 101852.

London, T., & Fay, C. (2016). Making money by fighting poverty. *ISE: Industrial & Systems Engineering at Work*, 48(11), 26–31. http://search.ebscohost.com/login.aspx?direct=true&db=bsh&AN=118903345&site=ehost-live

London, T., & Hart, S. L. (2004). Reinventing strategies for emerging markets: Beyond the transnational model. *Journal of International Business Studies*, 35(5), 350–370. https://doi.org/10.1057/palgrave.jibs.8400099

London, T. E. D. (2008). The base-of-the-pyramid perspective: A new approach to poverty alleviation. *Academy of Management Annual Meeting Proceedings*, 1, 1–6. http://10.0.21.89/AMBPP.2008.33716520; http://search.ebscohost.com/login.aspx?direct=true&db=bsh&AN=33716520&site=ehost-live

Maier, F., Meyer, M., & Steinbereithner, M. (2016). Nonprofit organizations becoming business-like: A systematic review. *Nonprofit and Voluntary Sector Quarterly*, 45(1), 64–86. https://doi.org/10.1177/0899764014561796

Malodia, S., Gupta, S., & Jaiswal, A. K. (2019). Reverse innovation: A conceptual framework. *Journal of the Academy of Marketing Science*, 1–21.

McMullen, J. S. (2011). Delineating the domain of development entrepreneurship: A market-based approach to facilitating inclusive economic growth. *Entrepreneurship: Theory and Practice*, 35(1), 185–193. https://doi.org/10.1111/j.1540-6520.2010.00428.x

Mezias, S., & Fakhreddin, M. (2015). Building boundary capabilities at the base of the pyramid. *Journal of Entrepreneurship and Public Policy*, 4(1), 111–133. https://doi.org/10.1108/JEPP-02-2013-0007

Mohr, J. J., Sengupta, S., & Slater, S. F. (2012). Serving base-of-the-pyramid markets: Meeting real needs through a customized approach. *Journal of Business Strategy, 33*(6), 4–14. http://10.0.4.84/02756661211281453; http://search.ebscohost.com/login.aspx?direct=true&db=bsh&AN=82894217&site=ehost-live

Montgomery, N., Peredo, A., & Carlson, E. (2012). *The BOP discourse as capitalist hegemony*. Academy of Management.

Moro, S., Pires, G., Rita, P., & Cortez, P. (2019). A text mining and topic modelling perspective of ethnic marketing research. *Journal of Business Research, 103,* 275–285.

Nahi, T. (2016). Cocreation at the base of the pyramid: Reviewing and organizing the diverse conceptualizations. *Organization and Environment, 29*(4), 416–437. https://doi.org/10.1177/1086026616652666

Nussbaum, M. C. (2001). *Women and human development: The capabilities approach* (Vol. 3). Cambridge University Press.

Porter, M. E., & Kramer, M. R. (2011). Creating shared value. *Harvard Business Review, 89* (1–2), 62–77. https://doi.org/10.1108/09600039410055963

Prahalad, C. K. (2004). Why selling to the poor makes for good business. *Fortune, 150*(10), 70–72. http://search.ebscohost.com/login.aspx?direct=true&db=bsh&AN=14963051&site=ehost-live

Prahalad, C. K. (2006). *The fortune at the bottom of the pyramid: Eradicating poverty through profits*. Pearson Prentice Hall.

Prahalad, C. K. (2012). Bottom of the pyramid as a source of breakthrough innovations. *Journal of Product Innovation Management, 29*(1), 6–12. http://10.0.4.87/j.1540-5885.2011.00874.x; http://search.ebscohost.com/login.aspx?direct=true&db=bsh&AN=67226477&site=ehost-live

Prahalad, C. K., & Hammond, A. (2002). Serving the world's poor, profitably. *Harvard Business Review, 80.*

Prahalad, C. K., & Hart, S. L. (2002). The fortune at the bottom of the pyramid. *Strategy+Business Magazine, 26,* 273. https://doi.org/10.2139/ssrn.914518

Raffaelli, R., Glynn, M. A., & Tushman, M. (2019). Frame flexibility: The role of cognitive and emotional framing in innovation adoption by incumbent firms. *Strategic Management Journal, 40*(7), 1013–1039.

Rashid, A. T., & Rahman, M. (2009). Making profit to solve development problems: The case of Telenor AS and the village phone programme in Bangladesh. *Journal of Marketing Management, 25*(9–10), 1049–1060. http://10.0.5.82/026725709X479363; http://search.ebscohost.com/login.aspx?direct=true&db=bsh&AN=46815129&site=ehost-live

Reinecke, J., & Ansari, S. (2016). Taming wicked problems: The role of framing in the construction of corporate social responsibility. *Journal of Management Studies, 53*(3), 299–329.

Ritz, A., Brewer, G. A., & Neumann, O. (2016). Public service motivation: A systematic literature review and outlook. *Public Administration Review, 76*(3), 414–426.

Rivera-Santos, M., Rufín, C., & Kolk, A. (2012). Bridging the institutional divide: Partnerships in subsistence markets. *Journal of Business Research, 65*(12), 1721–1727. https://doi.org/10.1016/j.jbusres.2012.02.013

Roxas, S. K., & Ungson, G. R. (2011). From alleviation to eradication: A reassessment of modernization, market-based, and communitarian solutions to global poverty. *Poverty & Public Policy, 3*(2), 1–25.

Savolainen, P., Ahonen, J. J., & Richardson, I. (2012). Software development project success and failure from the supplier's perspective: A systematic literature review. *International Journal of Project Management, 30*(4), 458–469.

Schwarz, C. (2018). ldagibbs: A command for topic modeling in stata using latent dirichlet allocation. *The Stata Journal, 18*(1), 101–117.

Sen, A. (1999). *Development freedom*. Anchor Books.

Sharma, G., & Jaiswal, A. K. (2018). Unsustainability of sustainability: Cognitive frames and tensions in bottom of the pyramid projects. *Journal of Business Ethics, 148*(2), 291–307.

Simanis, E. (2012, June). Reality check at the bottom of the pyramid. *Harvard Business Review.* https://hbr.org/2012/06/reality-check-at-the-bottom-of-the-pyramid

Simanis, E., & Hart, S. (2008). The base of the pyramid protocol: Toward next generation BoP strategy. *Innovations: Technology, Governance, Globalization.* https://doi.org/10.1162/itgg.2008.3.1.57

Simanis, E., Hart, S., & Duke, D. (2008). The base of the pyramid protocol: Beyond "basic needs" business strategies. *Innovations: Technology, Governance, Globalization, 3*(1), 57–84. https://doi.org/10.1162/itgg.2008.3.1.57

Snow, D. A. (2004). Framing processes, ideology, and discursive fields. *The Blackwell Companion to Social Movements, 1,* 380–412.

Sonenshein, S. (2010). We're changing – or are we? Untangling the role of progressive, regressive, and stability narratives during strategic change implementation. *Academy of Management Journal, 53*(3), 477–512.

UNDP. (2014). *Barriers and opportunities at the base of the pyramid – the role of the private sector in inclusive development.* www.iicpsd.undp.org/content/istanbul/en/home/library/reports/barriers-and-opportunities-at-the-base-of-the-pyramid-the-role/

Webb, J. W., & Morris, M. H. (2013). Microenterprise growth at the base of the pyramid: A resource-based perspective. *Journal of Developmental Entrepreneurship, 18*(4). https://doi.org/10.1142/S108494671350026X

World Bank. (2018). *World bank dataset.* https://data.worldbank.org/topic/poverty

Yunus, M., Moingeon, B., & Lehmann-Ortega, L. (2010). Building social business models: Lessons from the grameen experience. *Long Range Planning, 43*(2–3), 308–325. https://doi.org/10.1016/j.lrp.2009.12.005

Yurdakul, D., Atik, D., & Dholakia, N. (2017). Redefining the bottom of the pyramid from a marketing perspective. *Marketing Theory, 17*(3), 289–303.

4 Learning in Hybrid Organizations

A Systematic Literature Review

Kristian Marinov, Ashley Metz, Kelly Alexander, and Federica Angeli

Introduction

This chapter explores how learning occurs in hybrid organisations, such as social enterprises with dual financial and social goals. Learning is important in any organisation, but as hybrid organisations experience unique pressures and have multiple goals, how well organizations learn has potential implications for social and financial goal attainment. We bring the literatures on learning and hybrid organising in conversation through an integrated review, which categorises the types of organizational learning in hybrid organizations by types of logic tensions (Smith & Lewis, 2011). These logic tensions are discussed in light of the learning literature, highlighting the emergence, significance and resolution of the tensions for organisations and individuals.

Hybrid organisations are organisational forms which combine two different institutional logics, or sets "of belief systems and associated practices, [that] define the content and meaning of institutions" (Reay & Hinings, 2009, pp. 627–631). An institutional logic refers to the taken for granted assumptions, practices, and beliefs that guide actors activities through their fields of work (Friedland, 1991). Social enterprises are an "ideal type" of hybrid organisation (Battilana & Lee, 2014) incorporating two modes of value creation within a single organisation. The first is based on a commercial, for-profit logic aimed at ensuring financial self-reliance. The second is asocial, community-oriented logic, aimed at pursuing a social or environmental mission and attaining long-term impact (Battilana & Lee, 2014). The essence of the hybrid form does not merely stem from the combination of the two separate logics, but rather from the creation of an entirely novel hybrid logic and identity characterised by new organisational goals and strategies, expressed in "hybrid" behaviour (Knutsson & Thomasson, 2017)

Hybrid organisations face a multitude of challenges that are either unique to them or more easily resolved in other organisational forms. Conflicting logics can lead to challenges in scaling up processes (Fosfuri et al., 2016), tensions between social and financial goals (Battilana et al., 2015; Battilana & Dorado, 2010; Smith et al., 2013) and difficulties for employees and managers in prioritising activities (Argote, 2013; Greve, 2017). Other issues include the prioritisation of one logic over the other, or "mission drift" (Battilana & Dorado, 2010), possible financial deficits where charity logics dominate (Battilana et al., 2015), and splits in organisational identity (Smith et al., 2013). Finally, there are risks of external, as well as internal delegitimisation, due to the increased number and divergence of stakeholders' expectations (Lee et al.,

DOI: 10.4324/9780429243165-5
This chapter has been made available under a CC-BY-NC 4.0 license.

74 Kristian Marinov et al.

2017), and recurrent cognitive dissonance because of the constant challenging of beliefs related to multiple logics (Knutsson & Thomasson, 2017).

Organisations react to these challenges by *adapting*, for example, to pursue a greater fit with the demands of the environment (e.g. uncertain environment requires more structural flexibility), and an improvement of organisational processes (e.g. more flexible organisational structure) (Greve, 2017). To do so, they may interpret the problem caused by the challenges and break down established routines to refine or change the part of the organisation that is affected (Greve, 2017). Reshaping, and improving these routines requires an adaptation of the cognitive schemata (the mental maps that guide thoughts and behaviour) of the individuals engaging in them (Hahn et al., 2014), as well as an adaptation of the organisations' processes to achieve their goals (e.g. how teams work together; what management system is used) (Levinthal & March, 1981). By observing adaptations to practices and routines, it is possible to see organisational learning (Gherardi, 2019).

Adaptation is the result of learning in an organisation, seeking greater fit with the demands of the environment, and improving organisational processes (Greve, 2017). Organisational learning is the change in knowledge resulting from experience (Fiol & Lyles, 1985). Therefore, organisational adaptation refers to responsiveness to knowledge gained in the organisation through practice. Learning processes occur constantly within hybrid organisations. However, due to the fluid and overarching nature of learning, the majority of the hybrid organisation literature that refers to processes of learning does not explicitly recognize them as such. Rather, learning theory is woven implicitly into the hybrid (i.e. hybrid organisations) literature. For example, it has been called management of tensions (Smith et al., 2013), a reconciliation in institutional logics paradoxes (Jay, 2013), or a harnessing of productive tensions (Battilana et al., 2015). The result is a lack of conceptual integration between hybrid literature and organisational learning literature. To date, only two studies could be located that attempt to make this link explicit (Knutsson & Thomasson, 2017; Urban & Gaffurini, 2018). A more thorough exploration of this link is important, as hybrid organisational structures necessitate that organisational learning is geared towards improving organisational performance in both its aspects – social and economic – along with the balance between them.

Knowing how to learn and adapt to problems arising from these contradictory goals can be informed by theoretical insight provided by contemporary organisational learning theories. Simultaneously, hybrid organisations are poised to further develop the organisational learning literature, as learning from multiple contradictory goals is an underdeveloped topic that can bear fruitful exploration. This integration however requires that the two fields of literature communicate. Instead, while there has been a substantial body of literature developed concerning organisational learning in general (Argote, 2013; Argote & Epple, 1990; Bierly et al., 2000; Chiva et al., 2010; Easterby-Smith & Lyles, 2011; Greve, 2017), as well as various processes of adaptation, and learning in hybrid organisations (Battilana & Dorado, 2010; Dees, 2012; Jay, 2013; Smith et al., 2012, 2013), no study so far has categorised the range and types of organisational learning with hybrid organisations.

Bridging this gap, this systematic literature review serves to provide clarity with respect to several points. First, it aims to outline various forms of learning that hybrid organisations engage in. In doing so, it aims to create a model for learning in hybrid organisations by combining insights from the substantial body of literature concerning organisational learning (Argote, 2013; Argote & Epple, 1990; Bierly et al., 2000; Chiva et al., 2010; Easterby-Smith & Lyles, 2011; Greve, 2017), and processes of adaptation and learning in hybrid organisations (Battilana & Dorado, 2010; Dees, 2012; Jay, 2013; Smith et al., 2012, 2013). Learning literature informs the process models by highlighting the various forms of learning that may take place within organisations and by individuals, thus proving clarity to the way the process models unfold. Second, this research therefore aims to provide theoretical insight into the functioning and development of hybrid organisations. This insight is necessary given the unique challenges stemming from hybrids' novel organisational form – such as goal incongruence and conflicting interests (Knutsson & Thomasson, 2017). Third, this chapter aims to light the path for future possible research into both organisational learning and hybrid organisations. The research question guiding the research is:

> How are hybrid organisations able to adapt to tensions stemming from multiple institutional logics?

Learning in Hybrid Organisations

Theoretical insight from contemporary organisational learning theories informs our understanding of learning and adapting to problems arising from contradictory goals. The mechanisms by which organisational learning occurs are comprehension, adoption, and manipulation of organisational processes (Greve, 2017). One way to observe learning in organisations is by identifying changes in practices and routines (Gherardi, 2019). Another is via changes in performance, such as production and financial performance (Argote & Epple, 1990; Dutton & Thomas, 1984). Organisational learning drives knowledge creation – classified as declarative, explicit, or procedural (referring to skills and routines) (Argote, 2013).

Learning is an essential part of organisational survival and success, especially for organisations operating in complex environments and facing paradoxical tensions (Anderson, 1999; Jay, 2013; Senge, 1990). Yet Senge (1990) posits that the majority of organisations are poor learners, and by no accident. The design and management of organisations, workers' role perceptions, and how they are taught to think about, and interact with, the organisation, all serve to create a profound 'learning disability' (Senge, 1990). We outline various reasons for this, at both the individual and organisational levels, below.

Organisations are systems processing information and knowledge with interdependent elements and these dynamic elements are in constant flux (Senge, 1990) Individuals in organisations create shared meaning and understanding through dialogue (Senge, 1990). A systems dynamics approach focuses on the relationships between variables (Anderson, 1999; Senge, 1990), and provides a lens through which to view learning processes in hybrids. The impact of learning is traced to outputs that are greater than the sum of their inputs – indicating non-linearity and feedback loops (Hjorth & Bagheri, 2006). Organisations fluctuate between structure/order and disruptive chaos, and are composed of agents attempting to maintain a state of equilibrium (Anderson, 1999; Senge, 1990). Multiple logics in hybrid organisations influence, are interpreted, and enacted at various levels of the organisation (individual, team, department, organisation, environment) (Battilana et al., 2015; Battilana & Dorado, 2010; Smith et al., 2012).

76 *Kristian Marinov et al.*

Learning is the management of experiences (Glynn et al., 1992) and expansion of the range of possible behaviours available to actors. Learning itself occurs through processing previous knowledge, and forges new knowledge (Argote, 2013). In this system, organisational learning occurs through the sequential process of knowledge acquisition, information distribution, the collective interpretation of information, and consolidation into organisational memory (Huber, 1991). Whilst direct trial and error from experience is conducive to learning in everyday life, this form of learning is problematic in organisations (Senge, 1990). Often in organisations, behaviour and consequence are decoupled by time and space. Consequences of a decision made in one department can influence an entire organisation. Yet this impact is not always observed, as the system masks direct links, and consequences are not immediately apparent. Decoupling means that experience can be difficult to identify and learn from (Senge, 1990).

Within hybrid organisations, learning occurs at the individual and organisational levels. Organisational learning requires an adaptation of the processes organisations engage in to achieve their goals (e.g. how teams work together; what management system is used) (Levinthal & March, 1981). For individuals this means reshaping and improving routines and adapting cognitive schemata (mental maps guiding actors' thoughts and behaviour) of the individuals involved (Hahn et al., 2014).

Forms of Organisational Learning

Individual Learning

Individuals in organisations are viewed as agents with schemata – or perceptions of the environment, time and context – and act based on interaction between the environment and rules constructed within their 'mental map' (Anderson, 1999). That is, individuals are agents with free will, pursuing their own (implicit) goals, constrained by organisations' rules and controls (Anderson, 1999). Individuals act based on cognitive rules, and action is oriented towards the attainment of the goal(s) set by the agent, and a goal is considered an equilibrium state. The individual acts to maximise compliance with their environment – in pursuit of their goals. Cognitive rules are represented as 'genetic algorithms' that act on an *if, then* basis, flowing along a series of *if, then* clauses (Anderson, 1999; Senge, 1990). Based on this description, individual-level learning is the refinement of cognitive schemata, and an improvement, and/or expansion in thinking and behavioural patterns oriented towards achieving implicit goals (Hahn et al., 2014).

Organisational Learning

Learning on the organisational level differs from individual learning and is not simply the aggregation of the latter (Fiol & Lyles, 1985). Yet organisational learning is contingent upon the collective cognitive processes of individuals (Yeo, 2005). In contrast with individual learning, learning that occurs on the organisational level can be seen as preserved in the organisational memory. This memory contains and sustains behaviours, mental maps, norms, and values over time, whereas those of individuals are in constant flux (Hedberg, 1981).

Organisational memory is important for preserving lessons learned by organisations and allowing adaptations to occur in improvement of the organisation. Yet, in paradoxical fashion, punctuated points of organisational forgetting are crucial

(Easterby-Smith & Lyles, 2011). Organisations settle into routines, which are central in organisational memory – yet this does not imply that those routines always fit with the environment, or enhance organisational efficacy. Thus equilibrium states are dynamic and not static (Smith & Lewis, 2011). Therefore, when the equilibrium point shifts pushing an organisation out of fit, it becomes crucial to disrupt the status quo, unlearn routines, forget implicit assumptions, and incite a burst of innovation, renewal, and creative destruction. In this way adaptation may occur through innovation and adopting new routines (Easterby-Smith & Lyles, 2011).

This iterative process of learning and forgetting, creation and destruction, represents a cycle ranging from instability to systemic order. In this process, there are various learning mechanisms unfolding and changing system dynamics. Learning may be indirect – "learning through the failures of others" (Bledow et al., 2017, p. 1), experiential or direct (Argote, 2013); and learning may occur via performance feedback (Greve, 2017; Nason et al., 2018). It is through these types of learning that the organisational system adapts itself.

Therefore, we have seen that learning occurs through systems of feedback at the organisational and individual levels, and that this shapes the organisation and the way in which goal attainment occurs. Hybrid organisations manage complex dynamics, where multiple logics increase the managerial burden, and necessitate increased learning and adaption.

Hybrids Organisations' Adaptive Challenges

Hybrid organisations' adaptive challenges can be categorised as stemming from the logic tensions present in hybrids (Smith & Lewis, 2011). Such tensions can be categorised as paradoxes, dilemmas, and dialectical tensions. Paradoxes are defined as opposing forces, or elements, which are synergistic and connected in the larger system (Quinn & Cameron, 1988). An example of a paradox is one department focusing on financial gain, and another on social impact – creating seeming incompatibilities, ignoring the fact that, on a higher level, social value creation requires reliable financing, and that finances serve to support a goal (the social mission). Paradoxes can exist embedded in the hybrid as an emergent property of how the hybrid functions as a system; this is a form of latent paradox that needn't necessarily be noticed by the organisation. Paradoxes become noticeable when they are made cognitively relevant, or salient in the organisation. A paradox is more likely to become cognitively salient as divergent logics become enacted, a plurality of institutional viewpoints is present, organisational change is required, and scarcity sets in (Smith & Lewis, 2011). Dilemmas, on the other hand are competing choices with advantages and disadvantages (McGrath, 1982). Finally, dialectic tensions are contradictions resolved through synthesis or through the stressing of similarities, whilst neglecting value differences (Bledow et al., 2009).

Methods

Research Design

The review utilises a systematic, rather than a heuristic, approach to locating, selecting and analysing literature, based on the PRISMA guidelines (Moher et al., 2016) (see Figure 4.1). The systematic method is widely respected for creating a transparent,

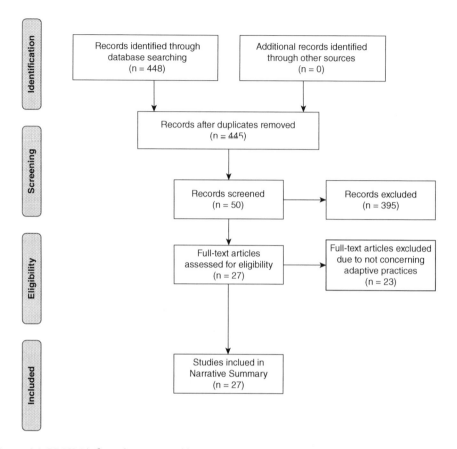

Figure 4.1 PRISMA flow diagram and literature review results.

complete and reproducible procedure, avoiding biases (such as incompleteness, or bias towards highly cited literature) inherent in other techniques (Moher et al., 2016; Tranfield et al., 2003). The methodological process of the review is conducted based on the work of Tranfield et al. (2003). We followed the three review stages: first engaging in planning – identifying the appropriate keywords; then conducting the actual search and completing the review; and finally reporting on the results and dissemination of these results.

The lack of paradigmatic consensus in the field (Rashman et al., 2009) leads to the adoption of a broad approach to the selection of literature that meets the criteria of answering the research question. The broad approach is typical in management and social sciences, where wide array of concept definitions and theories of learning are defined (Tranfield et al., 2003). Data collection has been done making use of key terms and a predetermined search algorithm (detailed in Figure 4.2).

In order to cluster the literature, we adopt the typology developed by Smith and Lewis (2011), which conceptually clarifies the full range of existing logic tensions. Tensions can relate to learning, organising, belonging, performing, or a combination of these ideal types. *Learning* tensions relate to building upon versus destroying the

Line	Keywords
1	'Hybrid Organi*ation*' OR 'Social Venture*' OR 'Social Enterprise*' OR 'Social Entrepeneurship' OR 'Benefit Organi'ation*' OR 'B Corp' OR 'B Corporation' AND 'Organi*ational Learning' OR 'Learning' OR 'Adaptation' OR 'Organi*ational Adaptation' OR 'Evolution' OR 'Change' OR 'Organi*ational Change' OR 'Organi*ation Change' OR 'Transformation' OR 'Organi*ational Transformation'
2	'Hybrid Organi*ation*' OR 'Social Venture*' OR 'Social Enterprise*' OR 'Social Entrepeneurship' OR 'Benefit Organi*ation*' OR 'B Corp' OR 'B Corporation' AND 'System Dynamics' OR 'Complexity Theory' OR 'Complexity'

* Denotes Any Variation in the search word: E.g. Organi*ation will include Organisation and Organization

Figure 4.2 Search Keywords

past to create the future. *Organising* tensions refer to competing designs, structures and processes oriented towards the achievement of a desired outcome. *Belonging* tensions relate to identity, and as it is formed by competing values, logics, and roles. Identity answers the questions of 'Who we are', and 'what we do', guiding behaviour in a desired direction(s) (Smith & Lewis, 2011). Finally, *performing* tensions relate to the divergence in notions of organisational success, as defined and guided by strategies, goals prescribed by different logics and stakeholders. Acknowledging the complex, cross-boundary nature of such tensions, we also consider that articles can cover multiple types of tensions. To capture the nuance and theoretical contribution illustrated in such cross-category articles, we integrate them into the ideal categories in order to show how they contribute to informing hybrid adaptive processes.

Search Strategy

Criteria for inclusion include articles investigating, and/or developing concepts, and/ or mechanisms in hybrid learning. We define hybrid organisations' learning as individual-level learning consisting of the development of the learning capabilities of individuals, and/or the refinement of their cognitive schemata, as well as organisation-level learning, consisting of shifts in the organisations structure, and processes. Learning is oriented towards the resolution of logic tensions, and the challenges stemming from them, at both the individual and organisational levels.

The literature search included peer-reviewed quantitative, conceptual, and qualitative papers, published in English. Purely normative, or prescriptive papers were excluded, as their advice risks being unsubstantiated (Rashman et al., 2009). Given the nascent nature of the hybrid field of scientific inquiry (Battilana, 2018), and the lack of previous reviews on the topic, this review sets no limit to its time horizon in search of the literature.

We searched Web of Science and key terms used to search the database focused on hybrid organisations mentioned in conjunction with organisational learning, or change, and separately with system dynamics keywords (see Figure 4.2). The search yielded 448 articles, decreasing to 445 after removal of duplicates. Initial screening and selection of the articles consisted of an analysis of the articles' title and abstracts for the keywords, yielding 50 articles. A secondary screening consisting of in-depth full text analysis yielded a final selection of 27 articles, which were included for review and synthesis. A flow diagram of the literature search can be found in Figure 4.1

According to geographical lines, the literature was primarily concentrated in developed countries (70%) including: the USA, UK, France, Italy, Belgium, Sweden, Germany, The Netherlands, Austria, Scotland, and Canada. A comparatively much smaller proportion of the literature focused on developing countries (15%) including: South Africa, Two Pacific Island Nations, Brazil, and India, and underdeveloped nations (7%) including Senegal and Cambodia. The remainder of the literature focuses on multiple contexts (7.4%).

A broad range of hybrid organisation types emerged from the literature, and across a number of sectors. Studies were conducted in the education sector (Ometto et al., 2019) corporate law firms (Mangen & Brivot, 2015), a 'global café' focusing on cultural education, and integration (Dobson et al., 2018), Work Integration Social Enterprises (WISEs) (Battilana et al., 2015; Pache & Santos, 2013), an industrial manufacturing/art firm (Dalpiaz et al., 2016), public-private partnerships (Reissner, 2019), the private-public healthcare sector (Bishop & Waring, 2016), and others. The common structural thread shared by all hybrid organisational forms is a multiplicity of varyingly contradictory institutional logics, and the implications these have for the subsystems comprising the organisations.

Data Synthesis

The aim of this review is to highlight the processes of learning in hybrid organisations in each paper, and synthesise these processes into a model. To accomplish this, this review utilises an empirically grounded approach (Crossan & Apaydin, 2010). For this purpose, we adopt the data synthesis method of narrative summary. Narrative summary is appropriate for both qualitative and quantitative research, and has the ability to make an account of complex, dynamic processes, taking into account sequence, and contingency through integration, and juxtaposition of narratives (Dixon-Woods et al., 2005; Kolb et al., 2018; Popay et al., 2005).

Results and Discussion

The following section details the results and we note that a system dynamics perspective emerges in the research, as feedback loops highlight the non-linear way in which learning and adaptation take place. System dynamics focus on the relationships between variables, adopting an integrated view, and taking a multilevel perspective (P. Anderson, 1999; Senge, 1990). System dynamics allow for describing each level of the system, and the interactions between levels. This lens is particularly suitable to view learning processes in hybrids – where the organisation is a system with interdependent elements and these dynamic elements are in constant flux. Thus, the impact of learning is traced to outputs that are greater than the sum of their inputs – indicating non-linearity, and creating loops of causality when aggregated (Hjorth & Bagheri, 2006). Based on Hjorth and Bagheri (2006), we create four dynamic systems models (see Appendices 1–4), clarifying the range of conditions which impact learning in four areas – Learning, Organising, Behaving, and Performing. This model creates an image of how the learning system operates by illustrating the influence variables have on each other – either reinforcing (+) or diminishing (–) the effect. This creates a web

Learning in Hybrid Organisations 81

of connections, and feedback loops, whose full influence can only be observed in a holistic view of the system (Hjorth & Bagheri, 2006).

Literature Clustering

We see the multiple pathways (e.g. through learning, structure) that hybrid organisations may take to achieve their goal of adaptation, and delivery of multiple organisational aims, as indicative of equifinality (Dzombak et al., 2014). This is evident in various means of adaptation – such as changes in the systemic order of the organisation (Chiva et al., 2010), and/or changes in the cognitive schemata of the agents in the organisation (Senge, 1990). The literature revealed this adaptation takes place in various contexts, organisational settings, levels of analysis, and according to various theories.

In clustering the literature, we adapted Smith and Lewis's (2011) typology, drawing out the variety of ideal-type logic tensions. Tensions can relate to learning, organising, belonging, performing, or a combination of these ideal types. Figure 4.3 represents the literature clustered according to the ideal-type logic tensions. In the figure, dark squares refer to the ideal-type logic tensions, while lighter squares highlight the dynamic interaction between different types of tensions as they combine and interact. We discuss each of these tensions in the following sections, with a discussion of how organisations adapt to each one. Acknowledging the complex, cross-boundary nature of such tensions, we also note that the literature highlights that organisations may be subject to multiple types of tensions. To capture the nuance and theoretical contribution illustrated in such cross-category articles, we integrate them into the ideal categories to show how they contribute to informing hybrid adaptive processes (see Figure 4.3).

Adapting to Tensions

Hybrid organisations are required to identify and adapt to the various types of tensions that their organisations face. Learning tensions relate to building upon the past to create the future (Smith & Lewis, 2011). Organising tensions refer to competing designs, structures and processes oriented towards the achievement of a desired outcome (Smith & Lewis, 2011). Belonging tensions relate to identity, and are formed by competing values, logics, and roles (Smith & Lewis, 2011). Finally, performing tensions relate to the divergence in notions of organisational success, as defined and guided by strategies to attain goals prescribed by different logics and stakeholders (Smith & Lewis, 2011). Each of these is discussed in the following sections.

Adapting to Learning Tensions

One way of learning tensions can be resolved by the development and exploitation of organisational capabilities (OC). The literature captures varying aspects of OC, each defined differently. However OC generally pertains to an organisations' ability to develop and leverage their internal potential, manifested as skills and resources, to enact organisational change. Eti-Tofinga et al. (2018, p. 620) view this internal potential, or OC as "sets of knowledge and skills that allow an organisation to perform tasks effectively". OC is comprised of operational and dynamic capabilities.

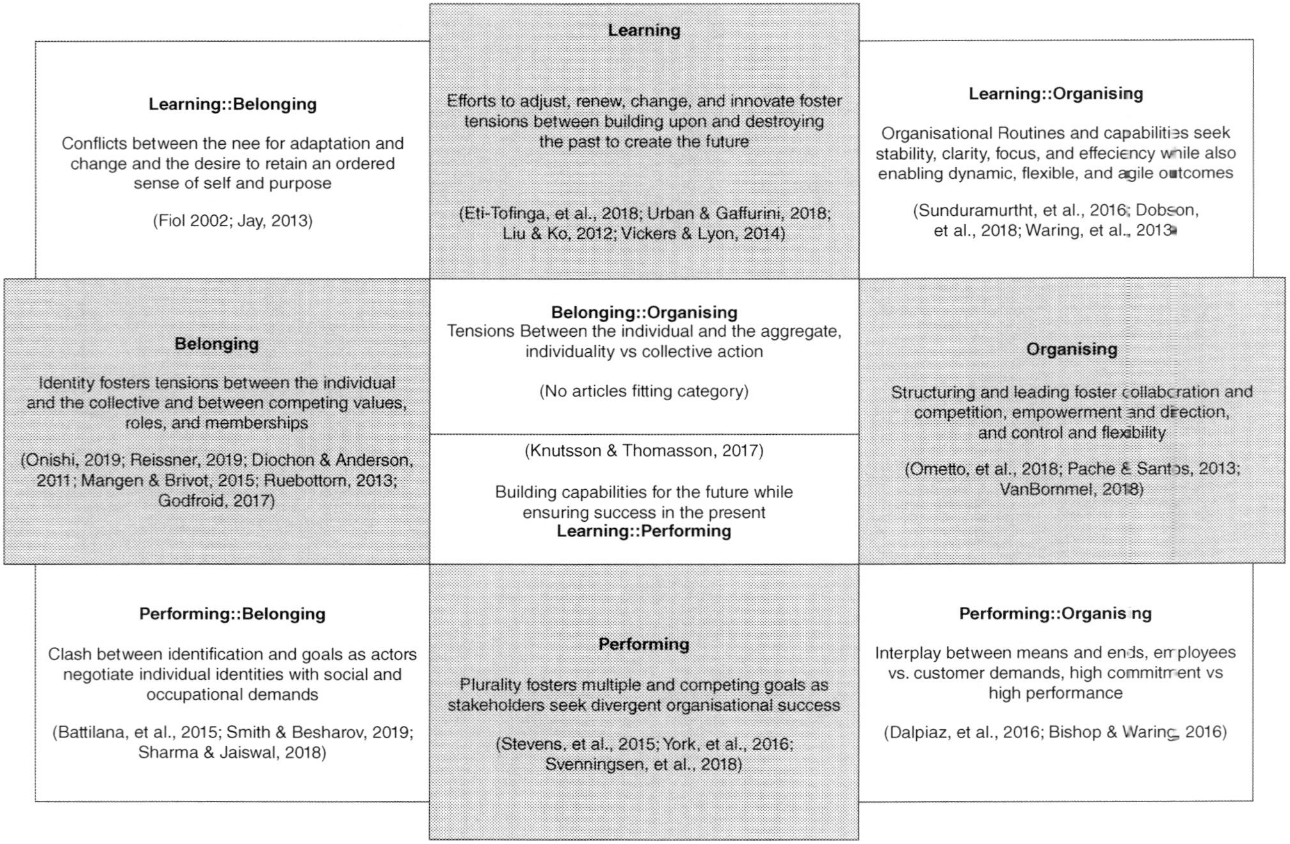

82 Kristian Marinov et al.

Learning::Belonging

Conflicts between the need for adaptation and change and the desire to retain an ordered sense of self and purpose

(Fiol 2002; Jay, 2013)

Learning

Efforts to adjust, renew, change, and innovate foster tensions between building upon and destroying the past to create the future

(Eti-Tofinga, et al., 2018; Urban & Gaffurini, 2018; Liu & Ko, 2012; Vickers & Lyon, 2014)

Learning::Organising

Organisational Routines and capabilities seek stability, clarity, focus, and effeciency while also enabling dynamic, flexible, and agile outcomes

(Sunduramurtht, et al., 2016; Dobson, et al., 2018; Waring, et al., 2013)

Belonging

Identity fosters tensions between the individual and the collective and between competing values, roles, and memberships

(Onishi, 2019; Reissner, 2019; Diochon & Anderson, 2011; Mangen & Brivot, 2015; Ruebottom, 2013; Godfroid, 2017)

Belonging::Organising

Tensions Between the individual and the aggregate, individuality vs collective action

(No articles fitting category)

(Knutsson & Thomasson, 2017)

Building capabilities for the future while ensuring success in the present
Learning::Performing

Organising

Structuring and leading foster collabcration and competition, empowerment and direction, and control and flexibility

(Ometto, et al., 2018; Pache & Santos, 2013; VanBommel, 2018)

Performing::Belonging

Clash between identification and goals as actors negotiate individual identities with social and occupational demands

(Battilana, et al., 2015; Smith & Besharov, 2019; Sharma & Jaiswal, 2018)

Performing

Plurality fosters multiple and competing goals as stakeholders seek divergent organisational success

(Stevens, et al., 2015; York, et al., 2016; Svenningsen, et al., 2018)

Performing::Organising

Interplay between means and ends, employees vs. customer demands, high commitment vs high performance

(Dalpiaz, et al., 2016; Bishop & Waring, 2016)

Figure 4.3 Types of logic tensions and literature results clustering. Adapted from "Toward a theory of paradox: A dynamic equilibrium model of organizing" by Smith and Lewis (2011). Model adapted to display article's placement by category.

Learning in Hybrid Organisations 83

Operational capabilities are low-level sets of knowledge, such as administration, governance practices, and routines. Dynamic capabilities are higher-order sets of knowledge and skills comprising the ability to modify the resource base of the organisation, and to transform and adapt behaviour and routines (Vickers & Lyon, 2014; Winter, 2003), and innovate (Urban & Gaffurini, 2018). A subset of OCs is directly concerned with learning – namely organisational learning capabilities (OLCs). Urban and Gaffurini (2018) posit OLCs are specific capabilities of knowledge conversion, participative decision-making, risk taking, and organisational dialogue. They view these as being positively related to innovative change efforts. OLCs are developed through organisational learning – including knowledge accumulation, articulation, and codification (Liu & Ko, 2012). Following codification, it is beneficial for hybrids to take a holistic view of the organisational system, to exploit these capabilities. For example, aligning OCs with organisational culture (e.g. democratic culture fits with democratic decision-making), and taking into account context and external environment (Eti-Tofinga et al., 2018). In short, OCs, and OLCs, developed through organisational learning can be used to enact change, or development with regard to market capabilities (Liu & Ko, 2012), organisational growth and expansion (Vickers & Lyon, 2014), social innovation (Urban & Gaffurini, 2018) as well as cultural change (Eti-Tofinga et al., 2018).

Two additional approaches in the literature consist in the resolution of learning tensions through organising approaches, and vice versa. Sunduramurthy et al. (2016) identify two modes of action, ingeneuring (systematic planning approach to resource use) and bricolage (making due with resources at hand). The characteristics of these modes of action relate to how the environment is conceptualised (non-acceptance/acceptance of limitations), how resources are approached (new uses for existing ones/use for intended purpose), nature of agency (concentrated/distributed stakeholders, or agents), and process mode (bias for action and making do/planning driven by vision). Successful hybrids were found to not accept limitations, to recombine existing resources into new resources, involve a diverse set of actors, and plan carefully – driven by the organisation's vision.

Dobson et al. (2018) depict how the challenges of scaling and expansion in hybrid organisations can be overcome through a highly locally adaptive, flexible approach focused on experimentation and business model innovation, whilst retaining a replicable core business model. This is only generalisable, however, to expansion in uncertain conditions (unknown contexts), where the hybrid business model does not require *a priori* proof of 'working', as it would in other contexts in order to have legitimacy.

Both studies show a reciprocal influence, where learning influences organising, and the way that the hybrid is organised determines learning capacities. For instance, seeing negative stereotypes about their students hindered students' studying capabilities (environmental limitation), the educational institution studied by Sunduramurthy et al. (2016) adopted a bricolage organising approach to reject and change those stereotypes. On the other hand, an organisation called ViaVia café (Dobson et al., 2018), created a flexible organising model to allow for the experimentation, learning, and adaptation that would be required in a new, uncertain international context when expanding the enterprise.

A dominant theme in the learning/tension resolution literature is that of OCs. OCs represent the capacity of an organisation to learn and adapt to the challenges facing it. OCs are developed through a learning process consisting of knowledge accumulation, knowledge articulation and understanding, and knowledge embedding or codification (Liu & Ko, 2012). In order for OCs and OLCs to reach desired outcomes they must be enacted, and this process of enactment leads to organisational adaptive outcomes.

We note the connection here between OCs, OC enactment, and adaptive outcomes. Together these three elements create a process of enactment, whereby OCs enable the flow of information through the system (see Figure 4.4). This information provides agents the dynamic skills to adapt their cognitive schemata, and the ability to engage in dialogue and decision-making, enabling agents to bring forth their adaptive capacities. OCs may also directly allow for adaptive outcomes, for instance in the development of market capabilities (Liu & Ko, 2012).

OC development precedes OC enactment aimed at resolving an adaptive problem. OC enactment consists of experimentation, and learning through feedback loops created by continuous enactment of adaptive practice. This process results in adaptive outcomes. An example is ViaVia Café (Dobson et al., 2018), who use their company's dynamic capabilities to scale up their business model through experimentation with new practices, such as holding art exhibitions. Learning from the successes and failures of that experiment – and further developing the practice to generate revenue, whilst fulfilling its mission of cultural education – ViaVia Café successfully overcame the learning tensions associated with scaling up.

There are two factors shaping the iterative enactment and feedback of OC development. Firstly, the one which is considered adaptive is in constant flux thus necessitating renewed adaptive efforts over time. Secondly, the development of systemic order informs how adaptation should be enacted in the future, and changes organisations' OCs by influencing the knowledge development and codification process responsible for developing OCs (see Figure 4.5).

Adapting to Organizing Tensions

The literature identifies a number of approaches which can be used to resolve organising tensions. Decoupling and compromising are seen as two traditional means of doing so (Pache & Santos, 2013). These approaches represent modes of thinking about, and dealing with tensions. They foster learning from tensions, and hybridisation to varying degrees. Compromise refers to a trade-off between logics, and risks that higher-level interdependencies, and synergies be ignored if employed extensively (Smith & Lewis, 2011). This creates the threat of mission drift, compartmentalisation, and potential difficulties with scaling.

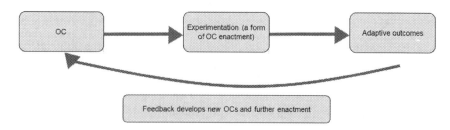

Figure 4.4 Process of OC enactment and adaptive outcome attainment.

Learning in Hybrid Organisations 85

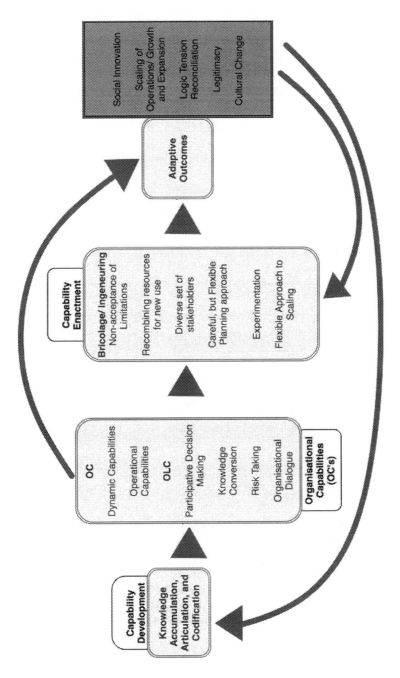

Figure 4.5 Learning tensions iterative adaptive process model.

Decoupling refers to the separation between operational and symbolic aspects of differing logics, adopting both at the same time, but only symbolically engaging and practicing one of them (Bromley & Powell, 2012). However, decoupling creates many of the same risks as compromise, with the addition of conflict between decoupled parts of the organisation as they pursue different goals which can come into contact as cross-boundary, or cross-functional interdependencies become salient. A refinement of this strategy is selective coupling, which advocates for the strategically selective and partial compliance with conflicting logic prescriptions, to maintain the perception of institutional compliance for internal stakeholders. In practice, this means enacting elements of different logics across some but not all areas. An example from the work of Pache and Santos (2013) is embedding the organisation in the local community, as prescribed by a social mission logic; but having a standard, formalised brand image across international contexts, as prescribed by a commercial logic. Through the perception of compliance created by this selective coupling, internal conflict is mitigated, and legitimacy gained from relevant stakeholders (Pache & Santos, 2013). Selective coupling requires direct learning through trial and error in order to identify how to couple individual logics with certain elements of the organisation. What is unclear is how these modes of coping affect the organisation as a whole.

Through a system dynamics perspective, engaging in these modes of coping shifts the order enacted in the organisation, changing it through direct engagement, making learning through direct experience possible. The shift in order creates a shift in the equilibrium state, which in turn produces system feedback regarding the fit of the adaptation. For example, TEMPORG, an organisation studied by Pache and Santos (2013) demonstrated selective coupling by adopting strict standardised procedures in some areas of it operations, and giving autonomy to other areas, thus meeting conflicting demands for autonomy and efficiency through standardisation in different departments. This mode of coupling allowed TEMPORG employees in different parts of the organisation to pursue the behavioural prescriptions inscribed in their cognitive schemata by different institutional logics. By allowing both of these logics to operate independently, hybridisation is achieved by separating the departmental level from the organisational level.

The literature notes several different approaches to organising and engage with hybrid logics through means of dialogue and internal negotiation. Bishop and Waring (2016) find that micro-level negotiations mediate the relationship between competing logics, organisational practice and form. Thus, negotiations help logics and performance goals to converge. In this mediation process, one can arrive at distributive negotiation outcomes (concessions favouring one logic over the other), or integrative ones (satisfying multiple logics at once) (Lewicki & Litterer, 1985). Such negotiations occur over specific elements of the organisation and specific areas of disagreement. Outcomes of negotiated settlements may be that logics blend and become more hybridised; or more segregated, depending on negotiation outcome (Bishop & Waring, 2016). One structural approach to enact negotiation is creating 'spaces of negotiation', providing face to face opportunities for employees to meet and engage in negotiation of the contradictory normative prescriptions of logics (Battilana et al., 2015; Ometto et al., 2019). This can occur provided there is a common understanding of the organisation's superordinate goal, and individuals acknowledge mutual interdependencies (Battilana et al., 2015; Ometto et al., 2019). However, spaces of negotiation are difficult to maintain whilst scaling up an organisation. In an attempt to deal with this, Ometto et al. (2019) propose 'herding spaces' as a solution. Herding spaces connect a hybrid to its institutional context, via for example meetings with hybrids of a similar nature, focus, or locality to discuss challenges, motivate individuals, affirm normative orientation, and thus avoid mission drift, especially when scaling up. See Figure 4.6.

Adapting to Belonging Tensions

Current identity research elaborates on how institutional logics inform behaviour and practice, the role of identity in influencing logics and practice, and how incompatibilities between identities and logics constrain organisations, and looks at the responses to identity (in)compatibilities (Onishi, 2019). Organisational identity was found to play a 'filtering', or mediating role between institutional logic and practice, such that identity influences what practices will be adopted, and how they will be enacted (Onishi, 2019). However, in the presence of the complex, contradictory multiplicity of institutional logics, where interpretation is ambiguous, a processes of sensemaking is required (Diochon & Anderson, 2011; Jay, 2013; Reissner, 2019). Sensemaking is needed to aid the organisation in arriving at an understanding, and reconciliation of seemingly mutually-exclusive practices (Diochon & Anderson, 2011; Jay, 2013; Reissner, 2019). Sensemaking is important and aids in transforming the organisational identity, as differences in identity can foster ongoing logic tensions (Smith & Besharov, 2019). Identity transformation facilitates the adoption of an organisational mind-set better able to understand and grapple with paradoxes inherent in hybrids, aiding the adoption of innovative practices and new organisational structures (Jay, 2013).

Considering both the individual and organisational levels, (Fiol, 2002) outlines a model of organisational identity transformation. The process consists of de-identification with the current identity, re-identification situated in work activities, eventually resulting in re-identification through practice with the core identity and guiding principles.

On the individual level, identity transformation unfolds as a breaking of trust, a temporary sense of connection to a new context of practice, building into a newly forged sense of trust. Identity is shaped by the cognitive frame, or understanding of the institutional logic in ones thinking (Sharma & Jaiswal, 2018). In addition, individuals' cognitive frames are shaped dynamically through interpersonal interaction and contestation over what logic 'should' be adopted and how (Sharma & Jaiswal, 2018). Values and motivations are an aspect of cognition, shaped by identity (Anderson, 2000). As such, identity transformations must take into account how cognition translates into motivation and values that drive individuals within the hybrid (e.g. prosocial, profit seeking, or both) (Diochon & Anderson, 2011; Godfroid, 2017). Motivations, and values determine how individuals (re)interpret their identity, resolve the ambiguity surrounding value conflicts, and what type of incentive would drive them to engage with the organisation (Diochon & Anderson, 2011; Godfroid, 2017). Specifically, tensions between values shape the organisational identity, and aid the capacity for innovation and change in coping with ambiguities and uncertainties (Diochon & Anderson, 2011). Time also plays a role in shaping cognitive frames. For instance, changing events can shift the perception of what type of goals should be adopted (e.g. as a project nears its end, short-term goals are adopted and long-term goals forgotten) (Sharma & Jaiswal, 2018).

88 *Kristian Marinov et al.*

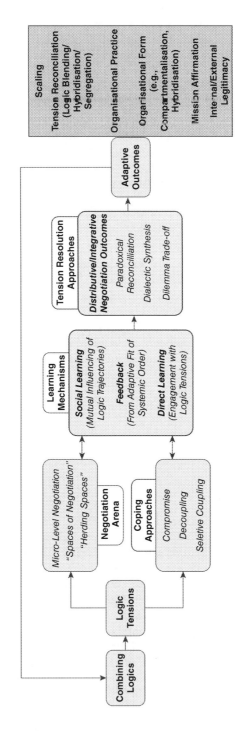

Figure 4.6 Organising tensions iterative model of adaptation.

Learning in Hybrid Organisations 89

At the organisational level, de-identification begins as disruption of operations, followed by fragmentation of efforts – as individuals and teams shift and focus on new experiments, or contexts of practice. This eventually results in re-stabilisation of routines and forging a new understanding of coherence. Founding logics partly determine the starting point for the formation of an organisational identity, and sets the trajectory for enacting dual missions. For instance, 'social imprinting', or an initial emphasis on the social mission will set that mission as a greater priority, at the expense of economic goals (Battilana et al., 2015; Pache & Santos, 2013). Interpreting the 'belonging tensions' literature, a stable identity in the context of ongoing institutional plurality and paradoxical contradiction is not feasible. Rather, the identity of hybrid organisations requires constant learning, sensemaking, and reinterpretation if it is to be conducive to an understanding of the organisation and its environment, and subsequently, to desired adaptive outcomes (Fiol, 1994; Jay, 2013; Sharma & Jaiswal, 2018; Smith & Besharov, 2019).

Several variables interject in the sensemaking process, shifting identification, and increasing complexity faced by hybrid organisations regarding the shaping of identity. Shaping and establishing a normative perception of identity takes place in conjunction with partnering organisations' form(s), and institutional logics (relational positioning), external stakeholders' and employees' expectations (discursive framing), and of employees' current identities and adopted logics (Jay, 2013; Reissner, 2019). Mangen and Brivot (2015) add power, discourse, and agency into this equation. Their findings show that different groups within the hybrid organisation struggle for power, and purposefully attempt to shape identities and interpretations of logics within the organisation to their benefit. These actors utilise discourse, as a way of discussing, and framing particular issues (Watson, 2001). This can result in groups whose identities have been challenged within the organisation, to go against one logic, thus shaping a new identity. Discussion and rhetoric are important, helping to shape and make sense of organisational identity, resolving ambiguities and logic tensions and creating shared meaning – captured by organisational meta-narratives – or overarching stories (Oakes et al., 1998; Ruebottom, 2013). All of these variables serve to inform identity formation via a multitude of learning mechanisms. For instance, power struggles and interpersonal influence are a form of social learning; experimentation a form of direct learning; stakeholder expectations a form of feedback; and observing the identities of others a form of indirect learning.

From a systems dynamics perspective, individual identity can be seen as directing, and partly shaping the cognitive schemata of individuals, reinforcing pathways of behaviour which appear most viable and aligned with identity. This shaping of cognitive schemata and influencing behavioural pathways results in adaptive outcomes and is a result of the various forms of learning inherent in identity formation. A similar line of reasoning holds at the organisational level, where identities inform the adoption of practices, and therefore influence the systemic order. An example to illustrate this is the Cambridge Energy Alliance (CEA) (Jay, 2013) whose organisational identity shifted from a 'one stop shop' to a 'laboratory' to a 'catalyst of sustainable energy'. These shifts were necessitated by the fact that the first two identities were not able to combine the CEA's two missions, for profit and sustainable energy, in a way so that both would sustain each other. Shifts in the meta-narrative of the organisation, took place through continuous experimentation and innovation upon practices. This adaptation culminated in the creation of a new identity that was able to hybridise the two missions. See Figure 4.7.

90 *Kristian Marinov et al.*

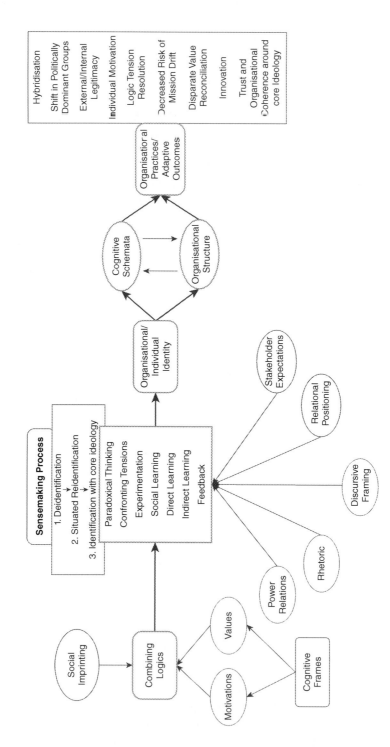

Figure 4.7 Belonging tensions model of adaptation.

Learning in Hybrid Organisations   91

Adapting to Performing Tensions

Divergent institutional logics create contradictory agendas and paths of action for actors (Smith & Lewis, 2011). Logic(s) adopted by different actors sustain the hybrid form to varying degrees. For example, a purely social mission-oriented logic would eventually compromise the financial viability of the hybrid. A hybrid logic – acknowledging the importance of both the social mission and financial viability – would better serve to sustain the hybrid form (Battilana et al., 2015). The creation of a hybrid logic also entails the instigation of 'hybrid behaviour' that is oriented towards reconciling institutional paradoxes by synthesising them. Such hybrid behaviour cannot be adopted solely through a shift to a hybrid structure, but must be enacted through organisational learning and change on multiple levels, challenging current practices. (Knutsson & Thomasson, 2017). Building on this notion, Smith and Besharov (2019) posit that adaptation of identity and disparate goals are necessary continuously recurring processes, as logic tensions persist over time, even after being resolved.

The literature posits multiple roads towards achieving a hybrid logic, ironing out performing tensions. Dalpiaz et al. (2016) discovered that Alessi, the manufacturing/art firm resolves performing tensions by shifting their notion of what their products are through a process called symbolic recomposition, systemically disrupting their habitual routines, reorganising themselves through experimentation, and adjusting their actions through feedback as they evolve. Smith and Besharov (2019) also place emphasis on resolving tensions through experimentation with new practices. The authors however place greater importance on identity as a cause of logic tensions under conditions of identity conflict, and the prism through which experimentation and new practices are interpreted. Additionally, Smith and Besharov (2019) emphasise working within the parameters of logic prescriptions, developing practices that conform to each logic, whilst Dalpiaz et al. (2016) depict a continuous transformation of how the institutional logics are interpreted, combined together and manifested in Alessi's products.

In a complementary work, York et al. (2016) focus on the macro and organisational levels in an attempt to describe how divergent logics contest and influence each other to arrive at a hybridised logic. York et al. (2016) posit that there exist dominant logics – widely adopted throughout the field (macro, sectoral level), and subordinate logics. Performing tensions stem from dominant and subordinate logics meeting, and their integration, establishing an equal footing is key to resolving these tensions. Integration is a procedure consisting of compromise between the two logics, followed by reframing of the position of the subordinate logic within the frame of the dominant logic, through political contestation. If successful, integration eventually results in the integration of the two logics, with both logics seen as legitimate and respected in practice.

At the individual level, there are multiple variables describing the tendency of individuals to hybridise. The tendency for logics to hybridise, as opposed to compromise or reject one logic, depends in part on the individuals' capital (relating to knowledge and skills; social ties and network; understanding of norms and mastery of language). The more of this type of capital one has, the more predisposed they are to hybridise (Svenningsen-Berthélem et al., 2018). Stevens et al. (2015) find empirically that values play a role in which mission will be prioritised, and under which circumstances. 'Other-regarding', pro-social values in management were positively associated with attention to the social mission; whilst utilitarian values, characterised by profit maximisation

92 Kristian Marinov et al.

and self-interest, were associated with the business mission. These foci vary with levels of firm performance. When performing well, more attention is devoted to social goals, whilst under conditions of economic adversity, existing ideas and schemas are emphasised (Ocasio, 1995).

In short, tensions relating to divergent ideas of organisational success, and conflicting adherence to logics can be resolved in various ways. One is the mobilisation of the agentic capacity of the organisation, attempting to shift logic enactment in practices and product development (Dalpiaz et al., 2016). A second path is the continuous reinterpretation of identity, and the adoption of new practices through experimentation, whilst respecting each logic (Smith & Besharov, 2019). Finally, organisations can embed conflicting logics into one another through a process of compromise, contestation, and legitimation (York et al., 2016).

Each of these pathways towards resolving performance tension represents an adaptive process paved by learning mechanisms. Every pathway is iterative and repeated efforts and attentions are required across time to sustain logic reconciliation and hybridity. Iteration of adaptive processes, and incremental experimentation to achieve logic legitimation and hybridisation, are core themes in resolving performance tensions. The process described by York et al. (2016) highlights hybridisation of field and organisation logics, through incremental adaptations. Feedback occurred when, for instance, environmental protests called for a greater emphasis on the ecological mission in the economic mission (York et al., 2016). Along similar lines, Dalpiaz et al. (2016) and Smith and Besharov (2019) describe resolving performing tensions through iterative implementation of new practices through experimentation. New practices are meant to better accommodate logics through hybridisation stemming from identity reinterpretation and working within boundaries of different logics (Smith & Besharov, 2019), and/or transforming the way logics are conceived and combined (Dalpiaz et al., 2016). For example, to serve their customer base, whilst allowing their artists to serve their artistic mission, Alessi combined logics. Combining logics of art and manufacturing allowed for loosening technical guidelines while maintaining technical feasibility – giving freedom to artists to create practical products 'enriched' with art. The result of this mode of combining logics is a more hybridised logic. Adaptation occurred in the studies by Dalpiaz et al. (2016) and Smith and Besharov (2019) as a result of direct exploration of, experimentation with, and learning from, new practices and ways of combining logics. Feedback from customers or workers unable to pursue their guiding mission (Dalpiaz et al., 2016) can be a trigger for adaptation, yet it is due to the direct experiential form of learning that new practices were adopted. See Figure 4.8.

Management Implications for Hybrid Organisations

This study highlights learning and adaptive mechanisms in hybrid organisations that are largely nascent in terms of organisational learning and system dynamics (Dzombak et al., 2014; Knutsson & Thomasson, 2017). Using Smith and Lewis' (2011) typology, we clustered the literature review results according to the types of logic tensions the articles focus on, arriving at several domains along which adaptation occurs in hybrids. These are organising, belonging, performing, and learning tensions. These types, and their cross-categories, highlight tensions in hybrid organisations. Adaptation to these can unfold through multiple – sometimes overlapping and complementary – pathways. Figure 4.9 positions the four types of tension according to

Learning in Hybrid Organisations 93

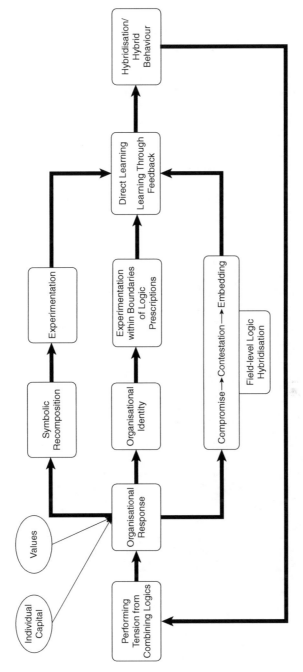

Figure 4.8 Performing tensions iterative model of adaptation.

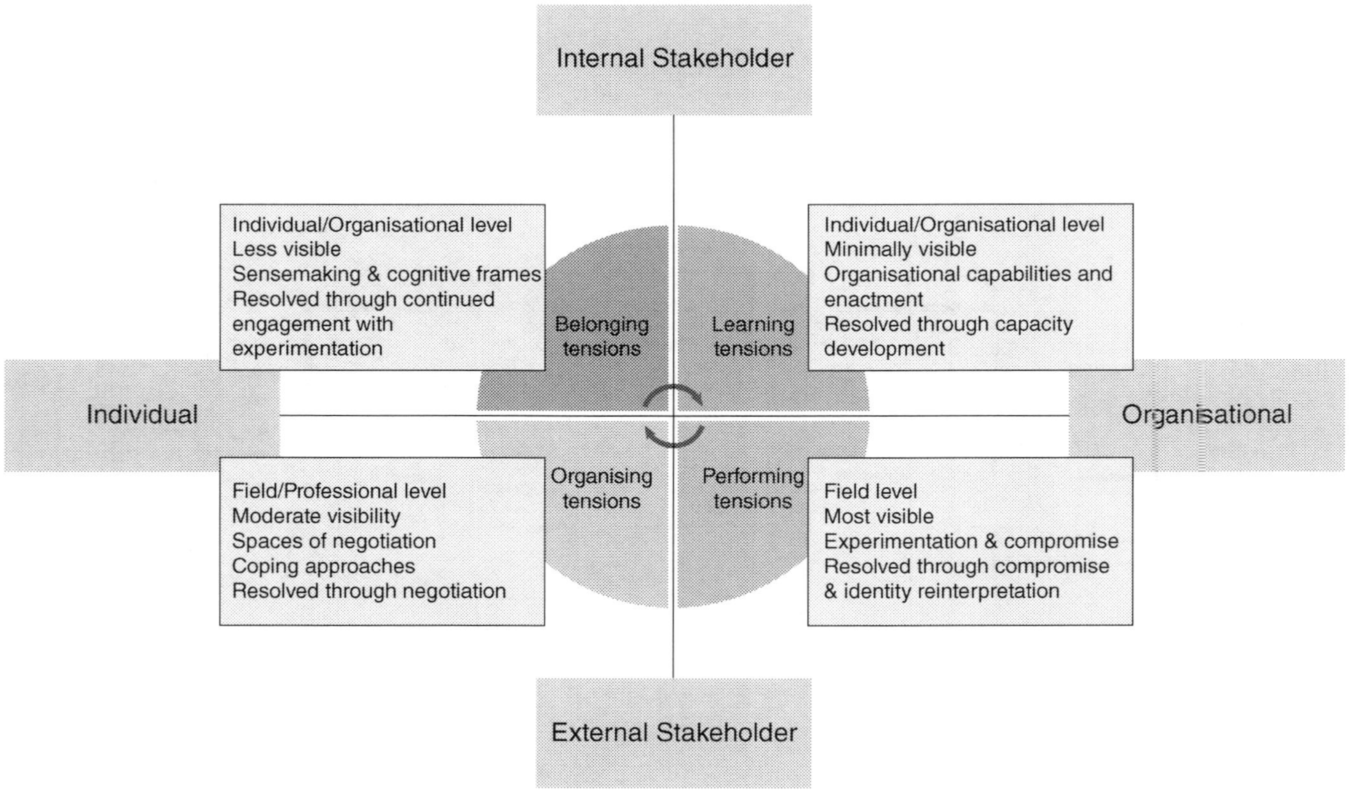

94   Kristian Marinov et al.

Figure 4.9 Mapping tensions in hybrid Organisations.

whether they are impact internal or external stakeholders and whether they occur at the individual or organisational levels. The visibility of each of these tensions is also highlighted, to assist managers in identifying these tensions and understand which methods can be implemented to resolve the tensions. *Organising* tensions are resolved through internal and external discussion and negotiation, and through the adoption of several modes of coping with logic tensions such as compromise, decoupling, and selective coupling. *Learning* tensions are resolved via the cultivation of an organisation's capabilities, followed by the enactment of those capabilities. *Belonging* tensions are resolved through the continuous reinterpretation of identity through experimentation, learning and the refinement of an agent's cognitive schemata. Finally, *performing* tensions are resolved through the hybridisation of logics, which is achieved through the process of compromise, contestation, and legitimation between logics, through the reinterpretation of identity much in the same way as with the resolution of belonging tensions, and through symbolic recomposition.

For organisations supporting, collaborating, funding, and establishing or running social enterprises, it is important to recognise the manifestation of different tensions within organisations. These tensions impact hybrid organisations – like social enterprises – in terms of scalability, sustainability, their accountability to diverse stakeholders, the transparency of the hybrids' operations, the talent retention and human resource strategies, and the reputation or legitimacy of these organisations. As social enterprises seek to balance goal attainment in the social and economic spheres, they need to remain mindful of the four types of tensions identified and manage these carefully. It is important to note that hybrid organisations will face different challenges at different stages of their lifecycle and development. Therefore, adapting to tensions is a continual process and the organisation is required to adapt and learn as it matures.

Finally, by exploring the potential present in the combination between hybrid, learning, and system dynamics theory, this review highlights pathways for future research on topics stemming from the marriage between these fields. The results of this chapter therefore serve to highlight the areas of focus for managers of social enterprises, to focus on the learning processes within organisations that can serve to address these challenges. Feedback loops that form and drive organisational learning need to be monitored to minimise mission drift and tensions are evident in each of the quadrants need to be managed and resolved. Should these tensions be allowed to deepen this can threaten the sustainability of the social enterprise

As societal challenges and wicked problems render themselves increasingly present with the ever-increasing complexity of the systems and environments in which we are embedded (P. Anderson, 1999; Jay, 2013; Senge, 1990), new solutions must be found. Hybrid organisations are part of that solution, as they fill the gaps in market failures where governments cannot intervene, and blend the free-market pursuit of profit with the ethical imperative required to create social value alongside monetary value. The informed management, and thorough theoretical understanding of hybrids, is therefore a necessity if hybrids are to be nodes of progress in societal systems seeking to address wicked problems.

References

Anderson, A. R. (2000). The protean entrepreneur: The entrepreneurial process as fitting self and circumstance. *Journal of Enterprising Culture*, 8(3), 201–234. https://doi.org/10.1142/s0218495800000127

Anderson, P. (1999). Perspective: Complexity theory and organization science. *Organization Science, 10*(3), 216–232. https://doi.org/10.1287/orsc.10.3.216

Argote, L. (2013). Organizational learning curves: Creating, retaining and transferring knowledge. In *Organizational learning* (2nd ed.). Springer. https://doi.org/10.1007/978-1-4614-5251-5_1

Argote, L., & Epple, D. (1990). Learning curves in manufacturing. *Science, 247*(4945), 920–924. https://doi.org/10.1126/science.247.4945.920

Battilana, J. (2018). Cracking the organizational challenge of pursuing joint social and financial goals: Social enterprise as a laboratory to understand hybrid organizing. *Management, 21*(4), 1278–1305. https://doi.org/10.3917/mana.214.1278

Battilana, J., & Dorado, S. (2010). Building sustainable hybrid organizations: The case of commercial microfinance organizations. *Academy of Management Journal, 53*(6), 1419–1440.

Battilana, J., & Lee, M. (2014). Advancing research on hybrid organizing – insights from the study of social enterprises. *Academy of Management Annals, 8*(1), 397–441. https://doi.org/10.1080/19416520.2014.893615

Battilana, J., Sengul, M., Pache, A. C., & Model, J. (2015). Harnessing productive tensions in hybrid organizations: The case of working integration social enterprises. *Academy of Management Journal, 58*(6), 1658–1685. https://doi.org/10.5465/amj.2013.0903

Bierly, P. E., Kessler, E. H., & Christensen, E. W. (2000). Organizational learning, knowledge and wisdom. *Journal of Organizational Change Management, 13*(6), 595–618. https://doi.org/10.1108/09534810010378605

Bishop, S., & Waring, J. (2016). Becoming hybrid: The negotiated order on the front line of public – private partnerships. *Human Relations, 69*(10), 1937–1958. https://doi.org/10.1177/0018726716630389

Bledow, R., Carette, B., Kühnel, J., & Bister, D. (2017). Learning from others' failures: The effectiveness of failure stories for managerial learning. *Academy of Management Learning and Education, 16*(1), 39–53. George Washington University. https://doi.org/10.5465/amle.2014.0169

Bledow, R., Frese, M., Anderson, N., Erez, M., & Farr, J. (2009). A dialectic perspective on innovation: Conflicting demands, multiple pathways, and ambidexterity. *Industrial and Organizational Psychology, 2*(3), 305–337. https://doi.org/10.1111/j.1754-9434.2009.01154.x

Bromley, P., & Powell, W. W. (2012). From smoke and mirrors to walking the talk: Decoupling in the contemporary world. *Academy of Management Annals, 6*(1), 483–530. https://doi.org/10.5465/19416520.2012.684462

Chiva, R., Grandío, A., & Alegre, J. (2010). Adaptive and generative learning: Implications from complexity theories. *International Journal of Management Reviews, 12*(2), 114–129. https://doi.org/10.1111/j.1468-2370.2008.00255.x

Crossan, M. M., & Apaydin, M. (2010). A multi-dimensional framework of organizational innovation: A systematic review of the literature. *Journal of Management Studies, 47*(6), 1154–1191. https://doi.org/10.1111/j.1467-6486.2009.00880.x

Dalpiaz, E., Rindova, V., & Ravasi, D. (2016). Combining logics to transform organizational agency: Blending industry and art at Alessi. *Administrative Science Quarterly, 61*(3), 347–392. https://doi.org/10.1177/0001839216636103

Dees, J. G. (2012). A tale of two cultures: Charity, problem solving, and the future of social entrepreneurship. *Journal of Business Ethics, 111*(3), 321–334. https://doi.org/10.1007/s10551-012-1412-5

Diochon, M., & Anderson, A. R. (2011). Ambivalence and ambiguity in social enterprise; narratives about values in reconciling purpose and practices. *International Entrepreneurship and Management Journal, 7*(1), 93–109. https://doi.org/10.1007/s11365-010-0161-0

Dixon-Woods, M., Agarwal, S., Jones, D., Young, B., & Sutton, A. (2005). Synthesising qualitative and quantitative evidence: A review of possible methods. *Journal of Health Services Research and Policy, 10*(1), 45–53. Sage Publications. https://doi.org/10.1258/1355819052801804

Dobson, K., Boone, S., Andries, P., & Daou, A. (2018). Successfully creating and scaling a sustainable social enterprise model under uncertainty: The case of viavia travellers cafés. *Journal of Cleaner Production, 172*, 4555–4564. https://doi.org/10.1016/j.jclepro.2017.09.010

Dutton, J. M., & Thomas, A. (1984). Treating progress functions as a managerial opportunity. *Academy of Management Review, 9*(2), 235–247. https://doi.org/10.5465/amr.1984.4277639

Dzombak, R., Mehta, C., Mehta, K., & Bilén, S. G. (2014). The relevance of systems thinking in the quest for multifinal social enterprises. *Systemic Practice and Action Research, 27*(6), 593–606. https://doi.org/10.1007/s11213-013-9313-9

Easterby-Smith, M., & Lyles, M. A. (2011). In praise of organizational forgetting. *Journal of Management Inquiry, 20*(3), 311–316. https://doi.org/10.1177/1056492611408508

Eti-Tofinga, B., Singh, G., & Douglas, H. (2018). Facilitating cultural change in social enterprises. *Journal of Organizational Change Management, 31*(3), 619–636. https://doi.org/10.1108/JOCM-12-2016-0296

Fiol, C. M. (1994). Consensus, diversity, and learning in organizations. *Organization Science, 5*(3), 403–420. https://doi.org/10.1287/orsc.5.3.403

Fiol, C. M. (2002). Capitalizing on paradox: The role of language in transforming organizational identities. *Organization Science, 13*(6), 653–666. https://doi.org/10.1287/orsc.13.6.653.502

Fiol, C. M., & Lyles, M. A. (1985). Organizational learning. *Academy of Management Review, 10*(4), 803–813. https://doi.org/10.5465/amr.1985.4279103

Fosfuri, A., Giarratana, M. S., & Roca, E. (2016). Social business hybrids: Demand externalities, competitive advantage, and growth through diversification. *Organization Science, 27*(5), 1275–1289. https://doi.org/10.1287/orsc.2016.1080

Friedland, R. (1991). Bringing society back in: Symbols, practices, and institutional contradictions. In *The new institutionalism in organizational analysis*. University of Chicago Press.

Gherardi, S. (2019). *Organizational knowledge: The texture of workplace learning* (J. Child & S. Rodriqures, Eds.). John Wiley & Sons, Blackwell Publishing. www.wiley.com/en-us/Organizational+Knowledge%3A+The+Texture+of+Workplace+Learning-p-9781405150361

Glynn, M. A., Milliken, F. J., & Lant, T. K. (1992). *Learning about organizational learning theory: An umbrella of organizing processes*. Academy of Management.

Godfroid, C. (2017). Are Microfinance loan officers closer to banking staff or to non-profit workers? A motivational approach. *Strategic Change, 26*(2), 117–132. https://doi.org/10.1002/jsc.2114

Greve, H. R. (2017). Organizational learning and adaptation. In *Oxford research encyclopedia of business and management*. Oxford University Press. https://doi.org/10.1093/acrefore/9780190224851.013.138

Hahn, T., Preuss, L., Pinkse, J., & Figge, F. (2014). Cognitive frames in corporate sustainability: Managerial sensemaking with paradoxical and business case frames. *Academy of Management Review, 39*(4), 463–487. https://doi.org/10.5465/amr.2012.0341

Hedberg, B. (1981). How organizations learn and unlearn. In P. Nystrom & W. Starbuck (Eds.), *Handbook of organizational design: Adapting organisations to their environment*. Oxford University Press.

Hjorth, P., & Bagheri, A. (2006). Navigating towards sustainable development: A system dynamics approach. *Futures, 38*(1), 74–92. https://doi.org/10.1016/j.futures.2005.04.005

Huber, G. P. (1991). Organizational learning: The contributing processes and the literatures. *Organization Science, 2*(1), 88–115. https://doi.org/10.1287/orsc.2.1.88

Jay, J. (2013). Navigating paradox as a mechanism of change and innovation in hybrid organizations. *Academy of Management Journal, 56*(1), 137–159. https://doi.org/10.5465/amj.2010.0772

Knutsson, H., & Thomasson, A. (2017). Exploring organisational hybridity from a learning perspective. *Qualitative Research in Accounting and Management, 14*(4), 430–447. https://doi.org/10.1108/QRAM-04-2016-0030

Kolb, H., Snowden, A., & Stevens, E. (2018). Systematic review and narrative summary: Treatments for and risk factors associated with respiratory tract secretions (death rattle) in the dying adult. *Journal of Advanced Nursing, 74*(7), 1446–1462. Blackwell Publishing Ltd. https://doi.org/10.1111/jan.13557

Lee, B. H., Hiatt, S. R., & Lounsbury, M. (2017). Market mediators and the trade-offs of legitimacy-seeking behaviors in a nascent category. *Organization Science, 28*(3), 447–470. https://doi.org/10.1287/orsc.2017.1126

Levinthal, D., & March, J. G. (1981). A model of adaptive organizational search. *Journal of Economic Behavior and Organization*, 2(4), 307–333. https://doi.org/10.1016/0167-2681(81)90012-3

Lewicki, R. J., & Litterer, J. A. (1985). *Negotiation*. Richard D. Irwin. Inc.

Liu, G., & Ko, W. W. (2012). Organizational learning and marketing capability development: A study of the charity retailing operations of British social enterprise. *Nonprofit and Voluntary Sector Quarterly*, 41(4), 580–608. https://doi.org/10.1177/0899764011411722

Mangen, C., & Brivot, M. (2015). The challenge of sustaining organizational hybridity: The role of power and agency. *Human Relations*, 68(4), 659–684. https://doi.org/10.1177/0018726714539524

McGrath, J. E. (1982). *Judgment calls in research (studying organizations) by Joseph E. McGrath (1982–10–01): Amazon.com: Books*. Sage Publications.

Moher, D., Shamseer, L., Clarke, M., Ghersi, D., Liberati, A., Petticrew, M., Shekelle, P., Stewart, L. A., Estarli, M., Barrera, E. S. A., Martínez-Rodríguez, R., Baladia, E., Agüero, S. D., Camacho, S., Buhring, K., Herrero-López, A., Gil-González, D. M., Altman, D. G., Booth, A., . . . Whitlock, E. (2016). Preferred reporting items for systematic review and meta-analysis protocols (PRISMA-P) 2015 statement. *Revista Espanola de Nutricion Humana y Dietetica*, 20(2), 148–160. https://doi.org/10.1186/2046-4053-4-1

Nason, R. S., Bacq, S., & Gras, D. (2018). A Behavioral theory of social performance: Social identity and stakeholder expectations. *Academy of Management Review*, 43(2), 259–283. https://doi.org/10.5465/amr.2015.0081

Oakes, L. S., Townley, B., & Cooper, D. J. (1998). Business planning as pedagogy: Language and control in a changing institutional field. *Administrative Science Quarterly*, 43(2), 257–292. https://doi.org/10.2307/2393853

Ocasio, W. C. (1995). The enactment of economic adversity: A reconciliation of theories of failure-induced change and threat-rigidity. *Research in Organizational Behavior*, 287–331.

Ometto, M. P., Gegenhuber, T., Winter, J., & Greenwood, R. (2019). From balancing missions to mission drift: The role of the institutional context, spaces, and compartmentalization in the scaling of social enterprises. *Business and Society*, 58(5), 1003–1046. https://doi.org/10.1177/0007650318758329

Onishi, T. (2019). Venture philanthropy and practice variations: The interplay of institutional logics and organizational identities. *Nonprofit and Voluntary Sector Quarterly*. https://doi.org/10.1177/0899764018819875

Pache, A. C., & Santos, F. (2013). Inside the hybrid organzation: Selective coupling as a repsonse to competing institutional logics. *Academy of Management Journal*, 56(4), 972–1001. https://doi.org/10.5465/amj.2011.0405

Popay, J., Roberts, H., Sowden, A., Petticrew, M., Britten, N., Arai, L., Roen, K., & Rodgers, M. (2005). Developing guidance on the conduct of narrative synthesis in systematic reviews. *Journal of Epidemiology and Community Health*, 59(Suppl 1), A7.

Quinn, R. E., & Cameron, K. S. (1988). *Paradox and transformation: Toward a theory of change in organization and management*. Ballinger Publishing Co., Harper & Row Publishers.

Rashman, L., Withers, E., & Hartley, J. (2009). Organizational learning and knowledge in public service organizations: A systematic review of the literature. *International Journal of Management Reviews*, 11(4), 463–494. https://doi.org/10.1111/j.1468-2370.2009.00257.x

Reay, T., & Hinings, C. R. (2009). Managing the rivalry of competing institutional logics. *Organization Studies*, 30(6), 629–652. https://doi.org/10.1177/0170840609104803

Reissner, S. C. (2019). "We are this hybrid": Members' search for organizational identity in an institutionalized public–private partnership. *Public Administration*, 97(1), 48–63. https://doi.org/10.1111/padm.12333

Ruebottom, T. (2013). The microstructures of rhetorical strategy in social entrepreneurship: Building legitimacy through heroes and villains. *Journal of Business Venturing*, 28(1), 98–116. https://doi.org/10.1016/j.jbusvent.2011.05.001

Senge, P. M. (1990). *The fifth discipline: The art and practice of the learning organization (Book, 1990) [WorldCat.org]*. Doubleday, Currency. www.worldcat.org/title/fifth-discipline-the-art-and-practice-of-the-learning-organization/oclc/21226996

Sharma, G., & Jaiswal, A. K. (2018). Unsustainability of sustainability: Cognitive frames and tensions in bottom of the pyramid projects. *Journal of Business Ethics*, 148(2), 291–307. https://doi.org/10.1007/s10551-017-3584-5

Smith, W. K., & Besharov, M. L. (2019). Bowing before dual Gods: How structured flexibility sustains organizational hybridity. *Administrative Science Quarterly*, 64(1), 1–44. https://doi.org/10.1177/0001839217750826

Smith, W. K., Gonin, M., & Besharov, M. L. (2013). Managing social-business tensions: A review and research agenda for social enterprise. *Business Ethics Quarterly*, 23(3), 407–442. https://doi.org/10.5840/beq201323327

Smith, W. K., & Lewis, M. (2011). Toward a theory of paradox: A dynamic equilibrium model of organizing. *Academy of Management Review*, 36(2), 381–403. https://doi.org/10.5465/amr.2009.0223

Smith, W. K., Lewis, M. W., & Tushman, M. L. (2012). Organizational sustainability: Organization design and senior leadership to enable strategic paradox. In *The Oxford handbook of positive organizational scholarship*. Oxford University Press. https://doi.org/10.1093/oxfordhb/9780199734610.013.0061

Stevens, R., Moray, N., Bruneel, J., & Clarysse, B. (2015). Attention allocation to multiple goals: The case of for-profit social enterprises. *Strategic Management Journal*, 36(7), 1006–1016. https://doi.org/10.1002/smj.2265

Sunduramurthy, C., Zheng, C., Musteen, M., Francis, J., & Rhyne, L. (2016). Doing more with less, systematically? Bricolage and ingenieuring in successful social ventures. *Journal of World Business*, 51(5), 855–870. https://doi.org/10.1016/j.jwb.2016.06.005

Svenningsen-Berthélem, V., Boxenbaum, E., & Ravasi, D. (2018). Individual responses to multiple logics in hybrid organizing: The role of structural position. *Management (France)*, 21(4), 1306–1328. https://doi.org/10.3917/mana.214.1306

Tranfield, D., Denyer, D., & Smart, P. (2003). Towards a methodology for developing evidence-informed management knowledge by means of systematic review. *British Journal of Management*, 14(3), 207–222. https://doi.org/10.1111/1467-8551.00375

Urban, B., & Gaffurini, E. (2018). Social enterprises and organizational learning in South Africa. *Journal of Entrepreneurship in Emerging Economies*, 10(1), 117–133. https://doi.org/10.1108/JEEE-02-2017-0010

Vickers, I., & Lyon, F. (2014). Beyond green niches? Growth strategies of environmentally-motivated social enterprises. *International Small Business Journal*, 32(4), 449–470. https://doi.org/10.1177/0266242612457700

Watson, T. J. (2001). *In search of management, chaos and control in managerial work* (1st ed.). Cengage Learning EMEA. www.amazon.com/Search-Management-Revised-Culture-Managerial/dp/1861525230

Winter, S. G. (2003). Understanding dynamic capabilities. *Strategic Management Journal*, 24(10), 991–995. https://doi.org/10.1002/smj.318

Yeo, R. K. (2005). Revisiting the roots of learning organization: A synthesis of the learning organization literature. *Learning Organization*, 12(4), 368–382. Emerald Group Publishing Limited. https://doi.org/10.1108/09696470510599145

York, J. G., Hargrave, T. J., & Pacheco, D. F. (2016). Converging winds: Logic hybridization in the Colorado wind energy field. *Academy of Management Journal*, 59(2), 579–610. https://doi.org/10.5465/amj.2013.0657

5 On NGOs and Development Management

What Do Critical Management Studies Have to Offer?

Emanuela Girei, Federica Angeli and Arun Kumar

Introduction

This chapter is about management of global development, or development management for short. In particular, we focus on Non-Governmental Organisations (NGOs) – a significant, prominent but not unproblematic type of actor in this field.

As is widely known, NGOs entered the development arena at the beginning of the 1980s with the promise of promoting bottom-up development, supposedly close to the needs and aspirations of the grassroots (Hearn, 2007). Four decades on, it is apparent that the NGOs' transformative promise has remained partly unfulfilled. The initial enthusiasm for NGOs has given way to a critical questioning of their role in international development and especially of their ability to articulate and implement an alternative to the neoliberal agenda (Chachage, 2005; Hearn, 2007; Manji & O'Coill, 2002; Shivji, 2007). Scholars have already identified a number of potential, and often competing, explanations of this shortcoming. For instance, some scholars have questioned the authenticity of NGOs' commitment given their self-serving interests (Manji & O'Coill, 2002), while others have drawn attention to the corruption within the wider non-profit sector (Smith, 2010). Contrary to their expected proximity to dispossessed communities, others have pointed to NGOs' inherent elitism (Lewis, 2017). Still others have explained the failures of NGOs with their lack of power (Michael, 2004) when compared to large donor agencies, governments, and corporate behemoths. Even as some scholars attribute many of the NGOs' failings to their lack of managerial capacity/experience (Brown & Kalegaonkar, 2002), others point to NGOs' uncritical embracement of technocratic and managerial approaches (Girei, 2016).

Interestingly, the definition of NGOs blends with the concept of civil society organisations. NGOs' role as the embodiment of civil society's voice is the basis of their legitimacy as "democratizers of development" (Banks et al., 2015; Bebbington et al., 2007). The changes of the aid industry over time, combined with the high relative influence of donors on NGOs with respect to the ultimate beneficiaries, has marked the evolution of the NGOs towards identifying organisations that can meet donors' requirements and satisfy strict accountability standards for a variety of funders, including private donors, governments, Northern NGOs and social impact investors (Angeli et al., 2020; Banks et al., 2015; Mohan, 2002). NGOs nowadays face a number of tensions such as the need to develop and maintain accountability systems towards the donors versus accountability systems towards beneficiaries; their adherence to donors' development agenda versus the specific needs of the communities they serve; their

DOI: 10.4324/9780429243165-6

This chapter has been made available under a CC-BY-NC 4.0 license.

focus on short-term, quantifiable outputs, versus longer-time structural and systemic impact, which is more much difficult to stimulate, monitor, measure and fund on an ongoing basis; their focus on short-term projects rather than long-term structural change (Angeli et al., 2020; Banks et al., 2015; Dicklitch & Lwanga, 2003).

Expectedly so, such debates raise an important question around definitional and typological issues. After all, the term NGO encompasses a plurality of meanings and organisational forms. The term NGO as applied in the mainstream management literature is ambiguous in itself (Srinivas, 2009, pp. 2–3; Tvedt, 1998, pp. 12–37). It refers to a set of organisations which differ greatly in size, budget, activities and ideological orientation – from transnational religious organisations that manage billions of dollars to secular community organizations that work locally and often on shoestring budgets. While some NGOs receive regular funding from a handful of established, institutional donors, others devote considerable resources in preparing and writing funding bids to ensure operational continuity. In an attempt at defining the term, Edwards and Fowler (2003, p. 2) focus on Non-Governmental Development Organisation (NGDO) that work "on poverty and injustice within 'developing' countries." Similarly, Lewis (Lewis, 2003, p. 1) defines NGOs as "the group of organisations engaged in development and poverty reduction work". Other authors further circumscribe the relation between NGOs and development, asserting that "NGOs are only NGOs in any politically meaningful sense of the term if they are offering alternatives to dominant models, practices and ideas about development" (Bebbington et al., 2007, p. 3). A relevant distinction is also made based on the type of work carried out by NGOs, which can be broadly classified into either operational or advocacy activities (Lewis, 2006). Charnovitz (1997, pp. 185–186) states that, "NGOs are groups of individuals organized for the myriads of reasons that engage human imagination and aspiration. They can be set up to advocate a particular cause, such as human rights, or to carry out programmes on the ground, such as disaster relief. They can have membership ranging from local to global." Advocacy NGOs thus aim to raise awareness and to thereby influence governments and corporations towards issues of societal relevance. Operational NGOs concentrate on designing and implementing development-related projects. Charnovitz also distinguishes NGOs according to their geographical orientation, which can be national, international, or community-based (Charnovitz, 1997).

Vakil (Vakil, 1997) further distinguishes NGOs from other third sector organizations. NGOs are "self-governing, private, not-for-profit organizations that are geared towards improving the quality of life for disadvantaged people" (Vakil, 1997, p. 2060). In this sense, NGOs pursue agendas focused on social, environmental and economic change, typically associate with the notion of 'development' and 'sustainable development'. The term 'private' distinguishes NGOs from governmental agencies, while the term 'not-for-profit' highlights the nature of NGOs as non-profit-redistributing. Finally, these organisations are self-governed, and hence autonomously managed.

Notwithstanding the tensions and extensive debates around what NGOs are and what their roles should be, they remain an important, even influential in some cases, organisational actor. In this chapter, we explore the role of NGOs within the wider developmental landscape. In particular, we focus on how NGOs as organisations structure and manage their roles, relationships, and responsibilities. Moving away from mainstream management orthodoxy, we focus on the extant and potential contribution of critical management studies (CMS), a three decade-long intervention that

102 Emanuela Girei, Federica Angeli and Arun Kumar

holds deep-seated scepticism towards mainstream Management and Organization Studies orthodoxy (Adler et al., 2007). In particular, CMS challenges the ideology of excessive managerialism that is built around the primacy of the market where managerialism serves as a global ideology that once learnt, "can be applied anywhere, to anything and on anyone" (Parker, 2002, p. 5). The chapter is structured as follows: first, we outline the rise and role of NGOs in global development. Next, we focus on development management that is the management of global development. In particular, we interrogate the potential and problems of managerialism in development. In the following section, we focus on how critical management studies can help us problematize and think about development management, followed by some concluding reflections.

The Rise of Development NGOs

The NGO phenomenon rose to global significance in the late 1980s, partly as a result of what is usually called the development "impasse" or "crisis" i.e. a widespread sense of disillusionment with, and sense of failure of, the current development thinking and practice at the time (Blaikie, 2007; Cliffe et al., 1985; Simon, 1997; Wai, 2007, p. 12). Critics focused in particular on two key tenets of development 'orthodoxy': the central role of the state in development and the primacy attributed to economic growth. By the 1980s, there was widespread disappointment with the state-led models that had characterised development interventions since the 1950s. On the one hand, the neoliberal Bretton Woods Institutions (BWIs) advocated a minimal state to remove a major obstruction to development (Gros & Prokopovych, 2005; Onis & Senses, 2005; World Bank, 1981). On the other hand, neo-Marxist critiques saw the state's role in development as oppressive and exploitative, especially in the light of rising military expenditure and the heavy taxation of peasants (Bernstein, 1990, p. 110; Hyden, 1994, pp. 316–317). In response to which, the aid industry began to focus on alternative organisational actors to lead, structure, and manage development, a role which NGOs came to assume.

Relatedly, there was also growing dissatisfaction with the obsession within development programmes with economic growth. After initial assumptions that growth would automatically translate into poverty reduction came undone, questions began to be asked in the 1980s about the primacy of growth as a fundamental driver in development thinking. More specifically, the neoliberal reforms which dominated the development agenda since the early 1980s attributed to the market the role of key-engine of development, assuming that economic growth and wealth would trickle down to the poor, hence eradicating poverty and inequality (Stewart, 1997, p. 16). However, in the 1980s Africa and more generally the Global South witnessed an economic decline, an increase in poverty levels and a deterioration in living standards (ECA, 1989). Even as poverty levels have since begun to decline, there has been a steady, significant increase of income inequalities. Oxfam Novib – a large development charity – reported that in 2018 the world's 26 richest billionaires owned as many as 3.8 billion people (50% of the world population) at the base of the income pyramid (Oxfam, 2021). According to the UN, while in 1950 GDP per capita in the developed world was seven times higher than in Africa, in 2001 the gap had more than doubled (22,825 compared to 1,489) (United Nations, 2006, p. 5).

Hence, disillusionment with top-down state-led development practices on the one hand, and critiques against a predominantly 'economistic' understanding of development on the other led, in turn to a flourishing of alternatives conceptions of development, including 'participatory development', 'human development', 'post-development' and 'rights-based development' (Pieterse, 1998; Schuurman, 2000; Simon, 2007). Despite the heterogeneity among and within these perspectives, most of them advocated alternative, 'bottom-up' development thinking and practices. Against this background, a wide consensus emerged around the potentially positive role of NGOs, seen as the "'magic bullet', the panacea to failed top-down development and the means to poor people's empowerment" (Hearn, 2007, p. 1096). NGOs were expected to bring about fundamental changes, by means of adopting participatory and emancipatory approaches focused on the development aspirations of grassroots communities, thus widening the development thinking and practices beyond economic growth. In addition to this, NGOs were also favoured by official development agencies, which considered them cheaper, more effective and less prone to political pressures than governments in the delivery and implementation of development programmes (Edwards & Hulme, 1996).

In the period between 1980 and 2010, the number of NGOs, national and international, in the Global South rose dramatically. Funding to NGOs and civil society organisations has steadily increased between 2002 and 2017. Figure 5.1 plots the official development assistance (ODA) financial flows in US million (reduced at current prices) disbursed in 2002–2017 (15 years) from all development assistance committee (DAC) countries (source: OECD statistics).

From the early 1990s onwards the faith in neo-liberal development policies started diminishing. First the World Bank and later the IMF revisited their approach, articulating what came to be known as the "post-Washington consensus" (Onis & Senses, 2005; Ruckert, 2006). The novelty of the post-Washington consensus lies in three key elements: the recognition of the role of the state in development processes; a new interest in democracy and "good governance"; and a renewed concern with poverty reduction (Onis & Senses, 2005, p. 276). All three key elements of the so-called post-Washington consensus as well as the concern for participation and ownership, have significant impacts on the work, identity, and role of NGOs within the development industry. From the new perspective, NGOs are expected to continue providing welfare services to the poor, but are also entrusted a key role in the good governance agenda

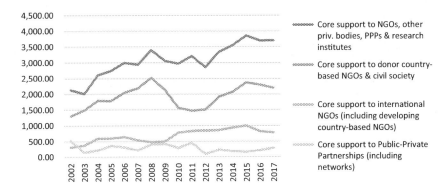

Figure 5.1 ODA financial flows in US millions, 2002–2017.

Source: OECD statistics

104 *Emanuela Girei, Federica Angeli and Arun Kumar*

and in the democratisation process (De Coninck, 2004). Our interest here, primarily, is to highlight that since the 1980s the prominence of NGOs has grown dramatically, so that today they are widely considered legitimate actors in development. They are actively involved in the implementation of development projects, usually participate in national and international policy-making and are allocated a significant portion of development funding.

However, four decades on, the increasing involvement of NGOs in global development does not seem to have brought the expected transformation in development thinking and practice (Blaikie, 2007; Cliffe et al., 1985; Simon, 1997; Wai, 2007, p. 12). Hence, the initial enthusiasm for NGOs has left room for a critical questioning of their role in development and their ability to make development more just and inclusive.

NGOs and Development Management: Why We Should Listen to CMS

As mentioned before, some scholars point out that many of the NGOs' failings are predominantly due to their lack of managerial capacity and experiences (Edwards & Fowler, 2003). According to them, the growing prominence that NGOs have acquired in the development field requires them to incrementally move away from being informal, voluntary-based organisations towards more professional and professionally-managed organisations, capable of differentiating themselves from other development actors. Underpinning such a view of NGOs' role are two key assumptions. One, that management studies, with a focus on a certain type of management, can make a significant contribution to development and sustainable development goals; and two, that there exists a distinctive realm of development practice known as development management (Brinkerhoff & Brinkerhoff, 2010; Lewis, 2003). For instance, Lewis argues that while NGOs are called on to "give priority to well-established management principles, most of which are drawn from the business world" (see also Dichter, 1989; Lewis, 2003, p. 340), while there are also distinctive features of NGO management, including relations with funders and a commitment to participation and empowerment (Lewis, 2006, pp. 189–200). Likewise, Thomas (Thomas, 1999, p. 51) points out that "the clearest examples of good development management will be those which use the enabling and empowerment mode of management to achieve development goals for the relatively powerless;" thus combining instrumental (goal-oriented) and developmental (empowerment-oriented) dimensions. Similarly, Fowler (Fowler, 1997) sees NGO management as a combination of instrumental, task-driven features with value and process-driven dimensions, where conventional management thinking and tools are adapted to fit the distinctive NGO context and mission.

These perspectives assume that conventional management theory and practice, somehow adapted to the NGOs' focus on social change rather than profit, is capable of delivering micro-changes at the organisational level, which can be aggregated and will result in wider societal changes. For instance, Edwards and Sen (Edwards & Sen, 2000), suggest that social transformation occurs by integrating changes at three levels: personal, organisational, and societal. They argue that personal transformation towards cooperative, caring and compassionate ways of thinking and behaving acts as a "well-spring of change in all other areas" (Edwards & Sen, 2000, p. 609) and as the basis of wider changes in the social and economic spheres. From this perspective, NGOs' effectiveness in promoting social change depends on their ability to

On NGOs and Development Management 105

integrate personal transformation into their programmes, activities, partnerships, and organisational praxis. This in turn requires them "to experiment more seriously with management practices, organisational structure and personnel policies that create the feedback loops we are looking for between personal change, institutional performance and wider impact" (Edwards & Sen, 2000, p. 614).

Consistent with the dominant performance culture permeating international development – the accountability and performance of NGOs have become central themes of development management. Proponents of development management argue that NGOs ought to invest in strategic planning, performance appraisal, and strengthening their accountability mechanisms (Fowler, 2003). The case *for* development management comes, according to the proponents, from the increasing pressure on NGOs to evidence the impact their work makes, the increasingly competitive nature of the development "industry" and issues of NGOs legitimacy towards donors and the public (Fowler, 1997, pp. 160–183). As donors' requirements and expectations differ from those of communities, NGOs are now expected to *manage* "multiple accountabilities", upwards and downwards, towards targets and towards participation (Ebrahim, 2003; Walsh & Lenihan, 2006), thereby experiencing tensions between the often clashing requirements of financial bookkeeping and social outcomes (Angeli et al., 2020)

Contrary to those propagating development management, some scholars take a more critical stance as they turn their attention to exploring the detrimental consequences of the *managerialisation* of the NGO sector: both to highlight the pervasiveness of management principles and techniques in NGO work (Wallace et al., 2007); and its detrimental effects. The critics address two particularly interesting issues on development management: the constraining impact of management thinking and practice on NGO work, and the furthering of inequalities within the NGO sector, especially between Southern and Northern NGOs, which we discuss next.

Critics of development management are, first and foremost, concerned about the pervasiveness of "rational" management thinking and tools (linear, logic models such as logical framework analysis or LFA and project cycle management); and their impact in terms of depoliticising development. Taking issue with the linear, rational, and deterministic conceptualisation of development management, critics of development management argue that such approaches result in the silencing of concerns that do not fit such a linear perspective, while it also turns the attention of development actors including NGOs towards a micro-level of analysis and intervention, thus losing sight of the bigger picture – that is, structural, substantial transformations (Wallace et al., 2007). Furthermore, critics argue that the obsession with results weakens the operational autonomy of NGOs, insofar as funding is usually constrained by the predefined plans, goals and priorities of donors (Bornstein, 2003; CDRN, 2004b). In this regard, several scholars have demonstrated how NGOs have progressively turned their efforts towards meeting donors' demands and requirements, so to ensure their survival, often drifting away from their original mission and their involvement with grassroots (Banks et al., 2015).

Still others have argued that the managerialisation of NGOs has exacerbated inequalities between Northern and Southern NGOs, leading to divisions within the NGO sector in the Global South (Mowles et al., 2008; Wallace et al., 2007). They argue that the unequivocal adoption of mainstream development management by international NGOs (INGOs) has increased the pressure on NGOs from the Global South to adopt specific management approaches, tools, and techniques. These include logframes and project cycle management, which – despite the rhetoric of partnership – are hardly

106 *Emanuela Girei, Federica Angeli and Arun Kumar*

ever negotiable (CDRN, 2004b; Wallace et al., 2007). Partly with a view to responding to the perceived lack of managerial capacity among NGOs from the Global South, some INGOs have taken on the burden of building and developing the capacity of their southern counterparts. Yet research suggests that these programmes do not focus on the capacity needs and aspirations identified by Southern NGOs. Instead, Northern NGOs tend to transmit management knowledge – on, say, strategic planning rather than on financial accountability, logframes or reporting – downwards on to their southern "partners" (Mowles et al., 2008). This is often done without investigating whether Southern NGOs consider it appropriate (see also Lewis, 2008). Finally, the excessive managerialisation of NGOs has led to the marginalization of those NGOs unable to keep pace with the fads and fashions of management jargon and techniques (Bornstein, 2003). In Uganda, for example, there seems to be an extensive rural "hidden sector", progressively obscured by urban-based, "sophisticated" NGOs (CDRN, 2004a, pp. 23–29).

The criticisms of development management are interesting for two main reasons. One, they suggest that technic-driven nature of development management, epitomised by the heavy deployment of standard tools and model and accountability to donors, has a detrimental impact on social change agenda. Two, such criticisms bring into relief the dominant role of actors from the Global North in how we *think about* and *do* development. That is, development management, far from enabling NGOs in fulfilling their transformative promise, re-inscribes and re-produces pre-existing asymmetries: such as those to do with North/South, urban/rural, etc. We summarize these external pressures and dynamics in the loop diagram represented in Figure 5.2. Donors' strict accountability requirements and focus on short-term solutions increase NGOs' pressures towards managerialism and professionalisation, leading to the adoption of managerial tools and technocratic practices borrowed from the private sector. This process strengthens NGOs' efforts to develop upward accountability and to meet donors' demands to the detriment of downward accountability towards beneficiary communities. The accountability shift negatively activates the second reinforcing loop, which becomes a cycle of progressively negative outcomes. The decreased involvement with grassroots reduces NGOs' adherence to their original civil society mandate and development mission, thereby decreasing their focus on beneficiaries' needs and their capability to design appropriate actions. This dynamic results in reduced NGOs' legitimacy within the target communities, to further impoverish their mission adherence.

While the detrimental impact of NGOs' heavy reliance on a technocratic understanding of management is evident, the fallacies it has created (in terms of disengagement from long-term social change agendas, progressive distancing from the grassroots, progressive proximity with donors' agendas and so on), cannot be answered simply by loosening the management requirements associated with development programmes. In this sense, critical perspectives from CMS might help us to identify ways through which NGOs' management can be understood and shaped so to serve social transformation, justice and equality.

Development Management: Learning from CMS

From the previous sections we have seen that NGOs have increasingly embraced conventional management approaches and practices in their operations, and that this has attracted growing criticism. In this section, we aim to go beyond existing critiques and explore how CMS can contribute to development management approaches, practices,

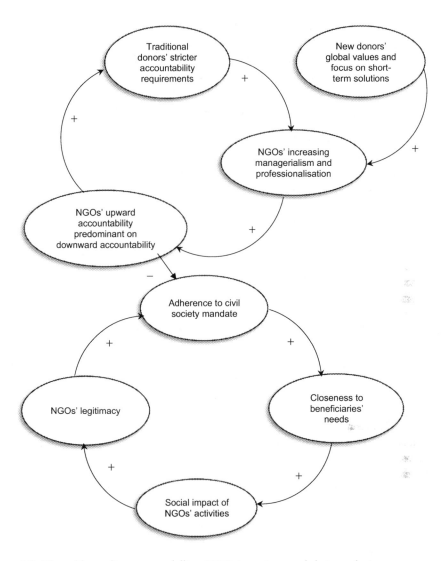

Figure 5.2 'Causal loop diagram modelling NGOs' tensions and their evolution.

and policies which are more suitable to support NGOs' engagement with social change, equality and justice. Among others, we focus on three in particular: (a) a sceptical attitude towards abstract universal management principles and approaches; (b) de-naturalisation of development management imperatives, and (c) consideration of how asymmetries of power shape NGOs management fads and fashions.

Scepticism

Similar to extant criticism of mainstream management orthodoxy – in particular, its emphasis on positivistic approaches and on an universalising and modernising

108   *Emanuela Girei, Federica Angeli and Arun Kumar*

impulse where context is rendered insignificant (Alvesson & Deetz, 2000; Alvesson & Willmott, 1996) – development management is no different. Applying CMS's questioning of management, we note that development management draws its strength from the following two features: one, its claim to its own "scientific", value- and bias-free, objective nature which renders social reality as fully knowable, predictable, and amenable to modelling. Two, development management draws its popularity from its own transformative, emancipatory promise – that is, it can lead to efficiencies while further societal betterment. Development management relies on the atomisation of social realities, where results and impact are taken to emerge from the aggregation of discrete micro-events, linked hierarchically and causally. Borrowing principles from physics and biology, development management explains social realities and human behaviour in mechanical terms, divorcing them from their social fabric where they are generated (Townley, 2002). This problematic conception of development management is evident from the managerialism that NGOs adopt, or are often made to under pressure from donor agencies. A clear example is the SDGs, where development is measured by counting individuals in discrete categories, whose sum is assumed to correlate with social phenomena associated with poverty.

Drawing on CMS, we would advocate for relentless questioning of the scientific character and neutrality attributed to development management. We would argue that the supposed and self-proclaimed universality and generalisability of mainstream development management are built upon an ideal "abstract management" (Townley, 2001, 2002), divorced not only from socioeconomic and political contexts but also from a historically situated cultural and relational texture. Variations (historical rather than economic, cultural rather than political) are thus obscured or manipulated to reflect the claimed universal validity of the model. This results in the neglect of important questions regarding, for instance, whose interests are being served by managerialist decision or approaches. The focus on micro-activities, micro-performances, and micro-results effectively discharges NGOs from analysing and reflecting on the history and the macro-level of international relations and political-economy where development takes – or should take – place.

Denaturalising Managerial Imperatives

One of CMS's most significant contribution relates to the questioning of the taken for granted nature of long-standing views, principles, and assumptions and calls for their "de-naturalisation". In the case of development management, this will include how key development management logics or imperatives are conceived. For instance, if we try to question and unfold the meaning of notions such as "value for money", output-based aid (OBA), payments-by-results (PbR), which allegedly support effective and efficient decision-making in key aspects such as resources allocation, we would begin to more clearly see that what are presented as "technical" and neutral decisions are often political decisions based on dominant and taken for granted ideas, which privileges certain dimensions and objectives over others (Frenzel et al., 2018). For example, the pursuit of managerial ends – for example, the number of users of a certain service over a set timeframe – tends to undermine other, more qualitative objectives, such as the quality of the service, sustainability of the service, engagement of user in the definition of the service and so on.

Of particular concern here is the progressive narrowing of perspectives resulting from the adoption of such models, and the constant exclusion of dimensions and dynamics that are intrinsically political, multi-faced, and shiftable and, as such, cannot be contained in the prescriptive models adopted in the aid industry.

Focussing on Power Asymmetries

A third insight coming from CMS concerns how global asymmetries shape development management knowledge and practice (Girei, 2017). Drawing on Said, we use the term "Orientalist" to characterise the way in which knowledge produced by the West about management in Africa rests explicitly or implicitly on a dichotomised and polarised definition of East and West. Binary thinking like this rests on the assumption that the West is the norm and the definition of the non-Western (the Other) based in what it lacks in comparison. Generic management and development management allow non-Western forms of organisation to emerge only with reference to the ways in which they differ from Western models, which generates mainly pejorative descriptions and labels ("traditional", 'corrupt", "backward") (Nuijten, 2005, p. 5; Prasad, 2003, p. 32). For instance, the good governance agenda rests on the assumption that Africa lacks management capacity, is inefficient and is not performance oriented, unlike the West, whose technical assistance and programmatic leadership is thus legitimised. From this perspective, then, the discourse of development management is Orientalist, portraying Africa as in dire need of guidance from the West and perpetuating the latter's dominant role in defining both needs and solutions.

More generally, it can be argued that development management maintains and reinforces unequal relations, through the domination of knowledge, tools, and techniques created and controlled by Westerners (Escobar, 1997; Kothari, 2005; Parpart, 1995). Given Europe's efforts to subjugate its colonies not only economically but also culturally (Mudimbe, 1988; Prasad, 2003), the neo-colonial dimension of development management can be traced within the apparently tireless effort to establish, under the guise of capacity development, the universality of Western worldviews and values at the expense of hindering and undermining possibilities for the development of alternative views.

The foregoing arguments also illuminate the geopolitical nature of the dominant management approaches, which is often overlooked in the mainstream debate on development management. As mentioned earlier, the technocratic and managerial nature of development management has been acknowledged and criticised by many scholars. Yet, the proposed solutions revolve around ever more and even "better management", which often results in further disregard of the inherently political nature of development and of development management (see, for instance, Wallace et al., 2007). However, these perspectives place the technical and the political as opposing poles, as if a technicist understanding of management could be improved by loosening its formalist requirements and adding an assumedly absent political agenda.

While the criticisms regarding the heavy reliance on techniques and tools can be shared, the claim that such perspectives lack a political agenda renders it questionable. Those management techniques and tools and their foundations, presented by their architects as scientific, neutral and thus already depoliticised, can instead be viewed as inherently political. They might be seen as sustaining not only the unequal global relations mentioned earlier, but also the dominant neo-liberal regime: development management, with its emphasis on results, individual measurements, and performance contributes to naturalising values, views, and practice which underpin the neoliberal (market) ideology, and, simultaneously to silence issues such as power, justice, and solidarity, just to name a few. The emphasis on standardised, quantitative approaches, metrics, and indicators reveals a dangerous de-contextualisation of development practices, which are instead deeply context-specific and require situated perspectives. In this sense, it becomes of utmost importance for NGOs and their ecosystems to develop accountability practices that are unique to their sectors, activities, and contexts, and that are co-created with both donors and grassroots communities. As highlighted in Figure 5.2, the adoption of managerial practices mutated by the private sector likely leads to a dangerous spiral voiding NGOs of their very distinctive mission and related legitimacy.

Against this already complex picture, the role of donors – and in particular the evolution of their relative power, ideology, agenda, and requirements – is of primary relevance to understand those upstream dynamics directly influencing NGOs' behaviours and outcomes (Banks & Hulme, 2014). NGOs face a general decline of available foreign aid from traditional donors and an increasing relative power of non-traditional donors (Kragelund, 2014), such as government new to the foreign aid landscape, as well as private donors, for example in the form of corporate philanthropists, also labelled as "philantrocapitalism" (McGoey, 2014). While traditional donors have collectively matured experience and expertise on how to shape development efforts, these new donors are likely to bring about potentially radically different views, with growing 'voice and political influence of unelected and unaccountable stakeholders in national and international development agendas' (Banks & Hulme, 2014, p. 187). Tensions between traditional and non-traditional donors have been documented, with the former fearing that the advancements they achieved in terms of accountability and transparency of development assistance funds could be "undone" by the new actors. Also in terms of focus, while traditional donors show a broad consensus on development priorities, such as poverty eradication, non-traditional donations seem more influenced by national leaders' agenda. Although financial flows from non-traditional donors appear to be still relatively low with respect to traditional channels, they are likely to alter the power dynamics between NGOs and their traditional sponsors.

An illuminating example is the Bill and Melinda Gates Foundation, whose action has significantly reshaped the global health landscape, and agenda-setting. By fuelling enormous amounts of private capital through an innovative model, the foundation has undoubtedly revamped the development sector and set an admirable example for many super-wealthy private donors. However, the fact that one private foundation – acting on the basis of its global value and priorities as opposed to local needs – has comparable or even larger bearing in setting the health policy of developing countries is undeniably concerning (Banks & Hulme, 2014; McGoey, 2014). Elsewhere, Kumar and Brooks (2021) have argued that even when philanthropic foundations are acting in "partnership" with other legitimate development actors, they are able to exercise influence disproportionate to their financial or personnel involvement. They suggest thinking of philanthropies' determining influence in international development in the form of metaphors: of bridges, interdigitates, leapfrogging, platforms, and satellites (Kumar & Brooks, 2021). The risk is high for such powerful international charities to

Table 5.1 Evolution of Private Donors' Development Financial Flows, Between 2009 and 2019 (US million dollars, current prices source OECD statistics)

Year	2009	2010	2011	2012	2013	2014	2015	2016	2017	2018
Private Donors Total	2620	1844	4332	2393	3496	3693	5472	4495	8284	6643
Arcus Foundation	..	..	..	..	..	..	15	16	15	17
Bernard van Leer Foundation	..	..	..	..	..	..	..	..	14	13
Bill & Melinda Gates Foundation	2620	1844	4332	2393	3335	3497	5279	4026	4838	3214
C&A Foundation	..	..	..	..	7	9	18	29	30	..
Carnegie Corporation of New York	..	..	..	..	..	..	..	..	24	18
Charity Projects Ltd. (Comic Relief)	..	..	..	..	38	57	59	44	47	25
Children's Investment Fund Foundation	..	..	..	..	..	..	..	..	207	219
Conrad N. Hilton Foundation	..	..	..	..	42	50	47	50	50	41
David & Lucile Packard Foundation	..	..	..	..	..	..	..	..	119	120
Ford Foundation	..	..	..	..	..	..	..	..	244	216
Gatsby Charitable Foundation	..	..	..	..	17	7	17	8	12	13
Gordon and Betty Moore Foundation	..	..	..	..	..	..	..	..	50	113
Grameen Crédit Agricole Foundation	..	..	..	..	..	..	..	..	39	36
H&M Foundation	..	..	..	..	5	25	7	12	31	7
John D. & Catherine T. MacArthur Foundation	..	..	..	..	..	..	..	..	240	100
MasterCard Foundation	..	..	..	..	..	..	..	..	77	54
MAVA Foundation	..	..	..	..	30	24	15	13	71	57
MetLife Foundation	..	..	..	..	22	23	14	9	28	18
Michael & Susan Dell Foundation	..	..	..	..	..	..	..	24	31	31
Oak Foundation	..	..	..	..	..	..	..	..	111	208
Omidyar Network Fund, Inc.	..	..	..	..	..	..	..	..	57	52
Wellcome Trust	..	..	..	..	..	..	..	..	254	261
William & Flora Hewlett Foundation	..	..	..	..	..	..	..	..	183	172
United Postcode Lotteries, Total	..	..	..	..	..	..	..	249	352	349
Dutch Postcode Lottery	..	..	..	..	..	..	..	228	244	234
People's Postcode Lottery	..	..	..	..	..	..	..	21	38	45
Swedish Postcode Lottery	..	..	..	..	..	..	..	..	70	70

overrule the local governments, and disempower local health systems and civil society in their primary role of design, implementation, and monitors of policies and programmes, thereby fundamentally failing in their development goals. Table 5.1 reports all private donors' development financial flows, between 2009 and 2019 (US million dollars, current prices – source OECD statistics).

Lessons for Policy and Practice: In Conclusion

In the previous sections, we have argued that the pervasive faith in supposedly scientific, rational management approaches is problematic and might hinder the same purposes for which they are adopted. In this sense, we think it is crucial to re-think what kind(s) of management knowledge and practice might support NGOs to strengthen their engagement with social change agenda, driven by a commitment to social justice and self-determination. For those practitioners and policy makers committed to these principles, a way forward would be that of engaging with pluriversality (a world within which many worlds fit) (Ndlovu-Gatsheni, 2015) and nurture the conditions of possibilities of various and alternative management and organisational approaches. Practically this could be done in several ways. For instance, Jammulamadaka (2013) proposes the embracement of what she calls "odd-ball" approaches, through which alternative management and organisational praxes can be discovered. Crucial in this sense, she suggests, is the initial suspension of both evaluation and search for causality in favour of an ideographic approach attentive and responsive to context-specific dynamics. Importantly, many NGOs especially those from the Global South already do so, especially after having been made to adopt largely impractical and unhelpful prescriptive models required by the aid industry. However, the ways through which they negotiate top-down managerial requirements in their day-to-day practice remains largely undocumented, and potentially transformative critiques emerging from civil society organisations (CSOs) practices are left underdeveloped and unexploited. In this sense, there is a dire need of bottom-up evidence and reflections on CSOs management approaches (especially in the Global South), so to enlighten how they revise and transform abstract managerialist imperatives and which approaches they adopt in their attempts to make sense and transform the contexts where they work.

An engagement with pluriversality also requires an appreciation of the political role of CSOs and the acknowledgment that management is not only about "how to do" but also, and often especially, about "what to do", thus making choices among different agendas, interests and priorities. Thus, the ubiquitous expectations for NGOs to be apolitical might need to be reconsidered. Interestingly, some actors have been already doing so, as for instance emerges from the Dutch government "Dialogue and Dissent" policy programme, which, by acknowledging the intrinsically political nature of development and underdevelopment, specifically aims at strengthening NGOs advocacy capacity in the Global South and their ability to contribute to transformative political processes (van Wessel, 2020). Interestingly, at the core of this programme, lies a critical assessment of managerialism, which is contrasted with a "social transformation logic", characterised by an appreciation of ambiguity and dissent and a commitment to challenge structural inequalities and to widening opportunities for CSOs to play an active political role (Kamstra, 2017).

This chapter has critically reviewed the debate on development management in the NGO sector. We have seen that, while contestations over development management are recognised along a spectrum, what changes is partly the extent to which such contestations are considered and partly how they are addressed. At the one pole, a problem-solving approach prevails which aims to advance the status of development management knowledge and practice. This position, by broadly supporting the primacy of effectiveness, seems to hinder NGOs' efforts at social transformation, insofar as the focus on results belittles the role of history and of the geopolitical context in which NGOs operate, thus narrowing opportunities to question who is served by development, who decides what the results are, how they are decided and what relevance these priorities and results have, locally and globally. At the opposite pole, the debate is more oriented towards a radical critique of the pervasiveness of management thinking and practice in development, illuminating its continuities with Western colonialism and imperialism.

By placing development management within the context of history and of global power asymmetries, not only do critical perspectives offer an interesting insight into how development management contributes to the expansion of the neoliberal agenda, for instance by naturalising certain values, views, and practices and simultaneously discouraging analysing beyond the micro-level, but they also make clear suggestions on how NGO management can be transformed to better serve NGOs commitment with issues of social change, justice, and equality.

References

Adler, P. S., Forbes, L. C., & Willmott, H. (2007). Critical management studies. *The Academy of Management Annals, 1*, 119–179.
Alvesson, M., & Deetz, S. A. (2000). *Doing critical management research*. Sage Publications.
Alvesson, M., & Willmott, H. (1996). *Making sense of management*. Sage Publications.
Angeli, F., Raab, J., & Oerlemans, L. (2020). *Adaptive responses to performance gaps in project networks*. Research in the Sociology of Organizations, in press.
Banks, N., & Hulme, D. (2014). New development alternatives or business as usual with a new face? The transformative potential of new actors and alliances in development. *Third World Quarterly, 35*(1), 181–195.
Banks, N., Hulme, D., & Edwards, M. (2015). NGOs, states, and donors revisited: Still too close for comfort? *World Development, 66*, 707–718.
Bebbington, A., Hickey, S., & Mitlin, D. (Eds.). (2007). *Introduction: Can NGOs make a difference? The challenge of development alternatives* (pp. 1–38). Zed Books.
Bernstein, H. (1990). Agriculture "modernisation" in the era of structural adjustment. In M. Griffon (Ed.), *Economie des filières en régions chaudes: Formation des prix et échanges agricoles* (pp. 103–119). CIRAD.
Blaikie, N. (2007). *Approaches to social inquiry*. Polity Press.
Bornstein, L. (2003). Management standards and development practice in the South African aid chain. *Public Administration and Development, 23*, 393–404.
Brinkerhoff, J., & Brinkerhoff, D. (2010). International development management: A Northen perspective. *Public Administration and Development, 30*(2), 102–115.
Brown, L. D., & Kalegaonkar, A. (2002). Support organizations and the evolution of the NGO sector. *Nonprofit and Voluntary Sector Quarterly, 31*(2), 231–258. https://doi.org/10.1177/0899764002312004
CDRN. (2004a). *Thoughts on civil society in Uganda*. CDRN.
CDRN. (2004b). *Working together or undermining each other? Development actors and funding flows: Implication for civil society organisation in Uganda*. CDRN.
Chachage, S. L. C. (2005, August 30). *CSOs in Tanzania: Challenges and developmental needs* (pp. 1–19). Paper presented to the Foundation for Civil Society "Away Day" Meeting.
Charnovitz, S. (1997). Two centuries of participation: NGOs and international governance. *Michigan Journal of International Law, 18*(2), 183–286.
Cliffe, L., Ishemo, S., & Williams, G. (1985). The review, intellectual & the left in Africa. *Review of African Political Economy, 32*(1–13).
De Coninck, J. (2004). The state, civil society and development policy in Uganda: Where are we coming from? In K. Brock, M. Rosemary, & J. Gaventa (Eds.), *Unpacking policy:*

114 *Emanuela Girei, Federica Angeli and Arun Kumar*

Knowledge, actors and spaces in poverty reduction in Uganda and Nigeria (pp. 51–73). Fountain Publishers.

Dichter, T. (1989). Development management: Plain or fancy? Sorting out some muddles. *Public Administration and Development*, *9*(4), 381–393.

Dicklitch, S., & Lwanga, D. (2003). The politics of being non-political: Human rights organizations and the creation of a positive human rights culture in Uganda. *Human Rights Quarterly*, *25*, 482.

Ebrahim, A. (2003). Accountability in practice: Mechanisms for NGOs. *World Development*, *31*(5), 813–829.

ECA. (1989). *African alternative framework to structural adjustment programmes for socio-economic recovery and transformation.* www.uneca.org/itca/ariportal/docs/aaf_sap.pdf

Edwards, M., & Fowler, A. (2003). Introduction: Changing challenges for NGDO management. In M. Edwards & A. Fowler (Eds.), *The Earthscan reader on NGO management* (pp. 1–10). Earthscan.

Edwards, M., & Hulme, D. (1996). Too close for comfort? The impact of official aid on non-governmental organizations. *World Development*, *24*(6), 961–973.

Edwards, M., & Sen, G. (2000). NGOs, social change and the trasformation of human relationships: A 21st-century civic agenda. *Third World Quarterly*, *21*(4), 605–616.

Escobar, A. (1997). The making and unmaking of the third world through development. In M. A. B. Rahnema Victoria (Ed.), *The post-development reader*. Zed Books.

Fowler, A. (1997). *Striking a balance: A guide to enhancing effectiveness of non-governmental organization in international development*. Earthscan Publication.

Fowler, A. (2003). Assessing NGO performance: Difficulties, dilemmas and a way Ahead. In M. Edwards & A. Fowler (Eds.), *The Earthscan reader on NGO management* (pp. 293–307). Earthscan.

Frenzel, F., Case, P., Kumar, A., & Sedgwick, M. W. (2018). Managing international development: (Re)positioning critique in the post-2008 conjecture. *Ephemera*, *18*(3), 577–604.

Girei, E. (2016). NGO, management and development: Harnessing counter-hegemonic possibilities. *Organization Studies*, *37*(2), 193–212.

Girei, E. (2017). Decolonising management knowledge: A reflexive journey as practitioner and researcher in Uganda. *Management Learning*, *48*(4), 453–470.

Gros, J. G., & Prokopovych, O. (2005). *When reality contradicts rhetoric: World bank lending practices in developing countries in historical, theoretical and empirical perspectives*. CODERESIA.

Hearn, J. (2007). African NGOs: The new compradors? *Development and Change*, *38*(6), 1095–1110.

Hyden, G. (1994). Changing ideological and theoretical perspectives on development. In U. Himmelstrand, K. Kinyanjui, & E. Mburugu (Eds.), *African perspective on development* (pp. 308–319). James Currey.

Jammulamadaka, N. (2013). What to stop doing in order to get things done?. In V. Malin, J. Murphy, & M. Siltaoja (Eds.), *Getting things done (dialogues in critical management studies* (Vol. 2, pp. 225–243). Emerald Group Publishing Limited.

Kamstra, J. (2017). *Dialogue and dissent theory of change 2.0. supporting civil society's advocacy role*. Netherlands' Ministry of Foreign Affairs.

Kothari, U. (2005). Authority and expertise: The professionalisation of international development and the ordering of dissent. *Antipode*, 425–446.

Kragelund, P. (2014). "Donors go home": Non-traditional state actors and the creation of development space in Zambia. *Third World Quarterly*, *35*(1), 145–162.

Kumar, A., & Brooks, S. (2021). Bridges, platforms and satellites: Theorizing the power of global philanthropy in international development. *Economy and Society*, *50*(2), 322–345.

Lewis, D. (2003). Theorizing the organization and management of non-governmental development organizations. *Public Management Review*, *5*(3), 325–344.

Lewis, D. (2006). *The management of non-governmental development organizations*. Routledge.

Lewis, D. (2008). Nongovernmentalism and the reorganization of public action. In S. Dar & B. Cook (Eds.), *The new development management: Critiquing the dual modernization* (pp. 41–55). Zed Books.

Lewis, D. (2017). Organising and representing the poor in a clientelistic democracy: The decline of radical NGOs in Bangladesh. *The Journal of Development Studies*, 53(10), 1545–1567. https://doi.org/10.1080/00220388.2017.1279732

Manji, F., & O'Coill, C. (2002). The missionary position: NGOs and development in Africa. *International Affairs*, 78(3), 567–583.

McGoey, L. (2014). The philanthropic state: Market – state hybrids in the philanthrocapitalist turn. *Third World Quarterly*, 35(1), 109–125.

Michael, S. (2004). *Undermining development: The absence of power among local NGOs in Africa*. James Currey.

Mohan, G. (2002). The disappointments of civil society: The politics of NGO intervention in northern Ghana. *Political Geography*, 21(1), 125–154.

Mowles, C., Stacey, R., & Griffin, D. (2008). What contribution can insights from the complexity sciences make to the theory and practice of development management? *Journal of International Development*, 20(6), 804–820.

Mudimbe, V. Y. (1988). *The invention of Africa: Gnosis, philosophy and the order of knowledge*. Indiana University.

Ndlovu-Gatsheni, S. J. (2015). The decolonial Mandela: Embodiment of peace, justice, and humanism. *Journal of Developing Societies*, 31(3), 305–332. https://doi.org/10.1177/01697 96X15590326

Nuijten, M. (2005, July 4–6). *The fallacy of systems thinking in development studies, a practice approach towards organisation and power*. Paper presented at the Critical Management Studies. http://ugle.svf.uib.no/svfweb1/filer/1550.pdf

Onis, Z., & Senses, F. (2005). Rethinking the emerging post-Washington consensus. *Development and Change*, 36(2), 263–290.

Oxfam. (2021). *The inequality virus*. https://oxfamilibrary.openrepository.com/handle/10546/ 621149

Parker, M. (2002). Against Management: Organization in the Age of Managerialism. Polity.

Parpart, J. L. (1995). Deconstructing the development "expert": Gender, development and the "vulnerable groups". In M. H. Marchand & J. L. Parpart (Eds.), *Feminist/postmodernism/ development* (pp. 221–243). Routledge.

Pieterse, J. N. (1998). My paradigm or yours? Alternative development, post-development, reflexive development. *Development and Change*, 29, 343–373.

Prasad, A. (2003). The gaze of the other: Postcolonial theory and organizational analysis. In A. Prasad (Ed.), *Postcolonial theory and organizational analysis: A critical engagement* (pp. 3–43). Palgrave Macmillan.

Ruckert, A. (2006). Towards an inclusive-neoliberal regime of development: From the Washington to the post- Washington consensus. *Labour, Capital and Society*, 39(1), 34–67.

Schuurman, F. J. (2000). Paradigma lost, paradigms regained? Development studies in the twenty-firts century. *Third World Quarterly*, 21(1), 7–20.

Shivji, I. G. (2007). *Silences in NGO discourse: The role and future of NGOs in Africa*. Fahamu.

Simon, D. (1997). Development reconsidered: New direction in development thinking. *Geografiska Annaler: Series B, Human Geography*, 79(4), 183–201.

Simon, D. (2007). Beyond antidevelopment: Discourses, convergences, practices. *Singapore Journal of Tropical Geography*, 28, 205–218.

Smith, D. J. (2010). Corruption, NGOs, and development in Nigeria. *Third World Quarterly*, 31(2), 243–258.

Srinivas, N. (2009). Against NGOs? A critical perspective on nongovernmental action. *Nonprofit and Voluntary Sector Quarterly*, XX(X), 1–13.

Stewart, S. (1997). Happy ever after in the marketplace: Non-government organisations and uncivil society. *Review of African Political Economy, 24*(71), 11–34.

Thomas, A. (1999). What makes good development management. *Development in Practice, 9*(1–2), 9–17.

Townley, B. (2001). The cult of modernity. *Financial Accountability & Management, 17*(4), 303–310.

Townley, B. (2002). Managing with modernity. *Organization, 9*(4), 549–573.

Tvedt, T. (1998). *Angels of mercy or development diplomats? NGOs and foreign aid.* Africa World Press.

United Nations. (2006). *World economic and social survey 2006: Diverging growth and development.* www.un.org/esa/policy/wess/wess2006files/wess2006.pdf

Vakil, A. C. (1997). Confronting the classification problem: Toward a taxonomy of NGOs. *World Development, 25*(12), 2057–2070.

van Wessel, M., Hilhorst, D., Schulpen, L., & Biekart, K. (2020). Government and civil society organizations: Close but comfortable? Lessons from creating the Dutch "strategic partnerships for lobby and advocacy". *Development Policy Review, Online First.* https://doi.org/10.1111/dpr.12453

Wai, Z. (2007). Whither African development? A preparatory for an African alternative reformulation of the concept of development. *Africa Development, XXXII*(4), 71–98.

Wallace, T., Bornstein, L., & Chapman, J. (2007). *The aid chain: Coercion and committment in development NGOs.* Practical Actions Publishing.

Walsh, E., & Lenihan, H. (2006). Accountability and effectiveness of NGOs: Adapting business tools successfully. *Development in Practice, 16*(5), 412–424.

World Bank. (1981). *Accelerated development in Sub-Sahara Africa: An agenda for action.* http://www-wds.worldbank.org/external/default/WDSContentServer/WDSP/IB/2000/04/13/000178830_98101911444774/Rendered/PDF/multi_page.pdf

6 Organizational Networks for Sustainable Development

Jörg Raab

Introduction

How can we tackle complex social and environmental problems in an interconnected world and achieve transformational change? One of the answers is through organizational networks or cross-sector/multi-sector partnerships understood as a group of three or more organizations very often from diverse backgrounds that address a joint problem that none of them could achieve individually. Whether it is about eradicating sickness through a sustained mass vaccination strategy (the GAVI vaccine alliance), making supply chains free of slave labor and improve workers' working conditions (Helfen et al., 2018) or making palm oil production more sustainable (Dentoni et al., 2018), tackling these social or environmental sustainability issues requires collaboration between a multitude of organizations. As a consequence, the extent of both the literatures on sustainability and on (organizational) networks, multi-, cross-sector or multi-stakeholder partnerships as novel organizational forms as well as their combination has dramatically increased in the last three decades.

While the empirical object, i.e. collaborative arrangements of multiple organizations from different societal sectors trying to achieve common goals with regard to sustainable development is often relatively similar, different literatures use different lenses to highlight certain characteristics of the empirical reality. In the "partnerships" literature, the emphasis is often on the roles of the different parties and studies are frequently conducted from a process perspective, i.e. how deliberation, decision-making and enforcement processes evolve over time. This chapter takes a somewhat different perspective and focuses on a more structural governance perspective as it has evolved in the public management literature in the last three decades and applies that to sustainable development. However, as we will see in the following sections, many studies on sustainable development have already made use of these insights. This chapter attempts to systematize these insights and make them accessible to students and scholars of sustainable development.

The growing awareness for sustainability issues coincided with a strong globalization push and the digital transformation of societies since the end of the 1980s. These processes triggered a series of developments. First, digitalization led to an increasing interconnectedness both nationally and internationally, which has been coined the network society (Castells, 2010). Second, due to the liberalization of trade and financial markets, the opening of countries and increased travel possibilities, global economic development accelerated enormously which however caused environmental damage and increased inequality. Carbon dioxide (CO_2) emissions from the burning of fossil

DOI: 10.4324/9780429243165-7

This chapter has been made available under a CC-BY-NC 4.0 license.

118 *Jörg Raab*

fuels for energy and cement production for the entire world rose from 22.7 billion tons in 1990 to 36.44 billion tons in 2019 annually (Ritchie & Roser, 2020). Through the economic development especially in South America and Asia some inequalities decreased but globally social and economic inequality remains extensive even though economists debate how much it has changed (The Economist, 2019). It has become apparent that global economic and technological progress is very unequally distributed and has created or at least made visible many unintended negative effects of this development with regard to social inequities and environmental degradation.

However, due to these changes and the increasing connectivity in the world also the consciousness began to shift among many scientists, business people and policy makers towards the recognition that a more holistic approach is necessary to move to more sustainable societies. The realization has been growing, albeit very slowly that major transformations in our societies to a more sustainable way of living are unavoidable. The current Covid-19 pandemic presumably has strengthened and accelerated this realization (Engler et al., 2021). As I will discuss in this chapter, organizational networks have become one of the major organizational forms, actors put their hope on in order to initiate and realize that transformation not least in the form of an own U.N. Sustainable Development Goal (SDG 17).

In economics, Raworth (2017) coined the concept of "Doughnut Economics". The doughnut is made up of an inner ring that symbolizes the minimum social foundation of a decent live and an outer ring that symbolizes the natural planetary boundaries, human activity should not cross to safeguard long-term survival. Therefore, human activity should lead to a state within this ring she calls the "save and just space of humanity". We thus have to operate between an ecological ceiling on the outside and the social foundations such as food, water, social equity, health, and education, on the inside. Similarly, first the UN millennium goals and later the agenda 2030 with the Sustainable Development Goals (SDG) emphasized the interconnectedness of social and economic development as well as environmental sustainability merged into a global perspective of sustainable development.

Within the policy sciences, the concept of wicked problems became increasingly prominent in the literature since the early 2000s. It coincides with the growing awareness and studies on environmental sustainability and here especially climate change (Danken et al., 2016). The wicked problems concept, originally coined by Rittel and Webber in 1973 describes a class of societal and policy problems that are highly resistant to resolution such as poverty, migration or climate change. They are often contested and cannot be solved through a technocratic or social engineering approach (Rittel & Webber, 1973). Head argued that these problems are characterized by high uncertainty, high complexity and high value divergence between the involved and affected actors (Head, 2008). All three dimensions make that actors often have difficulties to even agree on what the exact problem is, not even talking about finding a solution for a problem with many interdependent subproblems, which are again symptoms of other problems. Many scholars therefore agree, that wicked problems are not solvable in the sense that we just have to find the right solution, implement it and the problem will be gone for good, but that wicked problems rather have to be solved over and over again and that interventions can even have detrimental effects (Danken et al., 2016). In addition, Levin et al. (2012) suggest the term "Super Wicked Problems" for a new class of global environmental problems that need to be tackled under time pressure, because we are reaching irreversible tipping points in some areas such as climate change and biodiversity that will be impossible to reverse. Crucial to this class of global environmental problems is that there are only weak or non-existing central authorities on the global level to address these problems.

In the management literature, scholars recently have started to pay increasing attention to this type of problems under the label "Grand Challenges" (Eisenhardt et al., 2016; Ferraro et al., 2015; George et al., 2016) and the question how management and management research can contribute in tackling these problems. In that perspective, "Grand Challenges" are formulations of global problems that can be plausibly addressed through coordinated and collaborative effort" (George et al., 2016, p. 1880)

The 17 UN SDGs are 16 summary fields with complex interconnected social, political, environmental, economic and psychological issues as described earlier from different disciplinary perspectives and a 17th goal called "partnership for the goals", which is defined as

Enhance the global partnership for sustainable development, complemented by multi-stakeholder partnerships that mobilize and share knowledge, expertise, technology and financial resources, to support the achievement of the sustainable development goals in all countries, in particular developing countries.
(https://sdgcompass.org/sdgs/sdg-17/)

In some sense, SDG 17 is an odd one out, since it is not a substantial policy goal like the other 16 but more a tool to achieve the substantive policy goals, if we leave aside that it can be a goal of establishing better and more equal relations between the global south and north. However, it underscores the importance and prevalence that policy makers in practice put on the issue of partnerships and collaboration to reach the SDGs. In fact, when we look at these goals such as reducing poverty and hunger, increasing health and gender equality, gaining access to clean water, education, climate action and other environmental goals, etc., we can easily recognize that they overlap, influence each other and are interconnected in countless ways as is also evident in the concepts of Grand Challenges, Wicked Problems or the Doughnut Economy. As a demonstration of this interconnectedness, Kapucu and Beaudet (2020) for example showed the complex organizational network structure that evolved around the food-energy-water nexus within the SDGs.

Comparing the different concepts laid out earlier shows that they agree on the fact that sustainability issues in the broader sense and the narrower sense of environmental sustainability are very complex problems, often still characterized by a lack of information and knowledge and shifting over time and therefore are highly uncertain. In addition, the wicked problems concept emphasizes that these problems do not exist objectively but are perceived subjectively through various lenses that are formed by the different values people and organizations hold dear and strive for. Literature in public management, policy sciences and management and organization studies has collected ample evidence that neither hierarchies/the state nor the markets can tackle problems with such characteristics individually. Rather, it is collaborative arrangements in the form of organizational networks and partnerships that are the most promising governance or organizational form to address this type of problems (Gray & Purdy, 2018; O'Toole, 1997; Ostrom, 1990; Raab & Kenis, 2009). Examples of such collaborative arrangements in the area of the SDGs are for example the collaboration between the ICRC, Philips design and the Philips

120 Jörg Raab

Foundation as described in the case description in chapter 10 of this book, or the GAVI vaccine alliance (Bill and Melinda Gates foundation, UNICEF, WHO, World Bank and wider partners with civil society organizations, national governments, pharmaceutical industry, research and technical institutes in the health field (Gavi the Vaccine Allliance, n.d.); Climate Action Network Europe with over 170 member organizations such as Greenpeace, the WWF, Biovision in the area of climate change/action (https://caneurope.org/), the European Anti-Poverty Network (www.eapn.eu/poverty) with organizations such as Caritas, Salvation Army, European Federation of Food Banks or the European Federation for Street Children in the area of poverty alleviation. What is similar to all these collaborations is that they consist of a group of autonomous organizations from different sectors that try to achieve joint goals in the area of sustainability that none of them could do on their own.

As this organizational form becomes more and more prevalent, legitimate and important to tackle sustainability problems as signaled by the SDG 17 on cross-sector partnerships as well as the broader academic literature on wicked problems and sustainable development, the use and therefore the understanding of organizational networks in different forms and shapes are key to tackle these problems. Also, in the organization and management literature dealing with grand challenges, we clearly can see an emphasis on collaborative approaches. Given the importance and attention from many different disciplines, however, it does not come as a surprise that the literature on networks and partnerships for sustainable development is very diverse and distributed over many disciplines such as political science, management and organization studies, sociology, public and non-profit management and multi-disciplinary science combining social and natural sciences as well as (public) health. As a consequence, many different labels are used to describe and analyze similar types of collaborative arrangements, where actors from different sectors, backgrounds and with different organizational cultures work together to jointly address these problems. Labels and concepts that we can find in the different literatures are policy networks, cross-sector or stakeholder partnerships, cross-sector collaborations, collaborative governance, governance networks, social-ecological networks, alliances, consortia, public private partnerships or (inter-) organizational networks. In the following, I will use the term organizational networks as a generic term that describes groups "of three or more organizations that facilitate the achievement of a common goal, which none of the individual organizations could achieve on their own" (Provan et al., 2007; Provan & Kenis, 2008) for this group of collaborative arrangements. They are consciously created, i.e. not merely the aggregate of dyadic relationships, in which organizations are autonomous but interdependent and they jointly produce the network output. The organizations in these networks are often connected by multiplex ties such as financial flows, services or information exchange.

As we will see in the following, despite the high hopes and expectations in the literature in the 1990s and still expressed in SDG 17, such networks are no panacea for solving complex issues in general, including in the area of sustainable development. In fact, they are complex organizational arrangements whose success is conditional on different factors. The chapter will therefore discuss with regard to sustainable development why these networks exist, what types we can distinguish, how they can be governed and managed, under what conditions they might work and how they can be evaluated. In addition, I will discuss how they have been picked up in practice and their impact on the field, i.e. to what extent an organizational network perspective

Organizational Networks for Sustainable Development   121

contributes to our understanding of how we can effectively and efficiently organize for sustainable development.

Why Do Organizational Networks Exist?

The rationale for organizational networks to exist can be seen from a system and from an actor perspective. However, these two perspectives are heuristic categories and in practice are interlinked. From a system perspective, organizational networks come into being, because the problem space exceeds the capacities, competences, skills and resources of individual organizations, i.e. none of the organizations is able to tackle or even solve a problem sufficiently on its own. Therefore, organizations have to be mandated, incentivized or at least encouraged to collaborate and coordinate their activities in a way that will lead to the solution of that problem. For example, one of the major challenges to build a more sustainable economy is to make production, consumption and use as well as deposing of products much more circular. At this point in time, the main producers of consumer goods do not even know exactly all the (raw) materials that are in their products. Building a circular economy therefore requires collaboration from all the actors in the supply chain including the organizations dealing with recycling/deposing with the relevant government entities in a way that goes beyond the current sequential process, i.e. from raw materials to the garbage can. This is, because once we stop throwing things simply away and have to think and act from a circular system perspective, actors in a value chain will find themselves in pooled if not even reciprocal rather than sequential interdependencies (Thompson, 1967). Thompson's typology describes different types of interdependencies with an increasing complexity. In a sequential interdependency, the output of one actor is the input of another one. In a pooled interdependencies, actors bring their resources together to create a joint output. In the most complex form of interdependency, the reciprocal one, in- and outputs are mutual. Moving from the sequential to pooled to reciprocal requires ever more coordination and cooperation to successfully deal with these interdependencies. For multi-organizational systems, this will require elaborated collaboration and coordination in form of organizational networks that need to set up and maintain circular ecosystems around certain product groups or offerings (Cardoso de Oliveira et al., 2019). Moreover, these networks will also be embedded in such ecosystems, characterized by complementarities between organizations from the private, public and semi-public sectors (see for a recent discussion on networks and ecosystems Shipilov & Gawer, 2020). In that example, none of the individual producers will be able to do that on their own not even, if the organization is a powerful and large company, since it is likely to be dependent on a myriad of suppliers. Once it is responsible for the recycling of its products, the input and outputs of organizations after/before itself become part of a circle with pooled or reciprocal interdependencies.

Another argument from a system perspective frequently found in the literature for the existence of organizational networks is that governments find it difficult to respond to complex sustainability problems that often exceed their capacities in both scale and scope as well as exceed their territorial and institutional boundaries. Bodin (2017) shows that in socio-ecological systems such as maritime fisheries, ecosystems frequently exceed institutional boundaries whether it is organizational entities, organizations, sectors, countries or even continental boundaries. In order to keep such ecosystems intact and organize harvesting sustainably, organizations need to negotiate and collaborate. However, it is not only the mismatch of ecosystems and institutional spaces but also the nature of common pool resources that require collaboration. Common pool resources are characterized by the fact that people cannot be excluded naturally from consuming a resource. Since the resource is limited, it will be overused and eventually depleted, if participants individually maximize its use. As Ostrom (2015) shows, in order to avoid this "tragedy of the commons", the building of institutions through horizontal collaboration, not hierarchical fiat, is necessary and possible. This functional rationality from a system perspective is frequently so strong that it actually becomes a normative demand, so powerful that people rush to network formation without checking whether it is actually necessary and possible. On the other hand, network formation, even if desirable from a functional perspective, may not happen due to institutional barriers or lack of chemistry between individuals. This might especially be the case for more complex problem structures, where different actors working on different subproblems need to recognize the inter-dependencies and overcome various hurdles to collaborate (Hedlund et al., 2021).

As shown earlier, from an actor perspective, tackling overarching problems that can also contribute to better achieving one's own organizational goals can be a strong motivation and reward for participating and investing in organizational networks for individual organizations. However, there are different rationales on the organizational level that can explain why organizations join organizational networks despite the necessary additional effort, resources and potential constraints on their actions, strategy and autonomy. Different organization theories provide a theoretical basis for these motivations.

Social network theory implies that organizations join networks to strengthen their own (power) position by strategically forging ties with other organizations in their environment with positive performance effects (Zaheer & Bell, 2005). Resource dependence theory argues that organizations want to reduce uncertainty stemming from their resource dependency on other organizations. In the example of the circular economy laid out earlier, for example, organization would want to build longer lasting assured relationships in order to secure the inflow of necessary inputs and secure the outflow and sales of outputs (Pfeffer & Salancik, 1978). From an institutional theory perspective, organizations join networks because they can increase their legitimacy, especially when connecting with organizations that are seen as reputable, providing solutions or goods and services that people want and see as desirable (DiMaggio & Powell, 2000; Human & Provan, 2000). Participating in a network can also create access to knowledge and other resources as emphasized by the Resource Based Theory of the Firm (Lavie, 2006). Transaction Cost Theory, on the other hand, argues that in situations that are characterized by a medium frequency of transactions, asset specificity and uncertainty a hybrid governance form, i.e. network relations, is preferable to hierarchies or markets in order to minimize transaction costs. Last but not least, stakeholder theory claims that organizations have normative responsibilities toward other organizations and groups whose activities and lives they influence (Freeman et al., 2010), which can provide a motivation to participate in organizational networks to manage these effects (for an early review on theoretical perspectives on inter-organizational relations and networks, see Oliver & Ebers, 1998).

As argued in the beginning, the desire to achieve their own organizational goals or contribute to broader collective goals can also be a motivation for organizations to participate in networks (Kenis & Raab, 2020b). Such motivation can arise from strategic thinking but also from internal organizational pressures by professionals in the organization, who want to see certain problems tackled in an effective way and recognize that their own organizations and they themselves are not able to achieve that on their own. However, orientation towards a joint purpose and common goals does not mean that power asymmetries between organizations, interests and conflicts disappear in organizational networks and partnerships. By recognizing the interdependencies and couple themselves more tightly through collaboration, conflicts between organizations actually can become more pronounced and need to be managed. Power asymmetries can evolve due to different sizes of organizations, different resources and political influence. In addition, unequal resource dependencies might lead to power asymmetries where organizations gain power, whose output is essential for the operations of others in the network and these resources cannot easily be substituted (Pfeffer & Salancik, 1978). Organizations will also have to keep their organizational goals and interests in mind and conflicts might arise when network goals start to conflict with (some) organizational goals. Moreover, in the area of sustainable development, organizations might also be tied to certain political interests or ideologies and the leeway of organizational leaders is limited when working together with the (former) "enemy".

Building on these organization theories, Gray and Purdy (2018, pp. 27–33) distinguish between "legitimacy, resource, competency and society oriented motivations" for partnering with other organizations. "Legitimacy oriented motivations" encompass building reputation, image and branding or to attract and retain employees. "Resource oriented motivations" include gaining access to networks, build capacity or create innovative products and markets and secure funds. Gaining expertise, leverage diverse knowledge and identify issues and trends as well as growing awareness of complex social problems are part of "competency-oriented motivations". "Society-oriented motivations" encompass influencing policy development or responding to stakeholder and shareholder activism regarding local problems. Other organization level motivations that we can find in the literature are increased revenue and/or growth opportunities, reduced risks, risk sharing and/or costs (Mirvis & Worley, 2014).

These motivations are valid for both profit and non-profit organizations (Gray & Purdy, 2018) and to some extent even for government organizations. However, government organizations very often have a legal mandate to tackle sustainability problems. Therefore, gaining legitimacy is of less importance, but they rather seek additional resources and competencies as well as include or even co-opt societal stakeholders. In that context an interesting question is, whether organizational networks including organizations from different sectors can compensate for weak state capacity. Unfortunately, there is increasing evidence that state capacity and effective cross-sector organizational networks are more likely to be mutually reinforcing rather than that these networks of business and NGOs could compensate for weak state capacity in tackling complex sustainability problems (Lazzarini et al., 2020), i.e. a functioning state with administrative capacity is necessary to address sustainability problems, which can be aided and multiplied by cross-sector networks. The question therefore is whether the hope and expectation that SDG 17 symbolizes, is justified in weak or even failed state contexts.

What Types of Networks Can We Distinguish and How Do they Evolve?

As in the general literature on organizational networks, we can identify different types of networks in the literature with regard to sustainability issues as well. However, there is not one specific typology that could help us to categorize the different types of networks that we find in practice. We rather see distinctions based on different dimensions. The most basic distinction is between serendipitous and engineered networks (Doz et al., 2000; Raab & Kenis, 2009). Serendipitous networks are networks made up of the aggregate of groups of actors and their dyadic ties that exist in the eyes of the observer. Organizations in the network have only very little awareness about the extent and the composition of the network, they do not have joint network goals or a shared identity. Engineered networks, on the other hand, are groups of actors that come together to achieve joint network goals or tackle common problems. They are consciously created and governed and people operating in these networks might over time develop a shared consciousness and identity. In practice, however, this distinction is often not that clear cut. In a temporary perspective, networks might morph from serendipitous networks into engineered ones as actors gain increasing awareness of their interdependencies. From a structural perspective, we often see networks that consist of a very active core group of organizations and a broader periphery of organizations which are necessary to reach the network goals. The organizations in the periphery might, from their own perspective, have only limited stakes in achieving the network goals and might be connected more bilaterally to a core organization and are not really aware of the overall network goals. Rather, they might generally support the broader purpose of the network (Carboni et al., 2019). In such purpose oriented networks, we therefore find parts that might be more serendipitous and others which are more engineered. Bodin's social-ecological networks (2017) for example, encompass both types. The underlying eco-systems and the actors operating in them and harvesting resources create a serendipitous network that actually needs to be converted into conscious collaboration and coordination and therefore into engineered networks in order to manage such eco-systems sustainably (Bodin, 2017; Ostrom, 2009).

Another distinction is based on the mode of instigation. Here, we can distinguish between voluntary and mandated networks (Popp & Casebeer, 2015; Segato & Raab, 2019). Voluntary networks are networks where organizations come together on their own accord to tackle a sustainability issue. Very often this happens bottom-up through professionals within these organizations who then seek support from their organizations' leadership. Mandated networks are networks that are instigated top down by government organizations. Networks are then becoming more of a tool in implementing government policies. A mixed type is characterized by "bounded voluntariness" (Segato & Raab, 2019). These are networks that are not mandated but strongly incentivized through additional resource promises by the instigating actor(s). Such instigating actors often make the funding of networks conditional on a certain size, a specific composition of actors or a specific mode of governance. Instigating actors oftentimes are government bodies but can also be philanthropic organizations which want to see their programs implemented in a certain way. Examples for voluntary networks in the area of sustainability are the GAVI Vaccine partnership (Kamya et al., 2017), multi-party governance systems to manage ocean or water systems (Lubell et al., 2014) or the Nestlé Nespresso sustainable supply chain network (Alvarez et al., 2010). Sayles and Baggio (2017) report on a mandated network to restore Salmon stock in Puget Sound, Washington State, U.S.A. In this case, the living and breeding conditions of Salmon require actors whose actions affect river basins and ocean waters to collaborate. Collaboration is strongly driven by state and federally promoted initiatives, often coordinated through watershed planning bodies. Examples of bounded voluntariness can be found for example in areas, where network formation is part of larger government programs for example in the area of estuary protection and management (Schneider et al., 2003).

Yet another distinction is based on the time dimension. We can distinguish between networks that are set up to last for a certain period or until certain goals or a certain state are achieved (Kenis et al., 2009), networks that are in principle open ended and networks that switch between active and latent phases. The latter are networks that continue to exist as a basic structure and are (re-)activated when necessary. Temporary networks can occur in the form of "issue or opportunity networks, as a temporary constellation of organizations to pursue a specific purpose" (Mirvis & Worley, 2014). After that purpose is achieved the network dissolves.

Last but not least we can differentiate in networks that are formed around vertical production chains. They move resources from raw materials to the end consumer and can address business as well as sustainability issues (Mirvis & Worley, 2014). As indicated earlier, resource (inter)dependence is also a central feature for organizations within a circular economy but as discussed in Chapter 1 of this book on Corporate Responsibility is also a permanent topic with regard to the responsibility of multinational companies for social and environmental standards in their supply chains. Trying to internalize effects in the form of environmental pollution or questionable working conditions in their supply chains, companies are likely to have to interact with government actors, unions, NGOs, auditing organizations that form organizational networks (Fichter et al., 2011; Helfen et al., 2018).

How Can Consciously Created Organizational Networks Be Governed?

Provan and Kenis (2008) suggest three ideal modes to govern organizational networks which we can also find in the literature on collaboration in the area of sustainability implicitly or explicitly: a self-governed network, a lead organization network and a network with a network administrative organization.

In case of a self- or shared governed network, all participating organizations are jointly involved in decision-making, monitoring, implementation and the operational processes the network employs. In principle, all participants are directly connected with each other through strong relationships. Albareda and Waddock (2018) describe how global CSR standards in initiatives like the UN Global Compact (UNGC), the Global Reporting Initiative (GRI) or the ISO26000 by the International Integrated Reporting Council and the International Organization for Standardization were developed through "networked CSR governance" based on a shared governance framework. Here, "the whole network is governed by the network members themselves (companies, NGOs, governments and international organizations) with no separate and specific governance entity or central coordinating body" (Albareda & Waddock, 2018, p. 664).

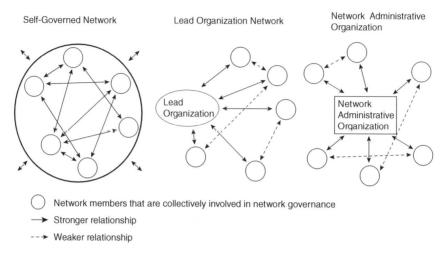

Figure 6.1 Ideal modes of network governance, based on Provan and Kenis (2008) (Popp et al., 2014).

The other two modes are brokered either by a lead organization or by a network administrative organization that is specifically set up for monitoring and coordination purposes. In case of a lead organization network, one of the organizations, very often the largest and most reputable one, takes on the coordination and monitoring tasks. The lead organization is then still part of the primary processes. Alvarez et al. (2010) describe the example of Nespresso as a lead organization. Over time in Nestle's Nespresso AAA sustainable quality program a network developed with Nespresso as the lead organization. This network encompassed 48 organizations such as coffee exporters and processing companies, NGOs and international development agencies on the local, national and global levels with the goal to make coffee production more sustainable.

In case of a Network Administrative Organization network, the central organization (the NAO) has merely coordination and monitoring tasks and does not participate in delivering services. While all organizations are directly connected to the NAO, not all the possible ties between the organizations are activated or need to be strong. Existence and strength of ties depend on the interdependencies between the individual organizations and which of them are actually necessary to achieve the network goals. Examples of NAO governed networks in the area of sustainability can be especially found in the international arena, where secretariats function as network administrative organizations for networks encompassing national governments, international NGOs, international organizations and research institutes. Poocharoen and Sovacool (2012) describe the Renewable Energy and Energy Efficiency Partnership (REEEP, now: www.reeep.org/) as such a NAO network. Members are European, the U.S., Australian and New Zealand governments, private actors such as Siemens, international organizations such as the UNDP and research institutes such as the Energy and Resources Institute (TERI) in India and the Mediterranean Renewable Energy Centre in Tunisia (Poocharoen & Sovacool, 2012). The network wants to contribute to areas

Organizational Networks for Sustainable Development 127

such as climate change mitigation, the reduction of greenhouse gas emissions; energy access and the diffusion of small-scale renewable energy technology to the rural poor (Poocharoen & Sovacool, 2012, p. 414).

In empirical reality, we often also find mixed types. For example, a few organizations jointly take the lead which would be a mix of a shared governance and a lead organization network. Another mixed type is, if NAO functions are located in a participating organization, because it is legally easier to formally have employment contracts with an existing organization, which would represent a mixture of a lead organization and an NAO network. The Gavi Vaccine Alliance on the global level for example represents a mixed type between a shared governance mode with a board for the strategic decisions and collaboration and an NAO with a secretariat of a few dozen people for policy development, coordination, monitoring and evaluation (www. gavi.org/our-alliance).

Subsequently, the central question becomes which governance mode is most effective under which conditions. Provan and Kenis (2008) suggest the following four contingency factors that form configurations with the governance mode: the size of the network, the trust density within the network, the level of goal consensus and the extent of the need for network level competencies. In case of small networks (about six participants) with high trust density between the organizations, high goal consensus and a low need for network level competencies, a self-governed network is likely to be effective. In case the network has a moderate size, low to medium trust density and moderate levels of goal consensus and need for network level competencies, a lead organization network is likely to be effective. For larger networks with moderate levels of trust, a high need for network level competencies and a moderately high goal consensus, a NAO network is likely to work best (Provan & Kenis, 2008). Therefore, it is not one mode that fits all, but the effectiveness of organizational networks depends on certain contingencies or situational factors in combination with the appropriate governance mode.

How Do Organizational Networks Function?

In general, there is no reason to believe that networks in the area of sustainability function differently than in other areas and therefore the insights from the general literature on networks and partnerships are in principle applicable. It is therefore not primarily the area or policy field that makes the use of organizational networks more or less necessary or prevalent but rather the type of problem. As Roberts (2000) argued, collaborative strategies are most likely to occur and be effective in situations where there is conflict about both the problem definition and the solution, where power is dispersed between multiple actors but not contested. These are typically situations with value divergence among the actors, uncertainty and high complexity as characterized by Head (2008) in his wicked problems framework.

In addition, one could argue, however, that in the area of environmental sustainability, the underlying ecological interdependencies reduce the flexibility for example with regard to the composition of the partnerships. If an actor group that harvests a species that plays a crucial role in the food chain in an ecosystem does not participate in a preservation network, it is very difficult to substitute for that. Such opt out can only be overcome either by threatening with hierarchical intervention by the state (stick in the window), by mandating the participation, or with considerable financial incentives.

128   *Jörg Raab*

All three responses to the opt-out threat, however, also have their drawbacks and limitations. Threats have to be credible and need to be enforced, if actors do not comply with potentially detrimental effects for collaboration between the actors. In mandated networks, collaboration may be more symbolic than real, because organizations respond to an avoidance strategy to institutional pressure using concealment strategies that disguise their non-conformity for example by blaming the other parties for lack of progress (Oliver, 1991, p. 152). In addition, without real commitment, learning is likely to be limited (Gray & Purdy, 2018, p. 101). As for financial incentives, we can regularly observe that networks often only keep existing as long as organizations receive these additional resources and stop, if the actors are asked to put up significant amounts of their own resources.

Depending on the specific field and situation, there are specific factors that influence the functioning of organizational networks and cross-sector partnerships. With regard to "super wicked problems" (Levin et al., 2012) as a class of complex global environmental problems time pressure is added to the mix. As difficult as many social problems are, we are facing environmental problems such as loss of biodiversity or climate change that after passing certain tipping points will change our living environment irreversibly. As larger transformations are necessary especially in the environmental sustainability areas, network decisions are likely to become more invasive for citizens and individual organizations with regard to behavioral changes. This inevitably leads to additional demands for legitimate decision-making and implementation as well as tensions with decision-making in parliamentary democracies that are difficult to resolve (Kenis & Raab, 2020a).

In addition, sustainability issues very often exceed institutional and territorial boundaries and therefore networks in that area present cross-level phenomena, i.e. they encompass actors from several layers from the global, the continental, national, regional to the local level that makes cross-level ties likely and necessary, which adds another layer of complexity to the governance and functioning of such networks (see also Gray & Purdy, 2018, p. 181).

Literature clearly shows that there is no size fits all set of "success factors" that would make organizational networks and partnerships for sustainability function effectively. What is needed is a situational approach based on specific contingencies. Literature suggests that these are dependent on (1) the type of the network, (2) the type of the problem and the underlying problem structure and (3) the development stage of the network.

(1) Type of the network

As stated earlier, we can distinguish between serendipitous and engineered organizational networks. The first type does not have explicitly formulated joint goals and organizations are not necessarily aware that they are part of a network. Such systems nonetheless produce outcomes and they might do better or worse depending on the underlying problem which will be discussed in the following. For engineered networks, we can distinguish between factors from a more structural and from a more process perspective. From a structural perspective, there is increasing evidence that it is the configurations of factors such as network size, trust density, network level competencies, goal consensus, mode of network governance, resource munificence, communication structure, formalization, system stability and support of the

Organizational Networks for Sustainable Development 129

community that play a role (Bryson et al., 2006; Provan & Kenis, 2008; Raab et al., 2015; Turrini et al., 2010). From a process perspective, certain network management tasks need to be fulfilled such as creating internal and external legitimacy, fostering commitment, managing conflicts, building leadership, adjusting the network governance to changing circumstances, ensuring and monitoring accountability and information provision (Bryson et al., 2006; Milward & Provan, 2006; Turrini et al., 2010). In addition, next to these tasks and processes for the management of networks, managers within the participating organizations have to adjust their activities as their organizations become members in organizational networks (management in networks). For example, managers need to monitor their organizations' role and contribution in the networks, build support for network engagement within their own organizations, deal with tensions between network activities and goals and those of their own organizations and stabilize or even institutionalize the network engagement within their own organizations to make them independent of specific individual persons (Milward & Provan, 2006).

(2) Type of the problem

Bodin (2017) suggests, that the type of problem influences what governance mode in case of engineered purpose oriented networks might work better: Coordination problems, where the actors "merely" have to acknowledge their interdependencies and plan and execute their activities are different from complex cooperation problems where limitations to or change of activities play a role and redistributive effects might occur. For low-risk coordination problems centralized networks, i.e. a lead organization mode, works better while dense collaborative structures, i.e. a shared governance mode, are better at addressing high-risk cooperation problems as they typically present themselves in wicked problems with high value divergence, uncertainty and complexity. However, as was discussed earlier, networks with a shared governance mode primarily work for relative small networks.

A different distinction is the one used by Milward and Provan (2006), who differentiate between learning and information diffusion networks, service delivery networks, problem solving networks and community capacity building networks. All these types appear in different areas of the sustainability goals and it has become clear that they require different structural configurations and processes. For example, a cross-sector partnership that represents an information diffusion network for health care information operates under very different conditions than a partnership whose goal it is to manage fish stock or water resources sustainably (problem solving network). Next to the different type and problems it is also the difference in underlying problem structures that creates different interdependencies between actors that need to be tackled differently in terms of designing the network governance and managing the processes (Hedlund et al., 2021).

For the partnerships for sustainability (SDG 17), that means that each partnership as an organizational network is specific. Not only do the 16 different goals represent very diverse policy areas, but the structure of a problem can be different within each goal itself with regard to the interdependencies of sub-problems and with other sustainable development goals as well as the number of actors with their interdependencies, goals and interests. In addition, the functions a partnership wants to fulfill can be different. Is it mainly to function as a network that distributes reliable and timely information

130 *Jörg Raab*

from and to the participants or does it want to design and implement solutions to tackle a problem? Does the network want to build problem solving capacity within a community so actors within the community can then autonomously tackle a sustainability problem or does the network want to deliver services itself? Problem structure, goals and function create different situational contexts and contingencies that require different governance modes and present different challenges for the instigation and the formation of a network. For example, a network whose members want to exchange information on the state of biodiversity can be run as a self-governed network even with a larger size. In contrast, increasing biodiversity with a larger number of members probably requires more coordination and a secretariat that takes on monitoring and coordination tasks as the network administrative organization.

(3) Development stage

The literature provides several life cycle models for organizational networks. Even though they do not always neatly follow the stages but rather repeat them or enter a recursive cycle of parts of the stages, there are clear differences in the evolution of these collaborative arrangements with regard to the situational factors. This in turn has consequences for how organizational networks work and function over time.

Ring and Van De Ven (1994) distinguish the phases of negotiation, commitment and execution. One could argue, however, that there is one stage that precedes the negotiation stage, since partners first have to be selected or self-select and convene before they can start to negotiate. In the negotiation stage, the participating parties develop joint expectations and goals, identify the interdependencies and tasks, distribute and allocate them. This stage therefore encompasses both formal bargaining and informal sense making. Part of formal bargaining is also, how activities and outcomes are monitored and assessed, who provides what resources as well as the decision-making structure, in short the design of the network and its governance structure. In the commitment stage, the terms and conditions of the governance structure are codified through either formal contracts or informal agreements among the parties. Very prominent are semi-legal agreements in the form of memoranda of understanding that exceed mere handshakes but do not reach the formality of legally binding contracts. In the execution stage, the agreements are implemented through coordinated organizational action to tackle the jointly defined problems and achieve the joint goals.

Gray and Purdy (2018) suggest a slightly more detailed framework with four phases: Convene, negotiate, implement the agreement and institutionalize the partnership with its structures and processes. While phases 1–3 are similar to the discussion in the previous paragraph on the basis of Ring and Van de Ven (1994), the institutionalization of the partnership receives more attention in a separate stage after the implementation. Depending on the duration and the necessary capabilities needed to achieve the joint goals and make partnerships sustainable, it is often required to make structures and processes both on the level of the partnership and the member organizations durable. This can happen through further formalization of organizational processes, budgets, monitoring rules and assessment procedures. Formalization can encompass the creation of functional profiles, the hiring of staff, setting the rules for rewards and information provision. Institutionalization also means altering practices and processes within the member organizations and making the functioning of the network independent of individual persons within the member organizations. However, there

Organizational Networks for Sustainable Development 131

is a big pitfall looming in this process. While some formalization might be necessary to create stability and make partnerships sustainable, participants have to be aware that making a partnership an own independent organization as the most extreme outcome, can have severe drawbacks as it seriously weakens some of the key features of networks that make them "lighter on their feet, i.e. more flexible than hierarchies" (Powell, 1990).

Whatever stage model we might apply, it becomes apparent that there are different developmental steps for organizational networks that require different managerial activities and different governance structures. In the convening stage, we will most likely see a shared governance approach, where all or at least the core partners will come together and then negotiate the terms and conditions. As we move to the implementation phase, the situational factors change and networks will move to implement and use the governance mode that is appropriate and necessary to effectively and efficiently achieve the network goals as discussed earlier. While in the beginning phases trust building is a central activity and the management of design will be important, the management of conflicts and accountability (Milward & Provan, 2006) will figure more prominently in later stages.

How Can Organizational Networks Be Evaluated?

Organizational networks are multi-level phenomena, i.e. they employ processes and activities on and have consequences for individual persons, teams and departments, individual organizations, networks as a hole and the wider communities they act in to address sustainability problems. Evaluation and assessment therefore can take place with regard to all these different levels. Provan and Milward (2001) suggest an evaluative framework that distinguishes between the community, the network and the level of the organization or participant. The key stakeholder groups and as a consequence, the assessment criteria are different for each level. For example, on the community level major stakeholders are the general public, politicians or funders. Assessment criteria are then the public perception of the development of the problem or changes in the incidence of the problem. On the network level, the primary stakeholders are the member organizations themselves. Criteria for that level can be network membership growth, ranges of services provided, integration and coordination of activities. For the level of the individual organization or participant, the main stakeholders are the member organizations' management and supervisory boards, staff members and individual clients. Evaluation criteria are for example enhanced legitimacy for the individual organization, resource acquisition or achievement of organizational goals.

In their evaluative framework, Emerson and Nabatchi (2015) distinguish between the unit of analysis and the performance level. Similar to Provan and Milward (2001), with regard to the level of analysis as the first dimension, they differentiate between the level of the participant organization, the network level or "collaborative governance regime" in their terminology and the "target goals" on what Provan and Milward (2001) called the "community level". These are goals that the network is trying to achieve with regard to the problem, condition, service or resource. Target goals vary considerably depending on their collective purpose, from environmental pollution problems to human made living conditions, safety or infrastructure issues (Emerson & Nabatchi, 2015). The second dimension, performance level, consists of "actions/outputs, outcomes and adaptation". Collaborative actions can be outputs in

132 *Jörg Raab*

the form of "educating constituents or the public, enacting policy measures (new laws or regulations), marshaling external resources, deploying staff, siting and permitting facilities, building or cleaning up, carrying out new management practices, monitoring implementation, or enforcing compliance" (Emerson & Nabatchi, 2015, p. 724). The second level is outcomes, i.e. results with regard to the change of problem conditions, i.e. closing the gap between the factual and the desired situation. The third level "adaptation" is systemic transformative changes in the collaborative governance regime/the network itself, which can be understood as adaptive responses to the outcomes of collaborative actions. For example, this would be the case, if the understanding between the parties and their coordination capacity in a socio-ecological system is positively altered. The two dimensions and three levels form a 3x3 table, in which each of the nine cells form an evaluative focus. For example the cell output/organization focuses on efficiency. Outcomes and network level focuses on external legitimacy, while outcomes and target goals would be effectiveness and adaptation/target goal focuses on the sustainability of the network (Emerson & Nabatchi, 2015, p. 724). It is vital to consciously distinguish these dimensions and levels when evaluating organizational networks, since it provides a more fine grained analytical framework that helps to identify shortcomings and to more clearly and better target subsequent interventions.

Next to the different levels and types of effects, that need to be taken into account when evaluating networks and partnerships, it is important to take time seriously. Networks and partnerships are no quick fix for complex sustainability problems. Building them takes time. In addition, it often takes years until any material effects of network activity (as with any other intervention in complex systems) are visible due to the time lag between interventions and effects. For example, the time required to restore biodiversity and bring back fish stocks in marine reserves may take years if not decades (Claudet et al., 2008). However, many partnerships are often characterized by short-time horizons of actors. Especially in areas where transformative change is needed like in the energy transition, longer time horizons are necessary or compensatory mechanisms have to be introduced for actors with shorter-time horizons (Horan, 2019).

Berrone et al. (2019) present a framework for the evaluation of public–private partnerships contributing to the sustainable development goals, which can also be applied more broadly to partnerships in general. They suggest to focus on six dimensions: (1) engagement of stakeholders; (2) increasing access to social interest services to the population; (3) scalability and replicability, i.e. the extent to which a partnership can become sustainable and applied in other contexts; (4) inclusiveness, i.e. the level of coverage that a partnership offers to diverse stakeholders; (5) economic impact, i.e. the impact of the partnership on the economy; and (6) resilience and environment, i.e. the ability of the partnership to build resilient and ecological communities. In this framework, the focus is clearly on the output and adaptation performance levels as well as the network and community levels/target goals and therefore very much focused on legitimacy, effectiveness, viability and sustainability. The organizational level is not looked at. As discussed earlier, it is not possible to focus on all levels and dimensions simultaneously all the time, but one should be aware of them and make conscious and well-argued choices. As discussed earlier about the motives of organizations to participate in networks, the question of rewards for the organizations is not trivial and can seriously hamper or even endanger the existence of a network in the long run.

Organizational Networks for Sustainable Development 133

One important complicating factor for the evaluation of networks in the case of complex social performance and long-term environmental sustainability in the group of wicked problems is that empirical contexts in which network activities take place are constantly in flux. Actors move in and out, the power dynamics between actors changes, the problem structure shifts and exogenous shocks might occur like violent conflicts, change in governments, natural disasters, etc. In a recent study on project networks in the area of humanitarian and development aid efforts, Angeli et al. (2020) argue that networks in such contexts face a performance paradox as they face difficulties first to reliably evaluate social performance, second to establish causal links between the network outputs, the outcomes and the wider community impact and third to deal with the tensions between social and financial performance. In order to deal with this paradox and with potential performance gaps, they develop adaptive responses in the form of adaptive monitoring and evaluative practices, collective goal setting and continuous renegotiation of aspiration levels. Part of this response is that "a fluid process of negotiating, monitoring and assessment tools emerges within the network, which dynamically keeps stakeholders on-board" (Angeli et al., 2020, p. 169). In addition, goals are negotiated and re-negotiated if circumstances change with the donor organizations and between the local and global levels of network organizations, which leads to a dynamic and collective adjustment of aspiration levels (Angeli et al., 2020).

The short overview in this section has demonstrated that we can assess networks on the basis of many different criteria. In the end, they are norms or "elements of value" (Simon, 1976) which we use as benchmarks to mirror the empirical outputs and outcomes. Norms are inherently normative, i.e. we cannot scientifically "proof" why one criterion/norm is better than the other. It is possible though to argue why certain criteria make sense and are appropriate in certain situations and contexts to engage in a realist evaluation that shows "what works for whom, in what circumstances, in what respects and how" (Fletcher et al., 2016).

However, even if we can identify these effects, it is often difficult to create a causal link between the network formation, its activity, the intervention and the effects, since complex sustainability problems are influenced by many factors with often difficult to understand interdependencies and feedback loops between various sub problems and actors. For many networks, it therefore remains a challenge to continuously and clearly proof their value to internal and external stakeholders, hereby safeguarding their internal and external legitimacy, even though there might be a general understanding that they are having a positive effect on dealing with a problem.

Discussion

Organizations come together in organizational networks to solve common problems, strive to fulfill shared purposes and achieve joint goals. However, working with other organizations beyond one's own organizational boundaries is "neither easy nor straightforward" (Gray & Purdy, 2018, p. 68). The idea that, if well meaning people are only willing to work together, good things will happen, is certainly sympathetic but neglects the complexities of these collaborative organizational arrangements. Willingness to cooperate or even to collaborate is very important, if not a necessary condition, but research on networks in general and in the area of sustainability in particular has demonstrated that it is certainly not sufficient. The high expectations

134 Jörg Raab

that are connected with such organizational arrangements are demonstrated in the SDG 17 "Partnerships for the Goals". One can therefore argue that the organizational concept of partnerships and networks is probably one of the most applied and impactful in practice from all the concepts discussed in this book, since it made it into the top level of the global framework on sustainability. Organizational networks have become a crucial part of the toolbox to advance sustainability in the different areas of the SDGs but they are certainly no panacea. Compared to markets and hierarchies as the other two main governance forms (Powell, 1990), networks are more complex and require more effort and conscious coordination by individual persons as well as organizations. One important finding from the research that many practitioners will also recognize is that partnerships and networks are frequently initiated with great enthusiasm and hope but that organizations and individuals often lose interest and commitment when the envisioned benefits and gains are not quickly realized (Gray & Purdy, 2018, p. 68). In fact, as stated earlier, setting up partnerships and being able to observe tangible results often takes years.

Increasing organizational coupling also enhances the chance that inherent tensions due to different organizational cultures, institutional fields and goals will become more pronounced and organizations find it difficult to address them in a productive manner. As a consequence, "many partnerships succumb to collaborative inertia, that is, they experience slow progress and truncate their efforts without any tangible outcomes (Huxham & Vangen, 2004)" (Gray & Purdy, 2018, p. 69). In fact, there is some indirect and anecdotal evidence that the majority of organizational networks do not fully achieve their self-declared goals. The reasons for that are manifold and it is important to recognize them in order to come to a realistic understanding of collaborative arrangements that will hopefully enable us to use them in contexts and in ways that will help us in making progress towards achieving the sustainability goals. After all, many of the problems are predictable and can be at least mitigated if they are anticipated and managed appropriately (Gray & Purdy, 2018, p. 69). In this context, it is also important to understand when *not* to use organizational networks as an organizational tool. One should for example be careful to use them, if the problem is not so complex after all and can be tackled either by an individual organization albeit with input from other organizations, jointly by two organizations or by creating incentives for a market response. In order to make progress in the application of organizational networks, one should therefore keep in mind, that,

1   . . . as with all organizational forms, their functioning and effectiveness is situational.
2   . . . they require more attention, energy and effort than markets or hierarchies.
3   . . . even though they form a response to complex problems they often add complexity themselves.
4   . . . decision times can be long.
5   . . . they are often difficult to sustain after initial enthusiasm.
6   . . . costs, benefits and rewards are often unclear and lagged. This makes it difficult to demonstrate their effectiveness with detrimental consequence for their legitimacy.
7   . . . they need to be managed on the network level *and* the organizational level (management *of* and management *in* networks) (Milward & Provan, 2006).

Network management is demanding. Networks are still often managed as if they are organizations.

8 ... power, interests and conflicts do not disappear in organizational networks, but can actually become more pronounced and need to be managed.

9 ... decision making can be intransparent and that networks potentially create a systemic conflict with decision making in representative democracies.

From a developmental policy perspective, there has been some hope that organizational networks in the form of cross-sector partnerships composed of NGOs, businesses and some state organizations might be able to compensate for weak state capacity and even contribute to the strengthening of that capacity to better tackle problems as reflected in the SDGs. This hope is based on the idea that know-how, creativity, ideas and resources can be transferred from non-state actors to state actors or at least be used in making up for the lack of state capacity to some extent supported by international donor organizations. As discussed earlier, there is some evidence that such a strategy might not work and that state capacity is essential to complement or even make NGO and business activity possible and a necessary condition to multiply their effects through cross-sector partnerships. One of the reasons could be that in strong state environments it is the state actors that often provide the legitimacy and anchor points through their lead organization role in such partnerships that state organizations in weak state contexts are not able to fulfil.

Conclusion

Organizational networks for sustainability come in many shapes and forms and with many different labels. Common to all of them is the idea that several organizations cooperate or collaborate in order to tackle a joint problem or achieve a shared purpose and joint goals that none of the organizations could achieve on their own. These organizational arrangements have become a crucial part of the sustainability toolbox as documented by their prominent status as the SDG 17 "Partnerships for the Goals" and in many policy documents and funding schemes of major donor organizations. It is therefore no surprise that they can be found in many different areas related to the sustainability goals, from alleviating poverty and hunger, improving health, addressing climate change, to managing the supply of clean water and preserving fish stocks. Therefore, they clearly represent an important, if not the only possible organizational response to complex (policy) problems with regard to sustainability albeit of course in combination with regulation and state activity. However, despite their ubiquity, they are no panacea and are very demanding for organizations and individuals alike. Engaging multiple organizations can actually add more complexity to the problem situation. Therefore, they should mainly be used for truly complex and not for complicated or simple problems (Westley et al., 2007). They require manifold management activities that are different from hierarchical organizations. When managing and evaluating them, one has to be aware of the multiple levels they operate and have impact on. Their development takes time and they are therefore no short term fix. Effects are regularly visible only after some time and often difficult to exactly attribute to specific network actions. They are frequently set up with great enthusiasm by actors who realize that they are interdependent with other actors. These actors recognize the need to collaborate in order

136 *Jörg Raab*

to make progress towards achieving the sustainability goals. Making organizational networks sustainable themselves and keeping them flexible and agile, however, is a challenge. Despite all these challenges and drawbacks, though, they are currently our best hope with regard to organizational forms when complex problems must be tackled. The most important question as we move forward is therefore not so much whether they work or not but when and in which contexts and in combination with which other organizational and governance forms as well as government engagement and intervention.

References

Albareda, L., & Waddock, S. (2018). Networked CSR governance: A whole network approach to meta-governance. *Business and Society, 57*(4), 636–675. https://doi.org/10.1177/00076 50315624205

Alvarez, G., Pilbeam, C., & Wilding, R. (2010). Nestlé Nespresso AAA sustainable quality program: An investigation into the governance dynamics in a multi-stakeholder supply chain network. *Supply Chain Management, 15*(2), 165–182. https://doi.org/10.1108/13598 541011028769

Angeli, F., Raab, J., & Oerlemans, L. (2020). Adaptive responses to performance gaps in project networks. In T. Braun & J. Lampel (Eds.), *Tensions and paradoxes in temporary organizing* (Vol. 67, pp. 153–178). Emerald Publishing Limited. https://doi.org/10.1108/ S0733-558X20200000067013

Berrone, P., Ricart, J. E., Duch, A. I., Bernardo, V., Salvador, J., Peña, J. P., & Planas, M. R. (2019). EASIER: An evaluation model for public-private partnerships contributing to the sustainable development goals. *Sustainability (Switzerland), 11*(8), 2339. https://doi. org/10.3390/su11082339

Bodin, Ö. (2017). Collaborative environmental governance: Achieving collective action in social-ecological systems. *Science, 357*(6352). https://doi.org/10.1126/science.aan1114

Bryson, J. M., Crosby, B. C., & Stone, M. M. (2006). The design and implementation of cross-sector collaborations: Propositions from the literature. *Public Administration Review, 66*(Suppl. 1), 44–55. https://doi.org/10.1111/j.1540-6210.2006.00665.x

Carboni, J. L., Saz-Carranza, A., Raab, J., & Isett, K. R. (2019). Taking dimensions of purpose-oriented networks seriously. *Perspectives on Public Management and Governance, 2*(3), 187–201. https://doi.org/10.1093/ppmgov/gvz011

Cardoso de Oliveira, M. C., Machado, M. C., Chiappetta Jabbour, C. J., & Lopes de Sousa Jabbour, A. B. (2019). Paving the way for the circular economy and more sustainable supply chains: Shedding light on formal and informal governance instruments used to induce green networks. *Management of Environmental Quality: An International Journal, 30*(5), 1095–1113. https://doi.org/10.1108/MEQ-01-2019-0005

Castells, M. (2010). *The rise of the network society* (2nd ed.). Wiley-Blackwell.

Claudet, J., Osenberg, C. W., Benedetti-Cecchi, L., Domenici, P., García-Charton, J. A., Pérez-Ruzafa, Á., Badalamenti, F., Bayle-Sempere, J., Brito, A., Bulleri, F., Culioli, J. M., Dimech, M., Falcón, J. M., Guala, I., Milazzo, M., Sánchez-Meca, J., Somerfield, P. J., Stobart, B., Vandeperre, F., . . . Planes, S. (2008). Marine reserves: Size and age do matter. *Ecology Letters, 11*(5), 481–489. https://doi.org/10.1111/j.1461-0248.2008.01166.x

Danken, T., Dribbisch, K., & Lange, A. (2016). Studying wicked problems forty years on: Towards a synthesis of a fragmented debate. *Der Moderne Staat – Zeitschrift Für Public Policy, Recht Und Management, 9*(1), 15–33. https://doi.org/10.3224/dms.v9i1.23638

Dentoni, D., Bitzer, V., & Schouten, G. (2018). Harnessing wicked problems in multi-stakeholder partnerships. *Journal of Business Ethics, 150*(2), 333–356. https://doi.org/10.1007/ s10551-018-3858-6

DiMaggio, P. J., & Powell, W. W. (2000). The iron cage revisited institutional isomorphism and collective rationality in organizational fields. *Advances in Strategic Management, 17*, 143–166. https://doi.org/10.1016/S0742-3322(00)17011-1

Doz, Y. L., Olk, P. M., & Ring, P. S. (2000). Formation processes of R&D consortia: Which path to take? Where does it lead? *Strategic Management Journal.* https://onlinelibrary.wiley.com/doi/10.1002/(SICI)1097-0266(200003)21:3%3C239::AID-SMJ97%3E3.0.CO;2-K

The Economist. (2019, November 28). Economists are rethinking the numbers on inequality. *The Economist.* www.economist.com/briefing/2019/11/28/economists-are-rethinking-the-numbers-on-inequality

Eisenhardt, K. M., Graebner, M. E., & Sonenshein, S. (2016). Grand challenges and inductive methods: Rigor without rigor mortis. *Academy of Management Journal, 59*(4), 1113–1123. https://doi.org/10.5465/amj.2016.4004

Emerson, K., & Nabatchi, T. (2015). Evaluating the productivity of collaborative governance regimes: A performance matrix. *Public Performance and Management Review, 38*(4), 717–747. https://doi.org/10.1080/15309576.2015.1031016

Engler, J. O., Abson, D. J., & von Wehrden, H. (2021). The coronavirus pandemic as an analogy for future sustainability challenges. *Sustainability Science, 16*(1), 317–319. https://doi.org/10.1007/s11625-020-00852-4

Ferraro, F., Etzion, D., & Gehman, J. (2015). Tackling grand challenges pragmatically: Robust action revisited. *Organization Studies, 36*(3), 363–390. https://doi.org/10.1177/0170840614563742

Fichter, M., Helfen, M., & Sydow, J. (2011). Employment relations in global production networks: Initiating transfer of practices via union involvement. *Human Relations, 64*(4), 599–622. https://doi.org/10.1177/0018726710396245

Fletcher, A., Jamal, F., Moore, G., Evans, R. E., Murphy, S., & Bonell, C. (2016). Realist complex intervention science: Applying realist principles across all phases of the medical research council framework for developing and evaluating complex interventions. *Evaluation, 22*(3), 286–303. https://doi.org/10.1177/1356389016652743

Freeman, R. E., Harrison, J. S., Wicks, A. C., Parmar, B., & de Colle, S. (2010). Stakeholder theory: The state of the art. In *Stakeholder theory: The state of the art.* Cambridge University Press. https://doi.org/10.1017/CBO9780511815768

Gavi the Vaccine Allliance. (n.d.). *About our alliance.* Retrieved June 8, 2021, from www.gavi.org/our-alliance/about

George, G., Howard-Grenville, J., Joshi, A., & Tihanyi, L. (2016). Understanding and tackling societal grand challenges through management research. *Academy of Management Journal, 59*(6), 1880–1895. https://doi.org/10.5465/amj.2016.4007

Gray, B., & Purdy, J. (2018). Collaborating for our future: Multistakeholder partnerships for solving complex problems. In *Collaborating for our future: Multistakeholder partnerships for solving complex problems.* Oxford University Press. https://doi.org/10.1093/oso/9780198782841.001.0001

Head, B. W. (2008). Wicked problems in public policy. *Public Policy, 3*(2), 101–118.

Hedlund, J., Bodin, Ö., & Nohrstedt, D. (2021). Policy issue interdependency and the formation of collaborative networks. *People and Nature, 3*(1), 236–250. https://doi.org/10.1002/pan3.10170

Helfen, M., Schüßler, E., & Sydow, J. (2018). How can employment relations in global value networks be managed towards social responsibility? *Human Relations, 71*(12), 1640–1665. https://doi.org/10.1177/0018726718757060

Horan, D. (2019). A new approach to partnerships for SDG transformations. *Sustainability (Switzerland), 11*(18), 4947. https://doi.org/10.3390/su11184947

Human, S. E., & Provan, K. G. (2000). Legitimacy building in the evolution of small-firm multilateral networks: A comparative study of success and demise. *Administrative Science Quarterly, 45*(2), 327–365. https://doi.org/10.2307/2667074

138 *Jörg Raab*

Huxham, C., & Vangen, S. (2004). Doing things collaboratively: Realizing the advantage or succumbing to inertia? *IEEE Engineering Management Review, 32*(4), 11–20. https://doi.org/10.1109/EMR.2004.25132

Kamya, C., Shearer, J., Asiimwe, G., Carnahan, E., Salisbury, N., Waiswa, P., Brinkerhoff, J., & Hozumi, D. (2017). Evaluating global health partnerships: A case study of a gavi HPV vaccine application process in Uganda. *International Journal of Health Policy and Management, 6*(6), 327–338. https://doi.org/10.15171/ijhpm.2016.137

Kapucu, N., & Beaudet, S. (2020). Network governance for collective action in implementing United Nations sustainable development goals. *Administrative Sciences, 10*(4), 100. https://doi.org/10.3390/admsci10040100

Kenis, P., Janowicz-Panjaitan, M., & Cambré, B. (2009). Temporary organizations: Prevalence, logic and effectiveness. In *Temporary organizations: Prevalence, logic and effectiveness*. Edward Elgar Publishing Ltd. https://doi.org/10.4337/9781849802154

Kenis, P., & Raab, J. (2020a). The multiplex democratic state as a response to complexity and uncertainty? In *Politische komplexität, governance von innovationen und policy-netzwerke* (pp. 37–50). Springer Fachmedien Wiesbaden. https://doi.org/10.1007/978-3-658-30914-5_5

Kenis, P., & Raab, J. (2020b). Back to the future: Using organization design theory for effective organizational networks. *Perspectives on Public Management and Governance, 3*(2), 109–123. https://doi.org/10.1093/ppmgov/gvaa005

Lavie, D. (2006). The competitive advantage of interconnected firms: An extension of the resource-based view. *Academy of Management Review, 31*(3), 638–658. https://doi.org/10.5465/AMR.2006.21318922

Lazzarini, S. G., Pongeluppe, L. S., Ito, N. C., Oliveira, F. de M., & Ovanessoff, A. (2020). Public capacity, plural forms of collaboration, and the performance of public initiatives: A configurational approach. *Journal of Public Administration Research and Theory, 30*(4), 579–595. https://doi.org/10.1093/jopart/muaa007

Levin, K., Cashore, B., Bernstein, S., Auld, G., Levin, K., Cashore, B., Bernstein, S., & Auld, G. (2012). Overcoming the tragedy of super wicked problems: Constraining our future selves to ameliorate global climate change. *Policy Sciences, 45*, 123–152. https://doi.org/10.1007/s11077-012-9151-0

Lubell, M., Robins, G., & Wang, P. (2014). Network structure and institutional complexity in an ecology of water management games. *Ecology and Society, 19*(4). https://doi.org/10.5751/ES-06880-190423

Milward, B. H., & Provan, K. G. (2006). *A manager's guide to choosing and using collaborative networks*. Networks and Partnerships Series.

Mirvis, P. H., & Worley, C. G. (2014). Organizing for sustainability: Why networks and partnerships? In *Building networks and partnerships* (Vol. 3, pp. 1–34). Emerald Group Publishing Limited. https://doi.org/10.1108/S2045-0605(2013)0000003005

Oliver, A. L., & Ebers, M. (1998). Networking network studies: An analysis of conceptual configurations in the study of inter-organizational relationships. *Organization Studies, 19*(4), 549–583. https://doi.org/10.1177/017084069801900402

Oliver, C. (1991). Strategic responses to institutional processes. *Academy of Management Review, 16*(1), 145–179. https://doi.org/10.5465/amr.1991.4279002

Ostrom, E. (1990). *Governing the commons: The evolution of institutions for collective action*. Cambridge University Press. https://doi.org/10.1017/cbo9780511807763

Ostrom, E. (2009). A general framework for analyzing sustainability of social-ecological systems. *Science, 325*(5939), 419–422. https://doi.org/10.1126/science.1172133

Ostrom, E. (2015). *Governerning the commons: The evolution of institutions for collective action* (2nd ed.). Cambridge University Press.

O'Toole, L. J. (1997). Treating networks seriously: Practical and research-based agendas in public administration. *Public Administration Review, 57*(1), 45. https://doi.org/10.2307/976691

Pfeffer, J., & Salancik, G. R. (1978). *The external control of organizations: A resource dependence perspective (Stanford business classics): Pfeffer, Jeffrey, Salancik, Gerald R.: 9780804747899: Amazon.com: Books.* Harper and Row.

Poocharoen, O., & Sovacool, B. K. (2012). Exploring the challenges of energy and resources network governance. *Energy Policy, 42*, 409–418. https://doi.org/10.1016/j.enpol.2011.12.005

Popp, J. K., & Casebeer, A. (2015). Be careful what you ask for: Things policy-makers should know before mandating networks. *Healthcare Management Forum, 28*(6), 230–235. https://doi.org/10.1177/0840470415599113

Popp, J., MacKean, G. L., Casebeer, A., Milward, H. B., & Lindstrom, R. R. (2014). *Inter-organizational networks: A critical review of the literature to Inform practice.* Report of the IBM Center for the Business of Government. Retrieved from: http://www.businessofgovernment.org/report/inter-organizational-networks-review-literature-inform-practice

Powell, W. W. (1990). Neither market nor hierarchy: Network forms of organization. *Research in Organizational Behavior, 12*, 295–336.

Provan, K. G., Fish, A., & Sydow, J. (2007). Interorganizational networks at the network nevel: A review of the empirical literature on whole networks. *Journal of Management, 33*(3), 479–516. https://doi.org/10.1177/0149206307302554

Provan, K. G., & Kenis, P. (2008). Modes of network governance: Structure, management, and effectiveness. *Journal of Public Administration Research and Theory, 18*(2), 229–252. https://doi.org/10.1093/jopart/mum015

Provan, K. G., & Milward, H. B. (2001). Do networks really work? A framework for evaluating public-sector organizational networks. *Public Administration Review, 61*(4), 414–423. https://doi.org/10.1111/0033-3352.00045

Raab, J., & Kenis, P. N. (2009). Heading toward a society of networks: Empirical developments and theoretical challenges. *Journal of Management Inquiry, 18*(3), 198–210. https://doi.org/10.1177/1056492609337493

Raab, J., Mannak, R. S., & Cambré, B. (2015). Combining structure, governance, and context: A configurational approach to network effectiveness. *Journal of Public Administration Research and Theory, 25*(2), 479–511. https://doi.org/10.1093/jopart/mut039

Raworth, K. (2017). *Doughnut economics: Seven ways to think like a 21st-century economist.* Random House Business Books.

Ring, P. S., & Van De Ven, A. H. (1994). Developmental processes of cooperative interorganizational relationships. *Academy of Management Review, 19*(1), 90–118. https://doi.org/10.5465/amr.1994.9410122009

Ritchie, H., & Roser, M. (2020, March 2). CO_2 *emissions.* https://ourworldindata.org/co2-emissions

Rittel, H. W. J., & Webber, M. M. (1973). Dilemmas in a general theory of planning. *Policy Sciences, 4*(2), 155–169. https://doi.org/10.1007/BF01405730

Roberts, N. (2000). Wicked problems and network approaches to resolution. *International Public Management Review: Electronic Journal, 1*(1), 1–19. www.ipmr.net

Sayles, J. S., & Baggio, J. A. (2017). Who collaborates and why: Assessment and diagnostic of governance network integration for salmon restoration in Puget Sound, USA. *Journal of Environmental Management, 186*(Pt 1), 64–78. https://doi.org/10.1016/j.jenvman.2016.09.085

Schneider, M., Scholz, J., Lubell, M., Mindruta, D., & Edwardsen, M. (2003). Building consensual institutions: Networks and the national estuary program. *American Journal of Political Science, 47*(1), 143–158. https://doi.org/10.1111/1540-5907.00010

Segato, F., & Raab, J. (2019). Mandated network formation. *International Journal of Public Sector Management, 32*(2), 191–206. https://doi.org/10.1108/IJPSM-01-2018-0018

Shipilov, A., & Gawer, A. (2020). Integrating research on interorganizational networks and ecosystems. *Academy of Management Annals, 14*(1), 92–121. https://doi.org/10.5465/annals.2018.0121

Simon, H. A. (1976). *Administrative behavior* (2nd ed.). New York Press.

Thompson, J. D. (1967). *Organizations in action; social science bases of administrative theory*. McGraw-Hill.

Turrini, A., Cristofoli, D., Frosini, F., & Nasi, G. (2010). Networking literature about determinants of network effectiveness. *Public Administration*, 88(2), 528–550. https://doi.org/10.1111/j.1467-9299.2009.01791.x

Westley, F., Patton, M. Q., & Zimmerman, B. (2007). *Getting to maybe: How the world is changed*. Vintage.

Zaheer, A., & Bell, G. G. (2005). Benefitting from network position: Firm capabilities, structural holes, and performance. *Strategic Management Journal*, 26, 1398–1438.

7 Impact Investing and New Social Funding

History, Actors and Promise

Laura Toschi and Ashley Metz

Introduction

The idea of "investing with the intention to generate positive, measurable social and environmental impact alongside a financial return,"[1] has gained momentum in recent years, though investing with various moral or at least non-financial principles has been around for a long time. The term "impact investing" emerged in a 2007 meeting of the Rockefeller Foundation.[2] Today, the term defines a group of organizations interested in enabling businesses' products and services that aim to make progress on social or environmental issues. The field brings together actors from philanthropic foundations interested in generating a return, as well as private investors interested in achieving a non-financial mission. These actors intend to address growing social and environmental challenges by deploying different forms of investment, not exclusively oriented to the generation of profit and financial returns (Arena et al., 2015; Calderini et al., 2018) and to encourage the development of companies with the objective to satisfy stakeholders, not only shareholders, at the expense of any other stakeholder (Dees & Anderson, 2003; Schaltegger et al., 2018).

The development of the impact investing phenomenon is part of a general rethinking of existing financial models in order to create a more sustainable economic system from a social and environmental point of view, aimed at offering a response to new challenges such as climate change, the aging of the population, the emergence of the "new poor" and the enormous polarization of income. As such, impact investing has captured the attention of both policy makers and researchers.

According to the Global Impact Investing Network (GIIN), since the introduction of impact investing in 2007, there are 1,340 impact investment organizations managing around US$502 billion in impact investing assets worldwide (GIIN, 2019a) and, in 2018, 13,000 investments, representing an overall value of more than US$33 billion, were financed. In 2020, the European Commission presented a communication entitled "A Strong Social Europe for Just Transitions"[3] highlighting the importance to define an ambitious social policy for implementing the European Pillar of Social Rights (that is, 20 principles and rights essential for fair and effective labour markets and welfare systems) and delivering progress at EU, national, regional and local level. The European Commission has also launched the Invest EU Programme[4] to support with approximately €50 billion in four policy areas: sustainable infrastructure, digitization, social entrepreneurship and social investment and skills. Other EU-level policies, funding programmes, and initiatives developed between 2010 and 2020 are the Social Investment Package (SIP) and Innovation Union Initiatives, the Social Business

DOI: 10.4324/9780429243165-8

This chapter has been made available under a CC-BY-NC 4.0 license.

Initiative (SBI), the EU Programme for Employment and Social Innovation (EaSI), the G8 Social Impact Investing Taskforce (SIIT), the European Fund for Strategic Investments (EFSI), the Social Impact Accelerator of the European Investment Bank (EIB), the EIB Social Impact Bond Co-investment Fund and many others.

In the academic literature, impact investing is still understudied (Hockerts et al., 2020). Much work has investigated the field's emergence with a focus on definitions (Höchstädter & Scheck, 2015), actor types (Mair & Hehenberger, 2014); and ideas that came to define and shape the field (Hehenberger et al., 2019; Moody, 2008; Nicholls, 2010). Others have investigated investment vehicles such as social impact bonds (Neyland, 2018), in which impact investors play a role. There have been fascinating studies that highlight regional relationships to finance, such as the role of the state in developing the field in China, (Yan & Ferraro, 2016). In a related stream, Arjaliès (2010), investigated the role of the Socially Responsible Investment (SRI) movement in changing mainstream asset management in France. Yet, much academic research is still fairly descriptive or written for a management audience (Hockerts et al., 2020)

In this chapter, we first introduce readers to the idea of impact investing and how its definition has evolved in the literature. Next, we introduce the organizational actors involved and the instruments they use. We conclude with a discussion of delivering on the promise of impact investing.

History and Definition of the Field

Impact Investing as Blended Value

The link between social impact and finance is not a modern idea. In one of the oldest examples, banking principles related to Islam date back to the 7th century and the early days of the religion. In England, 17th centuries' Quakers were among the first to align their investment with values in which they believed. In the 19th century, Shaker congregations in the United States of America financed businesses aligned with their religious values. More recently, 1970s' environmental concerns headed by Rachel Carson's Silent Spring book aimed at moving investments for the conservation of the planet harmed by pollution. In different forms, economic and social impact combined on the global market stage for centuries. However, a greater expansion of this investment strategy and its spread in the mainstream financial world has occurred in the last two decades with the introduction of the term *impact investing*, coined at the Rockefeller Foundation's Bellagio Center, on Lake Como, in 2007 (Rodin & Brandenburg, 2014), to identify investments that pursue the dual objective of generating both financial performance and social/environmental impact, generally labelled as blended value (Emerson, 2003).

The concept of *blended value* captures the idea that value is an indivisible integration of economic, social and environmental returns from investments (Emerson, 2003) and, thus, represents a new investment framework to support organizations with a focus on the value created not only in terms of economic returns, but also for people wellbeing and the conservation of the planet (Bugg-Levine & Emerson, 2011)

As suggested by Bose et al. (2019), it is possible to define a continuum of investment types (see Figure 7.1) with two extremes in terms of value generation: one oriented to the exclusive search for social impact (philanthropy) and the other focused totally on

	Philanthropy	Social investment	Program related investment	Impact investment	ESG investment	SRI	Traditional investment
Value generation	Social returns			Blended value (Social and economic return)	Economic return		
Actors	Foundations No-Profit Organizations			Foundations Venture Capital Private Equity Banks	Venture Capital Private Equity Banks		
Instrument	Grants			Equity Debt Subsidized debt	Equity Debt		

Figure 7.1 The continuum of impact investment types.

Source: Adapted by Bose et al. (2019)

obtaining economic and financial returns (traditional investment). Blended finance is positioned in the middle of this continuum, being geared towards generating a combination of the two different forms of value. The other existing investment approaches in the financial ecosystem emphasize more or less the generation of one type of value to the detriment of the other with different levels of intensity. In particular, *philanthropy* is purely social, without expectation of financial returns, *social investment* generates social impact first and, secondarily, may consider some financial returns, *program-related investments* generate social impact and expect at least a return of the principal. On the opposite side, *traditional investment* aims to maximize financial returns, *socially responsible investment* (SRI) excludes socially and environmental questionable companies and refers to an investor's moral obligation, while *ESG investment* focus on companies that track environmental (E), social (S) and governance (G) performance metrics, thus excluding in their screening process investments in those sectors that do not comply with ESG criteria (i.e. tobacco industry). Finally, *impact investors* are recognized as being those actors more inclined to generate blended value, because they typically emphasize the condition of positive screens, that is, investors' search for organizations that pursue a positive social impact (Brest & Born, 2013; Cooper, 2016; Harji & Jackson, 2012) and, at the same time, search for economic returns in order to redeploy the capital in successive rounds of investment and support the generation of measurable social impact (Block et al., 2021; Roundy, Brockman et al., 2017).

A further elaboration of the concept of impact investing has been provided by the EVPA (European Venture Philanthropy Association) which has proposed a distinction between investing *for* impact and investing *with* impact. The main difference between the two complementary approaches is that, on the one hand, investors *for* impact are capital providers that take risks that most others are not prepared to take, put the social organisation, the social innovation and the end beneficiaries at the centre, are highly engaged for the long-term and provide extensive non-financial support. Investors for impact are, hence, those that apply more extensively the venture philanthropy

144   *Laura Toschi and Ashley Metz*

approach. On the other hand, investors *with* impact are able to provide higher amount of resources, but, even if they consider the achievement of social impact, they have the need to guarantee a certain financial return on their investments. As a consequence, the level of risk they are ready to undertake is often limited.

The Evolution of the Impact Investing Definition

Despite the attempts to categorize and distinguish the various forms of financing, the boundaries between the aforementioned categories are blurred and the lack of a clear demarcation between approaches makes it difficult to provide a precise definition of the phenomenon of impact investing and the actors involved. While in the first period or birth of impact investing, the need to have a univocal definition was not a central topic, subsequently, with the exponential growth of the phenomenon, great attention has begun to be paid to the defining problem as its lack represents a barrier to the development of the field. The failure to come up with a shared and precise definition of what an impact investment means has let emerged *impact washing* purposes: actors moved by the goal to maintain their competitiveness on the market, by opportunistically leveraging on the sustainability trend, feed a bubble that diverge from the social and transformative mission which should, on the contrary, be the essential objective of these investments (Harji & Jackson, 2012; Höchstädter & Scheck, 2015).

Furthermore, the term evolved differently in the United States and in Europe, and the American perspective tends to assume that impact investing definitely involves a financial return, whereas the European perspective has included philanthropic or below-market return investing with a hands-on investment style. In addition, the dominant ideas underpinning the field of impact investing in Europe have evolved and solidified over time (Hehenberger et al., 2019). In Europe, ideas around the field's ambition, focus of investment, and how decisions were to be made, were in flux from around 2000 to the present day (see Hehenberger et al., 2019 for a history).

From a global academic perspective, the term impact investing has followed an evolution over time and it will evolve further as more research will be performed. In the following section, we outline three phases that follow *definitions* based in global literature, rather than particular regions. The phases proposed are summarized on the base of the publication date of the academic works reviewed (in practice, there is potential overlap). All the definitions highlight the combination of social value creation and maximization of social return on investment, even though the degree of return on investment varies between different definitions.

Phase 1

In the initial phase, impact investing was defined in a general and broad manner, often imprecisely classified as *social finance* (Moore et al., 2012; Rexhepi, 2016; Rizzi et al., 2018). Definitions mainly focused on differentiating impact investing from charity and venture capital (Battilana et al., 2012). Impact investing firms were recognized as those investors adopting venture capitalist strategies by investing in organizations with a clear social mission and whose primary purpose is to create social value (Geobey et al., 2012; Moore et al., 2012). This definition approximately highlights the importance of social and commercial goals (Alex Nicholls, 2010; Rangan et al.,

2011). However, it draws many similarities with other investment forms without a precise distinction that is, instead, required to demarcate the field from others.

Phase 2

Subsequently, the distinction in respect to other forms (like venture philanthropy, socially responsible investing, microfinance, and social impact bonds) becomes clearer in particular by highlighting the need of intention in creating social impact, high engagement, tailored financing, extensive support, organizational capacity building and performance measurement (Achleitner et al., 2011; Glanzel & Scheuerle, 2016; Hebb, 2013; Lazzarini et al., 2014; Rajan et al., 2014; Tekula & Shah, 2016; Weber, 2016). In particular, the Global Impact Investing Network (GIIN, 2013), reads: "Impact investments are investments made into companies, organisations, and funds with the intention to generate measurable social and environmental impact alongside a financial return". This definition is rooted in the principles of intentionality and measurability (Höchstädter & Scheck, 2015). *Intentionality* means inseparably incorporating the search for the solution into the business model, consciously accepting to sacrifice part of the economic result. By declaring the intention of generating impact, impact investing can be categorized as action-oriented, not only exclusion-oriented (like in the case of ESG investment and SRI), meaning that investors actively choose to invest in firms that 'do good' rather than avoiding investing in companies that deal arms or produce polluting products. The pillar of *measurability* suggests that the social impact objectives which were intentionally defined must be estimated – qualitatively and, if possible, quantitatively – along the entire phases of the investment process (at both the portfolio and transaction levels) in order to be able to verify whether and in what measure the goals have been achieved (OECD, 2019). As pointed out by Viviani and Maurel (2019), the willingness of impact actors to employ a measurable approach is a "sign of the professionalisation of the impact investing industry" (p. 2). However, the pillar of measurability is still an open issue as, while assessing environmental impacts is actually quite advanced (due to the quantitative nature of such impacts), the evaluation of social impacts is still under-developed and misses standardized and widely applicable methodologies (OECD, 2019). Nowadays, annual impact reports, quarterly key performance indicators (KPI) reporting or structured qualitative evaluations are the most diffused solutions. Some global networks, such as the GIIN and the Impact Investing Policy Collaborative, have started to introduce a set of new standards and metrics to evaluate social impact investments (the Impact Reporting and Investment Standards (IRIS) and the Global Impact Investing Rating System (GIIRS) (Ormiston et al., 2015). Recently, scholars have suggested that in addition to these two pillars, a third one has to be included, the one of additionality (Hebb, 2013; So & Staskevicius, 2015; Arena et al., 2015). *Additionality* is the motivation of impact investors to provide an additional social value, which would not have occurred without their involvement. More specifically, additionality "must increase the quantity or quality of the enterprise's social outcomes beyond what would otherwise have occurred" (Brest & Born, 2013, p. 24). Accordingly, impact investors should proactively and officially target disadvantaged areas for their investments, characterized by higher financial risks and lower return, lower levels of attractiveness, more severe capital constraints, when compared to ordinary financial transactions (Attridge & Engen, 2019; Calderini et al., 2018; Pereira, 2017). This principle is the

146 *Laura Toschi and Ashley Metz*

one that might guarantee a growth of the impact investing industry maintaining the aspiration to create systemic change that was at the root of this financial practice, thus limiting impact washing occurrences.

Phase 3

Finally, in recent years, the definition has become more specific and quantifiable and linked to the concept of *value creation*. In the financial field, this concept is linked to the trade-off between risk and return on investments (Markowitz, 1952): an investor generally expects a certain level of return in relation to the level of risk which is supported (the higher the risk, the higher the return). When the concept of value creation is applied to the field of impact investing, the financial dimension loses power, leaving the scene to the measurement of the social impact. However, social value, which refers to "wider non-financial impacts of programmes, organizations and interventions, including the wellbeing of individuals and communities, social capital and the environment" (Mulgan, 2010, p. 1) is "subjective, malleable and variable" (Watson & Whitley, 2017, p. 2) and, thus, difficult to measure and to compare among organizations (Viviani & Maurel, 2019). Among the others, the methodology of the social return on investment (SROI) is the most used. It estimates the monetary equivalent of social value generated by the investment and compares it to the monetary equivalent of input used. (Roundy, Holzhauer et al., 2017), for instance, provide a definition of impact investors based on interviews with active players in the field. From this exercise of self-identification, impact investors are described as those seeking both financial return on investment (ROI) and a social return on investment (SROI), so that investors seeking only one of the two may not be considered impact investors. Box 7.1 provides a summary of the main definitions of impact investing (in chronological order).

Box 7.1   Summary of the main definitions of impact investing (in chronological order).

Bugg-Levine & Goldstein, 2009

Impact investing helps to address the social or environmental problems while generating financial returns.

Rangan et al., 2011

Impact investing is an investment that creates social or environmental benefits while also providing a return of principal, with returns ranging from zero to market rate.

Brest & Born, 2013

Impact investing actively place capital in enterprises that generate social or environmental goods, services, or ancillary benefits (such as creating jobs), with expected financial returns ranging from the highly concessionary to above market.

Hebb, 2013

Impact investing is a sub-set of responsible investing. Here the investor intentionally invests to achieve positive social and environmental impact in addition to financial return.

GIIN, 2013

Impact investments are investments made into companies, organizations, and funds with the intention to generate measurable social and environmental impact alongside a financial return. They can be in both emerging and developed markets, and target a range of returns from below to market rate, depending upon the circumstance.

Weber, 2016

Definitions of impact investments are based on two common principles:

- The blended value principle, claiming that social finance products and services can and should achieve both financial and social returns (positive social impact).
- The principle of sustainable finance return, guaranteeing the long-term financial viability of social finance institutions.

Viviani & Maurel, 2019

Investments in enterprises with a both social and financial objective which can be justified only if those enterprises can provide for a higher performance than with a simple portfolio diversification (separate investment in two types of activity).

The Actors Involved

The impact investing market is a complex field where a large number of actors are at play such as, among others, national and local government agencies, non-profit organizations and foundations, for-profit corporations, asset managers and institutional investors (Littlefield, 2011; Tekula & Andersen, 2019; Tekula & Shah, 2016). This complexity can be analysed through two interrelated perspectives in order to depict the relations among all the players. First, the capital chain approach represents the flow of capital and focuses on the supply side (i.e. investors), the demand side (i.e. investees addressing social needs) and, in the middle, the financial and capacity-building intermediaries able to connect the other two dimensions. Second, the ecosystem approach, which enlarges the previous perspective by analysing all the actors (and their relations) active in the market which provide support to create an enabling environment through legal, regulatory and economic conditions.

The Impact Investing Capital Chain

In order to successfully create impact, a network of stakeholder relationships, representing the flow of capital, has to be navigated (see Figure 7.2). Each actor in the chain needs to understand the role of all the other players, from intermediaries to the ultimate users (Godeke & Briaud, 2020). *Asset owners*, such as retail investors, private foundations or sovereign wealth funds, hold the capital and decide about its allocation along the impact capital chain, thus deciding the impact orientation of the capital. *Intermediaries* sit between two parties to facilitate their connections, such as commercial and investment banks or investment funds. It is possible to identify two types of intermediaries: advisors and asset managers. Advisors are consultants who provide advices (services) to the asset owners on how to deploy their assets in exchange of fees, while asset managers, such as institutions and private investors, construct ad hoc products to meet specific investment goals defined by the clients. The beneficiaries of the capital are *enterprises* which intend to generate social impact and financial return. These enterprises can be non-profits, for-profits, and hybrid organizations where both a social and a financial orientation coexist. Finally, the impact created by the enterprises is directed towards the final *customers* and beneficiaries.

The most significant bottleneck in growing the impact investing market is the existence of the so-called funding gap: from the demand side, capital raisers claim that not enough capital is available, while from the offer side, investors perceive a lack of investable opportunities. It is, thus, important that all the actors of the impact capital chain work in concert in order to align goals and strategies among all the actors and increase the level of investment readiness (i.e., sufficient baseline of competences) in all the components of the chain.

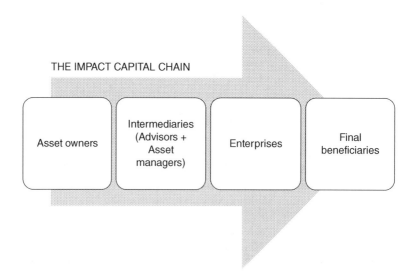

Figure 7.2 The impact capital chain.

Source: Adapted by Godeke and Briaud (2020)

The Impact Investing Ecosystem

In addition to the direct links among the actors of the supply chain of the impact investment market, other stakeholders are essential to create the desired impact, such as regulators, policy makers, incubator and accelerators. All these actors belong to an ecosystem, where each member plays a critical role in trying to mitigate the risk of impact investments and expand the pipeline of investable opportunities. In this context and given the complexity of driving social and environmental change, a collective action made of partnerships, collaborations and co-investments between the public and the private sectors is extremely relevant (Godeke & Briaud, 2020).

In order to develop impact investing is important to create solid infrastructures, a set of interconnected forces that promote and sustain the market. Schwartz et al. (2015) identify three main infrastructures which may facilitate impact investing functioning in a proper way. The first one is the *governmental infrastructure*, made of instruments available to governments to regulate or facilitate the development of the field (Addis, 2015; OECD, 2015): releasing legal constraints to favour the flow of money into the sector (Schwartz et al., 2015), supporting the growth of the market demand and the fundraising activities (Grieco, 2015; Oleksiak et al., 2015; Ormiston et al., 2015; Schwartz et al., 2015), being themselves social impact investors (Addis, 2015; Steinberg, 2015; Wells, 2012). A second element is the *facilitative infrastructure*, services to ensure readiness of both social investees and investors and facilitate interactions. Key players are generalist professionals, service firms and specialized consulting firms (Glanzel & Scheuerle, 2016; Hazenberg et al., 2014; Mendell & Barbosa, 2013; Schwartz et al., 2015). Also, the development and adoption of metrics and reporting methods (Addis, 2015; Clarkin & Cangioni, 2016; Mendell & Barbosa, 2013; Oleksiak et al., 2015; Ormiston et al., 2015; Schwartz et al., 2015) are relevant to allow players measuring the social performance of the investment and evaluating the social risk of investees (Mendell & Barbosa, 2013). The third pillar is represented by *transactional infrastructure* needed to lower transaction costs, which comprise capital providers for impact investing, financial intermediaries and financial instruments. Among capital providers, there are charities, foundations, development banks and high-net-worth individuals, but also impact investing funds, traditional institutional investors, retail investors, financial institutions and investment banks (Brandstetter & Lehner, 2015; Glanzel & Scheuerle, 2016; Lehner & Nicholls, 2014; Nicholls & Emerson, 2015; Oleksiak et al., 2015; Ormiston et al., 2015; Schwartz et al., 2015). In addition to the provision of capital, this type of infrastructure should also guarantee exit options for investors in order to repay the invested money (Addis, 2015; Mendell & Barbosa, 2013; Schwartz et al., 2015). Starting from these dimensions of the optimal impact investing market structure, Calderini et al. (2018) performed an analysis of the worldwide landscape: the results suggest that the impact investing market is still in a seed stage of development, where a small group of countries shows good infrastructures along the three dimensions and a vibrant ecosystem (US and UK), while the majority is still in an experimental phase (i.e., Canada, Australia, Japan, Portugal, Israel and France Italy, Mexico, Brazil and Germany).

Moreover, Roundy (2019) proposes a theory of impact investing ecosystems to explain geographical differences in the market. An impact investing ecosystem can be defined as a regional community generating high levels of impact investment for sustained periods of time. These ecosystems are hybrid as they integrate opposite logics of action (Lehner et al., 2018; Nicholls, 2010): the community logic, typical of the traditional philanthropy sector, the economic logic, characterizing the traditional venture investment and the regulative logic of the public sector (Figure 7.3).

To be effective, they need to be heterogeneous, coherent and coordinated. *Heterogeneous* ecosystems show high levels of diversity in their components. A relevant role is played by impact investor characteristics: (i) showing different expecting rates of returns (Lehner & Brandstetter, 2014; Roundy, Holzhauer et al., 2017) and methods to invest (privately, as part of self-organized groups or through "social" venture capital funds) (Block et al., 2018), (ii) targeting different types of investment in terms of size (from micro-finance to venture capital), grand challenges addressed (environmental, social or political problems), stage of development (from seed to later-stage), growth trajectories (micro business, organic growth, rapid scaling), legal structure (for-profit, non-profit and hybrid entities) and (iii) using different types of instruments (debt- or equity-based) (Glanzel & Scheuerle, 2016; Höchstädter & Scheck, 2015). *Coherence* may be defined as the degree of cohesiveness among all the components of the ecosystem, allowing them to be combined into an interconnected structure (Roundy, Brockman et al., 2017). The different logics represented in the impact investing ecosystem have distinct and sometimes conflicting goals, ownerships, organizational structures, accountability and resources which risk to leave activities within their distinct silos, undermining the growth of the ecosystem. For this reason, integration among the parts is a fundamental prerequisite. For impact investing ecosystems this may be translated in the existence of investors which are engaged in the same activities and are moved by the same goal of generating both social and financial returns (even if with different intensity among the two dimensions). A culture at the community level supporting this blended logic results being critical. Finally, *coordination* refers to the engagement of the players in deliberate and interconnected efforts to develop and support the ecosystem. To be vibrant, an ecosystem should rely on investors who are aware of the activities of their peers, develop a connected social network to facilitate information exchange among players and strengthen the collaboration among agents and co-investment activities. Co-investment allows investors to spread the risk among multiple actors

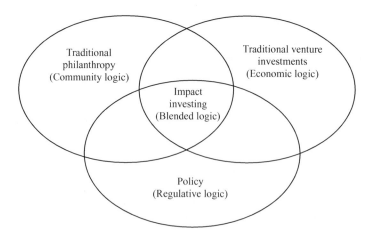

Figure 7.3 The impact investing ecosystem.

and increase the amount of capital provided, offers investee organizations larger networks, higher variety of expertise from different types of investors, lower dependence on one funding source and, more broadly, it promotes impact investing among a wider audience (EVPA Knowledge Centre, 2018). According to a recent survey performed by the EVPA, 87% of players co-invested at least once, however, not all communities are vibrant at the same intensity (EVPA Knowledge Centre, 2021). Indeed, co-investments may imply slower decision-making, more time-consuming management of relationships, potential misalignment of investment strategy. To avoid such risks and support cross-sector activities, clear expectations and incentives for collaboration are required and incubators, accelerators or impact-oriented support organizations may serve as suitable facilitators (GSG, 2018).

The Impact Investing Capital Providers

Similar to traditional investors, impact investors are also a heterogeneous group of actors (Bugg-Levine & Emerson, 2011), both individual and institutional, such as fund managers, development finance institutions, diversified financial institutions and banks, private foundations, pension funds, insurance companies, family offices, individual investors, NGOs, religious institutions. In order to better navigate this large number of actors, researchers have proposed different categorizations.

By taking in consideration the forms of capital provided, impact investors can be classified as equity or debt investors. The category of *equity investors* comprises entities such as venture capital or growth equity funds (e.g., Barber et al., 2021; Bugg-Levine & Emerson, 2011), is the most active in the market and primarily invest through impact investment funds. Equity investors are moved by financial interests since their objective is to achieve market-rate returns through positive exits from their investments (e.g., Barber et al., 2021; Brest & Born, 2013; Gray et al., 2016). They are generally labelled "pragmatic idealists" (Bocken, 2015), as they implement investment practices similar to those of the traditional VC industry, but at the same time are characterized by more patience in their exit strategy, a broader range of acceptable financial returns and a focus in businesses that are expected to tackle global social problems (education, microfinance, energy, housing, water procurement and healthcare). *Debt investors*, such as social banks, provide debt to their investee companies by searching for financial returns that are often characterized by below-market return expectations (Brest & Born, 2013). Other impact investors of this type are foundations or public institutions.

A second way to classify impact investors is the one distinguishing between *finance first* and *impact first*. To the first category belong investors who seek a market rate of return as first goal, while the second one is represented by investors who target investments primarily for their social or environmental impact (Monitor Report, 2009). The former group generally includes commercial investors, seeking investments which offer good financial returns and also yield social or environmental benefits, and pension funds, who are explicitly required to uphold a fiduciary standard. The second group, instead, accepts investments with below the market rate of return. Foundations are one of the more common examples of an impact-first investor.

A third categorization is the one splitting between *public* and *private* investors depending on the governance mode of the service provider. To the public category belong the government, development finance institutions, public pension funds or multilateral development bank, while the private category is populated by institutional investors, foundations, family offices or high net worth individuals.

Finally, Tekula and Andersen (2019) propose four categories of impact investing actors who are positioned along a spectrum with different degrees of alignment between market and impact goals, resembling a life cycle approach. *Enabling* actors operate in the nascent phase of the market with the role to create optimal infrastructure and increasing productivity. Government agencies and non-profit organizations operate through the provision of grants, while trade associations may develop comparable metrics. *Improving* actors address the issue of facilitating the matching between investors and investees. Governments aim to fix the market with specific regulations and supporting legislations, while trade associations and hubs, in addition to providing networks and research resources, help to grow the capacity of the market by educating and connecting talent to the field. Subsequently, *moving* actors have the role to move the market with an underlying market rationale around externalities, information imperfection and entry barriers. Government introduces tax credits, while non-profit or private actors provide patient capital. Finally, *launching* actors operate to support in moving assets to market, and developing them in order to yield growth. Both government and nonprofits may provide initial and seed capital, coupled with a more pronounced active engagement of private investors like banks, pension funds, family offices and large financial institutions. Box 7.2 provides a description of the main capital providers in impact investing.

Box 7.2   Description of the main capital providers in impact investing.

Commercial Markets

They prioritize returns over social impact and are important in later stages of scaling up impact investing industry sectors.

Community finance organizations

They provide access to capital to customers who may be unable to borrow from traditional financial institutions due to a lack of credit history or collateral.

Development Banks and Institutions

An excellent source of funding for impact innovators, but with a limited participation in high-risk and early-stage investing.

Ethical Banks

They work alongside impact companies and frequently invest in local initiatives, enabling them to create real change at both the local and global levels.

Foundations

They seek to align their investment philosophy with their public benefit purpose through mission-related investing (which use foundation capital to invest in businesses, non-profit organizations, charities and funds that generate positive social or environmental impact as well as financial returns) or programme-related investing (which invest using a foundation's programmatic funds to generate positive social or environmental impact and financial returns).

Governments

In addition to invest in traditional grants and contribution programmes, they target also financial returns, through direct financing, loans, loan guarantees and economic development programmes, and involve the measurement of social outcomes.

High Net-Worth Individuals

These investors (also known as angel investors) serve as pioneers of impact investing, providing high-risk capital to social businesses in the early stages of development, mainly in areas where they have maturated a personal interest or sectoral expertise. A valuable initiative is "The ImPact"[5], developed in New York City by a young generation of wealthy individuals (including Justin Rockefeller, Josh Cohen and Liesel Pritzker-Simmons), with the mission to create "a global community of families committed to aligning their assets with their values" and improve the flow of capital to support the development of businesses with a measurable social impact.

Microfinance Institutions

They provide financial services to the poor and are effective at reducing poverty in developing countries as they recognize that small loans may have a significant impact on low-income populations.

Private investors

They are mainly Venture Capital (VC) and growth equity funds, structured as traditional private equity funds but with the intentionality to produce social impact.

Social Stock Exchanges

Using social stock exchanges, investors can buy shares in a social business just as investors focused solely on profit would do in the traditional stock market. The four best known are the UK's Social Stock Exchange, Singapore's Impact Exchange, Canada's Social Venture Connexion, and the U.S.'s Mission Markets.

154   Laura Toschi and Ashley Metz

The Organizational Actors Served

Impact investing pursues the dual goals of creating social impact and ensuring net positive financial returns. To achieve this goal, their investments are focused on firms which create both social and commercial values (Roundy, Holzhauer et al., 2017) which are generally defined in the literature as *hybrid* organizations (Battilana & Dorado, 2010). Similar to the definition of impact investors, also these entities are characterized by the coexistence of a social and a commercial identity (Battilana & Dorado, 2010; Battilana et al., 2015; Haigh & Hoffman, 2014; Pache & Santos, 2013), where the first dimension refers to the achievement of certain levels of social impact, while the latter aims at obtaining profitability through a business activity (Haffar & Searcy, 2019). In general, the hybrid nature of social businesses poses some critical issues as it requires a constant management of the trade-offs between the two spheres, resulting in a high complexity in supporting their growth and attracting investors (Alter, 2006; Austin et al., 2006; Leadbeater, 2007; Wilson & Post, 2013). Indeed, the existence of a dual mission asks these organizations to manage the demands, expectations, goals and interests of multiple stakeholders, which may be reflected in competing logics and generate tensions in prioritizing the social or the economic dimension (Julie Battilana & Dorado, 2010; Doherty et al., 2014).

The landscape of hybrid entities is quite heterogeneous. Hybrid organizations may be positioned along a continuum where the social or the economic dimension results more or less important in respect to the other dimension. At one extreme, there are social-purpose organizations (also known as social enterprises) which can be generally defined as organizations whose main goal is reaching impact goals. These organizations, however, present a sustainable business model that makes them attractive to impact investors. On the other hand, we find traditional businesses which embed sustainability and social impact attentions in their business models. For definition, these entities prioritize the generation of profitability and thus have a sustainable and scalable business model.

The analysis of the business model is, thus, a driving factor in understanding the organizational actors targeted by impact investing capital providers and in differentiating them in respect to those targeted by other types of social finance. The importance of the *business model sustainability* as a driving factor to understand the actors served by impact investing is also highlighted by the EVPA (2018). On the one hand, for profit businesses with intentional social impact or social-purpose organizations with a proven financially sustainable business model are generally the target of investor *with* impact, due to the investors' research of some levels of financial returns. On the other hand, social-purpose organizations with a limited or inexistent sustainable business model are generally supported by investors *for* impact, as financial risk is not their primary concern in front of the potential to generate huge levels of social impact. Box 7.3 outlines the barriers for the development of impact investing in Europe.

Box 7.3   Barriers for the development of impact investing in Europe.

The European impact investing market has demonstrated rapid growth over the last decade but it has not yet reached its full potential and maturity as in

80% of the EU countries it is considered to be in its "infant" stages. Four main challenges have been identified as having the largest impact in preventing its development.

First, social enterprises might not be able to generate income levels aligned with investors' return expectations (Kickul & Lyons, 2015). This may due to the fact that their hybrid nature does not allow social ventures to charge market prices or target customers with high purchasing power (Karaphillis et al., 2010). As a consequence, the aim of addressing a social challenge leads to an unfavourable risk-return relationship (Nicholls & Emerson, 2015) making social enterprises unattractive for investors.

Second, similar to other forms of entrepreneurial ventures, the lack of track records and the existence of barriers to undertaking due diligence generate significant information asymmetry between the social entrepreneurs and possible external impact investing funders. The existence of such information asymmetries makes significant the cost of raising external financing as investors ask for higher interest rates and greater equity shares to compensate for the risk of funding an uncertain and unproven new venture (Watson & Wilson, 2002)

Third, the lack of collateral (Fielden et al., 2000; Scellato, 2007) due to the intangible nature of most high-tech investments, makes banks or other financial institutions generally unwilling to finance social new ventures because they hardly meet the criteria required to have access to standard forms of debt (Cassar, 2004).

Finally, it is more difficult for social ventures to demonstrate to potential investors their ability to generate social impact due to the absence of standardized and approved performance metrics for social risk and return (Bengo et al., 2016; Kickul & Lyons, 2015; Nicholls & Emerson, 2015).

The combination of these barriers could lead to the problem of "grant dependency" (Conathy, 2001; Fraser, 2007; Sunley & Pinch, 2012) so that social ventures can become reluctant to take on commercial finance and remain fixed in a charitable mindset.

The Financial Instruments

Impact investing can be applied across a broad range of asset classes: cash, fixed income, infrastructure, property, debt and equity. In practice, impact investors fund many asset classes using a broad range of instruments and merge different types of capital in innovative hybrid funding instruments for creating impact. In order to navigate this broad spectrum of options, the GIIN (2019b) has provided a classification of financial instruments (from debt-based to equity-based) along a return-rate spectrum ranging from *below market investments* (also known as concessionary) to *market rate investments*. The result is a rich and heterogeneous portfolio of opportunities in terms of tools to make investments and risk/return combinations across different asset classes. Grant support, equity, subordinated loans and senior loans are part of the former group, while guarantees, fixed income, public equity and private equity belong to the latter. These tools are generally distinguished between type of loan disbursed (equity or bond or mixed) and type of subjects financed (listed or unlisted companies, investments in intermediaries or direct). In the following, we present some of the most common financial instruments used in impact investing (Bugg-Levine et al., 2012; Chowdhry et al., 2013, 2016; Jackson, 2013; McHugh et al., 2013; Rizzello et al., 2016; Social Finance, 2009).

Social Investment Funds

Social investment funds are divided into two macro-categories: investments in organizations with a high socio-environmental impact (direct investments) and investments in funds or securities which in turn finance organizations with a high socio-environmental impact (indirect investments). In order to be defined as "impact", the funds must implement an investment strategy aimed at generating positive effects from an environmental and social point of view, with a consistent and transparent analysis methodology. Furthermore, impact investing provides for a measurement of results, which must be appropriately reported to investors through the impact report tool. Of course, the composition of the investment portfolio cannot disregard the analysis of traditional financial parameters such as risk, return and liquidity

Guarantees

Generally speaking, guarantees are risk reduction tools that protect investors against capital losses or provide credit enhancement. Loan guarantees is a particular type of guarantees consisting in a guarantor who agrees to pay any or all of the amount due on a loan instrument in case of non-payment by the borrower. Social impact guarantees are a further mechanism, which allow for a social market to be developed within a standardized market, by aligning lower financial returns to social investors when social outcomes are high, while simultaneously permitting greater monetary returns to financial investors for these same social outcomes

Green Bonds

One of the answers to the demand for instruments capable of financing activities with a positive impact on the environment is represented by green bonds. These are debt securities associated with the financing of projects with positive effects in environmental terms, such as renewable energy, sustainable management of waste and water resources, protection of biodiversity, energy efficiency. Green bonds represent an opportunity to increase the availability of capital necessary for the transition to a more sustainable economy and to reduce the cost of debt for projects with positive environmental repercussions.

Social Bonds

Social bonds are bond instruments used to finance projects with a positive social impact. The areas that can be financed may concern, for example, access to health and housing services, financial inclusion, food security and employment. At the European level, the Council of Europe Development Bank (CEB) launched a "social inclusion bond" worth €500 million, the proceeds of which will be used to finance projects in social housing, education and vocational training, and in the creation of jobs in small and medium-sized enterprises. Similarly, the Dutch Bank NBW has placed a social bond of €2 billion to finance social housing projects in the Netherlands.

Social Impact Bonds (SIBs)

SIBs are innovative impact investing tools intended for the implementation of public utility projects, with a remuneration of investors only in the event of actual generation of positive social impact, appropriately measured. For this reason, SIBs are considered bonds "Pay by Result (PbR)" or "Pay for Success". The structure of SIBs requires five stakeholders: a Public Administration (municipal, regional or national), the service providers (non-profit organizations or social enterprises), an investor, a specialized intermediary (generally third sector organizations or foundations) and an independent evaluator who measures the impact generated and the effectiveness of the obtained results. The first SIB was born in 2010 in the United Kingdom on the initiative of the Social Finance investment bank to support the reintegration of inmates from Peterborough prison with a sentence of less than 12 months, with the aim of reducing the recidivism rate.

Development Impact Bonds (DIBs)

Sharing similarities with SIBs, DIBs are generally implemented in developing countries and with developing country governments or donor agencies. Typically, an intermediary organization (a not-for-profit, NGO) coordinate the transaction, investors provide funds to roll out or scale up services and service providers deliver outcomes and funders (primarily public sector agencies from developing or donor countries) pay for results achieved.

Crowdfunding

Crowdfunding platforms allow collecting financing shares, even small ones, from a large number of subjects, by making information on the project to be financed public and shared. Crowdfunding is mainly divided into two main categories: (i) *non-financial models*, which do not provide for any form of economic return on the contribution of money (donation model) or, otherwise, the disbursement of small non-monetary rewards (reward model); (ii) *financial models*, which provide for an economic return on the investment and, in turn, are divided into *lending* and *equity crowdfunding*. Lending crowdfunding takes place through the subscription of a loan to which an interest rate is associated. It can be declined in various forms, such as *peer-to-peer lending*, where lenders can decide directly in which projects to invest, through loans to individuals (P2P) or to businesses (P2B), or *social lending* where the platforms mediate between debtors and widespread lenders who, in this case, cannot choose ex ante which projects to invest in. In equity crowdfunding, the aim is to raising venture capital from businesses. Later, the lender participates in and supports the start-up or growth of a business venture, benefiting from potential future dividends or capital gains.

Mission Related Investments (MRIs)

MRIs represent investments from a foundation's endowment that seek to achieve specific goals to advance a social mission, but also generally seeking financial returns. In contrast to Program Related Investments, MRIs are typically recorded as an investment asset rather than a grant asset.

Program Related Investments (PRIs)

Program Related Investments (PRIs) are a tool specific to foundations, used as an alternative to the traditional grant. They can effectively recycle grant money, grow the endowment, and provide the investee with significant unrestricted resources. These instruments can be an incredibly effective tool for bringing long-term financial stability to organizations – both investors and investees – while addressing critical social needs.

Concluding Thoughts

Where Is This Trajectory Taking Us?

Impact investing differs from other related investment approaches such as responsible finance, sustainable finance, social finance and ESG criteria. Responsible finance may refer to an investor's moral obligation; sustainable finance seems to lean more on environmental issues rather than on social issues (Bugg-Levine & Emerson, 2011) and ESG criteria (environmental, social and governance) can be used for negative screening, to exclude investments in those sectors that do not comply with ESG criteria (i.e. tobacco industry). Impact investing is action-oriented, not only exclusion oriented, meaning that investors actively choose to invest in firms that "do good" rather than avoiding investing in companies that do "harm". Impact investors have the intention of achieving both social and environmental positive impact along with financial returns (GIIN, 2019a, 2019b)

On the one hand, impact investing can be seen as a natural extension of these approaches and others in mainstream investing. Venture capital with its close relationship between investor and investee, though not always intentionally socially oriented, is not far from impact investing; its first activities started in the early 1950s in the USA (with the American Research and Development Corporation led by Georges Doriot). Early initiatives that show funds' intention to contribute to social good through finance. For example, the US Community Reinvestment Act, passed in 1977, was based on the banks "obligation" to answer the needs for credit of low/middle income communities, and the Mondragon Corporation in Spain, a federation of workers cooperatives guided by social and solidarity principles operating in several sectors including finance, founded in 1956. Furthermore, in recent times, the traditional investing world is experiencing trends towards sustainability. Switzerland, once considered a place to bank if transparency was not of interest, is gaining a reputation as place for triple-bottom-line visibility (3BL).[6] Also, as of 2020, the climate crisis is increasingly considered a serious investment risk, drawing greater attention to sustainability in investing.

On the other hand, impact investing can be understood as a natural component of rationalization processes in the social sector, along with the trend towards social entrepreneurship. There has been much academic interest in how the social sector is becoming "business-like" (Maier et al., 2016), or the rationalization, professionalization (Hwang & Powell, 2009) and marketization (Eikenberry & Kluver, 2004) of organizations, including funding organizations and membership associations (Mair & Hehenberger, 2014). Scholars have unpacked how nonprofit organizations have adopted rhetoric, organizational practices and goals from business (Dart, 2004; Mair & Hehenberger, 2014) imported through professionals (Hwang & Powell, 2009; Suarez, 2010), resource providers (e.g. Rogers, 2011) and actors and models guided by logics from the financial world (Mair & Hehenberger, 2014; Pache & Santos, 2013).

Yet, during the last decade, societal problems have become more frequent, complex and with a global resonance (OECD, 2015). A situation which further worsened due to the Covid-19 pandemic crisis and the associated economic crisis undermined the well-being of the entire society on a global scale. In addition, the financial crisis of 2007–2009 has triggered numerous doubts about the effectiveness of the financial system in creating a benefit for the whole society (Shiller, 2013; Zingales, 2015). These developments have stimulated the necessity not only for new terms and approaches, but complete overhaul.

The relevant questions at this point are: *What will this overhaul take? And where is the field going?*

A telling quote about the state of impact investing in 2014 was:

> *It is too early to tell which social issue or which social group will put impact investment firmly on the map. Will it be 'children', 'unemployed youth', 'the elderly poor', 'reoffenders', 'health' or 'International Development'?*
> (Comment made by Sir Ronald Cohen at GSG meeting, 2014)
> (From Hehenberger et al., 2019)

At that time, the field was not yet sure of itself and was looking for success stories of its practices. During the research study (ibid), the authors (including one on this chapter) identified this quote as illustrative of the mechanism of *reordering*, reordering the hierarchy of priorities to prioritize means over ends – "positioning practices as more important than outcomes" (p. 1703). We had identified concerns that the field might focus on practices and less on the social purpose organizations and their interests, and a "mismatch between the interests of those with resources and tools and those who implement them." Yet, at the time of finalizing this chapter in 2021, the world is arguably in a very different place. The COVID-19 crisis, along with growing acceptance of climate change as a fact and also a problem to solve, has shaken norms and values, as well as needs. Increasingly, it is taken for granted that organizations will have to create impact and a range of financing approaches will be necessary to serve them. It is perhaps no longer a question of "putting impact investing on the map", but necessarily, urgently, finding and supporting solutions using the enormous resources in the global financial markets that have been accumulated in the last decades. The risk of a focus on tools or resource providers arguably dissipates when problems are so urgent they simply need to be addressed by any means necessary (though scholars and practitioners can still be well-served to focus on beneficiary needs and solving problems over promoting tools).

The impact investing overhaul needs to be approached in order to develop a broad response to the global crisis, able to accelerate the flow of capital by leveraging on the assets of the global impact investing industry. The imperative now is collaboration: different actors have to "work together across different networks to really maximize the role that impact investing can play in crisis response, recovery, and resilience"[7] (Giselle Leung, GIIN, 2021). Under this vein, the GIIN has recently launched a platform named "Response, Recovery, and Resilience Investment Coalition" (R3 Coalition)[8] where foundations, family offices, development finance institutions, other public and private investors fund managers work together and share deals. Only under the principle of collaborations, the recovery will be inclusive and sustainable. A global and multi-stakeholder collaboration implies combining different sources not only of financial capital, but also of human capital and expertise. From the dialogue among different stakeholders, it will be possible to understand the most efficient and leanest structure to give to collaboration in the field that will allow to create a society and an economic system more resilient to future crises. Muhammad Yunus asserted that the scale of the disasters wrought around the world by the COVID-19 pandemic is staggering, but, despite the enormous damage, we are facing the unprecedented opportunity to redesign our society, without bringing it back to the situation it was in before the crisis because that starting point was not good. In front of this *tabula rasa*, the impact investing industry may have a huge role in supporting the design of a new society.

Therefore, the next trick for impact investing may not be achieving awareness, but achieving seamless integration in the financial system, along the spectrum of return profiles. Future research may investigate what is facilitating or hindering this transition. For example:

- *What is the future of* impact investing *as a field and as a label? Do labels and definitions help or create artificial divides? And when is impact investing not the best approach? Where does it sit next to government funding?*

Impact investing is an evolving field that offers much promise and the term and ideas within the field continue to evolve. When does "impact investing" merge with mainstream investing? Impact investing can be understood as an issue field (Hehenberger et al., 2019), which thus may be a "mechanism" for changing an exchange field (Zietsma et al., 2017, p. 424), in this case, of mainstream investing. To what extent do labels like impact investing still matter in the future? Scholars may instead trace the integration of financial mechanisms into mainstream finance and study topics like how some are easily adopted while others are not. Further study may also help explain how II financing can be "a tool in the toolbox" adopted across governments and private firms. On a higher level, further investigation of the blurring of sector boundaries may be interesting to put this in perspective.

- *Do impact investors have valuable opportunities to invest in?*

The topic of investment readiness of enterprises pursuing social goal is well known in both literature and practice (Brandstetter & Lehner, 2015; Burand, 2014; Freireich & Fulton, 2009; Ormiston et al., 2015). In addition to support the development of the impact investing industry from the supply side, it will be also crucial to develop measures from the demand side of the funding gap in order to support social enterprises in

Impact Investing and New Social Funding   161

their capacity building process and become more attractive to investors. The challenge becomes, thus, to design the right programmes able to address this issue.

* *Do impact investors have the possibility to exit from their investments?*

Without the systematic availability of exit strategies from investments, impact investing will not reach the desired level of attractiveness for large institutional investors (Harji & Jackson, 2012; Mendell & Barbosa, 2013; Saltuk, 2015). Secondary markets, that allow for liquidity, and exchange platforms, created to connect investors with their peers and with valuable opportunities, will play an essential role for the field to flourish.

* *How should social impact be measured?*

The current impact measurement literature has mainly focused on outcomes/results (see Chapter 8 on Social Impact Evaluation). However, this approach creates tensions between investors and investees due to the trade-off in terms of profit (the economic dimension) and purpose (the social dimension). Recent studies suggest that social impact measurement should not be exclusively framed in terms of metrics, but also as an organizational learning tool and a means for improving the relationship between investors and investees (Bengo et al., 2021; Lall, 2017). The integration of a transactional perspective (based on outcomes) with a relational one (Chen & Harrison, 2020) should guide future research in the field. This approach emphasizes the importance of long-term strategic relationships and the co-design of new proprietary impact measurement tools which become fundamental to keep the process flowing productively, addressing the traditional economic-social tensions.

With this chapter we intended to summarize the main literature investigating the topic of impact investing and provide a preliminary landscape of this financial market. From this exercise, we can highlight the existence of a severe dilemma to which academics and policy makers should direct their attention. On the one hand, a primary condition for achieving the full effectiveness of the market is the development of a proper set of financial instruments, organizational forms, processes and infrastructures which may connect people with valuable opportunities and enable them to make a significant difference. Only with a wide spectrum of alternatives it will be possible to provide enough capital to new companies, moved by the mission to solve social and environmental problems, and to support existing companies, working to scale up their business and generate huge impact for the society. On the other hand, the consequences of a further rationalization, monetarization and marketization of the recipient organizations are still not clear and could generate severe side effects, distorting the original nature of inclusiveness and engagement. This tension needs to be addressed in order to allow the impact investing field to effectively progress, without completely shifting towards a commercial logic and losing its important features of volunteer desire to contribute to the generation of social value.

Notes

1 https://thegiin.org/impact-investing/need-to-know/
2 www.rockefellerfoundation.org/our-work/initiatives/innovative-finance/

162 Laura Toschi and Ashley Metz

3 https://ec.europa.eu/commission/presscorner/detail/en/qanda_20_20
4 https://ec.europa.eu/commission/presscorner/detail/lt/memo_19_2135
5 www.theimpact.org/
6 Social, economic and environmental bottom-line; the expression is based on the 3BL expression (people, planet and profit) proposed by J. Elkington in 1994.
7 www.fordfoundation.org/just-matters/just-matters/posts/impact-investors-respond-to-covid-19/
8 https://thegiin.org/r3coalition

References

Achleitner, A. K., Heinecke, A., Noble, A., Schoning, M., & Spiess-Knalf, W. (2011). Unlocking the mystery: An introduction to social investment. *Innovations*, 6(3), 41–50.

Addis, R. (2015). The roles of government and policy in social finance. In A. Nicholls, R. Paton, & J. Emerson (Eds.), *Social finance* (pp. 383–459). Oxford University Press.

Alter, S. K. (2006). Social enterprise models and their mission and money relationship. In A. Nicholls (Ed.), *Social entrepreneurship: New models of sustainable social change.* Oxford University Press.

Arena, M., Azzone, G., & Bengo, I. (2015). Performance measurement for social enterprises. *Voluntas*, 26(2), 649–672. https://doi.org/10.1007/s11266-013-9436-8

Arjaliès, D. L. (2010). A social movement perspective on finance: How socially responsible investment mattered. *Journal of Business Ethics*, 92(suppl 1), 57–78. https://doi.org/10.1007/s10551-010-0634-7

Attridge, S., & Engen, L. (2019). *Blended finance in the poorest countries: The need for a better approach.* Overseas Development Institute (ODI).

Austin, J., Stevenson, H., & Wei-Skillern, J. (2006). Social and commercial entrepreneurship: Same, different, or both? *Entrepreneurship: Theory and Practice*, 30(1), 1–22. https://doi.org/10.1111/j.1540-6520.2006.00107.x

Barber, B. M., Morse, A., & Yasuda, A. (2021). Impact investing. *Journal of Financial Economics*, 139(1), 162–185. https://doi.org/10.1016/j.jfineco.2020.07.008

Battilana, J., & Dorado, S. (2010). Building sustainable hybrid organizations: The case of commercial microfinance organizations. *Academy of Management Journal*, 53(6), 1419–1440.

Battilana, J., Lee, M., Walker, J., & Dorsey, C. (2012). In search of the hybrid ideal. *Standford Social Innovation Review*, 10(3), 51–55.

Battilana, J., Sengul, M., Pache, A. C., & Model, J. (2015). Harnessing productive tensions in hybrid organizations: The case of working integration social enterprises. *Academy of Management Journal*, 58(6), 1658–1685. https://doi.org/10.5465/amj.2013.0903

Bengo, I., Arena, M., Azzone, G., & Calderini, M. (2016). Indicators and metrics for social business: A review of current approaches. *Journal of Social Entrepreneurship*, 7(1), 1–24. Routledge. https://doi.org/10.1080/19420676.2015.1049286

Bengo, I., Borrello, A., & Chiodo, V. (2021). Preserving the integrity of social impact investing: Towards a distinctive implementation strategy. *Sustainability*, 13(5). https://doi.org/10.3390/su13052852

Block, J. H., Colombo, M. G., Cumming, D. J., & Vismara, S. (2018). New players in entrepreneurial finance and why they are there. *Small Business Economics*, 50(2), 239–250. https://doi.org/10.1007/s11187-016-9826-6

Block, J. H., Hirschmann, M., & Fisch, C. (2021). Which criteria matter when impact investors screen social enterprises? *Journal of Corporate Finance*, 66, 101813. https://doi.org/10.1016/j.jcorpfin.2020.101813

Bocken, N. M. P. (2015). Sustainable venture capital – catalyst for sustainable start-up success? *Journal of Cleaner Production*, 108, 647–658. https://doi.org/10.1016/j.jclepro.2015.05.079

Bose, S., Dong, S., & Simpson, A. (2019). *The financial ecosystem: The role of finance in achieving sustainability.* Palgrave Macmillan.

Brandstetter, L., & Lehner, O. M. (2015). Opening the market for impact investments: The need for adapted portfolio tools. *Entrepreneurship Research Journal, E5*(2), 87–107.

Brest, P., & Born, K. (2013). Unpacking the impact in impact investing. *Stanford Social Innovation Review*. https://law.stanford.edu/publications/unpacking-the-impact-in-impact-investing/

Bugg-Levine, A., & Emerson, J. (2011). Impact investing: Transforming how we make money while making a difference. *Innovations: Technology, Governance, Globalization, 6*(3), 9–18. https://doi.org/10.1162/inov_a_00077

Bugg-Levine, A., & Goldstein, J. (2009). Impact investing: Harnessing capital markets to solve problems at scale. *Community Development Innovation Review*, (2), 30–41.

Bugg-Levine, A., Kogut, B., & Kulatilaka, N. (2012). A new approach to funding social en- terprises – unbundling societal benefits and financial returns can dramatically increase investment. *Harvard Business Review, 90*(1–2), 118–123.

Burand, D. (2014). Resolving impact investment disputes: When doing good goes bad. *Journal of Law and Policy, 48*(55), 55–88.

Calderini, M., Chiodo, V., & Michelucci, F. V. (2018). The social impact investment race: Toward an interpretative framework. *European Business Review, 30*, 66–81.

Cassar, G. (2004). The financing of business start-ups. *Journal of Business Venturing, 19*(2), 261–283. https://doi.org/10.1016/S0883-9026(03)00029-6

Chen, S., & Harrison, R. (2020). Beyond profit vs. purpose: Transactional-relational practices in impact investing. *Journal of Business Venturing Insights, 14*, e00182. https://doi.org/10.1016/j.jbvi.2020.e00182

Chowdhry, B., Davies, S. W., & Waters, B. (2013). *Designing markets for impact investing in social businesses*. UCLA Anderson School of Management.

Chowdhry, B., Davies, S. W., & Waters, B. (2016). *Incentivizing impact investing*. Social Science Research Network.

Clarkin, J. E., & Cangioni, C. L. (2016). Impact investing: A primer and review of the literature. *Entrepreneurship Research Journal, 6*(2), 135–173. Walter de Gruyter GmbH. https://doi.org/10.1515/erj-2014-0011

Conathy, P. (2001). *Homeopathic finance – equitable capital for social enterprises*. New Economics Foundation.

Cooper, C. (2016). *Fat activism: A radical social movement*. HammerOn Press.

Dart, R. (2004). The legitimacy of social enterprise. *Nonprofit Management and Leadership, 14*(4), 411–424. https://doi.org/10.1002/nml.43

Dees, J. G., & Anderson, B. B. (2003). For-profit social ventures. *International Journal of Entrepreneurship Education, Special Issue on Social Entrepreneurship, 2*, 1–26.

Doherty, B., Haugh, H., & Lyon, F. (2014). Social enterprises as hybrid organizations: A review and research agenda. *International Journal of Management Reviews, 16*(4), 417–436. https://doi.org/10.1111/ijmr.12028

Eikenberry, A. M., & Kluver, J. D. (2004). The marketization of the nonprofit sector: Civil society at risk? *Public Administration Review, 64*(2), 132–140. John Wiley & Sons, Ltd. https://doi.org/10.1111/j.1540-6210.2004.00355.x

Emerson, J. (2003). The blended value proposition: Integrating social and financial returns. *California Management Review, 45*(4), 35–51. https://doi.org/10.2307/41166187

EVPA Knowledge Centre. (2018). *A practical guide to venture philanthropy and social impact investment* (4th ed.). EVPA.

EVPA Knowledge Centre. (2021). *The 2020 investing for impact survey: How social investors support positive societal change*. EVPA.

Fielden, S. L., Davidson, M. J., & Makin, P. J. (2000). Barriers encountered during micro and small business start-up in North-West England. *Journal of Small Business and Enterprise Development, 7*(4), 295–304. https://doi.org/10.1108/EUM0000000006852

Fraser, S. (2007). *Finance for small and medium-sized enterprises: A report on the 2006 UK survey of SME finances social enterprise booster survey*. Centre for Small and Medium-Sized Enterprises.

Freireich, J., & Fulton, K. (2009). *Investing for social and environmental impact: A design catalysing an emerging industry.* Monitor Group.

Geobey, S., Westley, F. R., & Weber, O. (2012). Enabling social innovation through developmental social finance. *Journal of Social Entrepreneurship, 3*(2), 151–165. https://doi.org/10.1080/19420676.2012.726006

GIIN. (2013). *What you need to know about impact investing.* https://thegiin.org/impact-investing/

GIIN. (2019a). *Sizing the impact investing market.* https://thegiin.org/research/publication/impinv-market-size

GIIN. (2019b). *What you need to know about impact investing.* https://thegiin.org/impact investing/need-to-know/#what-is-impact-investing

GIIN. (2021). *Impact investors respond to COVID-19.* https://www.fordfoundation.org/just-matters/just-matters/posts/impact-investors-respond-to-covid-19/

Glanzel, G., & Scheuerle, T. (2016). Social impact investing in Germany: Current impediments from investors' and social entrepreneurs' perspectives. *Voluntas: International Journal of Voluntary and Nonprofit Organizations, 27*(4), 1638–1668.

Godeke, S., & Briaud, P. (2020). *Impact investing handbook: An implementation guide for practitioners.* Rockefeller Philanthropy Advisors.

Gray, J., Ashburn, N., Douglas, H., Jeffers, J., & Geczy, C. (2016). *Great expectations: Mission preservation and financial performance in impact investing* (D. Musto, Ed.). https://socialimpact.wharton.upenn.edu/wp-content/uploads/2016/09/Great-Expectations-Mission-Preservation-and-Financial-Performance-in-Impact-Investing.pdf

Grieco, G. (2015). *Assessing social impact of social enterprises: Does one size really fit all?* Springer International Publishing.

GSG. (2018). *The impact principle: Widening participation and deepening practice for impact investment at scale.* GSG.

Haffar, M., & Searcy, C. (2019). How organizational logics shape trade-off decision-making in sustainability. *Long Range Planning, 52*(6), 101912. https://doi.org/10.1016/j.lrp.2019.101912

Haigh, N., & Hoffman, A. J. (2014). The new heretics: Hybrid organizations and the challenges they present to corporate sustainability. *Organization and Environment, 27*(3), 223–241. https://doi.org/10.1177/1086026614545345

Harji, K., & Jackson, E. T. (2012). *Accelerating impact: Achievements, challenges and what's next in building the impact investing industry.* Rockefeller Foundation.

Hazenberg, R., Seddon, F., & Denny, S. (2014). Intermediary perceptions of investment readiness in the UK social investment market. *Voluntas: International Journal of Voluntary and Nonprofit Organizations, 26*(3), 846–871.

Hebb, T. (2013). Impact investing and responsible investing: What does it mean? *Journal of Sustainable Finance & Investment, 3*(2), 71–74. https://doi.org/10.1080/20430795.2013.776255

Hehenberger, L., Mair, J., & Metz, A. (2019). The assembly of a field ideology: An idea-centric perspective on systemic power in impact investing. *Academy of Management Journal, 62*(6), 1672–1704. Academy of Management. https://doi.org/10.5465/amj.2017.1402

Höchstädter, A. K., & Scheck, B. (2015). What's in a name: An analysis of Impact investing understandings by academics and practitioners. *Journal of Business Ethics, 132*(2), 449–475. https://doi.org/10.1007/s10551-014-2327-0

Hockerts, K., Hehenberger, L., Farber, V., & Schaltegger, S. (2020). Impact investing – critical examinations of motivations, processes and results. *Call for Papers for a Special Issue of the Journal of Business Ethics, 33.*

Hwang, H., & Powell, W. W. (2009). The rationalization of charity: The influences of professionalism in the nonprofit sector. *Administrative Science Quarterly, 54*(2), 268–298.

Jackson, E. T. (2013). Evaluating social impact bonds: Questions, challenges, innovations, and possibilities in measuring outcomes in impact investing. *Community Development, 44*(5), 608–616. https://doi.org/10.1080/15575330.2013.854258

Karaphillis, G., Asimakos, S., & Moore, S. (2010). *Financing social economy organizations*. Canadian Social Economy Research Partnerships.

Kickul, J., & Lyons, T. S. (2015). Financing social enterprises. *Entrepreneurship Research Journal*, 5(2), 83–85.

Lall, S. (2017). Measuring to improve versus measuring to prove: Understanding the adoption of social performance measurement practices in nascent social enterprises. *Voluntas*, 28(6), 2633–2657. https://doi.org/10.1007/s11266-017-9898-1

Lazzarini, S. G., Cabral, S., Ferreira, L. C. D. M., Pongeluppe, L. S., & Rotndaro, A. (2014). *The best of both worlds? Impact investors and their role in the financial versus social performance debate* (No. 2015-06). A Research Agenda for Social Finance.

Leadbeater, C. (2007). *Social enterprise and social innovation: Strategies for the next ten years: A social enterprise think piece for the office of the third sector*. Cabinet Office of the Third Sector.

Lehner, O. M., & Brandstetter, L. (2014). *Impact investment portfolios: Including social risks and return*. ACRN Oxford Publishing House.

Lehner, O. M., Harrer, T., & Quast, M. (2018). Legitimacy and discourse in impact investing: Searching for the holy grail. *Academy of Management Proceedings*, 10935.

Lehner, O. M., & Nicholls, A. (2014). Social finance and crowdfunding for social enterprises: A public-private case study providing legitimacy and leverage. *Venture Capital*, 16(3), 271–286. https://doi.org/10.1080/13691066.2014.925305

Littlefield, E. (2011). Impact investing: Roots & branches. *Innovations: Technology, Governance, Globalization*, 6(3), 19–25. https://doi.org/10.1162/inov_a_00078

Maier, F., Meyer, M., & Steinbereithner, M. (2016). Nonprofit organizations becoming business-like: A systematic review. *Nonprofit and Voluntary Sector Quarterly*, 45(1), 64–86. https://doi.org/10.1177/0899764014561796

Mair, J., & Hehenberger, L. (2014). Front-stage and backstage convening: The transition from opposition to mutualistic coexistence in organizational philanthropy. *Academy of Management Journal*, 57(4), 1174–1200. https://doi.org/10.5465/amj.2012.0305

Markowitz, H. (1952). Portfolio selection. *Journal of Finance*, 1, 77–91.

McHugh, N., Sinclair, S., Roy, M., Huckfield, L., & Donaldson, C. (2013). Social impact bonds: A wolf in sheep's clothing? *Journal of Poverty and Social Justice*, 21(3), 247–257. https://doi.org/10.1332/204674313X13812372137921

Mendell, M., & Barbosa, E. (2013). Impact investing: A preliminary analysis of emergent primary and secondary exchange platforms. *Journal of Sustainable Finance and Investment*, 3(2), 111–123. https://doi.org/10.1080/20430795.2013.776258

Monitor Report. (2009). *Investing for social & environmental impact*. Monitor Report.

Moody, M. (2008). "Building a culture": The construction and evolution of venture philanthropy as a new organizational field. *Nonprofit and Voluntary Sector Quarterly*, 37(2), 324–352. https://doi.org/10.1177/0899764007310419

Moore, M. L., Westley, F. R., & Brodhead, T. (2012). Social finance intermediaries and social innovation. *Journal of Social Entrepreneurship*, 3(2), 184–205. https://doi.org/10.1080/19420676.2012.726020

Mulgan, G. (2010). Measuring social value. *Stanford Social Innovation Review*, 8(3), 38–43.

Neyland, D. (2018). On the transformation of children at-risk into an investment proposition: A study of social impact bonds as an anti-market device. *Sociological Review*, 66(3), 492–510. https://doi.org/10.1177/0038026117744415

Nicholls, A. (2010). The legitimacy of social entrepreneurship: Reflexive isomorphism in a pre-paradigmatic field. *Entrepreneurship: Theory and Practice*, 34(4), 611–633. https://doi.org/10.1111/j.1540-6520.2010.00397.x

Nicholls, A., & Emerson, J. (2015). Social finance: Capitalizing social impact. In A. Nicholls, R. Paton, & J. Emerson (Eds.), *Social finance* (pp. 207–249). Oxford University Press.

OECD. (2015). *Social impact investment: Building the evidence base.* OECD Publishing. www.oecd.org/publications/social-impact-investment-9789264233430-en.htm

OECD. (2019). *Social impact investment 2019: The impact imperative for sustainable development.* OECD Publishing.

Oleksiak, A., Nicholls, A., & Emerson, J. (2015). Impact investing: A market in evolution. In A. Nicholls, R. Paton, & J. Emerson (Eds.), *Social finance* (pp. 207–249). Oxford University Press.

Ormiston, J., Charlton, K., Donald, M. S., & Seymour, R. G. (2015). Overcoming the challenges of impact investing: Insights from leading investors. *Journal of Social Entrepreneurship,* 6(3), 352 378. https://doi.org/10.1080/19420676.2015.1049285

Pache, A. C., & Santos, F. (2013). Inside the hybrid organzation: Selective coupling as a repsonse to competing institutional logics. *Academy of Management Journal,* 56(4), 972–1001. https://doi.org/10.5465/amj.2011.0405

Pereira, L. (2017). Climate change impacts on agriculture across Africa. In *Oxford research encyclopedia of environmental science.* Oxford University Press.

Rajan, A. T., Koserwal, P., & Keerthana, S. (2014). The Global epicenter of impact investing: An analysis of social venture investments in India. *The Journal of Private Equity,* 17(2), 37–50.

Rangan, V. K., Appleby, S., Moon, L., & Schervish, P. G. (2011, November). The promise of impact investing. *Harvard Business Review,* 1–21.

Rexhepi, G. (2016). The architecture of social finance. In O. M. Lehner (Dir. & Ed.), *Routledge handbook of social and sustainable finance* (pp. 35–49). Routledge.

Rizzello, A., Migliazza, M. C., Carè, R., & Trotta, A. (2016). Social impact investing: A model and research agenda. In O. Weber (Ed.), *Routledge handbook of social and sustainable finance.* Routledge.

Rizzi, F., Pellegrini, C., & Battaglia, M. (2018). The structuring of social finance: Emerging approaches for supporting environmentally and socially impactful projects. *Journal of Cleaner Production,* 170, 805–817. https://doi.org/10.1016/j.jclepro.2017.09.167

Rodin, J., & Brandenburg, M. (2014). *The power of impact investing, putting markets to work for profit and global goods.* Wharton Digital Press.

Rogers, R. (2011). Why philanthro-policymaking matters. *Society,* 48, 376–381.

Roundy, P. T. (2019). Regional differences in impact investment: A theory of impact investing ecosystems. *Social Responsibility Journal,* 16(4), 467–485. https://doi.org/10.1108/SRJ-11-2018-0302

Roundy, P. T., Brockman, B. K., & Bradshaw, M. (2017). The resilience of entrepreneurial ecosystems. *Journal of Business Venturing Insights,* 8, 99–104.

Roundy, P. T., Holzhauer, H., & Dai, Y. (2017). Finance or philanthropy? Understanding the motivations and criteria of impact investors. *Social Responsibility Journal,* 3, 419–512.

Saltuk, Y. (2015). *Eyes on the horizon: The impact investor survey.* Global Impact Investing Network.

Scellato, G. (2007). Patents, firm size and financial constraints: An empirical analysis for a panel of Italian manufacturing firms. *Cambridge Journal of Economics,* 31(1), 55–76. https://doi.org/10.1093/cje/bel006

Schaltegger, S., Beckmann, M., & Hockerts, K. (2018). Collaborative entrepreneurship for sustainability: Creating solutions in light of the UN sustainable development goals. *International Journal of Entrepreneurial Venturing,* 10(2), 131–152. https://doi.org/10.1504/IJEV.2018.092709

Schwartz, R., Jones, C., & Nicholls, N. (2015). Building the social finance infrastructure. In A. Nicholls, R. Paton, & J. Emerson (Eds.), *Social finance* (pp. 488–517). Oxford University Press.

Shiller, R. J. (2013). Capitalism and financial innovation. *Financial Analysts Journal,* 69(1), 21–25. CFA Institute. https://doi.org/10.2469/faj.v69.n1.4

So, I., & Staskevicius, A. (2015). *Measuring the 'impact' in impact investing*. Harvard Business School.

Social Finance. (2009). *Social impact bonds: Rethinking finance for social outcomes*. Social Finance.

Steinberg, R. (2015). What should social finance invest in and with whom? In A. Nicholls, R. Paton, & J. Emerson (Eds.), *Social finance* (pp. 64–95). Oxford University Press.

Suarez, D. F. (2010). Street credentials and management backgrounds: Careers of nonprofit executives in an evolving sector. *Nonprofit and Voluntary Sector Quarterly, 39*, 696–716.

Sunley, P., & Pinch, S. (2012). Financing social enterprise: Social bricolage or evolutionary entrepreneurialism? *Social Enterprise Journal, 8*(2), 108–122. https://doi.org/10.1108/17508611211252837

Tekula, R., & Andersen, K. (2019). The role of government, nonprofit, and private facilitation of the impact investing marketplace. *Public Performance & Management Review, 42*(1), 142–161. https://doi.org/10.1080/15309576.2018.1495656

Tekula, R., & Shah, A. (2016). Funding social innovation. In O. M. Lehner (Ed.), *Routledge handbook of social and sustainable finance* (pp. 125–136). Routledge.

Viviani, J. L., & Maurel, C. (2019). Performance of impact investing: A value creation approach. *Research in International Business and Finance, 47*, 31–39. https://doi.org/10.1016/j.ribaf.2018.01.001

Watson, K. J., & Whitley, T. (2017). Applying social return on investment (SROI) to the built environment. *Building Research and Information, 45*(8), 875–891. https://doi.org/10.1080/09613218.2016.1223486

Watson, R., & Wilson, N. (2002). Small and medium size enterprise financing: A note on some of the empirical implications of a pecking order. *Journal of Business Finance and Accounting, 29*(3–4), 557–578. https://doi.org/10.1111/1468-5957.00443

Weber, O. (2016). Introducing Impact Investing. In O. M. Lehner (Ed.), *Routledge handbook of social and sustainable finance*. Routledge, Taylor Francis Group.

Wells, P. (2012). Understanding social investment policy: Evidence from the evaluation of futurebuilders in England. *Voluntary Sector Review, 3*, 157–177.

Wilson, F., & Post, J. E. (2013). Business models for people, planet (& profits): Exploring the phenomena of social business, a market-based approach to social value creation. *Small Business Economics, 40*(3), 715–737. https://doi.org/10.1007/s11187-011-9401-0

Yan, S., & Ferraro, F. (2016). State mediation in market emergence: Socially responsible investing in China. In *How institutions matter!* (Vol. 48B, pp. 173–206). Emerald Group Publishing Limited. https://doi.org/10.1108/S0733-558X201600048B005

Zietsma, C., Groenewegen, P., Logue, D. M., & Bob Hinings, C. R. (2017). Field or fields? Building the scaffolding for cumulation of research on institutional fields. *Academy of Management Annals, 11*(1), 391–450. https://doi.org/10.5465/annals.2014.0052

Zingales, L. (2015). Presidential address: Does finance benefit society? *Journal of Finance, 70*(4), 1327–1363. https://doi.org/10.1111/jofi.12295

8 Social Impact Evaluation
Moving From Method to Realist Strategy

Gorgi Krlev and Federica Angeli

Introduction

Impact is now everywhere. In view of the sustainable development goals, organisations – across sectors – are increasingly expected to prove and communicate the social impact they are creating (Howard-Grenville et al., 2019) or in other words the contributions they make towards those goals. Measuring social impact refers to assessing which effects organizations have on their immediate target group or wider stakeholders (Barnett et al., 2020; Beer & Micheli, 2018; Wry & Haugh, 2018). The need for measuring social impact is especially important for organizations invested with a social mandate, whose very purpose lies in contributing to the global goals of social and environmental sustainability. Innovative healthcare enterprises seek to improve the wellbeing of people without access to care, advocacy NGOs want to raise awareness for the needs of disadvantaged groups, and green tech start-ups strive for stopping environmental degradation. In reference to such organizations, gathering evidence on impacts achieved serves three primary functions: First, measuring impact enhances organizational learning and improves organizations' "operational capacity to deliver the value" (Moore, 2000, p. 183) they promise. It also helps organizations embrace "big strategy" (Whittington, 2012, p. 23) radiating beyond the organization rather than small strategy focusing on questions of efficiency, for example. Second, it enables existing and future stakeholders of such organizations, be they customers, donors or investors (Bonini & Emerson, 2005, p. 7), assess whether and how value is created and thus whether they should choose to support the organization. Third, measuring impact serves to signal accountability towards field regulators, such as the state, especially when new vehicles of public service contracting such as social impact bonds are being applied (Edmiston & Nicholls, 2018).

Due to the variety of organizations it matters to, and the breadth of functions it serves, measuring social impact is promoted by global organizations ranging from the social enterprise network Ashoka to the World Economic Forum (World Economic Forum, 2020). In the past two decades, significant progress has been made with regard to gathering and presenting evidence able to corroborate social impact. Impact analysts started with scattered and individualized hands-on approaches to assessing impact and have now arrived at a series of shared standards (Social Impact InvestmentTaskforce, 2014). The Impact Management Project (2021), supported by a range of global institutions and network organizations, is one of the most visible results of those efforts. Shared standards have emerged on the background of tools for measuring social impact such as the Social Return on Investment (SROI) (Emerson, 2003) or

DOI: 10.4324/9780429243165-9

This chapter has been made available under a CC-BY-NC 4.0 license.

the Best Alternative Charitable Option (BACO) (Brest et al., 2009). SROI provided a structured guide of how to identify and assess economic, socio-economic and social effects (Kehl et al., 2018; Maier et al., 2014), while BACO offered a heuristic approach to holding alternative organizational activities against each other in relation to some impact key performance indicators, to choose the best alternative. However, despite this evolution, we are still far away from a common understanding of how social impact measurement should be practiced. Part of the reasons why a gap in understanding how to practice measurement persists, is that from the start organizational and institutional actors in the field have insisted on developing and branding their individualized approaches (Tuan, 2008). Another reason is that organizations practicing impact measurement tend to apply a bricolage approach of pick and mix between tools and analytic strategies (Molecke & Pinkse, 2017), which make comparisons across organizations difficult if not impossible.

So, while the advancements in the field may have helped practitioners grasp the difficulties of impact measurement by providing methodologies, they might also have blurred deeper conceptual insights into effective strategies for gathering robust evidence on impact. In particular, tools and guidelines may have suggested an oversimplified image of what it entails to capture impact, in part denying impact complexities and promoting reductionist approaches to capturing it. Some observers claim that methods, indicators and standards are not the next frontier in impact measurement (Ruff & Olsen, 2016). Ruff and Olsen (2016) instead stress that, for generating and processing impact information, we need more analysts and stakeholders who are fluent in the impact language and capable of translating what specific figures and narratives of evidence mean. Having such ability matters to make sense of presented findings against the inchoate state of agreed standards and practice in the field described initially. The need for promoting the reflexive ability Ruff and Olsen describe does not only hold from the perspective of impact practice, but seems to apply from that of research in the area of impact, too. Recent reviews of management papers, which judged by their title and abstract claim to be dealing with measuring impact, show that the large majority of this research is not focusing on improved intervention outcomes or impacts for target groups (Barnett et al., 2020; Wry & Haugh, 2018). Instead and as the authors show, much of this "impact research" deals with prosocial certification of organizations, the challenges of measurement, or stops at the input or output level of the classic "logic model" in evaluation theory (Weiss, 1972, 1998) rather than with the assessment of social outcomes or systemic change. The logic model (Kaplan & Garrett, 2005, p. 167) is "a graphic display or 'map' of the relationship between a programme's resources, activities, and intended results, which also identifies the programme's underlying theory and assumptions." Among the intended results, the logic model distinguishes between outputs (tangible, quantifiable short-term results of the programme activities), outcomes (improvements at individual level among the programme recipients) and impact (community-wide, systemic benefits, often with a long-term perspective) (Ebrahim & Rangan, 2014). The lack of research genuinely focusing on impact is to a large part owed to the methodological and conceptual challenges of measuring impact, among which the measurement and attribution problems stand out (see the discussion in Krlev et al., 2019). These problems point at the difficulty of operationalizing impact and the difficulty of ascribing impact to specific organizational actions. Economics and political science have proposed ways to deal with them. Experimental studies are used to judge the effectiveness of development projects (Banerjee & Duflo, 2012; Clemens & Demombynes, 2011) or political anti-poverty programmes (Blattman et al., 2018)). But such studies also have downsides. Critics have highlighted that the fine-grained, technical approach of experiments is limited in providing suggestions on how to actually solve a problem such as global poverty (Ravallion, 2012), not to speak of the ethical problems randomization might evoke (Deaton & Cartwright, 2018). It also reduces the types of questions that can be asked (Reddy, 2012) and the types of evidence that can be gathered (Kabeer, 2019). So, there is a continuous struggle about how to best assess the social impact organizations are creating. We believe the methodology-driven, technical approach to social impact needs to be counter-balanced by a realist approach, which lays out the challenges at a more conceptual level and proposes a more comprehensive strategy of how to deal with them.

Why is developing such a realist approach important? First, because our social and environmental challenges are manifold and we are in dire need of understanding how organizations can contribute to addressing them in various ways (George et al., 2016). Second, because the performance literature suggests that the quality of evidence used in performance management increases direct effects on actual performance (Gerrish, 2016). Unfortunately, to date we have a strong divide between impact measurement being practiced as some sort of derivative to regular performance management with relatively poor quality of adequate evidence, and impact measurement explicitly focusing on the creation of social value (Beer & Micheli, 2018). In the worst of cases impact measurement is practiced "as a form of impression management" (Molecke & Pinkse, 2020) rather than to actually contribute to external accountability (Ebrahim, 2019) or to organizational learning. Importantly, organizations are known to learn from performance feedback, and to interpret underperformance or overperformance as cues to inform organizational change towards desired performance level (Greve, 2003; Nason et al., 2018; Ryan, 2004). However, this mechanism is influenced by the very definition of performance and its measurement. To spur beneficial organizational adaptation towards improved social impact, we therefore need to provide organizations with effective strategies, rather than only methods, of how to measure social impact, and advance the theory of impact measurement. Developing such a perspective is the purpose of this chapter.

We first outline the reasons why we are so fascinated with impact and the potential downsides of malpractice in measurement. We then present important analytic categories in the measurement process, which are often confused, before we outline different strategies in assessing organizational impact.

Why this Fascination with Impact?

Two main drivers are responsible for the present scholars' and practitioners' fascination with impact measurement. The first factor is higher standards of accountability. Over the past years, the focus of accountability has shifted from the aspects of responsibility (following the rules) and controllability (fulfilling your principal's expectations) towards transparency (revealing performance outcomes) and the subsequent liability for keeping this performance up (Ebrahim, 2019; Koppell, 2005). The second factor is more and more forceful calls for a higher effectiveness of investments for the "public good" in view of more challenging and complex social problems and the limitedness of public resources (Edmiston & Nicholls, 2018). At the very least, organizations are seeking to make sure and prove that they are doing no harm (Voegtlin & Scherer, 2017). These factors have arisen against a long tradition of practical developments and research on social accounting (Busco & Quattrone, 2018; Gray, 2002), integrated reporting (Nicholls, 2009) that seek to capture and communicate (positive and negative) social and environmental effects organizations are producing in addition to their financial performance.

While measuring social impact is thus of concern to essentially all types of organizations, nonprofits, social enterprises or non-governmental organizations have experienced particular pressures to deliver proof of their contributions to society beyond reports that communicate organizational activities or efficiency in employing funds. Fuelling such expectations are concepts such as Social Business (Yunus et al., 2010) and Venture Philanthropy (Mair & Hehenberger, 2014). These concepts try to merge two different worlds characterized by distinct principles. The collision of worlds is inherent in the very term "social impact measurement", and evokes a number of critical questions. How can you measure "the social"? Isn't measurement something that is restricted to the natural sciences and the business world? Should the social not be left untouched to preserve its grace? Is trying to measure the social not an act of "unsocializing"? Most economists have obviously negated these questions. Cost-benefit analysis for instance has quite a long tradition dating back to the 1980s and before (Drèze & Stern, 1985). It attempts to compare the costs a social project evokes with the positive – minus the negative, often unintended – effects it produces. This idea has been picked up and developed further by what was to become one of the first impact measurement tools in the nonprofit world: the Social Return on Investment (SROI) (Emerson, 2003). As its name suggests, it does not only follow the cost-benefit logic, but has the ambition of capturing more genuine social returns. Thereby and as per the logic model (Weiss, 1998), it tries to link the investment (inputs) directly to the yield they are creating (return). The analogy to the logic of financial returns has been driven by Anglo-Saxon, liberal democratic thinking (Maier et al., 2014). However, there is an ever greater interest in the tool in nation states with other welfare and economic traditions, for instance across Continental Europe (Kehl et al., 2018). Despite its proliferation, even after ten years of usage, there were major challenges in SROI practice, which we outline in the following as exemplary for the practice of impact measurement more widely.

Social Impact Measurement Malpractice and Its Consequences

An extensive analysis of SROI studies published between 2002 and 2012 showed a range of key limitations (Krlev et al., 2013). The results are admittedly somewhat dated, but we do not know of any comparable and updated effort that investigates measurement practice in depth. What is more, the general findings about practices have been confirmed in individual case studies (Wilson & Frederick Bull, 2013), research using survey and interview data (Millar & Hall, 2013) or conceptual considerations (Arvidson et al., 2014; Maier et al., 2014). What is more, very recent research shows that impact measurement is often practiced for symbolic rather than substantive reasons (Beer & Micheli, 2018; Molecke & Pinkse, 2020), supporting the suggested limitations. Our discussion of past practice in SROI is therefore meant to be exemplary for the current challenges of impact measurement research and practice, independent of tools or methods applied, or in fact the specific field

172 Gorgi Krlev and Federica Angeli

or sector (for-profit, nonprofit or public) in which the research is situated (see also (Barnett et al., 2020; Wry & Haugh, 2018).

The Focus on Outputs and Challenges of Attribution

A major problem revealed in the cited analysis related to the indicators applied. Analysts mostly focused on the sheer number of people who used a service or reported to benefit from it in one way or another. In the case of public health intervention to strengthen healthcare delivery in rural areas for example, this approach would reflect into tracking the number of people who visited a clinic. In a development project aimed to improve access to clean water and sanitation would translate to an increase in the number of toilets installed, or the number of wells dug up. In the case of a humanitarian relief project, this perspective would amount to focusing on the number of blankets being distributed, or temporary shelters built. Although informative, these performance indicators provide only the starting point to impact generation and fall short to provide effective information on whether these infrastructural improvements actually translated into benefits for individuals and communities. This approach is effectively limited to monitoring outputs rather than outcome or impact figures. What was essentially missing is the inclusion of the questions: (1) Did the target groups use these services? and (2) How did the target groups who used the service benefit from it? There are certainly cases where a mere increase in the number of people is sufficient to denote impact. Take for instance the number of people who have found a new job through a work integration effort. Although job satisfaction and retention should play a role, the fact that the person has moved from joblessness into a job is sufficient to derive subsequent major effects for the most part: public savings in personal transfers, the creation of new income and independence for the person, the rise in taxes. The same would apply for the visitors to a clinic, who at least benefit by receiving a health consultation that would not have taken place otherwise. If we take a youth centre however, the mere increase in numbers of people going in and out would not tell us much. What if more young people visit the center only because they are forced to do so in one way or another? Which services did they use and have they really benefitted from them? What if an increase in new visitors makes the services offered less effective for the youth who always used to go there? In the case of the development intervention above, the mere installation of toilets or wells does not automatically mean that the target groups will (properly) use them, an outcome that is often moderated by complex socio-cultural circumstances.

Another example is community engagement projects. The stimulation of interaction in a community is a virtue in itself (Arvidson et al., 2014). To estimate its value, however, we need to establish a causal link to for instance the independence of individuals in acting within this community (choice) or the empowerment of people (voice). Thus, it is not sufficient to stress the increase in numbers of people who report that they engage more strongly in the community. It is important to know how much more they are engaged as compared to the situation before (baseline), and how much this has increased their independence or that of other community members. To get to this, analysts have to be precise with regard to the description of indicators. The SROI study often found vague categories such as "a decrease in support need" or "the acquisition of special industry knowledge", which lacked further specification that would have been meaningful for a proper analysis.

Monetization and Challenges of Measurement

Most of the SROI reports analysed were related to work integration, where as out-lined earlier output measures might be sufficient to approximate impact. Besides and as mentioned earlier, monetization of the effects, a key feature of SROI, is rather straightforward. However, in other fields it is much more difficult to apply appropriate measures, not to speak of moving from measures to monetization of the effects. These cases include life coaching and assistance, comprising for example crime prevention and personality building for youth, teenage pregnancies, women affected by violence, other family conflicts, people in mental distress due to challenging life situations, or communities targeted in development and humanitarian interventions. The analysed reports dealt with this issue in two ways. The first strategy was to pretty much ignore all these aspects. Despite being acknowledged, they were not systematically incorporated in the analysis (neither quantitatively nor qualitatively). As a consequence, the respective studies concentrated mostly on the socio-economic dimension such as indirect public savings through decreased expenditures. An example is the reduction of workload for public bodies like the police through reduced crime rates by crime prevention programmes. While useful, this does not help measuring direct effects on individuals or surrounding communities.

Another part of the analysed studies paved overly creative ways to forceful monetization. For example, in one report the value of a challenging work environment after job integration was approximated financially by an event that was supposed to result in similar positive feelings: the cost of a two-day adventure trip. While creative, this strategy clearly is unable to establish any authentic connection between input and triggered social impact at all. Thus, if applied inappropriately, monetization does not contribute to increasing accountability of social organizations by introducing "hard figures" to assess their performance. The contrary will be the case, with additionally the risk of undermining the legitimacy of any such endeavour. Both strategies taken together suggest that the "social effects", postulated as particularly important in SROI, were not adequately captured.

Types of Data and Research Designs

While about 80% of the studies provided some qualitative information about such effects and 40% analysed social effects quantitatively, most of the provided evidence was poor. The most frequent qualitative evidence were single case studies – to put it more precisely a short anecdote on how a person's life had changed by taking part in an intervention. What we would actually expect to see instead is a cross-case comparison of observations or an analysis of interview data as often done in qualitative research. The situation was even worse as with regard to quantitative evidence. Out of the reports that provided quantitative evidence at all, less than 40% presented some kind of survey data and analysis, while 60% only provided some descriptive statistics, often related to output measures as described earlier.

No matter what kind of evidence is gathered, the chosen research design needs to be executed in a rigorous fashion, but this was not the case and maybe the greatest deficiency detected in the systematic SROI review. Not even 3% of the SROI studies analysed had applied an observational control group design – not to speak of randomization – and less than 20% had performed any ex ante – ex post observation. That

174 Gorgi Krlev and Federica Angeli

is most studies were cross-sectional, often without attempts of tracking influence of an intervention over time. The low quality of many studies in these regards is not particular to SROI and might even be worse in fields with other traditions of evaluation. Development assistance is one such field, where reviewers find that "[o]f the hundreds of evaluation studies conducted in recent years, only a tiny handful were designed in a manner that makes it possible to identify program impact" (Savedoff et al., 2006, p. 17). Recent reviews of research on the impacts of corporate social responsibility come to a very similar conclusion, stating that not a single study could be identified that focused explicitly on the measurement impact as opposed to outputs for example (Barnett et al., 2020).

Forming a Realist Impact Assessment Strategy

The observations given earlier suggest that we might need to take a step back and analyse in a more systematic way how organizations would best go about measuring their social impact. We have mentioned earlier that there is a struggle between the experimental approach to measurement in economics, and partly also in political science, and a hands-on approach in management practice as well as a discourse in management research that is focused more on meta-reflections about rather than actual measurement of impact. In order to find a middle ground between the two, it seems beneficial to turn to evidence-based medicine. Originally, the very blueprint of evidence-based studies in economics, evidence-based medicine, is now moving towards becoming more "realist" (Greenhalgh & Papoutsi, 2018; Wong et al., 2013). This development occurs, since complex health interventions (Byford & Sefton, 2003), where effects depend on a large number of factors that initiate several coinciding causal processes, and defy the logic of clearly controlled quantitative designs. Mirroring this realization, observers of evidence-based decision-making, especially in the social sector, have been calling for it to become more holistic and contextual (Brooks, 2016; Moss et al., 2020). Realist evaluation, as applied to evaluate complex health interventions, recognizes the role of context, and the interaction between the theoretical mechanism underlining the intervention and its context to produce the desired outcome. In this sense, many equivalent causal processes (as defined by the interplay between mechanisms and context) can lead to the same outcome, depending on the specificities of the setting. The transformation of practice in evidence-based medicine has served as inspiration to derive six analytic steps, which we suggest analysts of impact should go through when they are setting up, and executing their impact measurement and reporting. The steps integrate different types of evidence and a variety of research designs (see Glasziou & Heneghan, 2009 for an overview), depending on what impact analysts, be they from within our outside the investigated organization, want to find out and what kind of data the analysts can get hold of.

The main premise here is that impact analysts seek to assess a specific organizational activity, be it a product, service, or advocacy effort for example. Gauging impact at the level of an organization across a range of different activities, will either need to try and aggregate insights gained at the level of these activities, or estimate impact in a much more aggregated and sketchy way. Rather than robust proof of impact, such an approach would result in weighing of impact potential or promise, as is the case in certification of B Corp status for instance (Ballesteros-Sola et al., 2018).[1]

Step 1: Accounting for Complexity and Clarifying the Goal of the Measurement

First of all, anyone attempting to analyse the social impact created by a specific organisational activity, has to decide whether or not the complexity of the intervention's (1) "theory of change" or "logic model", and (2) operational strategy (see Ebrahim & Rangan, 2010) require the assessment of impact at all. Certain interventions – as we will see below – can be assessed by more straightforward means.

Any organizational activity can be conceptualized as intervention, aimed at triggering some behavioural change. Interventions are traditionally underpinned by a logic model, which lays out the expected change (in terms of outputs, outcomes and impact) in view of specific input resources and activities (Figure 8.1).

Operational complexity refers to activities that are multi-pronged or where several processes happen in parallel (see Glouberman & Zimmerman, 2002; Rogers, 2008 for a conceptualization of what is complex, for example as opposed to complicated). In line with this, complex interventions feature a high number of interacting components within the experimental and control interventions; require difficult and multi-faceted behavioural change of those delivering and/or receiving the intervention; target many groups or organizational levels; address many and potentially variable and context-dependent outcomes; require a high degree of flexibility to tailor to the intervention to the specificities of the receiving setting (Craig et al., 2008). From a logics model point of view instead, Rogers (2008) highlights how logic models may be simple or complex. What makes an intervention complex – whether it is a new public policy programme or a new product introduced in the market – is recursive causality and emergent outcomes. Most logic models rely simplistically on iteration of the intervention, instead, many socially-oriented interventions aim at creating a reinforcing (hopefully, virtuous) cycle "where an initial success creates the conditions for further success" (Rogers, 2008). Instead, emergent outcomes occur when unexpected, unpredicted phenomena manifest as a result of the intervention. These are typical in case of interventions that

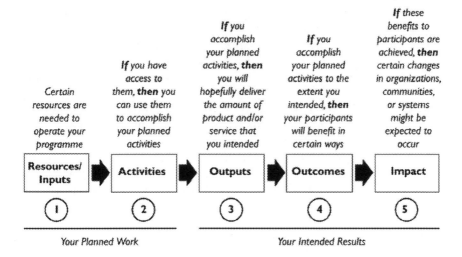

Figure 8.1 A simple logic model (Kellogg Foundation, 2004; Rogers, 2008).

address systemic challenges or "wicked problems", which behave as complex adaptive systems (Angeli & Montefusco, 2020; Dentoni et al., 2020). A logic model for a complex intervention – in this case a multi-strategy community intervention for reducing maternal and child health inequalities in India – is represented in Figure 8.2. Although the recursive paths and the emergent outcomes are not pictured, both have been observed during the mixed-method evaluation process (Gupta et al., 2017). The logic model represented nevertheless highlights the operational complexity.

Organizations will not have to address social impact at all, so Ebrahim and Rangan (2010) argue, if unless both their logic model and their operational strategy – that is the ways in which an intervention is executed – are complex, in line with the definitions of complex interventions, complex operational strategies. The effects of organizations where both dimensions are simple rather than complex can be captured reasonably well by simply looking at "what the organizations have done". While Ebrahim and Rangan refer to such measures as inputs, activities, outputs (and partly outcomes), we use "activities" only, as the term describes comprehensively and sufficiently what organizations need to account for, when they assess their effects as shown in Figure 8.3. Figure 8.3 presents four quadrants with different levels of complexity and provides examples for such constellations.

A simple logic model and operational strategy are found for instance in a food kitchen. There is a clear need (hunger) and a simple organizational activity (providing food). Although not solving the systemic issue leading to hunger, food kitchens serve a need that is straightforward and that is perceived as such by the recipients. To judge the effects of the latter, it would be sufficient to look at how many meals have been served. The same logic applies to other organizational activities, such as disaster relief or the life-saving organizational activities of sea rescue services. They can be assessed by the number of shelters provided, or the number of lives saved. A simple logic model and a complex operational strategy are also fairly easily identified. Think about an immunization campaign. It will be more complex than in a food kitchen to reach out, inform and attract people (operational strategy), but the impact of the organizational activity can be quite simply evaluated, in that performing the vaccination directly provides protection from the disease and thus a health gain. Water hygiene initiatives would be another example in this regard. They could be assessed by the number of chlorine tablets distributed, but people need to be convinced to use them once they have them. This circumstance gives organizations less control than in the immunization case over important factors that may moderate whether the outcome even has the chance to materialize or not, but can still be allocated reasonably well into this quadrant.

It is harder to find a good example for a simple operational strategy in combination with a complex logic model. We disagree with Ebrahim and Rangan (2010) that organizational activities which promote "rights and freedom" or "good governance" belong into that category. In our view, those are complex at both levels and should thus be assessed by impacts and not merely by quantifying activities. The best example we could think of are drug withdrawal programmes. Although the organizational activity needs to be multi-faceted and it can be hard to achieve effective behavioural change in patients, many such programmes work with a rather standard protocol of how to promote abstinence and thus pursue a straightforward operational strategy. However, there are alternatives to these standard models that have only been recognised recently, which focus on "controlled consumption" of illegal drugs instead

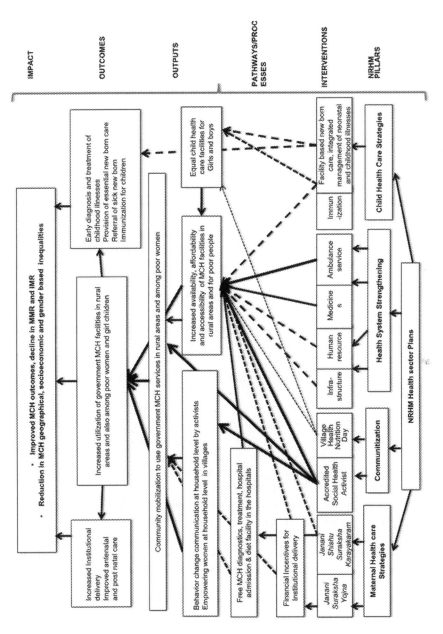

Figure 8.2 Intervention logic model illustrating pathways of change of a multi-strategy community intervention for reducing maternal and child health inequalities in India.

Source: Gupta et al. (2017)

		Activities	Activities
Logic model	Complex	*Example:* *Drug withdrawal*	*Examples:* *Violence prevention* *Empowerment activities* *Community development*
	Simple	Activities	Activities
		Example: *Food kitchen*	*Example:* *Immunisation initiative*
		Simple	Complex
		Operational strategy	

Figure 8.3 Differences in the complexity of interventions. Own illustration in relation to (Ebrahim & Rangan, 2010).

and challenge the status quo in many ways (Bergmann, 2014). They modify both the operational strategy and the logic model and thereby move such organizational activities to a doubly complex state. There are also other "in between cases" with a tendency of being more complex in both regards. HIV/AIDS campaigns promoting safer sex for instance share more commonalities in terms of operational strategies with the immunization or sanitation campaigns, but will need to effectuate impact through a more complex process of change in the behaviour of the individuals targeted and their surrounding environment than the water hygiene example discussed earlier.

Other organizational activities are inarguably complex on both levels. A violence prevention programme, independent of whether it targets the family or some wider social group, will have to seek out and intrude the social setting at risk, and try to effectuate change of a behaviour that might have deep root causes. The empowerment of women in deprived or traditional societies will need to span many different levels, from self-determination in various regards to the ability and acceptance of women to participate in public life. In a similar way, yet with an even more multifaceted target group and goal set, community development initiatives will need to become active at different levels and employ diverse modes of organizational activity.

The difficulty of finding good examples for organizational activities that are simple in at least one dimension outlines that the question about social impact is justified in relation to most social purpose organizations and the work they do, since interventions aiming to change human behaviours are inherently complex endeavours. It is worth noting that there may be assessments whose primary interest is not in impact, but in other aspects such as cost-effectiveness, the professionalism with which the organizational activity has been executed or other dimensions of performance. Analysts of social impact will have to decide whether the assessment of impact is actually at the centre of the investigation or whether it serves a complementary function and by which other measurement components it should be accompanied. Once this decision is made, the following procedural steps help draft and perform the corresponding measurement and attribution.

Step 2: Defining Scope and Measures

The impact analyst has to identify which intended effects are central to the investigated organizational activity. In this it is important to consider a range of stakeholders and the different effects they might benefit from, as highlighted in basically every guide to social impact measurement (Nicholls, 2009; Schober & Then, 2015; Social Impact InvestmentTaskforce, 2014). It is equally important though, not to let this effort distract the focus of the analysis as proposed earlier. Finding focus should be guided by the two rationales of: (1) delimiting the range of the stakeholders under study and (2) delimiting the range of (follow-up) up effects considered. With regard to the first aspect, direct beneficiaries should be at the centre of attention. This is because the analysis of impact should be located at the point that is most meaningful for answering whether and which effects have been achieved. If an organizational activity is not effective in making a difference for their target group, its overall impact is seriously impeded, and positive follow-up effects matter little.

With regard to the second aspect, the measurement components have to be tied to the core goals articulated in the organization's mission. Since social impact is a way of measuring the performance of organizations in contributing to social productivity, any measurement pertaining to it needs to refer back to the place where the supposed main dimensions of performance are defined. The danger otherwise is that the variables to be measured are so manifold and at such a distance that they exponentiate the identified assessment problems, in particular attribution. Causal attribution is particularly difficult in evaluating social impact, in view of the longer time-frame required to evaluate social effects and the potentially intervening factors, such as the effects achieved by others (alternative attribution), the effects that would have happened anyway (deadweight), for negative consequences (displacement) and for effects declining over time (drop off) (GECES Sub-group on Impact Measurement, 2014).

Step 3: Choosing the Appropriate Measurement Design

In a third step and to further improve attribution, the measurement or research design needs to be drafted by the analysts. This means analysts will need to clarify how they want to find out whether a specific social outcome has materialized, and whether the observed effect can be actually linked to the investigated organizational activities. As already mentioned, experimental designs may clash with feasibility, pragmatic or ethical considerations, which is why impact analysts may have to rely on observational measurement designs. These exist in a variety of outfits, which need to be selected based on how effectively they are applicable to the specific context. As mentioned previously evidence-based medicine can provide important guidance in this regard (Glasziou & Heneghan, 2009).

Designs with a Control Group

Controlled designs, i.e. designs that compare effects between an intervention group, buying the product or receiving the service for example, and a control group with no access to the product or service, require several specifics from the research context. First, there needs to be a meaningful control group, which is a group of people not affected by the organizational activity that is as similar as possible, in every other respect, to the group of people affected by it. The control group should be subject to some other "intervention", if two alternative organizational activities are to be compared as to their impact (for example, two alternative coaching programmes helping disadvantaged groups in financial need). Second, the recruitment of a control group

180   *Gorgi Krlev and Federica Angeli*

needs to be feasible, that is there needs to be sufficient ground to assume members of a potential control group will be willing to participate in the study. Where this is impossible, comparisons might be drawn between the general population using data from citizen surveys, to see whether those affected by the organizational activity experience different effects. Third, the insights achieved through the comparison should be valuable. Sometimes, it does not make sense to have a control group, since the transformation process an organizational activity seeks to trigger is so individual that getting in-depth insights, with qualitative methods, into whether and how the change has occurred should have priority over quantitative controlled designs. Fourth, efforts put into the analysis, including time, human and financial resources, need to be commensurate with the size and capacity of the organization as well as with the scope of the organizational activity under study.

Designs with a (within group) Pre-Post Comparison

If one of the above criteria does not hold, within group comparisons of those addressed by the organizational activity, before and after the organizational activity affected them, with a careful account of potential confounding factors are an alternative. They might generally be the design of choice where a multitude of confounding factors could be responsible for an effectuated change, for instance in fast changing environments or where organizational activities are hard to delineate strictly from other social influences, which are likely to vary across contexts or even individuals. This applies for instance to any normative education programme for children. Every child has a different position within the larger setting of the school she goes to, a different individual family background, or a different embedding in her peer groups. The social settings and changes over time are likely to be more variable for children than for other target groups. Even if groups of children are similar at face value, they are likely more affected by confounding factors than other individuals and reliable inference of impact from group comparisons is harder. Where such circumstances apply, it seems furthermore advisable to use a rather short time frame between pre- and post-assessment, since time might lever confounding so much that a longer duration deteriorates the precision of the analysis more than it offers to demonstrate the sustainability of effects.

Designs with a Focus on the Transformation Process

Educational research on bullying in school offers some illustrative insights on both points, namely the influence of context and changes over time. There typically is a significant "age decline" in reports about being bullied from the age of 8 to 16, that occurs without any specific intervention. Already some time ago Smith et al. (1999) have found support for two potential explanations for the observed decline. The first one is that when children are younger, there are more peers older than them attending school, who could potentially bully them. The second reason is that children only come to acquire the social skills and assertiveness needed to deal with bullying as they grow older. Thus, social context matters strongly and individual psychological development occurs even without any directional force steering the process. If we now realize that this social learning process does not occur in a linear fashion and in the same way for each and every individual, we need to be aware that any behavioural changes detected in an impact study might be caused by (changes in) group composition or

Social Impact Evaluation   181

(episodes of) external social influences. Such factors are hard to control for, even in quasi-experimental or experimental designs. Finally, when pre-post observations are practically hard to realize, for instance when it would require too much time to form a sufficiently large panel for the study, an option is to make use of retrospective accounts. This means for example to ask participants explicitly on whether their social activity has increased through a neighbourhood support initiative, and for example hold this against how socially connected the affected people used to be throughout their lives to see whether the initiative made a difference.

A Realist Approach to Designs

It is crucial to note here that pre-post types of evaluation that try to replicate a randomized control trial logic in social settings have in fact been questioned in their suitability to evaluate complex social organizational activities. A "realist" approach to evaluation instead seems more comprehensive and valuable, in that it not only takes into account outcomes indicators (outcome evaluation) but also tries to capture the influence of contextual factors and of the implementation process in a qualitative way through a process evaluation (Fletcher et al., 2016; Gupta et al., 2017). As a realist evaluation tries to assess '"what works for whom, in what circumstances, in what respects and how" (Jagosh et al., 2015), if follows that the implementation process of a designed organizational activity – for example the adoption process of a specific product or service – is highly relevant in explaining its outcomes. In the example of an education programme for children, the influence of the organizational activity on children's social skills would depend on the design of the organizational activity but also on the interaction between teachers in the programme and specific children, along with their unique school and family circumstances, learning curves, age and personal factors.

After decisions on the design have been made, we need to think about what types of data will need to be generated and assessed.

Step 4: Types of Data

The fourth step is to compose instruments to generate different types of data, namely quantitative or qualitative data, which are useful, valid and reliable enough to address the measurement problem (on validity and reliability of measures Cronbach, 1990, including in qualitative research (Morse et al., 2002). As mentioned before, both are very much at the centre of heated debates between proponents of supposedly clearer and more robust quantitative analysis (Banerjee & Duflo, 2012), or supposedly richer and more contextualized qualitative insights (Kabeer, 2019). Instead of favouring one over the other, here we are trying to outline the applicability as well as possibilities and limitations of either type of data in advancing insights into impact.

Quantitative data will mostly be generated by primary surveys or drawn from secondary data sources, while qualitative data will emerge from original interviews or observations. Quantitative methods are often more valid and reliable than qualitative ways of assessment, since some of the applicable measures have been tested extensively in previous research across a variety of contexts. They may also appear to be more objective by their use of numbers. However, King et al. (1995, p. 4f) for instance have long promoted the argument that "differences between quantitative and qualitative traditions are methodologically and substantively unimportant" and that both, if

182 Gorgi Krlev and Federica Angeli

rigorously applied, are able to arrive at "valid causal inference." They make the last statement in relation to historical research. In terms of explanation, qualitative methods offer more in-depth insights into a matter and are more easily adaptable during the research process. The impact analyst can probe issues right away and flexibly narrow down or extend the range of questions during one interview and carry the adaptions made to the next. Questionnaire items can also be adapted, but only after a larger number of questionnaires have been completed and analysed as to gaps or inconsistencies in the knowledge they generate.

Qualitative methods are particularly useful under three conditions. First, they offer to generate insights where we can say only little about the supposed effects of a specific organizational activity, that is, where we have little experience with it or related activities. Second, they offer room for differentiation and probing where effects differ remarkably across different types of beneficiaries or settings. Organizational activities meant to prevent violence in schools for instance, are likely to differ with regard to pupils with higher and lower initial levels of behavioural problems. Third and most importantly, qualitative methods should be applied where we seek direct insights into change processes or dynamics and we seek to carry out a process evaluation – and thus where a steady state comparison of measures across groups does not offer enough such evidence.

Longitudinal quantitative data also enables us to follow changes in measures over time (outcome evaluation), but in contrast to qualitative data it is hardly able to uncover the underlying mechanisms or understand and describe the interactions between effects. In consequence, qualitative data is often better at establishing links between the range of performed activities and changes in the measures. In other words, it offers to address the additional question of *how* changes have come about rather than only *if* they have occurred. This very link can be pivotal to organisational learning and the subsequent (re-)design in the components of what an organization does. Maxwell (2012, p. 31f) mentions causal inference is better ensured by quantitative testing. But at the same time, he makes the case for qualitative methods. He does so by relating to research in educational contexts from the 1980s and 1990s that suggests the effects of educational research on educational practice had been restricted by the fact that most of it was quantitative and lacking practical context and appeal.

Mixed methods and data are usually superior to either of the above approaches alone, but time, finance and circumstance might not always permit such comprehensive studies, which is why impact analysts need to make choices. After having identified which types of methods and data will offer the best evidence under an organization's given circumstances, we enter the most important phase in the measurement of social impact, which is the selection, adaption or design of the measures to be applied.

Step 5: Refining Measures

The first step in the development of measures is a thorough differentiation of the individual components. The exact measures are derived from what is stressed in the organizational mission. Depending on that mission, the measures can take on different outfits. And depending on the distinct focus, the drafting of individual measures has to relate to different points of reference in existing research. Practitioners have designed comprehensive data bases to showcase previous use of impact indicators for specific organizational activities (Global Impact Investing Network (GIIN), n.d.; Social Value UK, 2020). Given the social science grounding of this chapter and its orientation at realist evaluation, we argue impact investors, social entrepreneurs or corporate social responsibility managers would be well advised to also consult measurement practice in a variety of research fields. Standard and validated scales from psychology, sociology, economics or political science can be a useful resource, independent of whether the applied methods in the measurement of social impact are quantitative or qualitative. In case a qualitative approach is applied, questionnaire items must be translated into a (semi-)structured, and in rare cases unstructured, interview guide (Gubrium & Holstein, 2001). If the study is quantitative, no such conversion needs to be made. However, it is mostly useful to shorten, adapt, revise or combine existing sets of questions to match the specific field or country context of the analysed organizational activity and the focus in the knowledge to be produced. One of the reasons for performing some revision is the practicality of the measurement. It has to be feasible, in particular for smaller or less resource rich organizational activities. It often also has to be repeatable over time, for instance for being implemented into periodical social reporting (Nicholls, 2010), or for replicating the analysis by increasing participant numbers, or under varying context conditions.

In some cases measures will have to be drafted anew, since no previous research exists that can be applied directly, which is the case when the impact assessment is great in depth, large in scope, particularly original, placed in an unusual regional or field context, or located at a level typically not addressed in previous research in an adequate way. There will not always be a perfect fit between the goals of the measurement and previous research. However, it is very likely that some guidance can be found in the questions and scales applied on the micro level, for example in social psychology (see, for instance, Mruk, 2006, on the vast array of theories and measures of self-esteem alone) or on the macro level in large social surveys (for example European Social Survey, General Social Survey, World Values Survey, and many national surveys). Whenever new questions and scales are developed or existing ones revised for the measurement of organizational social impact, it is advisable to test their reliability and validity in a pre-test.

Step 6: Pre-testing and executing the study

Pre-tests do not only help validate measures. They also serve another, very central function, namely that of establishing a focus on beneficiaries' perspectives. The way measures are assessed has to be meaningful, not only judged against organisational mission, but also based on the viewpoints of the target group. This principle is embodied for instance in "user-oriented evaluation" of social service provision (Beresford & Carr, 2012; Martin, 2011). It ensures that the performed analysis is "material", that is relevant, to the served target group. Materiality towards target groups as well as other stakeholders, such as investors, is an imperative in social impact measurement (Nicholls, 2018; Social Impact Investment Taskforce, 2014). Thus, impact analysts need to find out whether the derived and developed measures work well with regard to their perceived importance to the affected target group.

For developing a good understanding of the latter, the analyst has to engage with these groups. Since discussions with the individuals targeted by the research might bias the effects measured later, the researcher may need to find other individuals who are reasonably close to the situations the target groups find themselves in. Factors to be considered include similarity on a variety of dimensions: institutional settings, age

184 *Gorgi Krlev and Federica Angeli*

composition, socio-economic status, etc. A study placed in a school setting, could simply test measures with other pupils and would also best include the opinion of teachers on the relevance of the instruments, their practical applicability, the meaningfulness of the analysis and potential ambiguities. Pre-tests can and should involve quantitative and qualitative means of assessment, which is an explicit testing of survey items but also a one-to-one discussion of the developed questionnaires, interview guides or other means of assessment.

Where it is very difficult, hardly possible, or extremely resource-intensive to test the assessment with beneficiaries or groups similar to those to be studied, it is the more important to engage closely with the organisation under investigation. The staff of the organisation will usually know better than an external analyst about the characteristics of specific user groups and their potential views on the organization's work and how that might affect measurement results. Taking this step is indispensable for developing a measurement concept that is comprehensive and concise at the same time. When engaging with the organization, it is however important to maintain a neutral distance between the analyst executing the study and the studied organization, which may have a biased standpoint. In case the analysis is performed by someone from within the organization, those analysts will need to try to behave as objectively as possible during all stages of the assessment. At any rate, the impact assessment should be iterative in character and allow for the revision of measurement components based on insights gained during the research process. This includes the revision or complementation of existing measures just as the inclusion of new ones in case new dimensions turn out to be relevant.

Implications for the Theory and Practice of Impact Measurement

Nowadays, all organizations across economic sectors and types of activities face a compelling call to evaluate the social and environmental effects of their operations, and hereby demonstrate their effectiveness and gain legitimacy. The task of developing an evaluation strategy that takes into account all the socially intended and unintended social and environmental externalities, while encompassing a feasible and efficient data collection, that is validated by all the relevant stakeholders and particularly "material" to the beneficiaries is admittedly a particularly daunting one.

With the idea to highlight common mistakes as well as suitable practices, this chapter has drawn attention on four main aspects of impact measurement in the realm of management theory and practices. First, social impact evaluation requires a paradigm shift from the traditional performance measurement associated with business and management studies. Taking into account social and environmental outcomes requires embracing a much more complex and nuanced performance framework, where goals are interdependent and possibly conflicting and where organizational activities (which range from programmes for behavioural change to traditional products or services) are likely to sort effects at multiple levels of analysis (individual, organizational, communities) and over time. A new cross-level, inter-temporal perspective is therefore salient in social impact evaluation (Hahn et al., 2015), in stark contrast with traditional performance measurement. For this reason, social impact measurement tools derived from traditional accounting as well as related attempts to monetize social impact and its measurement may often be unsuitable, as for many fields and regions, they reflect a reductionistic and narrow logic and fail to recognise the complexity aspects of social impact.

The second aspect that this chapter highlights is that while evaluating social impact should be appreciated in the realm of complexity and complexity thinking, interventions can be placed on a gradient of complexity, depending on their logic model (mechanism to induce behavioural change) and operational strategy (implementation process). When both logic model and operational strategy are straightforward, simpler impact evaluation approaches, closer to traditional accounting techniques or managerial performance management tools (Kaplan & McMillan, 2021), might be suitable. However, when both logic model and operational strategy are complex, the evaluation strategy needs to consider the inter-temporal and cross-level dimensions of social impact, the context-specificity of the organizational activity and its outcomes, the challenges of causal attribution and the necessity to devise measurement and indicators that are salient for all stakeholder. In other words, a complex, "realist" evaluation strategy should be devised.

The third aspect, related to the points above, considers how the data collection and data analysis underpinning the evaluation should be considered against their feasibility and suitability. In line with the complex intervention theory and with a "realist" approach to evaluation, a proper research design for assessing social impact needs to consider both qualitative and quantitative components. The main message here is that the chosen type of data and research design will need to follow from the question to be answered, rather than the other way around (Krlev, 2019). Pre-post quantitative testing is useful to appreciate outcomes based on standard indicators. Qualitative data collection and analysis are crucial to appreciate change dynamics and processes triggered by organizational activities, to include the contextual conditions and specificities of beneficiary groups and implementation agents, or to evaluate an organizational activity whose outcomes are largely unknown or likely to manifest over an extended and uncertain timespan.

Finally, when defining measures and evaluation frameworks for social impact it is of utmost importance to include users' perspectives, and to embed a "materiality" perspective (Nicholls, 2018). Both the measurement indicators and the evaluation process need to be relevant and acceptable to beneficiaries, who stand at a vantage point to highlight salient outcomes, flag specificities of the implementation process, guide the suitability of data collection tools, and validate data analysis processes, especially in the case of qualitative evidence.

These four aspects together pave the way for appropriately complex, yet feasible, acceptable and relevant approaches to social impact evaluation, while sensitizing practitioners about the necessary trade-offs that are inherent to assessing social and environmental impact of their operations. Only by making sure all four aspects apply, can impact measurement unfold its three primary goals outlined at the very beginning. Understanding a process deeply, for instance by embracing performance feedback or social and historical comparison, is a powerful way to enable actual organizational learning. Shifting power from investors or other funders, who may be reported to as an exercise in due diligence, to those affected by organizational activities, with a genuine interest if target groups experience superior social value, will eventually serve to improve investment decision and allocations. By illustrating the variety of ways in which organizations make valuable contributions to society or the natural environment (or harm them), in a rigorous fashion, we can not only push accountability towards those governing and regulating fields, but also identify the most potent sources of social innovation, and ultimately progress towards sustainable development.

186 *Gorgi Krlev and Federica Angeli*

Note

1 Organisations undergo an impact certification process to achieve a B Corp label, which marks them as in pursuit of high social and environmental performance. The label is awarded by B Lab, a nonprofit organisation that operates globally.

References

Angeli, F., & Montefusco, A. (2020). Sensemaking and learning during the Covid-19 pandemic: A complex adaptive systems perspective on policy decision-making. *World Development, 136*, 1–4.

Arvidson, M., Battye, F., & Salisbury, D. (2014). The social return on investment in community befriending. *International Journal of Public Sector Management, 27*(3), 225–240. https://doi.org/10.1108/IJPSM-03-2013-0045

Ballesteros-Sola, M., Stickney, M., & Trejo, Y. (2018). To B or not to B? The journey of "coding autism" toward the B corp certification. *Entrepreneurship Education and Pedagogy, 1*(2), 194–204. https://doi.org/10.1177/2515127418774035

Banerjee, A. V., & Duflo, E. (2012). *Poor economics: A radical rethinking of the way to fight global poverty.* PublicAffairs.

Barnett, M. L., Henriques, I., & Husted, B. W. (2020). Beyond good intentions: Designing CSR initiatives for greater social impact. *Journal of Management, 46*(6), 937–964. https://doi.org/10.1177/0149206319900539

Beer, H. A., & Micheli, P. (2018). Advancing performance measurement theory by focusing on subjects: Lessons from the measurement of social value. *International Journal of Management Reviews, 20*(3), 755–771. https://doi.org/10.1111/ijmr.12175

Beresford, P., & Carr, S. (2012). Research highlights in social work series. *Social Care, Service Users and User Involvement, 55.*

Bergmann, J. (2014). Der sanfte Kämpfer. *Brand Eins, 11,* 132–136. www.brandeins.de/archiv/2014/scheitern/joachim-koerkel-der-sanfte-kaempfer-kontrolliertes-trinken-abstinenz-dogma/

Blattman, C., Emeriau, M., & Fiala, N. (2018). Do anti-poverty programs sway voters? Experimental evidence from Uganda. *Review of Economics and Statistics, 100*(5), 891–905. https://doi.org/10.1162/rest_a_00737

Bonini, S., & Emerson, J. (2005). *Maximizing blended value: Building beyond the blended value map to sustainable investing, philanthropy and organizations.* Springer.

Brest, P., Harvey, H., & Low, K. (2009, Winter). Calculated impact. *Stanford Social Innovation Review,* 50–56. www.ssireview.org/articles/entry/calculated_impact

Brooks, J. (2016). Making the case for evidence-based decision-making. *Stanford Social Innovation Review.* https://ssir.org/articles/entry/making_the_case_for_evidence_based_decision_making

Busco, C., & Quattrone, P. (2018). Performing business and social innovation through accounting inscriptions: An introduction. *Accounting, Organizations and Society, 67,* 15–19. https://doi.org/10.1016/j.aos.2018.03.002

Byford, S., & Sefton, T. (2003). Economic evaluation of complex health and social care interventions. *National Institute Economic Review, 186,* 98–108. https://doi.org/10.1177/0027 95010300100114

Clemens, M. A., & Demombynes, G. (2011). When does rigorous impact evaluation make a difference? The case of the millennium villages. *Journal of Development Effectiveness, 3*(3), 305–339. https://doi.org/10.1080/19439342.2011.587017

Craig, P., Dieppe, P., Macintyre, S., Michie, S., Nazareth, I., Petticrew, M., Health, P., Unit, S., Michie, S., Nazareth, I., & Petticrew, M. (2008). Developing and evaluating complex interventions: New guidance. *BMJ (Clinical Research Ed.), 337,* a1655. https://doi.org/10.1136/bmj.a1655

Deaton, A., & Cartwright, N. (2018). Understanding and misunderstanding randomized controlled trials. *Social Science and Medicine, 210*, 2–21. https://doi.org/10.1016/j.socscimed.2017.12.005

Dentoni, D., Pinkse, J., & Lubberink, R. (2020). Linking sustainable business models to socio-ecological resilience through cross-sector partnerships: A complex adaptive systems view. *Business & Society.* https://doi.org/10.1177/0007650320935015

Drèze, J., & Stern, N. (1985). The theory of cost-benefit analysis. In A. J. Auerbach & M. S. Feldstein (Eds.), *Handbook of public economics* (pp. 909–990). North-Holland Publication Company.

Ebrahim, A. (2019). *Measuring social change: Performance and accountability in a complex world.* Stanford University Press.

Ebrahim, A., & Rangan, V. K. (2010, November 30). Putting the brakes on impact: A contingency framework for measuring social performance. *Academy of Management 2010 Annual Meeting – Dare to Care: Passion and Compassion in Management Practice and Research, AOM 2010.* https://doi.org/10.5465/ambpp.2010.54500944

Ebrahim, A., & Rangan, V. K. (2014). What impact? A framework for measuring the scale and scope of social performance. *California Management Review, 56*(3), 118–141. https://doi.org/10.1525/cmr.2014.56.3.118

Edmiston, D., & Nicholls, A. (2018). Social impact bonds: The role of private capital in outcome-based commissioning. *Journal of Social Policy, 47*(1), 57–76. https://doi.org/10.1017/S0047279417000125

Emerson, J. (2003). The blended value proposition: Integrating social and financial returns. *California Management Review, 45*(4), 35–51. https://doi.org/10.2307/41166187

Fletcher, A., Jamal, F., Moore, G., Evans, R. E., Murphy, S., & Bonell, C. (2016). Realist complex intervention science: Applying realist principles across all phases of the medical research council framework for developing and evaluating complex interventions. *Evaluation, 22*(3), 286–303. https://doi.org/10.1177/1356389016652743

GECES Sub-group on Impact Measurement. (2014, November). Proposed approaches to social impact measurement in European Commission legislation and in practice relating to EuSEFs and the EaSI. *Geces, 65.*

George, G., Howard-Grenville, J., Joshi, A., & Tihanyi, L. (2016). Understanding and tackling societal grand challenges through management research. *Academy of Management Journal, 59*(6), 1880–1895. https://doi.org/10.5465/amj.2016.4007

Gerrish, E. (2016). The impact of performance management on performance in public organizations: A meta-analysis. *Public Administration Review, 76*(1), 48–66. https://doi.org/10.1111/puar.12433

Glasziou, P., & Heneghan, C. (2009). A spotter's guide to study designs. *Evidence-Based Medicine, 14*(2), 37–38. https://doi.org/10.1136/ebm.14.2.37-a

Global Impact Investing Network (GIIN). (n.d.). *IRIS+: Impact metrics database and resources.* https://iris.thegiin.org/

Glouberman, S., & Zimmerman, B. (2002). Complicated and complex systems: What would successful reform of medicare look like? Changing health care in Canada. In G. Forest, G. Marchildon, & T. McIntosh (Eds.), *The Romanow papers* (pp. 21–53). University of Toronto Press.

Gray, R. (2002). The social accounting project and accounting organizations and society privileging engagement, imaginings, new accountings and pragmatism over critique? *Accounting, Organizations and Society, 27*(7), 687–708. https://econpapers.repec.org/RePEc:eee:aosoci:v:27:y:2002:i:7:p:687-708

Greenhalgh, T., & Papoutsi, C. (2018). Studying complexity in health services research: Desperately seeking an overdue paradigm shift. *BMC Medicine, 16*(1), 1–6. BioMed Central Ltd. https://doi.org/10.1186/s12916-018-1089-4

Greve, H. R. (2003). *Organizational learning from performance feedback*. Cambridge University Press. https://doi.org/10.1017/CBO9780511615139

Gubrium, J. F., & Holstein, J. A. (2001). *Handbook of interview research: Context & method*. Sage Publications.

Gupta, M., Bosma, H., Angeli, F., Kaur, M., Chakrapani, V., Rana, M., & Van Schayck, O. C. P. (2017). Impact of a multi-strategy community intervention to reduce maternal and child health inequalities in India: A qualitative study in Haryana. *PLoS One*, *12*(1). https://doi.org/10.1371/journal.pone.0170175

Hahn, T., Pinkse, J., Preuss, L., & Figge, F. (2015). Tensions in corporate sustainability: Towards an integrative framework. *Journal of Business Ethics*, *127*(2), 297 316. https://doi.org/10.1007/s10551-014-2047-5

Howard-Grenville, J., Davis, G. F., Dyllick, T., Miller, C. C., Thau, S., & Tsui, A. S. (2019). Sustainable development for a better world: Contributions of leadership, management, and organizations. *Academy of Management Discoveries*, *5*(4), 355–366. https://doi.org/10.5465/amd.2019.0275

The Impact Management Project. (2021). *The impact management project*. https://impactmanagementproject.com/

Jagosh, J., Bush, P. L., Salsberg, J., Macaulay, A. C., Greenhalgh, T., Wong, G., Cargo, M., Green, L. W., Herbert, C. P., & Pluye, P. (2015). A realist evaluation of community-based participatory research: Partnership synergy, trust building and related ripple effects. *BMC Public Health*, *15*(1), 725. https://doi.org/10.1186/s12889-015-1949-1

Kabeer, N. (2019). Randomized control trials and qualitative evaluations of a multifaceted programme for women in extreme poverty: Empirical findings and methodological reflections. *Journal of Human Development and Capabilities*, *20*(2), 197–217. https://doi.org/10.1080/19452829.2018.1536696

Kaplan, R. S., & McMillan, D. (2021). Reimagining the balanced scorecard for the ESG era. *Harvard Business Review*, *3*.

Kaplan, S. A., & Garrett, K. E. (2005). The use of logic models by community-based initiatives. *Evaluation and Program Planning*, *28*(2), 167–172. https://doi.org/10.1016/j.evalprogplan.2004.09.002

Kehl, K., Krlev, G., Then, V., & Mildenberger, G. (2018). Adapting the measuring rod for social returns in advanced welfare states: A critique of SROI. In A. Lindgreen, B. Hirsch, C. Vallaster, & S. Yousafzai (Eds.), *Measuring and controlling sustainability: Spanning theory and practice*. Routledge.

King, G., Keohane, R. O., & Verba, S. (1995). *Designing social inquiry: Scientific inference in qualitative research* (3rd ed.). Princeton University Press.

Koppell, J. G. S. (2005). Pathologies of accountability: ICANN and the challenge of "multiple accountabilities disorder". *Public Administration Review*, *65*(1), 94–108. https://doi.org/10.1111/j.1540-6210.2005.00434.x

Krlev, G. (2019). *If we're serious about changing the world, we need to get our evidence right – A comment on the 2019 nobel prize in economics*. LSE.

Krlev, G., Anheier, H. K., & Mildenberger, G. (2019). Introduction: Social innovation – what is it and who makes it? In H. K. Anheier, G. Krlev, & G. Mildenberger (Eds.), *Social innovation: Comparative perspectives*. Routledge.

Krlev, G., Münscher, R., & Mülbert, K. (2013). *Social return on investment (SROI): State-of-the-art and perspectives*. www.researchgate.net/publication/280664441_Social_Return_on_Investment_SROI_state-of-the-art_and_perspectives_-_a_meta-analysis_of_practice_in_Social_Return_on_Investment_SROI_studies_published_2002-2012

Maier, F., Schober, C., Simsa, R., & Millner, R. (2014). SROI as a method for evaluation research: Understanding merits and limitations. *Voluntas*, *26*(5), 1805–1830. https://doi.org/10.1007/s11266-014-9490-x

Mair, J., & Hehenberger, L. (2014). Front-stage and backstage convening: The transition from opposition to mutualistic coexistence in organizational philanthropy. *Academy of Management Journal*, 57(4), 1174–1200. https://doi.org/10.5465/amj.2012.0305

Martin, G. P. (2011). The third sector, user involvement and public service reform: A case study in the co-governance of health service provision. *Public Administration*, 89(3), 909–932. https://doi.org/10.1111/j.1467-9299.2011.01910.x

Maxwell, J. A. (2012). Qualitative research design: An interactive approach. In *Applied social research methods series* (3rd ed.). Sage Publications.

Millar, R., & Hall, K. (2013). Social return on investment (SROI) and performance measurement: The opportunities and barriers for social enterprises in health and social care. *Public Management Review*, 15(6), 923–941. https://doi.org/10.1080/14719037.2012.698857

Molecke, G., & Pinkse, J. (2017). Accountability for social impact: A bricolage perspective on impact measurement in social enterprises. *Journal of Business Venturing*, 32(5), 550–568. https://doi.org/10.1016/j.jbusvent.2017.05.003

Molecke, G., & Pinkse, J. (2020). Justifying social impact as a form of impression management: Legitimacy judgements of social enterprises' impact accounts. *British Journal of Management*, 31(2), 387–402. https://doi.org/10.1111/1467-8551.12397

Moore, M. H. (2000). Managing for value: Organizational strategy in for-profit, nonprofit, and governmental organizations. *Nonprofit and Voluntary Sector Quarterly*, 29(suppl.), 183–204. https://doi.org/10.1177/0899764000291s009

Morse, J. M., Barrett, M., Mayan, M., Olson, K., & Spiers, J. (2002). Verification strategies for establishing reliability and validity in qualitative research. *International Journal of Qualitative Methods*, 1(2), 13–22. https://doi.org/10.1177/160940690200100202

Moss, I. D., Coffman, J., & Beer, T. (2020). Smart decision-making. *Stanford Social Innovation Review*. https://ssir.org/articles/entry/smart_decision_making#

Nason, R. S., Bacq, S., & Gras, D. (2018). A behavioral theory of social performance: Social identity and stakeholder expectations. *Academy of Management Review*, 43(2), 259–283. https://doi.org/10.5465/amr.2015.0081

Nicholls, A. (2009). "We do good things, don't we?": "Blended value accounting" in social entrepreneurship. *Accounting, Organizations and Society*, 34(6–7), 755–769. https://doi.org/10.1016/j.aos.2009.04.008

Nicholls, A. (2010). The legitimacy of social entrepreneurship: Reflexive isomorphism in a pre-paradigmatic field. *Entrepreneurship: Theory and Practice*, 34(4), 611–633. https://doi.org/10.1111/j.1540-6520.2010.00397.x

Nicholls, A. (2018). A general theory of social impact accounting: Materiality, uncertainty and empowerment. *Journal of Social Entrepreneurship*, 9(2), 132–153. https://doi.org/10.1080/19420676.2018.1452785

Ravallion, M. (2012). Fighting poverty one experiment at a time: A review of abhijit banerjee and esther duflo's poor economics: A radical rethinking of the way to fight global poverty. *Journal of Economic Literature*, 50(1), 103–114. https://doi.org/10.1257/jel.50.1.103

Reddy, S. G. (2012). Randomise this! On poor economics. *Review of Agrarian Studies*, 2(2), 60–73. https://econpapers.repec.org/RePEc:fas:journl:v:2:y:2012:i:2:p:60-73

Rogers, P. J. (2008). Using programme theory to evaluate complicated and complex aspects of interventions. *Evaluation*, 14(1), 29–48. https://doi.org/10.1177/1356389007084674

Ruff, K., & Olsen, S. (2016). *The next frontier in social impact measurement isn't measurement at all*. https://ssir.org/articles/entry/the_next_frontier_in_social_impact_measurement_isnt_measurement_at_all

Ryan, A. (2004). Organizational learning from performance feedback: A behavioral perspective on innovation and change. *Administrative Science Quarterly*, 49(3), 490–494.

Savedoff, W. D., Levine, R., & Birdsall, N. (2006). *When will we ever learn?: Improving lives through impact evaluation*. Center for Global Development.

190 *Gorgi Krlev and Federica Angeli*

Schober, C., & Then, V. (2015). *Praxishandbuch social return on investment: Wirkung sozialer Investitionen messen*. Schäffer-Poesche.

Smith, P. K., Madsen, K. C., & Moody, J. C. (1999). What causes the age decline in reports of being bullied at school? Towards a developmental analysis of risks of being bullied. *Educational Research*, 41(3), 267–285. https://doi.org/10.1080/0013188990410303

Social Impact InvestmentTaskforce. (2014). *Measuring impact*. Subject Paper of the Impact Measurement Working Group. https://gsgii.org/reports/measuring-impact/

Social Value UK. (2020). *Global value exchange*. www.globalvaluexchange.org/

Tuan, M. T. (2008). *Measuring and/or estimating social value creation: Insights into eight integrated cost approaches*. www.gatesfoundation.org/learning/documents/wwl report measuring-estimating-social-value-creation.pdf

Voegtlin, C., & Scherer, A. G. (2017). Responsible innovation and the innovation of responsibility: Governing sustainable development in a globalized world. *Journal of Business Ethics*, 143(2), 227–243. https://doi.org/10.1007/s10551-015-2769-z

Weiss, C. H. (1972). Evaluation research: Methods for assessing program effectiveness. In *Prentice-Hall methods of social science series*. Prentice-Hall.

Weiss, C. H. (1998). *Evaluation: Methods for studying programs and policies* (2nd ed.). Prentice Hall.

Whittington, R. (2012). Big strategy/small strategy. *Strategic Organization*, 10(3), 263–268. https://doi.org/10.1177/1476127012452828

Wilson, D., & Frederick Bull, M. (2013). SROI in practice: The wooden canal boat society. *Social Enterprise Journal*, 9(3), 315–325. https://doi.org/10.1108/sej-03-2013-0013

W. K. Kellogg Foundation (2004) Logic Model Development Guide. Battle Creek, MI: W. K. Kellogg Foundation. Available at http://www.wkkf.org/Pubs/Tools/Evaluation/Pub3669.pdf

Wong, G., Greenhalgh, T., Westhorp, G., Buckingham, J., & Pawson, R. (2013). Rameses publication standards: Realist syntheses. *BMC Medicine*, 11(1), 1–14. https://doi.org/10.1186/1741-7015-11-21

World Economic Forum. (2020). *Toward common metrics and consistent reporting of sustainable value creation: Consulting draft*. World Economic Forum.

Wry, T., & Haugh, H. (2018). Brace for impact: Uniting our diverse voices through a social impact frame. *Journal of Business Venturing*, 33(5), 566–574. https://doi.org/10.1016/j.jbusvent.2018.04.010

Yunus, M., Moingeon, B., & Lehmann-Ortega, L. (2010). Building social business models: Lessons from the grameen experience. *Long Range Planning*, 43(2–3), 308–325. https://doi.org/10.1016/j.lrp.2009.12.005

9 Fix Forward – Building Experts: An exemplary case of a hybrid organization and its quest for financial independence

Kelly Alexander and Jörg Raab

Notes

This case, set in South Africa, is based on a larger research project on Social Enterprises in the education sector in Sub-Saharan Africa (South Africa, Ghana, Kenya and Ethiopia). The case description is based on an interview held with the CEO and Founder of Fix Forward, Joshua Cox, in January 2019. In addition, survey data from a Qualtrics survey completed by Joshua Cox in January 2019, and follow-up information attained via email correspondence in February, June and October 2020, was used. Secondary data from the website and interviews conducted by South African media outlets have also been used.

The United Nations' (UN's) Sustainable Development Goals (SDGs), established in 2015, aim to address grand challenges that face the world today – such as inequality, poverty, education and health (UNDP.org). Grand challenges represent interconnected issues requiring work on all 17 goals, with the intention of leading to improved livelihoods globally by 2030 (UNDP.org). In South Africa, two of these goals – Quality Education (#4) and Decent Work and Economic Growth (#8) – are closely related. Quality Education refers to structural elements such as establishing effective infrastructure conducive to learning – including access to water, internet and electricity.[1] This goal extends to adult education and access to "quality technical, vocational and tertiary education" (UN[2], 2020, #Envision2030 Goal 4: Quality Education, N.p.). The goal of Decent Work is to reduce informal employment, improve the number of employment opportunities and ensure that work environments adhere to human rights principles. This goal aims to develop policies that stimulate economic development, and lead to "decent job creation, entrepreneurship, creativity and innovation, and encourage the formalization and growth of micro-, small- and medium-sized enterprises" (UN[3] 2020, #Envision2030 Goal 8: Decent Work and Economic Growth, N.P.). The work of the social enterprise 'Fix Forward', presented in this case, serves to address these challenges.

Introduction

Education and employability are major issues in South Africa which contribute to extreme levels of unemployment in the country. These are challenges that social enterprise *Fix Forward* tries to address. This case explains the context in which they operate, challenges they face and provides an illustration of how management

DOI: 10.4324/9780429243165-10
This chapter has been made available under a CC-BY-NC 4.0 license.

192 Kelly Alexander and Jörg Raab

Figure 9.1 Job Done Guarantee, Photograph from Fix Forward website.

Source: Fix Forward, image. Retrieved 17 January 2020, from fixforward.com

Figure 9.2 Sustainable development goals addressed in this chapter.

Source: SDG image. Retrieved 17 January 2020, from http://www.un.org/development/desa/disabilities/wp-content/uploads/sites/15/2015/10/SDG-Poster.png

theory on hybrids can offer a lens for understanding issues such as mission management and financing.

The South African economy is characterised by poor education and relatedly, limited employment opportunities and unemployability of a large percentage of the population. In 2019, before the Covid-19 pandemic, 29.1% of the population were unemployed (Stats SA[4], 2019). A lack of education and training are significant barriers to economic growth and development of the country – particularly for previously disadvantaged and low-income communities (Rwigema et al., 2010). This is despite concerted efforts to bring about reform in the education sector, improvements in policy and curriculum and the substantial resources allocated to the sector (Albertyn et al., 2015).

UNICEF notes that 2017 marks the start of a decline in the "historically high" amount of government money directed to education in South Africa (UNICEF, 2017, p. 6). This left many organisations in the position of needing to bridge funding gaps, after reliance on the government as a source of funding prior to this. In addition, there were historically high levels of funding from International Non-Governmental Organisations which had also started to decline in the early 2000s. The racial segregation of Apartheid policies extended to education and training, and the shadow of these policies is still prevalent (see Table 9.1) – with stark inequalities in quality of, and access to, education and training and the levels of funding available (Urban, 2015).

Current performance of South African children is significantly lower that than of peers in countries in a comparable economic grouping, indicating there have not been strong improvements in education in the country in the last two decades (Clarke, 2015, in Albertyn et al., 2015). Almost 50% of students who entered the system in Grade 1 in 2001, did not complete 12 years of schooling and finish the final year of high school (matriculate) in 2018 (see Table 9.1) (Trialouge, 2019). Table 9.1 highlights the discrepancy between the performance of Private schools (Independent Examination Board) and Government-funded schools (National Senior Certificate) for matriculants.

The lack of improvement in education results in high levels of adult illiteracy, and a high percentage of the population with low skill levels (Urban, 2015). These challenges are the focus of considerable spending on further education and training programmes, at a rate that exceeds that of basic education expenditure (UNICEF, 2017, p. 10). This obviously impacts the nature of available employment prospects, and narrows the scope of work opportunities for many people (see Figure 9.3). Limited

Table 9.1 Matric Results 2018. (Adapted from Albertyn et al., 2015, p. 185.)

Matric Results 2018		
INDEPENDENT EXAMINATION BOARD		*NATIONAL SENIOR CERTIFICATE*
12 372	Candidates	630 360
98.9%	Pass rate	78.2%
90%	Candidates who qualified for admission to degree studies	35%

Source: Department of Basic Education (South Africa)

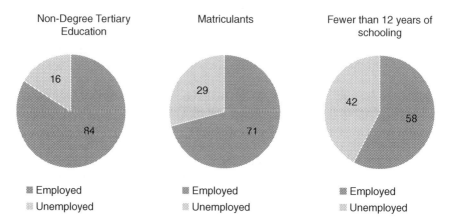

Figure 9.3 Unemployment levels in South Africa by education. (Adapted from Albertyn et al., 2015, p. 35.)

skills and illiteracy confines people to low-skilled and often precarious work, with limited advancement opportunities. Without addressing these issues, current patterns of inequality will be exacerbated and further entrenched.

According to Herrington et al. (2010, p. 46), the 2008 Global Entrepreneurship Monitor (GEM) report indicates that South African experts are more negative than experts in most other efficiency-driven countries[5] studied, regarding extra-curricular training and entrepreneurship training both within schools and at the school leaving stage. "Of particular concern was the quality of training after school, where South Africa achieved the lowest rating of all countries in the sample of efficiency driven countries" (Herrington et al., 2010, p. 46), and for Ramukumba (2015), the low levels of technical skills are a major impediment to employment in the country (in Albertyn et al., 2015).

Finally, there are still major inequalities in terms of the quality of public schooling, compared to private school education in the country, with only 35% of matriculants qualifying for admission into degree programmes at higher education institutions, perpetuating cycles of poverty (compared to 90% of private school matriculants) (see Table 9.1) (Albertyn et al., 2015). It is evident that these continuous inequalities present complex challenges, as societal inequality and a weak education system are locked in a negative cycle, with multiple antecedents, interacting and reinforcing each other, and with numerous actors and stakeholders involved.

Institutional Context

South Africa currently has a heavy reliance on the state and large corporations to address challenges of inequality and high unemployment levels, partly due to legislation and ruling African National Congress (ANC) government promises regarding reform and redress of inequalities (Littlewood & Holt, 2018). The South African government has limited engagement with NGOs and is often distrustful of these organisations, given perceptions of competing priorities and has lowered funding directed to these organisations (Urban, 2015). Simultaneously, following the Global Financial Crisis of 2008, 'donor fatigue' resulted in limited funds for socially oriented organisations, while South Africa's upper-middle income status (The World Bank[6], 2020) results in a relatively low level of Overseas Development Assistance (ODA) (UNICEF, 2017).

The emergence of social enterprises (SE) occurs in relation and response to global and local institutional frameworks (Urban, 2013). Though the government and corporations are seen as the main providers of social services, the Apartheid legacy has meant that socially oriented organisations in the country are common – there is awareness of the needs of others and the role of organisations in improving the quality of life of others. For example, the Broad Based Black Economic Empowerment (BBBEE) codes in the country encourage corporates to invest in Enterprise Development and Skills Development programmes, providing them with BBBEE points. Based on corporates' CSR and BBBEE spending with accredited BBBEE partners/organisations, they receive Skills Development and Enterprise Development points under the BBBEE codes, which improve access to government contracts for example. However, SEs do not have distinct legal forms; "Certain aspects of South African law approximate some of the features of European social enterprises, albeit that no explicit and distinct structure is provided for the social enterprise" (Urban, 2015, p. 276).

The perception that government and large businesses should act to address these systemic challenges (Urban, 2015) has meant, organisations with the potential to make a positive impact on employment and economic growth in their communities, such as "small businesses, are overlooked – particularly. . . [from] township areas. . . . It's an area that needs a lot more focus and attention, and that's what we're trying to do" (Cox, 2018, Radio Interview 702[7]). This is due to individuals favouring larger organisations and funders lacking confidence in smaller businesses, despite their often unique view into the needs of the communities that they serve (Urban, 2013).

Fix Forward is a social enterprise (SE) based in Cape Town, South Africa. The organisation's by-line – 'building experts' – speaks to both the mission of the organisation and the focus of their work. Fix Forward (FF) works with specialist tradesmen – particularly builders, carpenters and cabinet-makers, tilers, pavers and plumbers who have experience in the industry – providing further training, and connecting tradesmen with clients. FF's purpose notes that, "We aim to help build an equal and just society by creating opportunities for contractors from low-income communities to develop and thrive" (Annual Review, 2019). Based on referrals and a strong vetting process, independent contractors from low-income communities are invited to join the Fix Forward programme. CEO, Joshua Cox, notes that "Fix Forward is a social enterprise that's disrupting the building industry, to delight clients, and help talented contractors from low-income communities grow their businesses" (Fix Forward, 2020). Through entrepreneurial development training, contractors are upskilled and educated on customer engagement, quoting, pricing, invoicing and service delivery (Interview, 2019). Contractors and potential clients are connected via an online marketplace platform, and FF focuses "first and foremost [on] selling a quality service – and almost as a bonus people get to support tradesmen from lower income areas" (Fix Forward[8], 2020). FF goes beyond simply providing a matchmaking service by providing training and a "job done guarantee", ensuring that the work will be a satisfactorily completed (Interview, 2019).

FF hopes their work will result in money flowing into underserved and low-income communities and – through the provision of business education and training – that

196 Kelly Alexander and Jörg Raab

Table 9.2 Fix Forward's Mission. (Adapted from 'Annual Review, 2019'.)

FIX FORWARD'S THREE-FOLD MISSION		
Contractors	*Clients*	*Fix Forward*
To provide opportunities for business skills development and personal growth and fair access to the market.	To provide a quality building service that gives people the opportunity to contribute to social upliftment.	To grow and live our passion and purpose through our work.

Source: Company document, email correspondence 2020/06/29

small businesses will have the opportunity to grow (Interview, 2019). Consequently, they will be able to increase the number of employment opportunities in these low-income contexts, increasing access to decent jobs. FF has a dual mission – aiming to be financially viable, and create social impact – "our mission is really to create opportunities for contractors, like tradespeople basically, from low income areas to develop and thrive" (Interview, 2019). FF's positioning differs relative to other organisations as

> we are driven primarily by our social mission rather than a profit motive. We are different to other non-profits in that we have a strong commercial model which helps us move away from being overly reliant on donors; this creates potential to scale up both our impact and our business.
>
> (Fix Forward, 2020)[9]

Box 9.1   Contractor Profile. (Adapted from, Fix Forward, 2020.)

Profile 1: Anack Amini (Builder)
FF: How long have you been with Fix Forward?
AA: I've been with Fix Forward for one year now. It started out as just me and an apprentice in a broken down bakkie. Now I employ six people and have two company vehicles!
FF: How have the e-learning materials benefitted you?
AA: The courses really helped me to handle my projects and day-to-day business better. I've also improved my planning and the way I deal with clients now.
FF: What has been the most valuable thing you [sic] learnt?
AA: Learning about project management, the break down and guidelines provided were very useful and still are today!
FF: Has Fix Forward made a difference when it comes to gaining new and returning clients?
AA: Yes! Since joining I have had a lot more of my quotes approved. For example, I recently landed a very large tender in Constantia so I am very happy about my journey here.

Fix Forward, Q&A with the Founder. Retrieved January 17, 2020, from https://fixforward.com/qa-with-fix-forward-founder-joshua-cox/

The problem that FF identified and intends to solve is that there is a lack of trust in small contractors, and so they struggle to get work in larger projects. In addition, there is large information asymmetry between customers and builders regarding the nature of the work to be completed and a fair price for such work. FF sought to solve this challenge by providing training on effective quoting, and offer a 'Job done guarantee', in which the organisation ensures that if the work is not successfully and satisfactorily completed by a particular builder, FF will ensure that the project is then completed. FF will then supervise this process – eliminating any risk and uncertainty for the clients, and providing credibility to their contractors. However, as of February 2020 FF no longer offers a guarantee and do not supervise projects as they realised that this approach attracted too much liability for the organisation – in the rare instance where things went wrong.

The business relies on a pool of well-trained contractors, who are able to execute the work. In 2019 FF engaged with 100 contractors, and Cox reported this "meets our expectations" (Survey, 2019). In a review of their 2019 performance, FF notes that the organisation modified their programme and had 50 contractors attend in Cape Town, as well as relaunching their operations in the Gauteng province in 2018, after a period of absence in this province (Annual Review, 2019). In January 2019, there were 40 contractors who joined FF in Gauteng and an additional 12 in Cape Town (Email correspondence, Annual Review, 2019). All contractors have prior experience of at least a number of years working with private clients, completing entire projects with these clients. Contractors on the programme and platform undergo a rigorous and comprehensive vetting procedure. Contractors need to apply or are referred, their references are checked and they complete an in-depth, one-on-one interview (Interview, 2019). "Throughout that process we're evaluating their communication, their reliability and so on. Their industry knowledge" (Interview, 2019). The training element of the programme has been revised from monthly for 10 months, to monthly for 6 months, and now "we have longer sessions that are done weekly for four weeks" (Email correspondence, 2020), and attendance is mandatory. The reason for condensing the training timeframe is due to the need that contractors have to balance their work and businesses with the learning. The training takes place at the FF offices, or where there are larger groups (more than 10 people) training takes place in a hired venue. Once contractors begin work on a project, monitoring site visits are conducted – particularly on larger construction or renovation projects, while new contractors generally start on smaller projects (Interview, 2019).

Box 9.2   2018 Economic Impact Highlights (Adapted from Fix Forward Annual Review, 2019)

1   We surveyed 31 contractors to gather feedback and data
2   Combined, the 31 contractors employed 133 people labourers at the start of the programme and 177 by the end of it
3   44 new jobs created from just 31 of the 50 contractors supported last year (business growth of 33% on average within just one year)
4   Ishmaeel Karriem, one of our carpenters went from employing one person to employing seven, including one woman and one disabled person

> 5   One of our electricians went from employing two people, to employing four. Three of the four employees are youth
> 6   One contractor, Cassiem Madatt, had never gotten a project over R100, 000 in value before joining Fix Forward. He undertook two projects for G4S security. The first project was worth R145, 000 and the second worth R156 000. Both projects were a huge success and he was able to purchase a bakkie for his business within just 3 months of joining Fix Forward.
> 7   Kevin Fortune, a builder grew from four to six employees, and when asked as to how he benefited from Fix Forward he said:
>
> "I have more work and can provide my workers with a better quality of living for all of them."
>
> Company document, email correspondence 2020/06/29

FF's business model is based on facilitating a connection between contractors and the market, and providing support and surety for the work to be completed. The organisation provides 12 months of practical training, consisting of monthly workshops in the initial 6 months, followed by mentoring and monthly coaching for the contractors. The coaching is both personal and professional, aiming to develop contractors' ability to solve problems and mitigate challenges that they may face, helping contractors "to realize their potential" (Interview, 2019). Mentoring, which takes place monthly is held for one hour, face to face with an "experienced business mentor" (Annual Review, 2019, p. 1). Mentorship focuses on the contractors' businesses and is "about imparting knowledge, skills, providing guidance, and really helping people work on specific aspects within their business" (Interview, 2019). One of the builders on the FF programme noted,

> We went through very good financial management courses, I can comfortably tell you now that, these finances are for the business and these are my personal finances. The business can comfortably pay me a salary, which is a great thing. I wasn't able to do that before I came to Fix Forward.

One distinct advantage of the FF programme is that contractors are not employed by FF, remaining independent and are able to grow their businesses – facilitating job creation and financial independence of the SMMEs. Of the contractors who complete their training, approximately 40% remain on the FF platform deciding to continue to work with FF, with a total of approximately 100 contractors in Cape Town and the province of Gauteng[10], (Interview, 2019).

FF originated as Cox's side project and in 2012, after two years as a personal project, the company was formally established, and currently operates as both a non-profit trust and a private company (Interview, 2019). FF's hybrid organisational structure – combining a NPO legal entity (a non-profit trust) which owns a separate for-profit business. "The company earns money from the trust – there's a sort of a service arrangement there. The trust pays the company to facilitate market access

Fix Forward – Building Experts 199

Figure 9.4 Shepherd. Photograph from Fix Forward website.
Source: (Shepherd, 2020, Fix Forward). Retrieved February 9, 2020, from https://fixforward.com/shepherd-mtyatya-the-fix-forward-model/

for the contractors" (Cox, Interview, 2019). The trust earns income from corporate social investment and BBBEE related enterprise development spending on the part of corporates (Cox, Interview, 2019). This dual organisational structure provides the organisation with a number of advantages. For example, it can operate like "a business – trading without limitation, taking equity investment, whilst ensuring the mission is protected by ownership and control from the NPO. The NPO can also raise grant funding, rather than having to raise equity capital or debt upfront" (Survey, 2019). The dual structure allows the organisation to balance value creation (through the benefit of training and increased market access and earning potential for the builders) and value capture (through profit generation and an earned income strategy). However, a downside of this hybrid structure is the managerial complexity due to additional administration requirements of managing two sets of financials (Survey, 2019).

In this way, FF is able to generate revenue, in the for-profit arm of the organisation, through taking a 10–15% commission of the project value for each successful project, "so if they don't win we don't earn, . . . and that incentivizes us to ensure that they win as many projects as possible because it's good for our business" (Interview, 2019). All of the revenue earned by the organisation is through this commission. FF's dual aims are concurrently served through organisational action. Looking at total revenue generation, FF earned between 1.5 million and R 5 million (US$113,293–US$377,634) in 2018, of which less than R500,000 (US$37,764) was surplus. In addition to this, the training, which is conducted by the NPO-Trust is funded by corporates' CSR and BBBEE spending to earn Skills Development and Enterprise Development points. Of the total revenue generated by FF, between 26% and 50% was from grants and donations, indicating that the organisation is still reliant on grants and donations. The majority of the organisation's funding is from corporate and government donations, given FF's registration and accreditation to attain this funding. "We are a registered Enterprise Development Intermediary and a Public Benefit Organisation. This allows corporates to make tax-deductible donations and to give us money from their Enterprise Development spend, to improve their [BB]BEE scorecard" (Email correspondence, 2020). Yet Cox noted that the organisation had grown quickly in 2018, with an increase of more than 15% in terms of customers in the 12 months preceding taking the survey in January 2019 – increasing FFs value creation. This is an indication that they will be able to shift increasingly to value capture, generating a higher percentage of income independently.

Challenges

Like many emerging organisations, FF has faced a number of difficulties. One of the challenges was human capital, and Cox noted that in areas like marketing, FF lacked the required in-house expertise. This led to a challenge in terms of "growing brand awareness . . . so we relied a lot on external people, . . . both as advisors and . . . service providers to help us . . . drive that awareness" (Interview, 2019). Similarly, FF struggled with 'access to support and advisory services' (Survey, 2019). This was specifically linked to a lack of in-house marketing or tech expertise, which has "dramatically hampered our ability to put the right tech solutions in place, as well as to grow brand awareness and lead generation. We've struggled to find the right advisors in these two areas" (private email correspondence, 29 June 2020). FF also struggled with "Recruiting executive committee members/non-executive directors or trustees" due to the inability to pay competitive salaries for top talent (Survey, 2019). One of the major drivers behind FF aiming to become fully profitable and financially self-sustaining is the ability to compete for top talent in the market (Interview, 2019). "We know our model works, but our programme is not as effective as it could be and the earnings per contractor from Fix Forward are below where we would like them to be" (Survey, 2019).

Another challenge related to training – linked to the social mission – was an e-learning platform which was discontinued. The e-learning had 10 modules, which were similar in content to the workshops that are held, yet there was limited engagement from the contractors as the platform was not "particularly engaging or, kind of interactive . . . we were not getting maximum value out of it" (Interview, 2019). Cox continued to note that "I think e-learning as a concept can add a lot of value, but then you have to have the right tool, you have to have the right content, you have to have the right format. And I don't think we had any of those" (Interview, 2019). The e-learning was discontinued in the short term, and replaced with a mentorship program (Interview, 2019).

In addition, Cox notes that the primary challenges for the organisation relate to perfecting the business offering – as distinct from the strong business model (Interview, 2019). There have not been any major changes to the business model, only to the "mechanics, . . . the sort of value proposition to customers. So, defining that, executing that, finding what that looks like, what that should look like?" FF's current challenge is trying to better understand what will best serve the market, to correctly identify customers' needs and to meet that demand effectively (Interview, 2019). This is a typical business challenge, and links to the profit-oriented, value capture, mission of the organisation.

A related challenge linked to the business side of the organisation, is the standardisation of quoting, as projects vary and contractors are "unique in terms of how they cost out a project and put together a quote", resulting in vast differences from contractors (Interview, 2019). As a result, FF are in the process of developing a more consistent method for quoting that will allow for a standardised and fair price for both parties, to improve the percentage of quotes that are won (Interview, 2019). This will assist the organisation in growing the proportion of self-generated revenue. However, the organisation currently wins approximately 50% of the quotes they send out – above the industry average (Interview, 2019).

A significant challenge in the building and contracting industry is the fact that clients are unwilling to pay for a high service level when they expect a lower one (Interview, 2019). FF recognizes the need to challenge that way of thinking and develops an understanding that there is a price fair to both clients and contractors (Fix Forward[11], 2020). The challenge is to do this without leveraging the fact that the contractors are from low-income communities, with the associated perception that the job will be 'cheap' – FF "is all about positioning our service as a quality service, not a cheap one" (Fix Forward[12], 2020).

Funding, financial independence and sustainability is a major challenge for FF, and the organisation is "still quite heavily reliant on funding, obviously with a view to . . . building [achieving] full self-sustainability". Yet in the South African context and more broadly there are few SEs that are able to sustain themselves financially through their trading activities. Cox indicates there are few examples of successful SEs, perhaps with the exception of Grameen Bank, or organisations like Tom's Shoes and Warby Parker – the latter of which, however, have had adverse impacts in the communities in which they operate (Interview, 2019). "I mean, there's not a lot of social enterprise that I'm aware of that, that trade in the market place. . . [and] that trading is directly linked to their mission, and where the revenue from their trading activities covers their costs" (Interview, 2019).

In addition, ensuring that the business is able to scale, by expanding the pool of vetted and trained contractors, was problematic for FF. "I think finding . . . the right systems and mechanisms to feed the pipeline of contractors has definitely been a challenge . . . particularly when we need to get big numbers. How do we go about finding those people?" (Interview, 2019). Cox framed this as a challenge if it transpires that demand for FF's training offering is lacking – and noted that contractor recruitment was an area of the business that had received a lot of attention, yet had not delivered the expected results as yet (Interview, 2019). Thus without contractors trained and in place to execute the work, FF may struggle to meet future growing demand.

FF's future plans include potential international expansion, and they have had preliminary discussions regarding operating in Colombia, and other Sub-Saharan African countries where there is a similar need. Furthermore, the organisation is considering engaging closely with South Africa's Sectoral Education and Training Authorities (SETAs), to provide accredited training for the contractors. This would allow the contractors to have a more formal skills qualification, which would assist them in the expansion of their individual businesses. Resolving the challenges of the business model and ensuring a steady pipeline of contractors will be issues that they will need to have resolved, and then ensure they can mitigate in other contexts as well.

Similarly, the need to offer accredited training in other countries will need to be investigated, with an appropriate adjustment of the training on offer.

Finally, it is typically thought that the institutional environment in a country like South Africa would have challenges relating to the rule of law and corruption. However, this did not emerge as an issue, with Cox noting that there is some support for SEs from both government and the business community, and that issues such as graft and corruption do not feature as challenges for the organisation.[13]

A Theoretical Analysis of Fix Forward

Fix Forward: Through the Lens of Hybrid Organising

Looking at FF through the lens of theory about hybrid organising helps us to see the ways in which the tensions in hybrid organisations can be managed, as well as highlighting some of the challenges involved in delivering on the goals of a dual mission, and financial sustainability. Hybrid organisations combine elements or logics of not-for-profit and for-profit ways of organising – existing on a continuum between organisations seeking profit and those delivering only a social mission (Haigh et al., 2015; Battilana et al., 2017, p. 142). Logics are assumed and stable social conventions, norms and values, that facilitate individuals' understanding of their environment of their situation by providing implicit guidelines on acceptable actions and behaviour (Greenwood et al., 2010). Hybridity refers to the various "activities, structures, processes and meanings by which organizations make sense of and combine aspects of multiple organizational forms" (Battilana & Lee, 2014, p. 389). In this way, social enterprises, like FF, are hybrid organisations combining multiple organisational identities – emphasising both 'social' and 'business' – as well as having a hybrid legal structure – as the non-profit trust owns the private company (Moss, Short, Payne, & Lumpkin, 2011; Interview, 2019).

Hybrid organisations intend to alter patterns of financial dependence on donors and grants experienced by NGOs and other social value creating organisations. Hybrid organisations seek to introduce a focus on delivering social value in parallel with economic value – as core to their organisational mission (Mair & Rathert, 2020). Financial independence is important for hybrid organisations – supporting the creation of social value (Holt & Littlewood, 2015). Yet, hybrid organisations are required to work conscientiously towards this goal, often initially reliant on donors and grants, seeking to reduce this as the organisation matures.

Theoretical discussion about HO structures can help us to see how an organisation may or may not experience certain challenges. A typology presented by Santos et al. (2015) reviews various HO structures, regarding contingent or automatic value spillover. Positive value spillover – which hybrid organisations would seek to maximise – refers to the additional positive benefits arising from a transaction, beyond the immediate product or service (Santos et al., 2015). Contingent spillovers require additional intervention from the organisations – for example in the form of "training, raising awareness and mentoring" (Santos et al., 2015, p. 42). In terms of spillover, FF exhibits features of both contingent and automatic value spillover. More business for FF as an organisation and a higher conversion of quotes to business, results in higher profits for the organisation and obviously more work for the contractors involved – this is an automatic process. The contingent component of the organisation's spillover is evident in the training, mentoring and upskilling of the contractors – which is required to ensure that there is a consistent standard of work delivered.

Davies and Doherty (2019) extend the value spillover notion and review the extent to which the organisation's activities are differentiated or integrated. Differentiated organisations are those in which there is some decoupling between the customers and beneficiaries, or where the activities take place in different units or organisational structures (Davies & Doherty, 2019). Both organisational missions are concurrently served in integrated organisations, through the same organisational actions (Davies & Doherty, 2019). Integrated organisations are thought to be less influenced by mission drift – which refers to the prioritisation of either the social or economic mission, to the detriment of the other (Ebrahim et al., 2014). In addition to integration, human capital and governance are crucial. Having the correct governance structure and human capital in place can also serve to limit the risk of mission drift. As noted earlier, FF struggled with the recruitment of executive committee members/non-executive directors or trustees, which is a potential area of weakness for the organisation as they seek to attain and uphold this balance (Interview, 2019).

For Cox it is "critical for social enterprise to generate revenue through [integrated] activities . . . that are missional linked" (Interview, 2019). Cox gives the example of an organisation with the mission to tutor "high school youth to help them improve their pass mark, and on the side you're selling soap to try and fund that, you know, then the selling of the soap can detract from what you're doing" (Interview, 2019). In the case of FF, "the more money we earn, the better our contractors do. And so, in earning money we're actually achieving our mission" (Interview, 2019). FF's revenue generation activity is aligned fully with their mission, thus the more work they have the more impact they have. It follows that there are theoretically fewer operational tensions to be resolved between the two areas of focus for an integrated organisation, allowing for a more focused organisation, with a clear path to scale.

The Sustainable Funding Dilemma

Cox's intention to be financially independent and to generate income through profit-oriented activities may be challenging to achieve. However, increasingly, as hybrid organisations, SEs are turning to mixed strategies for funding and investment. This situation has been accelerated by the "Great Recession [2008] and its aftermath [which] forced non-profits to seek out new and different ways to address their challenges" (Reilly, 2016, p. 297). This situation has been exacerbated by Covid-19, which has also led to social enterprises needing to be more flexible in the use and allocation of funding (Darko & Hashi, 2020) This results in reliance on government or other funding and donations being an increasingly unreliable and unsustainable funding strategy (Reilly, 2016; Lumpkin et al., 2013). For Lumpkin et al., (2013), resource constraints are not necessarily unique to SEs, with many commercial entrepreneurial ventures experiencing similar challenges. However, a unique challenge is access to resources, as the additional social mission held by SEs may be less attractive to traditional investors (Lumpkin et al., 2013).

There are a variety of new forms of funding that have emerged in support of shifts in the global economy, and an increased awareness of the need to support organisations seeking to generate social value. For example, the rise of impact investing aims to support projects that deliver measurable social or environmental yield, in addition to financial profits, and is supported by both individual and institutional investors (The Global Impact Investing Network[14] 2020). However, there may be a "financial dead zone" for SEs that exist in the middle of the spectrum (Carpenter & Lauritzen, 2016, p. 4). Organisations that identify more clearly as fully blended with an equal focus on both the social and profit motive may be seen as too "profit driven" for philanthropic organisations, or too "socially oriented" for more traditional investors (Carpenter & Lauritzen, 2016).

The South African funding landscape is unique, shaped by the institutional framework of the country. Policies such as BBBEE incentivise corporates to direct their CSR spending to Skills or Enterprise Development, to gain preferential access to government contracts. Aligning with the BBBEE policy framework provides an avenue of funding for SEs if they: support Enterprise and Supplier Development through "preferential procurement, supply chain development and growth of small black-owned business"; engage in socio-economic development – aimed at improving levels of inclusion through grants or donations; or if SEs engage in Skills Development programmes – particularly to youth and previously disadvantaged people (Greater Capital, 2016, p. 9). This leads to a substantial amount of money flowing into these sectors (see Figure 9.6). Education – including vocational skills and training – receives approximately 50% of CSR spend in South Africa (Trialogue, 2019). This impacts the way in which SEs operate in the country, as they are often able to sell their services to corporates, in exchange for the BBBEE points that the corporate receives through this type of transaction. For Cox, there is doubt as to whether this reflects a truly market-driven approach to funding in the long-term:

> people spin it different ways, . . . so people say, *Oh, well, you know, corporate's buying my services.* So . . . they say, *Well, I'm totally self-funded,* but if it's coming from someone's CSI [Corporate Social Investment] budget or . . . enterprise development budget or whatever, that's not, in my view. I mean, we could make the same case. We could say we're an educational institution, and corporates pay us money to deliver training. So we count that as revenue and we 100% self-funded. . . . You can make a case for the fact that you're delivering enterprise development services and then that means that it's revenue and not a grant. But the reality is, my views is, it's a grant, unless you are trading in the market place where you have CUSTOMERS who are purchasing a product or service, if it's someone who is funding you because they're going to get [BB]BEE points or some kind of tax break, that's not a – I don't think you can count that as earned revenue. That's my view. Other people hold a different view.
>
> (Interview, 2019)

FF have a dual-income generation strategy where South African corporates pay for skills training (offered by the NFP Trust) – linked to the BBBEE scorecards, and the company earns money for each construction project that contractors complete. This close link between the contractors' success and the financial success of FF means that the organisation is intent on ensuring that contractors are well skilled and supported (Interview, 2019). While the majority of their funding is from corporates, FF also received donations from local foundations and trusts, with a large initial grant from "government, from the IDC [Industrial Development Corporation of South Africa]" and from Nedbank, a local bank, who provided R3.4 million (US$256,797) to FF, in

Fix Forward – Building Experts 205

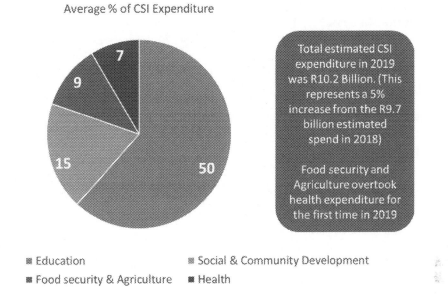

Figure 9.5 CSI Spend in South Africa, 2019. (Adapted from Trialogue 2019 Business in Society Handbook.)

line with the bank's pledge to support economic growth and job creation in the country (Interview, 2019; Fix Forward[15], 2020).

Currently FF are working towards being self-sustaining, and covers about 40–50% of its costs. At the group level this translates into the commercial operations' sales revenue, "covering about . . . 25% of our total costs [for 2018], but the company earns money from the banks, from the trust as well" (Interview, 2019). For Cox, revenue generation is the most important focus for the organisation – to facilitate growth and improved human capital (Interview, 2019). Financial independence is seen as the 'lifeblood' of success, and Cox compared FF to prior positions he held in the NPO sector, noting,

> unless you've . . . been in a pure non-profit sector, with no earned revenue at all, . . . the shift to . . . money come in that we've earned ourselves that is unallocated, unrestricted, it is the most liberating thing ever because, it means that we can direct that money to exactly where it needs to go. And we don't need to justify to anyone, we don't need to report on it. We don't need all these things that, you know, um, that slow organizations down. Um, and, and, and limit them . . . you don't spend all this time reporting on and trying to justify writing proposals.
> (Interview, 2019)

Cox continues to state that funding is much more difficult to manage as it is not consistent, "you know, we could earn nothing this month and have 3 million [Rand] come in next month. You're not going to have that in business" (Interview, 2019).

206 Kelly Alexander and Jörg Raab

The imperative to be financially sustainable is linked to the ability to attract funders to the organisation, for investment in support of scale, as well as social returns and value creation (Interview, 2019). When SEs prioritise self-generated revenue, their "core mission is thereby freed from total dependence upon the decisions of donors" (Reilly, 2016, p. 297). FF's business model means that investment into the organisation will extend beyond the immediate impact of support or training for a set number of contractors for a limited period of time, but the sustained and broader impact that FF will be able to have as it scales its operations (Interview, 2019). This business model is "a strength ... it's an internal thing, but it links to an external opportunity where funders are specifically looking to fund organizations that can become self-sustaining" (Interview, 2019).

This is seen to contrast many SEs' approach. Cox mentioned one SE that raises significant funding, but that the revenue earned is from the sale of free inputs, "so they're getting [inputs] donated, which they sell. . . . You can't compare them to another organization that is manufacturing . . . and selling . . . 'cause they're getting these free inputs and they are earning off that" (Interview, 2019). So, for Cox this did not represent an earned revenue generation strategy (Interview, 2019). In such a case, should the donated inputs fail to materialise, the business model would be put in jeopardy.

Conclusion

Hybrid organisations like FF, attempting to balance dual missions, need to identify a business model that will allow for revenue generation and the attainment of social goals. This is a challenging task and may lead to much uncertainty – particularly in the early stages of the business – as it prepares to scale and is reliant on diverse sources of funding. The earned revenue generation strategy has repercussions for the type of funders that will ultimately invest in the organisation, the competitiveness of the organisation, and the ability to compete with other SEs, as well as regular for-profit organisations, for human capital that the organisation is able to retain – particularly in terms of salaries. This is further influenced by the institutional context in which the organisation is operating, and the resource constraints, legitimacy and legal/regulatory framework. The institutional context may vary, with considerable latitude in how 'self-sustaining' and 'market-generated revenues' are defined and understood. This is often context specific, and shaped by the organisation's goals. When considering theoretical point of view, this indicates that hybrid organisations' dual mission and multiple organisational identities – i.e. 'social' and 'business' – may be more mutable and fluctuate based on environmental changes (Moss et al., 2011).

Cox is confident that FF has the right business model, and that its integrated activities balance the dual organisational goals. However there remains uncertainty regarding market engagement and at the group level, FF is still predominantly reliant on non-earned revenue. However, there is a clear business case and strong intention to increase self-generated revenue, with the associated benefit of increasing FF's social impact. This highlights an important lesson for social enterprises and policy makers, regarding social enterprises' funding models. The revenue mix that social enterprises make use of as they start and ultimately scale, are heavily influenced by the institutional environment, and the type of resources available. Yet it is important that organisations carefully review the potential downsides of certain forms of funding, which could adversely affect their ability to be profitable at a later stage. This raises the question of best structures, mechanisms and incentives to support social enterprises in their value creation and value capture activities. As Cox notes, BBBEE and CSR funding in South Africa may result in organisations claiming to have 100% earned income without this being linked to market-based activities (Interview, 2019). This may influence the competitiveness of social enterprises in the long-term.

A staged model of funding, relying on different sources of funding at different stages of the social enterprise's growth may be useful, and revenue diversification has been noted to be beneficial (Zhao & Li, 2019). We present a staged model of funding for hybrid Organisations such as FF, which plots a path to financial sustainability (see Figure 9.6). Yet there may also be drawbacks to this model, particularly reliance on donations and grants which could lead to dependency (Coupet, 2018). Thus although an abundant resource environment – due to policies such as BBBEE or simply a munificent donor environment – may be thought to be positive in enabling the emergence and success of a social enterprise, it may also hamper the development and resilience of social enterprises. This may lead social enterprises to become over-reliant on this type of funding. While there remains a place for the work of NGOs, social enterprises by definition aim to be self-funded and financially viable. It is thus important, particularly at the start-up phase, for social enterprises to establish organisational practices that will support the attainment of this goal. While FF currently makes use of a mixed-revenue model, Cox is intent on ensuring the organisation is able to shift towards 100% self-sustaining and profit driven business model.

As noted, there are two broad types of social enterprises – those with differentiated and integrated business models. The adoption of an integrated business model by FF has been central to the organisation's identity and critical to their success. The close coupling of the organisational goals and the activities of the organisation has limited the potential for issues such as mission drift to arise in the organisation. This strategy is more likely to lead to sustainable income generation – independent of donor fatigue and changes in funders' priorities. In addition, the close coupling of social and economic value generation allows for focus in the organisation. In terms of human capital requirements, FF's integrated business model indicates that there is not a need to hire staff with separate and specialised skills, as the economic value creation activities automatically lead to social value creation spillover. For FF, as they are working with independent contractors with existing businesses that they are attempting to help to scale and grow, this model is very effective. FF has also been cautious of the positioning of their organisation, as working with highly skilled contractors – not drawing on the social value creation aspect too heavily. By avoiding the association with the development aspect of the SE, which may be associated with connotations of charity

Figure 9.6 Staged model of funding, a drive to independence.

and potentially less skilled contractors, FF position themselves as a competitive and effective business and minimise the potential for tension regarding the organisation's legitimacy to arise.

FF thus represents an organisation with the potential to scale and have a large impact, creating jobs, improving livelihoods. Through an integrated business model, this HO is able to effectively create social and economic value concurrently, mitigating the risk of mission drift, maintaining a clear focus on becoming increasingly profitable, and lowering their reliance on grants and donations. The organisation will retain the elements of both contingent and automatic value spillover, needing to focus on both goals of the organisation. FF has been able to ensure that there is consistency for the organisation through donations received by the NFP Trust, which creates income stability; while it is possible to test and revise the revenue generation model without disrupting the organisation. This allows the organisation to develop and progress along a number of stages, where at each stage it is able to lower its grant dependence, sharpen the revenue generation model and interface with the market, with the goal to ultimately lead to financial independence. This may indicate that other hybrid organisations and SEs seeking to meet dual aims, could consider this approach to aid in initially getting established through grants, and with time transfer increased responsibility for revenue generation to the for-profit arm of the organisation. This may aid in ensuring that the social and economic goals – or value creation and capture – are closely linked from the hybrid organisations' inception, and allow organisations to transform as they mature from donor dependence to profitable, independent organisations. Box 9.3 provides discussion questions for further reflection on the case.

Box 9.3   Discussion questions.

1   Given the staged model of funding for sustainability: 1. what are the risks of this in terms of dependence on donors; 2. and the applicability of this model in different contexts?

2   To what extent is Fix Forward working to bridge institutional voids in the context of South Africa – given that it's characterised by large corporate organisations and a strong drive by the government to address wicked problems?

3   Would you suggest that Fix Forward simplify their legal model and adopt a single legal form, to minimise complexity, given that the organisation's hybridity and dual goals is clearly articulated within the organisation?

4   Given the unique operational environment in South Africa (with Broad Based Black Economic Empowerment and established CSR practices), would you expect that Fix Forward's business model would work in a different emerging market context?

5   What advice would you give to Fix Forward to ensure they are able to successfully scale in South Africa, across Africa and potentially into Latin America?

Notes

1 Sustainable Development Goals Knowledge Platform. (n.d.). Retrieved January 24, 2020, from https://sustainabledevelopment.un.org/sdg4
2 United Nations: Department of Economic and Social Affairs. Retrieved January 24, 2020, from www.un.org/development/desa/disabilities/envision2030-goal4.html
3 United Nations: Department of Economic and Social Affairs. Retrieved January 24, 2020, from https://www.un.org/development/desa/disabilities/envision2030-goal8.html
4 Statistics South Africa. Retrieved January 24, 2020, from www.statssa.gov.za/?p=12689. The level of unemployment has increased due to the pandemic, with some studies indicating as much as a 40% decline in active employment, with the potential that 50% this loss being permanent, even once the pandemic has ended
5 Efficiency driven economies are characterised by industrialisation, and the establishment of institutions in support of increased productivity. The Global Entrepreneurship Monitor report classifies countries as either Factor-driven Efficiency-driven or Innovation-driven, based on GDP and reliance on the primary sector (Herrington et al., 2010).
6 World Bank Country and Lending Groups. Retrieved January 30, 2020, from https://datahelpdesk.worldbank.org/knowledgebase/articles/906519-world-bank-country-and-lending-groups
7 Joshua Cox. (2018). *702 radio interview*. Retrieved January 17, 2020, from www.702.co.za/articles/323513/fix-forward-creates-opportunities-for-tradesmen-from-poor-areas-to-grow
8 Fix Forward video. Retrieved January 17, 2020, from https://fixforward.com/our-story/
9 Fix Forward, Q&A with the Founder. Retrieved January 17, 2020, from https://fixforward.com/qa-with-fix-forward-founder-joshua-cox/
10 Gauteng is the most populated province of South Africa which contains the capital, Pretoria, and Johannesburg, the largest city.
11 Fix Forward, Q&A with the Founder. Retrieved January 17, 2020, from https://fixforward.com/qa-with-fix-forward-founder-joshua-cox/
12 Fix Forward, Q&A with the Founder. Retrieved January 17, 2020, from https://fixforward.com/qa-with-fix-forward-founder-joshua-cox/
13 Data attained from research survey completed in January 2019, using Qualtrics.
14 The Global Impact Investing Network: Impact Investing. Retrieved February 2, 2020, from https://thegiin.org/impact-investing/
15 Fix Forward, Q&A with the Founder. Retrieved January 17, 2020, from https://fixforward.com/qa-with-fix-forward-founder-joshua-cox/

References

Albertyn, L., Swart, C., & Bonnici, F. (2015). *South African education innovators review*. Bertha Centre for Social Innovation & Entrepreneurship, University of Cape Town Graduate School of Business.

Battilana, J., Besharov, M., & Mitzinneck, B. (2017). On hybrids and hybrid organizing: A review and roadmap for future research. *The Sage Handbook of Organizational Institutionalism*, 2, 133–169.

Battilana, J., & Lee, M. (2014). Advancing research on hybrid organizing – insights from the study of social enterprises. *The Academy of Management Annals*, 8(1), 397–441.

Carpenter, G., & Lauritzen, J. R. K. (2016). *Promoting social enterprise financing: Discussion paper*. Danish Technological Institute:, Centre for Policy and Business Analysis.

Clarke, J. (2015). South African education overview. In L. Albertyn, C. Swart, & F. Bonnici (Eds.), *South African education innovators review*. Bertha Centre for Social Innovation & Entrepreneurship, University of Cape Town Graduate School of Business.

Coupet, J. (2018). Exploring the link between government funding and efficiency in nonprofit colleges. *Nonprofit Management and Leadership*, 29(1), 65–81.

Cox, J. (2019). *702 radio interview*. Retrieved January 17, 2020, from www.702.co.za/articles/323513/fix-forward-creates-opportunities-for-tradesmen-from-poor-areas-to-grow

Darko, E., & Hashi, F. M. (2020). *Innovation and resilience: British council 2020.* Retrieved January 20, 2021, from www.britishcouncil.org/sites/default/files/socialenterprise_covidres ponsesurvey_web_final_0.pdf

Davies, I. A., & Doherty, B. (2019). Balancing a hybrid business model: The search for equilibrium at cafédirect. *Journal of Business Ethics*, *157*(4), 1043–1066.

Ebrahim, A., Battilana, J., & Mair, J. (2014). The governance of social enterprises: Mission drift and accountability challenges in hybrid organizations. *Research in Organizational Behavior*, *34*, 81–100.

Fix Forward. (2020). Retrieved January 17, 2021, from https://fixforward.com/our-story/

Fix Forward, Q&A with the Founder. Retrieved January 17, 2021, from https://fixforward. com/qa-with-fix-forward-founder-joshua-cox/

The Global Impact Investing Network: Impact Investing. (n.d.). Retrieved February 2, 2020, from https://thegiin.org/impact-investing/

Greater Capital. (2016). *A guide to finance for social enterprises in South Africa.* International Labour Organization.

Greenwood, R., Díaz, A. M., Li, S. X., & Lorente, J. C. (2010). The multiplicity of institutional logics and the heterogeneity of organizational responses. *Organization Science*, *21*(2), 521–539.

Haigh, N., Kennedy, E. D., & Walker, J. (2015). Hybrid organizations as shape-shifters: Altering legal structure for strategic gain. *California Management Review*, *57*(3), 59–82.

Herrington, M., Kew, J., Kew, P., & Monitor, G. E. (2010). *Tracking entrepreneurship in South Africa: A GEM perspective* (pp. 1–174). Graduate School of Business, University of Cape Town.

Holt, D., & Littlewood, D. (2015). Identifying, mapping, and monitoring the impact of hybrid firms. *California Management Review*, *57*(3), 107–125.

Littlewood, D., & Holt, D. (2018). Social entrepreneurship in South Africa: Exploring the influence of environment. *Business & Society, 57*(3), 525–561.

Lumpkin, G. T., Moss, T. W., Gras, D. M., Kato, S., & Amezcua, A. S. (2013). Entrepreneurial processes in social contexts: How are they different, if at all? *Small Business Economics*, *40*(3), 761–783.

Mair, J., & Rathert, N. (2020). *Let's talk about problems: Advancing research on hybrid organizing, social enterprises, and institutional context.* Research in the Sociology of Organizations.

Moss, T. W., Short, J. C., Payne, G. T., & Lumpkin, G. T. (2011). Dual identities in social ventures: An exploratory study. *Entrepreneurship Theory and Practice, 35*(4), 805–830.

Ramukumba, K. (2015). Pathways to employment. In L. Albertyn, C. Swart, & F. Bonnici (Eds.), *South African education innovators review.* Bertha Centre for Social Innovation & Entrepreneurship, University of Cape Town Graduate School of Business.

Reilly, T. (2016). Are social enterprises viable models for funding nonprofits? *Human Service Organizations: Management, Leadership & Governance*, *40*(4), 297–301. https://doi.org/10 .1080/23303131.2016.1165047

Rwigema, H., Urban, B., & Venter, R. (2010). *Entrepreneurship theory in practice.* Oxford University Press.

Santos, F., Pache, A. C., & Birkholz, C. (2015). Making hybrids work: Aligning business models and organizational design for social enterprises. *California Management Review*, *57*(3), 36–58.

Sustainable Development Goals Knowledge Platform. (n.d.). Retrieved January 24, 2020, from https://sustainabledevelopment.un.org/sdg4

Trialogue Business in Society Handbook. (2019). *The trialogue business in society handbook* (22nd ed.). Trialogue Publication.

United Nation Children's Fund (UNICEF). (2017). *Education budget South Africa 2017/2018.* UNICEF.

United Nations: Department of Economic and Social Affairs. (n.d.). Retrieved January 24, 2020, from www.un.org/development/desa/disabilities/envision2030-goal4.html

Urban, B. (2013). Social entrepreneurship in an emerging economy: A focus on the institutional environment and social entrepreneurial self-efficacy. *Managing Global Transitions: International Research Journal*, 11(1).

Urban, B. (2015). An exploratory study on outcomes of social enterprises in South Africa. *Journal of Enterprising Culture*, 23(2), 271–297.

World Bank Country and Lending Groups. (n.d.). Retrieved January 30, 2020, from https://datahelpdesk.worldbank.org/knowledgebase/articles/906519-world-bank-country-and-lending-groups

Zhao, E. Y., & Li, Y. (2019). Institutions and entrepreneurship: Broadening and contextualizing the institutional theory in entrepreneurship research. *Quarterly Journal of Management*, 4(2), 15–25.

10 Value Co-Creation Through Multi-Stakeholder Collaborations for Health in Fragile Settings

The Case of the High-Risk Pregnancy Referral Tool

Simona Rocchi, Zahra Sultany, Federica Angeli, Patray Lui, Stephanie Saraswati Cristin and Koen Joosse

The article represents the authors' views; it does not necessarily reflect the views of their affiliated institutions

Introduction

Access to healthcare and maternal mortality are major issues particularly in in low-middle-income countries such as in Sub-Sahara Africa. Even when healthcare services are available, these are often underutilized due to numerous cultural, social, religious and economic barriers. These are challenges that a multi-stakeholder collaboration including International Committee of the Red Cross, the Philips Foundation, and Philips Experience Design, joined forces to address. The case discussed in this chapter represents an ideal example of how a multi-stakeholder collaboration has evolved to address antenatal care in low-middle-income countries (LMICs). This case examines the fragile environment the project is focused on, the process of establishing the cross-sector collaboration, and the way in which the tool created was developed, tested and implemented. The chapter then turns to theory, outlining the critical components required for a successful project and the way in which these played out empirically in the case – highlighting the advantages of cross-sector collaborations in addressing wicked problems. The SDGs at the centre of this case (SDG 3, 5 and 10) are highlighted in the images in Figure 10.1.

The World Health Organization (WHO) and the World Bank estimate that half the world's population lacks access to essential health services they need (World Health Organization & World Bank, 2017). It is therefore unsurprising to learn that in 2017, about 810 women died during and following pregnancy and childbirth every day. Of all maternal deaths, 94% occurred in low-middle-income countries (LMICs), especially in Sub-Saharan Africa, which alone accounted for roughly two-thirds of them (WHO, 2019). It is however disturbing to discover that the majority of those maternal deaths were associated with preventable causes, and could have been avoided with simple antenatal care services. This fact was brought forward by the United Nations (UN) in the section *Reproductive, maternal, newborn and child health* of Sustainable Development Goal 3 (SDG3), which aims to 'ensure healthy lives and promote well-being for all at all ages' by 2030 (UN, 2019). Addressing the maternal

DOI: 10.4324/9780429243165-11

This chapter has been made available under a CC-BY-NC 4.0 license.

Figure 10.1 SDGs addressed in this case.

mortality and particularly the antenatal care challenge is complex, and connected to that progress on the Millennium Development Goal 5 (gender equality) has been slow (WHO, 2014). Evidence highlights that, even when healthcare facilities, trained midwives and healthcare professionals are present in disadvantaged areas to provide antenatal care services, these often remain underutilized because of a complex nexus of cultural, social, religious and economic barriers (Das et al., 2018; Dey et al., 2018). Deeply rooted gender inequalities (SDG5) lead to a situation of disadvantage for many women in fertile age, who lack sufficient health literacy and decision-making power to access adequate healthcare support. The difference in maternal mortality between Global North and Global South closely reflects rampant socio-economic inequalities (WHO, 2019) and illustrates a co-evolution between SDG3, SDG5 and SDG10 (Reduce inequalities).

In LMICs, antenatal care is consequently a high healthcare priority for many local governments and humanitarian programmes. Foremost within the humanitarian space, the International Committee of the Red Cross (ICRC) argues that antenatal care is one of the most challenging areas for both professional healthcare workers and informal care givers, such as traditional birth attendants (TBAs, operating in fragile environments such as conflict zones, post-conflict zones, displacement areas and areas affected by natural disasters (Du Mortier, 2017)). These contexts of operation often lack essential healthcare services and/or sufficient medical personnel. Facilities, if in place, are often difficult to reach due to infrastructural conditions. If facilities do exist they may be damaged, or not properly functioning due to insufficient medical equipment or poor maintenance. They may suffer from insufficient medical supplies, and have no, or very limited, access to electricity and connectivity. On top of these barriers, local cultural beliefs, traditional practices and generally low healthcare awareness among local communities also play an important role in preventing pregnant women from seeking healthcare services (Kopp, 2017).

214 *Simona Rocchi et al.*

The interdependency of these factors in fragile environments qualifies antenatal care as a classic example of a societal 'wicked problem' to tackle; a problem that due to its systemic nature requires commitment and coordinated actions from multiple stake-holders in the private, public and civil society sectors, who share resources and jointly create value (Macdonald, 2016). Health and wealth in low-resource settings go hand-in-hand, as indicated in the report Tracking Universal Health Coverage: 2017 Global Monitoring (World Health Organization & World Bank, 2017). About 100 million people are still being pushed into 'extreme poverty' (living on US$1.90 or less a day) for out-of-pocket spending.[1] The case discussed in this chapter represents an ideal example of how a multi-stakeholder collaboration has evolved to address antenatal care in LMICs.

Cross-sector Collaboration for Antenatal Care: The Case of Philips Experience Design, Philips Foundation and the International Committee of the Red Cross

The complexity of delivering postnatal and antenatal care, like many other wicked problems and challenges addressed via the UN sustainable development agenda, can-not be solved by one sector alone. Interventions carried out by stakeholders operating in isolation, who rely only on their own financial resources and capabilities, have not yet produced sufficiently encouraging results to progress the societal goals expressed in the 2030 targets. Global investment needed to address the SDGs is in the order of US$5 trillion to US$7 trillion per year. Estimates for investment needs in developing countries alone range from US$3.3 trillion to US$4.5 trillion per year, mainly for basic infrastructure, food security, climate change mitigation and adaptation, health, and education (UNCTAD, 2014). This is why SDG 17 explicitly flags 'partnership for the goals', encouraging cross-sector cooperation and partnership formation. In this respect, collaboration between non-profits and businesses is increasing and becoming more strategically important (Austin, 2000). These collaborations do not seek only to combine financial resources around societal challenges and ambitious common goals, but also to bring together complementary expertise and assets that are essential to boost joint innovations and synergistic interventions able to amplify impact on the ground.

Setting Up a Cross-Sector Collaboration for Antenatal Care in Fragile Settings

It was in this spirit that in 2015 the International Committee of the Red Cross (ICRC), the Philips Foundation (PF) – the non-profit organization of Philips – and Philips Experience Design (PED) – the design team of Philips, the healthcare technology company – joined forces around their commitment to SDG3 (Good Health and Wellbe-ing), to focus on the antenatal care challenge in fragile settings of Sub-Sahara African countries. The basis of the partnership, which was established between the ICRC and the PF, was to engage in an experimental approach for 'value co-creation', namely the creation of value that benefits all parties involved and particularly takes on board the beneficiaries' needs and values through a bottom-up approach (e.g. Angeli & Jaiswal, 2016). The goal of the first joint initiative was to develop low-cost innovations able to support the delivery of effective, quality antenatal care services to local communities living in these difficult settings. The approach would combine the ICRC's medical expertise and insights into the local population's needs coming from the humanitarian world with innovation and design capabilities from the private healthcare sector, channelled into the partnership via the PF (see Figure 10.2). The specific occasion behind this teaming up was the celebration of 90 years of design within Philips, at the end of 2015, when 120 designers (donating their time pro-bono) were gathered together with experts from the ICRC and Philips Foundation representatives for a series of 2-day-ideation workshop in different locations around the world (The Netherlands, Singapore, USA, India and China), over a period of a couple of months. The goal of the event was to combine Philips design expertise, temporarily removed from their day to day work, with ICRC knowledge of antenatal issues in multidisciplinary teams to develop ideas for the Philips Foundation to pursue. This series of workshop kick-started a process of co-creation, design, testing and implementation of the new solution that lasted roughly two years to achieve full development and another year to full deployment and start scaling.

The 'Co-creation' Process

Initially, a team of designers and researchers connected with doctors and midwives from the ICRC to support preparation of the design briefs used to guide the first large-scale workshop. Virtual and face-to-face interviews and working sessions were essential to gather insights on contextual requirements, socio-cultural conditions and people's priority needs, from both a health delivery and a health-seeking perspective. The interests and motivations for collaboration were openly shared and discussed

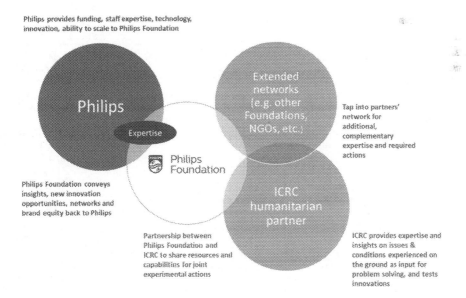

Figure 10.2 Visualization of tripartite cooperation (Philips Foundation, Philips and ICRC) sharing assets and resources for joint actions to strengthen healthcare systems and community care in fragile settings.

Source: Courtesy of Philips Foundation

216 Simona Rocchi et al.

among the various stakeholders at the beginning of this experimental path. ICRC's interest was to come up with easy-to-use tools that could support the work of midwives, traditional birth attendants (TBAs) – generally members of the local community that help women to deliver at home – and/or Community Healthcare Volunteers (CHVs), who deliver a wide range of healthcare services, when providing antenatal care in contexts often confronted with no, or very limited, access to electricity and connectivity. The Philips Foundation wanted to move away from its traditional formulas of financial donations to general humanitarian causes, since the impact and results of such donations are difficult to assess. Instead, it sought to leverage Philips' innovation power and expertise as a unique resource. Its objective was to support access to quality care to disadvantaged pregnant women living in difficult conditions by equipping its humanitarian partner (ICRC) with appropriate and context-specific tools necessary to carry out their work (see Table 10.1). Philips Experience Design wanted to contribute to a humanitarian cause by leveraging its creative workforce (doing good for the world) while advancing Philips' agenda of improving people's lives in underserved communities, and gaining new contextual insights into unfamiliar market geographies, which could put in place some 'seeds' for portfolio development in the years to come (doing well for the company).

Design thinking and people-centric design methodologies were applied all along the 'value co-creation' process: from the establishment of a common understanding of the challenge to address on the ground and common objectives ('discovery' and 'framing' phases) to the shaping and testing of potential solutions ('ideation' and 'building' phases).

Table 10.1 Overview of Missions of the Three Parties in the Cooperation

ICRC	Philips Foundation	Philips (Philips Experience Design)
The ICRC is an independent, neutral organization ensuring humanitarian protection and assistance for victims of armed conflict and other situations of violence. It takes action in response to emergencies and at the same time promotes respect for international humanitarian law and its implementation in national law. Established in 1863, the ICRC is at the origin of the Geneva Conventions and the International Red Cross and Red Crescent Movement (ICRC, 2020)	Philips Foundation's mission is to reduce healthcare inequality by providing access to quality healthcare for disadvantaged communities. The Philips Foundation is a registered charity that was established in July 2014 – founded on the belief that innovation and collaboration with key partners around the world can help solve some of the world's toughest healthcare challenges and make essential impact (Philips Foundation, 2014, 2020).	Philips Experience Design is the design group of Philips, a company that strives to make the world healthier and more sustainable through innovation. Philips's purpose is to improve the health and well-being of 2.5 billion people a year – including 400 million in underserved communities – by 2030. The company was founded in 1891. Today Philips is a leading health technology company focused on improving people's health and enabling better outcomes across the health continuum from healthy living and prevention, to diagnosis, treatment and home care (Philips, 2020a, 2020b)

Value Co-Creation Through Multi-Stakeholder Collaborations   217

Thanks to the contextual knowledge of the ICRC medical staff and the creative power of PED workforce, the ideation resulted in a wide range of innovative solutions. Ideas and concepts were then ranked by the ICRC for their relevance and practical application, and a few were selected for further development. Among those, this chapter presents only the case of the High-Risk Pregnancy (HRP) Referral Cards: a low-tech, low-cost checklist to support the identification and communication of symptoms that can lead to risky pregnancies, before they become life-threatening (see Box 10.1).

Box 10.1   The High-Risk Pregnancy Referral Cards: Tool description.

Earlier risk detection in pregnancy will lead to earlier referrals from the community to the first level of care, and from primary healthcare to hospitals. This time factor plays a crucial role when working on the high number of maternal morbidity and mortality in areas where the access to quality healthcare is hampered due to low coverage of healthcare services, war, displacement, insecurity, lack of infrastructure, lack of skilled healthcare providers and lack of awareness and knowledge.

Ms. Sigrid Kopp – Former Supra Regional Midwife, International Committee of the Red Cross, 2015.

Responding to this need, the HRP referral cards are designed to train traditional birth attendants and community healthcare workers in:

- recognising and explaining the signs of high-risk pregnancies (red cards) to women living in various socio-cultural and geographical contexts, to encourage them to approach the closest healthcare centers;
- educating and raising awareness of practices for healthy pregnancy, and on the importance of antenatal check-ups (green cards).

The tool is easy to understand for audiences with different levels of literacy. The graphics respect local cultural and religious sensitivities (e.g. no representations of unclothed women's bodies) and the content – currently available in English, French and Swahili – can be easily adapted to other languages and another look and feel to accommodate different contextual requirements.

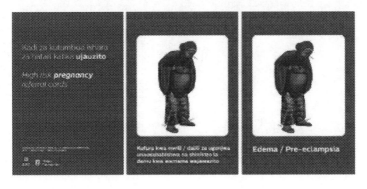

Value Co-Creation Through Multi-Stakeholder Collaborations   219

Images usage: courtesy of the ICRC

220   *Simona Rocchi et al.*

Table 10.2 Overview of Countries Reached by the ICRC with the Deployment of the HRP Referral Tool between 2017 and 2018

Country	Number of Traditional Birth Attendants reached	Number of HRP cards distributed
Nigeria	>1,200	1,300
CAR	105	200
Mali	160	200
Niger	82	100
South Sudan	230	450
Cameroun	No data	100
Total	Approx. 1,800	2,350

Implementing the HRP referral tool

In the course of 2017 and 2018, the ICRC deployed the final tool: 2,350 sets of referral cards (see Table 10.2) were distributed in six African countries – Cameroon, CAR, Mali, Niger, Nigeria and South Sudan – reaching approximately 1,800 traditional birth attendants (lay healthcare givers). Figure 10.3 represents the co-creation process underpinning the development of the HRP tool.

The use of the tool has been monitored over time by the ICRC to assess its benefits in relation to the project's original ambition. Qualitative observations and positive experiences have been traced by collecting quotes from the ICRC health field officers (HFOs) and local traditional birth attendants (TBAs) despite the difficulties of the working conditions. An HFO operating in Nigeria mentioned that: *The cards are very useful for the TBAs – as we can see from the data, they are able to identify the various risks demonstrated in the cards and offer timely referrals. In fact, some of the TBAs come with their cards with the mother they have identified to have a certain condition.* Another quote from a TBA in Central African Republic (CAR) mentioned that: *With the HRP cards it is easier for me to convince the mother and the family about the importance of being referred to a health facility. I can show them the pictures and because it has the logo of the ICRC, the community has more trust.*

Now, the tool is being scaled up. The ICRC has integrated the HRP Referral Cards into its Primary Health Care (PHC) resource centre for further use by all ICRC health delegates (to print/use as needed). A downloadable customizable version is also available on request to accommodate translation into local languages/dialects. The positive results have also encouraged the Philips Foundation to enter into a new partnership with the Red Cross Kenya for disseminating the HRP referral cards in new geographies affected by a similar challenge and contexts. In 2019, distribution of the tool started in rural and nomadic areas of four Kenyan counties with the ambition of reaching 250,000 women and family members. The objective is not only to amplify the impact but also to measure potential outcomes in the healthcare referral system linking communities to primary and higher level of care facilities.

Testing and refining outcome: the HRP tool

The HRP referral tool was shaped, tested and re-shaped iteratively through joint activities that took place over the course of almost two years. The tool is relatively

Value Co-Creation Through Multi-Stakeholder Collaborations 221

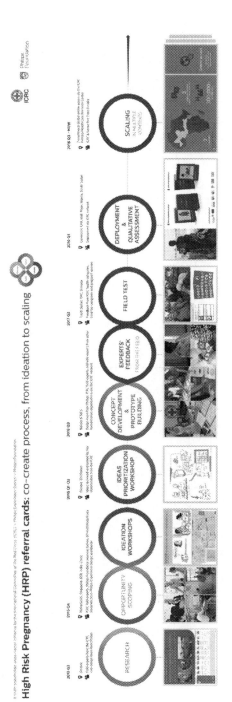

Figure 10.3 Visualization of the 'co-create' process adopted to mobilize multiple stakeholders (including local communities) in various phases, from research to ideation and prototype development, and from testing and finalization to dissemination.

Source: Courtesy of Philips Experience Design, Philips Foundation, & ICRC

222 *Simona Rocchi et al.*

simple to produce, but its development involved extensive consolidation and validation by medical expertise, as well as identifying and testing a graphical language that is appealing to the majority of the targeted local communities living in fragile settings of different geographies. A quote from Stephane Du Mortier, former Head of the Primary Health Care Services at the ICRC, acknowledges the time and effort put into its development: *innovation is not improvisation.* This statement becomes particularly true when the innovation is generated by multiple stakeholders coming from different sectors who need to bring together different expertise and synchronize activities around a complex goal.

Via collaborative online and face-to-face sessions, the initial concept of the HRP Referral Cards was matured into a prototype, which proposed a variety of formats and graphical representations. Between 2016 and 2017, the ICRC collected insights from the field of operation in Somalia, Nigeria, South Sudan and DRC to shape the tool's content and the visuals. Formal testing of the complete prototype was conducted in two facilities in South Sudan over a three-month period to gather feedback from both healthcare givers and the beneficiaries. This iterative process was important to come up with a solution that was truly meaningful and appropriate to its contexts of use. Marking a last milestone, the tool was finalized in a workshop organized in Nairobi with a core team of designers, midwives from the ICRC, and other midwives from the ICRC's network of local NGOs also dealing with the challenge of antenatal care.

Multi-stakeholder Partnerships and Value Co-Creation: A Theoretical Analysis of Trust Formation and Consolidation

The SDG17 strongly supports the value of partnerships between national governments, the international community, civil society, private businesses, and other sectors to achieve sustainable development goals. A cross-sector partnership involving multiple stakeholders is a collaboration between two or three sectors with interconnected problems and interests, with the aim to pool complementary resources and competences in the pursuit of a common goal. At the heart of this collaboration is the co-creation of a solution, as the HRP tool case very well illustrates. "Over the last decade, stakeholders tried to co-create innovative solutions in cross-sector partnerships at the base of the economic pyramid (BoP)" (Venn & Berg, 2014). Therefore, the collaboration between nonprofit and businesses is becoming more strategically important (Austin, 2000). However, partnering across societal sectors is challenging, as it requires bringing organizations with different approaches, cultures, interests, and values together and finding an equitable approach that delivers value for all. The organizational identities, missions, values, and way of workings – in one concept, the organizational cultures – might restrain partners' willingness and ability to adapt to these contingencies and to overcome role conflict in their relationship. Sloan and Oliver (2013) asserted that "lack of trust is a key problem in these arrangements".

Trust-building is a long process and is only developed over time (Das & Teng, 1998; Pennink, 2017; Sloan & Oliver, 2013). The literature on trust-building in cross-sector partnerships focuses on the relational practices to trust-building. These practices include frequent interactions (Sloan & Oliver, 2013) or continued communication and information exchange (Das & Teng, 1998), interdependence (Pennink, 2017), risk-taking (Das & Teng, 1998; Sloan & Oliver, 2013) interfirm adaptation (Das & Teng, 1998), open-mindedness, flexibility and transparency (Dentoni et al., 2018) that may help partners overcome and leverage key differences in the partnership. However, partner stereotypes (Sloan & Oliver, 2013) and other factors such as missions, structure and pattern of activities (Ber, 2010) that define an organizational culture are barriers to trust development.

In the case of a multi-stakeholder partnership aiming to achieve social impact in fragile settings, the challenges inherent to trust formation are even more acute than in traditional collaboration arrangements. To reach consensus on the very definition of the collaboration goals in itself requires intense cooperation and exchange between the involved parties, as health outcomes and community impact are difficult to define and measure (Dentoni et al., 2018; Nason et al., 2018). Moreover, different organizational cultures are involved, which see for example a potential clash between profitability-oriented firms and philanthropic organizations from the third sector and which imply different expectations, goals, ways of working and conceptualizations of success. In these contexts, a process of co-creation is therefore necessary, not only to design solutions, but also to define the problems (Alford & Head, 2017; Head & Alford, 2015). In the base-of-the-pyramid literature, the necessity of a co-creation approach has been widely recognized (Dahan et al., 2010; Kolk et al., 2014; Reypens et al., 2016), and particularly embedded into a business model thinking through a phase of value discovery (Angeli & Jaiswal, 2016). However, how this is achieved is less explored, and evidence is still meagre about which organizational models can best serve a co-creation purpose.

This case study provides a first-hand illustration of how co-creation can be successfully achieved through a multi-stakeholder collaboration. Moreover, it highlights how relationship between trust and organizational culture change is iterative and evolves in the partnership process, as trust and cultural emergence occur at the partnership interface after the cross-sector partnership is implemented (Parker & Selsky, 2004). That means that while trust is formed, cultural change occurs within each organization, which in turn influences the consolidation of trust, smoothens processes of goal-setting, and favours the design and implementation of the desired solution. A new, multi-stakeholder culture is formed, that recognizes the valuable contribution of each partner and underlines how the underlying collaboration has been instrumental to its impact. In the words of ICRC and Philips Foundation

The HRP cards are the result of a simple, yet meaningful, co-creation process. Following feedback from both staff and communities, the cards have been updated and now can be seamlessly integrated into ICRC's primary health care resource center and be made available to all health delegates to leverage in operations.

Esperanza Martinez – Head of Health, ICRC

Philips Foundation's mission is to reduce healthcare inequality by providing access to quality healthcare for disadvantaged communities, in support of UN Sustainable Development Goal 3. I'm proud to see that- in partnership with the ICRC-, we developed and deployed the HRP cards. We are committed to help scale the impact of the referral cards on the basis of further deployment in relevant settings.

Ronald de Jong – Chairman Philips Foundation

224 *Simona Rocchi et al.*

The next sections delve more in-depth into the literature addressing cross-sector partnership, organizational culture and their co-evolution, and connects these insights with examples from the HRP case.

Multi-stakeholder (cross-sector) Partnerships: Definitions

"Cross-sector partnerships are formed when at least two organizations from public, private, or civil society sectors agree to work together to achieve mutual goals or address a shared problem" (MacDonald, 2016). In these types of partnerships, because more than one partner from any of the three sectors is involved, therefore, is also referred to as multi-stakeholder partnerships. In the existing studies, these terms are often used interchangeably. For instance, terms such as multi-stakeholder partnerships (Brouwer et al., 2016), collaboratives/collaborative groups (Bryson et al., 2006), multi-stakeholder initiatives (Krawchuk, 2013) and multi-stakeholder networks (Bäckstrand, 2006) all refer to similar collaborative arrangements. The Center of Development for Innovation (CDI)[2] defines multi-stakeholder partnership as "A process of interactive learning, empowerment and participatory governance that enables stakeholders with interconnected problems and ambitions, but often differing interests, to be collectively innovative and resilient when faced with the emerging risks, crises, and opportunities of a complex and changing environment."

This definition notes the importance of both the social and strategic value of multi-stakeholder partnerships. First, for its social value because partners are attracted to each other based on 'synergistic goals' and 'opportunities' that address a specific problem that is beyond the ability of one single organization (Stott, 2017). Second, for its strategic value that multi-stakeholder partnership is an iterative process in which stakeholders "assess the present situation, plan, implement, review, adjust, and again plan ahead" (Brouwer et al., 2016). Therefore, as Le Ber (2010) argues "neither success nor failure is absolute" in a multi-stakeholder partnership. It depends on the extent partners are flexible and resilient in their strategic planning to adapt to the changing environment and sustain that momentum towards success. Austin and Seitanidi (2012) argue that "accepting adaptive responsibilities and co-design mechanisms" increases the chance of success. The evolution of the partnership between PED, PF and ICRC highlights in fact how the focus on co-design, the emphasis on frequent interactions and on a flexible adaptation of roles and responsibilities over time allowed for trust-building, while engaging all partners in a journey of successful product development and partnership consolidation. Therefore, partners constantly and iteratively may need to adjust their roles and facilitate or/and manage the partnership together. The partners' interactions become crucial to planning that may help to sustain success or triggering a failure. However, the relational process and interactions between parties do not just happen as a result of partnership and those interactions do not necessarily lead to an effective partnership. Foley et al. (2017) assert that "Trust in people and the process of collaboration is a key feature of successful/effective multi-stakeholder partnerships". Therefore, trust plays an important role in the success of partnership and partners' relationships.

Trust in multi-stakeholder partnerships

In general terms "trust is expressed as an optimistic expectation on the part of an individual about the outcome of an event or the behavior of a person" (Pennink,

2017). Trust in people and in the process become important particularly in a network structure where partners can learn from each other (Airike et al., 2016). Trust building is an iterative process that is developed continuously and gradually (Sloan & Oliver, 2013). In general, in social exchange, one partner voluntarily provides benefits to another partner. On the part of the partner, a sense of obligation triggers to provide some benefit in return. The social exchange is a result of direct contact or recurrent exchange in the long run between partners (Pennink, 2017). Because partners are frequently engaged in a social exchange relationship this act of reciprocity encourages engagement and trust. Managing expectation, frequent interactions (Sloan & Oliver, 2013) or continued communication and information exchange (Das & Teng, 1998; Pennink, 2017) interdependence (Pennink, 2017), equity preservation, interfirm adaptation (Das & Teng, 1998) open-mindedness, flexibility, transparency (Dentoni et al., 2018) are the elements that can trigger reciprocity and build trust among stakeholders over time, as "Trust builds slowly and incrementally through repeated interactions" (Venn & Berg, 2014). Amongst all, communication and information exchange, open-mindedness and flexibility are critical to partners' trust, commitment and improving working culture in multi-stakeholder partnerships.

This point is well illustrated through the interview data:

It is essential to talk and discuss the subject and not to walk around it: to address it and acknowledge that it might be a bit distrustful, but to prove that we are in it for the same outcome. In the end, it is a matter of establishing long-term relationship and gaining trust. How do we do that? By communicating, by talking a lot and discussing what the options are and not avoiding the subject.

Interview data also suggests that trust builds and is facilitated in different stages of collaboration, as abstract ideas start to transition into concrete actions and differences in organizational culture become less relevant:

Issues of trust typically arise in the phase when the collaboration is still abstract – in the conceptualization phase, in contracting discussions, in discussing things like IP, which often occurs on partnership management level. As soon as this phase is over and people actually start working together on the ground, they discover each other's drive and passion towards common goals and experience the added value they can bring to each other, and then trust is quickly built.

Participant from the Philips Foundation

Once we began the process of using and leveraging the HRP cards in the selected primary health care districts, the focus quickly shifted to the affected expecting mothers that stood before us and the abstract structural elements of the multi-stakeholder collaboration blurred away in the background. It became about the patients, and thus the crystallization of the common goal helped seal any issues of mistrust or organizational differences that had previously arose.

Participant from the ICRC

226   *Simona Rocchi et al.*

Organizational Culture in Multi-Stakeholder Partnerships

Organizational culture is defined as "a system of shared values and norms that define appropriate attitudes and behavior for organizational members" (Das & Teng, 1998). More comprehensively, Schein (2010) defines culture as:

> A pattern of shared basic assumptions learned by a group as it solved its problems of external adaptation and internal integration, which has worked well enough to be considered valid and therefore, to be taught to new members as the correct way to perceive, think and feel concerning those problems.

To understand an organization's culture, this can be analysed on three levels. (1) Artefacts, (2) Values and (3) Assumptions. Each level rests on the other, meaning that artefacts such as organizational structures, processes, procedures, practices, routines and behaviour patterns of the members of organizations (Meirovich, 2012; Reid, 2016) exist based on its values. Values are those norms such as strategies, goals that organizations are likely to share. Assumptions are the thoughts and feelings, view of how the work should be done that underpins the organization's operations (Meirovich, 2012). These assumptions provide a basis for why and how the organizational values are built. Traditionally, the humanitarian sector is grounded on values and principles of humanity, neutrality, impartiality and independence, which provide a basis for organizational structures and practices and lead to assumptions with respect to the role of the private sector. The autonomy of humanitarian action, or its independence from political, economic, military or other objectives, is a key point of the broader cross-sectorial partnership debate within the sector – and was no exception in the decision to collaborate on the HRP cards. The participants in the Philips interview sometimes noted stigma around the underlying reasons for collaboration, further pointing to a generalized perception that the private sector's sole aim is towards profit generation and commercial objectives. Philips Experience Design and the Philips Foundation were very eager to collaborate to develop innovations with the ICRC. ICRC representatives in turn, while acknowledging the potential added value for those in need, were initially apprehensive to face traditional stereotypes linked to private sector collaboration. An interviewee from the Philips Foundation explained:

> *I think the NGO sector was traditionally reluctant to work with the private sector as they think it would influence their work and challenge their independence. It feels as though we have successfully overcome that in this project with the ICRC. More generally speaking, I believe that the trust that collaboration with the private sector can add to the quality and impact of their work has grown among the NGO sector, in line with the notion that the SDGs can only be realized with strong global partnerships and cooperation (SDG17).*

Although traditional organizational cultural traits of both the humanitarian and private sector naturally guided perceptions and initial conversations, it is important to note that progress and trust building was led individually by champions who saw the added value of the collaboration and sought to break the traditional moulds. It was only with the one-on-one conversations with the primary health care programme manager and the midwife that the project started to take shape. The initial stages of the collaboration were characterized by countless onboarding meetings aimed to defining a common language to achieve a common goal. It simply takes time for partners to develop a mutual understanding of working culture, ways of planning and operating, as well as addressing or even discussing a problem or solution each in their own jargon. One Philips participant commented:

> *In the beginning our ICRC counterparts didn't really know what we mean by co-create. They didn't know what kind of benefits to expect by conceptualizing insights from their experts and leveraging tools like design thinking.*

As the partnership took hold, it became evident that different priorities and ways of working would additionally influence the product delivery timeline and the setting of key performance indicators. As an organization working in volatile conflict-affected settings, the ICRC is traditionally more accustomed to cater to acute crises and immediate needs of populations across a wide portfolio of humanitarian support and interventions. An interviewee from PED emphasized that this has often caused difficulties in understanding when progress could be made. Similarly, an ICRC representative asserted:

> *I think communicating expectations of when delivery is possible and feasible, then how to progress from there in case of either internal or external delays is critical in these partnerships- with a huge emphasis on the importance of flexibility and adaptability. The HRP Cards - however important - are just one small element of a broader primary healthcare program under an even larger health strategy in countries of our operations. The development or implementation is thus difficult for our colleagues in the field who are often dealing with acute emergencies to systematically prioritize among many different needs and initiatives. Furthermore, the environments in which the ICRC operates are volatile, so it is often difficult to predict appropriate security conditions or availability of staff conducive to meet the timelines set with partners at the global level.*

Co-evolution of Trust and Organizational Culture in MSPs

Organizational culture and trust in the relationship are not static but rather iterative and evolving aspects, as the people in organizations or within a partnership make decisions, take actions and interact with each other and are in turn influenced by others' culture (Reid, 2016). Problems however might occur when partners are unable to reconcile cultural differences, which may impact partnership success and partners' relations. Cultural clashes might occur because partners are not well aware of possible differences between organizational cultures and their impact on the partnership or they are unable to respond to cultural differences. Therefore, first of all, "partners have to identify the core strengths of their organizations and their comparative advantage over others" (Reid, 2016) and accept the cultural differences between them. Meirovich (2012) studied cultural differences and similarities in strategic alliances, and his conclusions are also applicable to the multi-stakeholder partnerships. In his paper, he suggests that "differences at the beginning of a relationship should be considered as input, which may be altered by the deliberate or unintentional activities of the parties involved". The first step in the relationship-building is that partners appreciate other's cultural trait and accepting it as valuable as their own, and approach each other with the right attitude, open-mindedness, responsive to their changing needs (Dentoni et al., 2018) that is very essential when interacting with partners with different backgrounds. "When cultures are mutually appreciated, differences will lead to success; otherwise, cultural differences will create cultural conflict and hamper performance" (Meirovich, 2012).

The concept of "emergent culture" by Parker and Selsky (2004) underlines the importance of the *blended culture* that emerges between partners as the collaboration consolidates. The authors indicate that identifying both similarities and dissimilarities in the partnership allows for a third, or emergent, culture to develop. In this type of culture, partners share value and negotiate the meaning of the partnership over time and involve in a dialogue (Stöteler et al., 2012) to jointly develop and discuss routines for tasks and processes (Parker & Selsky, 2004) while at the same time holding to their basic assumptions.

While organizational culture between partners evolves, it is important to note that new practices are often formed on the basis of not only explicit rules and regulations but also a set of ethical habits and reciprocal moral obligations internalized by each of the partners (Sambasivan & Yen, 2010). The case illustrated in this chapter highlights two main mechanisms that allowed for the emergence of a blended culture in the partnership: *pursuing compromise and flexibility, and emphasizing co-creation.*

Pursuing Compromise and Flexibility

Managing expectations becomes very important when partners have different interests and values. The HRP case shows that when partners were responsive to each other needs and expectations, this encouraged mutual learning, engagement, and trust in the relationship. A participant from PED illustrated that because they were able to listen and understand their partners' needs and requirements (The ICRC), they were able to deliver a tool answering to their partners' expectations. The ongoing dialogue triggered a sense of commitment to the collaboration and to the outcomes on both sides. This implies that *the* partnership is flexible enough to respond to the various needs of the stakeholders involved as well as adjust joint-efforts towards the expected results. Das and Teng (1998) argue that the relationship between flexibility and building trust reinforces mutual adaptation. Therefore, in cross-sector partnerships, stakeholders need to iteratively discuss and align their requirements and expectations to move the relationship forward. However, it is important to keep in mind that interactions between stakeholders, particularly in a cross-sector partnership, are often hindered by divergence in their organizational structure, organizational identities and patterns of activities (Ber, 2010); *together* these elements form the organizational culture. An example from the interview data highlights this point:

> I think trust developed by being able to deliver what was expected from all the partners at different stages of the project, but most importantly thanks to the fact that we were eager to engage in a dialogue with the ICRC to truly understand their needs and take on board their specific challenges. We listened to them, we understood their contextual requirements, and we translated learnings and

insights into a meaningful solution for them, the beneficiaries that they reach, and all parties involved.

Participant from Philips Experience Design

Thus, partners were not only able to deliver on expectations but also aware of the changes in their expectations over time and adapted accordingly. Partners argued that compromises may be needed from any stakeholders' side to move forward and adapt to changing circumstances.

Co-innovation is giving and taking. On the one hand it is cross-stimulation and cross fertilization, on the other hand it requires willingness to compromise and finding common grounds to accommodate one another' needs as mentioned by a participant from Philips Experience Design.

Emphasizing co-creation approaches

The 'co-create' methodology applied by Philips Experience Design during the project execution facilitated also the definition of a shared, equitable goal for the partners. The methodology supported the alignment of all stakeholders involved since the start of the cooperation. It helped in building a good relationship, develop trust, and establish commitment between stakeholders and positively influenced the partnership.

Co-creation, namely the process of co-designing solutions by incorporating multiple views, is advocated by many scholars as necessary in the innovation process leading to solutions for disadvantaged, fragile settings. This HRP tool case highlights the need to generate a valuable solution for all partners involved, especially ICRC, as an important representative of the beneficiaries' point of view. The collaborative project started with gathering insights from the ICRC health delegates from the field of operation and to identify antenatal care issues faced in relation to the local infrastructural, socio-economic and cultural challenges. Then, all these contextual insights where shared in the large scale ideation workshop that was bringing together designers, the ICRC healthcare experts and Philips Foundation representatives. After the workshop, the design outcomes were clustered based on different challenges and filtered as previously described. From the results, three co-related concepts were prioritized to be developed to be materialized in the short term. Here, stakeholders started to develop mutual learning as they exchanged information frequently.

I really liked to interact with people who are working in the field; listening to their experiences helped me to better understand the context and wear their shoes during the co-design process, highlighted an interviewee from a representative of Philips Experience Design.

Based on feedbacks, a final solution direction was defined for development. Partners were open to listen and understand each other's needs and expectations to accommodate changes. A representative of the ICRC mentioned that the co-create activities helped partners in enhancing trust and commitment over time.

The co-create activities helped a lot to have a better common understanding of the added value that we can generate with joint-efforts. They helped a lot to build the relationship.

Participant from ICRC

230   Simona Rocchi et al.

In the next step, the improved solution was then ready for field trial. Field trial framework and questions were set up by the ICRC and conducted in two facilities in South Sudan; the tool was also reviewed and validated by the ICRC health delegates and local lay healthcare providers in other locations. Their feedback was consolidated to finalize the tool in two versions for deployment in the countries of operation of ICRC first and later in some contexts of operation of the Red Cross Kenya. *By that time everyone was committed not because we had to – due to formal agreements – but because we believed in it. And then the cooperation resulted much more natural at that point"*, as noted by a participant from ICRC.

During and after the tool deployment stage, the ICRC gathered qualitative data in the form of feedback, confirming that the tool was well accepted by their beneficiaries; thanks to these positive results ICRC integrated the tool into its primary health care resource centre. Figure 10.4 shows the challenges encountered and enablers put in place through the HRP project; it may help stakeholders to improve existing partnerships and/or in setting new collaborative initiatives by leveraging value co-creation processes able to take into account multiple views and perspectives. These factors are derived from both primary (interviews) and secondary (archival data) sources of analysis.

Practical implications

The HRP case illustrates how cross-sector collaborations can benefit by combining capabilities and expertise but also how they are challenged by cross-cultural conflicts, which can significantly influence and possibly hamper the partnership's success and the partners' relationship. Against this backdrop, the case highlights the importance of favouring the emergence of a *blended culture* within cross-sector collaborations, as a set of values, beliefs and practices idiosyncratic to the collaborative endeavour. The starting point is partners' awareness of their culture and of the partners' culture, to identifying differences and potential sources of conflict. Next, they should acknowledge and accept differences, value complementarity and mutually accept each other's view and expectations in an equitable fashion. The cross-cultural differences, if not properly understood, reconciled and managed can be a barrier to trust-building and partners' commitment to the partnership and/or collaborative initiative. This implies that partners must frequently communicate and manage partnership expectations, and engage in trust-building practices to ensure the achievement of a common goal. In line with earlier studies (Das & Teng, 1998; Pennink, 2017), the stakeholders involved in the relationship should constantly and transparently share information that facilities mutual learning and cross-cultural fertilization.

This case also provides the opportunity to advance current literature and provide useful indications to managerial practice. Interestingly, while most of the previous studies have looked at the evolution of trust in multi-stakeholder partnerships and of organizational culture in strategic alliances separately, the co-evolution of trust and organizational culture in cross-sector partnerships – organizational arrangement that by definition bridge cultural differences – has received far less attention. This case illustrates the importance of two mechanisms that help partners overcome cultural difference, stimulate a positive cycle of mutual learning, foster the emergence of an idiosyncratic common culture and ensure a positive outcome. First, the use of compromise

Value Co-Creation Through Multi-Stakeholder Collaborations 231

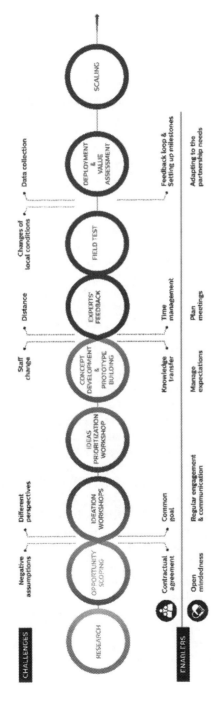

Figure 10.4 Challenges and Enablers throughout the MSP (HRP project).

232 *Simona Rocchi et al.*

and flexibility, hence keeping goals and practices particularly adaptable to changes in contextual conditions, but also enabling fluidity in partners' expectations, as mutual understanding evolves and challenges and benefits surface during the collaborative endeavours. Second, the emphasis is on a co-creation character of the partnership. The value co-creation aspect has emerged as particularly effective to favour partners' commitment, and the development of ownership and mutual trust. In contrast with previous work – which acknowledges the importance of co-creation practices but remains abstract in relation to how these can be achieved (e.g. Kolk et al., 2014) – this case provides concrete and vivid indications on how co-creation could look like in the context of a BOP cross-sector collaboration, not as just one-time workshop encounter but as a continued virtual and face-to-face engagement over time. Given the huge amount of information and interests involved when dealing with collaborative actions around the SDGs, it was important to establish a way of working that was iterative and transformative by nature. The adoption of an ongoing 'value co-creation' process (see Figure 10.3) was considered instrumental in tackling historical barriers preventing cross-sector efforts.

At the start, the 'value co-creation' process helped to change conventional mindsets and overcome prejudices to create long-lasting impact such as: business activities focus only on maximizing profits without sufficiently considering people's most pressing needs and requirements (from the NGO side); humanitarian sector organizations are anchored to philanthropic actions and charity instead of focusing on the empowerment of local communities and their social fabric to drive effective changes (from the business side). Since the beginning of the joint initiative, the organization of regular meetings and working sessions among the stakeholders who came together to share expertise and define a clear shared goal, has helped foster understanding of each other's strengths, weaknesses and ways of working. Most importantly, it has opened a dialogue that has revealed sometimes conflicting interests and allowed for all the parties to debate their various expectations.

Regular workshops and interactions between the various global and local teams have further facilitated listening to multiple voices and the mobilization of resources. This has led to a more inclusive democratic decision-making process which is essential for developing trust – a key factor, since lack of trust is a barrier frequently encountered in cross-sectors partnerships. Balancing long-term ambitions with short-term actions to show progress and intermediate results was an equally important ingredient of this tri-partite collaboration. Moreover, a broader lesson emerged: if the scope of a collaboration is too narrow, interventions will struggle to scale. However, if the scope of a joint effort is too broad, and it is not sufficiently underpinned by concrete solid actions on the ground, interventions will have difficulty in keeping stakeholders motivated and creating impact. Partnerships and multi-stakeholder collaborations are resource-intensive and time-consuming, especially if they include joint-innovation activities. However, by combining capabilities, expertise and multi-disciplinary team efforts, they can amplify impact on the ground and help to pursue better access to quality care for all, moving forward the SDG3 (Health and Well-being), while promoting progress also on SDG5 (Gender inequities), SDG10 (Reduce inequalities) and SDG17 (Partnerships for the Goals).

Some discussion questions are proposed in Box 10.2.

Box 10.2 Discussion questions for the chapter.

1 Discuss how cross-cultural conflicts can influence a partnership. Provide examples from the case.
2 Discuss the role of trust in the multi-stakeholder partnership. Why is building trust potentially difficult in the context of socially-oriented multi-stakeholder partnerships?
3 What practices can be involved in building trust? How was trust built in this case?
4 Discuss the idea of a blended culture within cross-sector collaborations. How can it work? What is your view on some challenges and benefits involved?
5 Understanding an organization's culture is stated to involve analysis of (1) Artefacts, (2) Values and (3) Assumptions. Thinking about various types of research methods, how might you understand an organization's culture? Would you use this method as a practitioner working with or in a multi-stakeholder partnership? If so, what could be gained or why would you opt not to?

Notes

1 www.who.int/health_financing/topics/financial-protection/key-policy-messages/en/#:~:text=About%20100%20million%20people%20are,to%20pay%20for%20health%20care
2 The Centre of Development Innovation (CDI), of Wageningen University & Research Centre. www.managingforimpact.org/event/cdi-seminar-design-and-facilitation-multi-stakeholder-partnerships-msps

References

Airike, P. E., Rotter, J. P., & Mark-Herbert, C. (2016). Corporate motives for multi-stakeholder collaboration- corporate social responsibility in the electronics supply chains. *Journal of Cleaner Production, 131,* 639–648. https://doi.org/10.1016/j.jclepro.2016.04.121

Alford, J., & Head, B. W. (2017). Wicked and less wicked problems: A typology and a contingency framework. *Policy and Society, 36*(3), 397–413. https://doi.org/10.1080/14494035.2017.1361634

Angeli, F., & Jaiswal, A. K. (2016). Business model innovation for inclusive health care delivery at the bottom of the pyramid. *Organization and Environment, 29*(4), 486–507. https://doi.org/10.1177/1086026616647174

Austin, J. E. (2000). Strategic collaboration between nonprofits and businesses. *Nonprofit and Voluntary Sector Quarterly, 29*(suppl.), 69–97. https://doi.org/10.1177/0899764000291s004

Austin, J. E., & Seitanidi, M. M. (2012). Collaborative value creation: A review of partnering between nonprofits and businesses: Part I. Value creation spectrum and collaboration stage. *Nonprofit and Voluntary Sector Quarterly, 41*(5), 726–758. https://doi.org/10.1177/0899764012450777

Bäckstrand, K. (2006). Multi-stakeholder partnerships for sustainable development: Rethinking legitimacy, accountability and effectiveness. *European Environment, 16*(5), 290–306. https://doi.org/10.1002/eet.425

Ber, M. L. (2010). *Cross-sector models of collaboration for social innovation*. Electronic Thesis and Dissertation Repository. https://ir.lib.uwo.ca/etd/10

Brouwer, J. H., Woodhill, A. J., Hemmati, M., Verhoosel, K. S., & van Vugt, S. M. (2016). *The MSP guide*. Practical Action Publishing Ltd.

Bryson, J. M., Crosby, B. C., & Stone, M. M. (2006). *The design and implementation of cross-sector collaborations: Propositions from the literature* (Vol. 66, pp. 44–55). John Wiley & Sons, Ltd.

Dahan, N. M., Doh, J. P., Oetzel, J., & Yaziji, M. (2010). Corporate-NGO collaboration: Co-creating new business models for developing markets. *Long Range Planning, 43*(2–3), 326–342. https://doi.org/10.1016/J.LRP.2009.11.003

Das, M., Angeli, F., Krumeich, A. J. S. M., & Van Schayck, O. C. P. (2018). The gendered experience with respect to health-seeking behaviour in an urban slum of Kolkata, India. *International Journal for Equity in Health, 17*(1), 24. https://doi.org/10.1186/s12939-018-0738-8

Das, T. K., & Teng, B. S. (1998). Between trust and control: Developing confidence in partner cooperation in alliances. *The Academy of Management Review, 23*(3), 491–491. https://doi.org/10.2307/259291

Dentoni, D., Bitzer, V., & Schouten, G. (2018). Harnessing wicked problems in multi-stakeholder partnerships. *Journal of Business Ethics, 150*(2), 333–356. https://doi.org/10.1007/s10551-018-3858-6

Dey, A., Hay, K., Afroz, B., Chandurkar, D., Singh, K., Dehingia, N., Raj, A., & Silverman, J. G. (2018). Understanding intersections of social determinants of maternal healthcare utilization in Uttar Pradesh, India. *PLoS One, 13*(10). https://doi.org/10.1371/journal.pone.0204810

Du Mortier, S. (2017). *Former head of the primary health care services – ICRC*. Video interview on antenatal care challenge in fragile environment on the joint-innovation process with the Philips Foundation and Philips.

Foley, R. W., Wiek, A., Kay, B., & Rushforth, R. (2017). Ideal and reality of multi-stakeholder collaboration on sustainability problems: A case study on a large-scale industrial contamination in Phoenix, Arizona. *Sustainability Science, 12*(1), 123–136. https://doi.org/10.1007/s11625-016-0393-1

Head, B. W., & Alford, J. (2015). Wicked problems: Implications for public policy and management. *Administration & Society, 47*(6), 711–739. https://doi.org/10.1177/0095399713481601

ICRC. (2020). *Mandate and mission*. ICRC.

Kolk, A., Rivera-Santos, M., & Rufin, C. (2014). Reviewing a decade of research on the "base/bottom of the pyramid" (BOP) concept. *Business & Society, 53*(3), 338–377. https://doi.org/10.1177/0007650312474928

Kopp, S. (2017). *Former supra regional midwife – ICRC*. Video interview on antenatal care challenge and on joint-innovations process with the Philips Foundation and Philips.

Krawchuk, F. (2013). *Multi-stakeholder collaboration: How government, business, and non-governmental leaders transform complex challenges into new possibilities*. http://oefresearch.org/sites/default/files/documents/publications/msc-digital-final-r.pdf

Macdonald, A. (2016). *Multi-stakeholder partnerships for community sustainability plan implementation: Understanding structures and outcomes at the partner and partnership levels*. https://uwspace.uwaterloo.ca/handle/10012/10362

Meirovich, G. (2012). *Cultural similarities and differences: Impacts on performance in strategic partnerships*. Emerald Group Publishing Limited.

Nason, R. S., Bacq, S., & Gras, D. (2018). A behavioral theory of social performance: Social identity and stakeholder expectations. *Academy of Management Review, 43*(2), 259–283. https://doi.org/10.5465/amr.2015.0081

Parker, B., & Selsky, J. W. (2004). Interface dynamics in cause-based partnerships: An exploration of emergent culture. *Nonprofit and Voluntary Sector Quarterly, 33*(3), 458–488. https://doi.org/10.1177/0899764004266016

Value Co-Creation Through Multi-Stakeholder Collaborations   235

Pennink, C. (2017). *The trust cycle: The process of trust building, and the influence of trust on risk and outcomes in public-private partnerships*. Erasmus University.

Philips. (2020a). *About the company*. www.philips.com/a-w/about/company

Philips. (2020b). *Access to care*. www.philips.com/a-w/about/sustainability/access-to-care.html

Philips Foundation. (2014). *About us*. www.philips-foundation.com/a-w/about-us.html

Philips Foundation. (2020). *Mission*. www.philips-foundation.com/a-w/our-mission.html

Reid, S. (2016). *The partnership culture navigator – the partnering initiative*. Retrieved November 24, 2020, from https://thepartneringinitiative.org/publications/toolbook-series/the-partnership-culture-navigator/

Reypens, C., Lievens, A., & Blazevic, V. (2016). Leveraging value in multi-stakeholder innovation networks: A process framework for value co-creation and capture. *Industrial Marketing Management*. https://doi.org/10.1016/j.indmarman.2016.03.005

Sambasivan, M., & Yen, C. N. (2010). Strategic alliances in a manufacturing supply chain: Influence of organizational culture from the manufacturer's perspective. *International Journal of Physical Distribution and Logistics Management*, 40(6), 456–474. https://doi.org/10.1108/09600031011062191

Schein, E. H. (2010). *Organizational culture and leadership* (Vol. 2). John Wiley & Sons.

Sloan, P., & Oliver, D. (2013). Building trust in multi-stakeholder partnerships: Critical emotional incidents and practices of engagement. *Organization Studies*, 34(12), 1835–1868. https://doi.org/10.1177/0170840613495018

Stöteler, I., Reeder, S., & van Tulder, R. (2012). *Cross-sector partnership formation: What to consider before you start? – The intersector project*. Retrieved November 24, 2020, from http://intersector.com/resource/cross-sector-partnership-formation-what-to-consider-before-you-start/

Stott, L. (2017). *Partnership and social progress: Multi-stakeholder collaboration in context*. https://era.ed.ac.uk/handle/1842/22948

UN. (2019). *SDGs: Sustainable development knowledge platform*. Retrieved November 24, 2020, from https://sustainabledevelopment.un.org/topics/sustainabledevelopmentgoals

UNCTAD. (2014). *World investment report 2014 – investing in the SDGs: An action plan*. https://unctad.org/en/PublicationsLibrary/wir2014_en.pdf

Venn, R., & Berg, N. (2014). The gatekeeping function of trust in cross-sector social partnerships. *Business and Society Review*, 119(3), 385–416. https://doi.org/10.1111/basr.12038

WHO. (2014). *Maternal mortality progress towards achieving the fifth millennium development goal*. www.who.int/topics/millennium_development_goals/maternal_health/en/

WHO. (2019). *Maternal mortality*. Retrieved November 19, 2020, from www.who.int/newsroom/fact-sheets/detail/maternal-mortality

World Health Organization & World Bank. (2017). *Tracking universal health coverage: 2017 global monitoring report*. www.who.int/healthinfo/universal_health_coverage/report/2017/en/; https://apps.who.int/iris/bitstream/handle/10665/259817/9789241513555-eng.pdf

11 Medical Device Innovation at the Base of the Pyramid

General Electrics' India Strategy to Make Healthcare Affordable[1]

Anand Kumar Jaiswal and Federica Angeli

Introduction

The healthcare need in India is sizeable and growing, with a large segment of the population significantly underserved. Private sector actors, such as General Electric, can play an important role in bridging the gap between growing healthcare needs and stalling government investments. With a large and growing population, and an increased incidence of non-communicable diseases (NCDs), governments are increasingly unable to meet the needs of their population. General Electric has delivered significant innovation in this context, addressing the resource-constrained base of the pyramid (BOP) market. In this chapter, we review the challenges in the Indian healthcare sector – outlining the need for the development of – and access to – affordable medical devices (AMD), in line with addressing SDG 3 and SDG 1. We highlight the innovations required within the organization – developing new ways of operating in order to develop an innovative and affordable AMD. We then turn to the processes of ensuring ease of use and developing an effective distribution strategy. Finally, we discuss GE' approach as an exemplar of effective BOP strategy from a theoretical perspective. Figure 11.1 highlights the SDG addressed in this chapter.

India has the second-largest population in the world, after China. With 1.37 billion inhabitants in 2019, India is expected to become the most populous country globally by 2027 (United Nations, 2019). India's median age of the population is significantly lower than the other BRICS countries (Brazil, Russia, China and South Africa), as most people in the country are in the 15 to 64 years age group, with only about 5% of its population older than 64 years in 2019 (Statista, 2019). However, due to the increasing urbanization and changing lifestyles, India faces a dual burden of contagious and non-contagious diseases, making the pursuit of SDG 3 – Good Health and Well-being, particularly challenging. There is a serious concern among practitioners, experts and policymakers that contagious illnesses such as Malaria, Dengue, AIDS and more recently, COVID-19, will continue to create a major burden for country's healthcare system. At the same time, due to the growing incidence of lifestyle diseases related to high blood pressure, obesity, poor diet, tobacco and alcohol consumption, the demand for specialized health care services to treat non-communicable diseases (NCDs) is accelerating beyond India's traditional health problems. NCDs are currently responsible for around 60% of deaths in the country (NATHEALTH, 2018). The country is facing the pressure of a double burden of malnutrition, with both underweight and overweight segments of the population, in combination with its epidemiological transition from communicable to non-communicable diseases (Sengupta

DOI: 10.4324/9780429243165-12

This chapter has been made available under a CC-BY-NC 4.0 license.

Medical Device Innovation at the Base of the Pyramid   237

Figure 11.1 SDGs addressed in this chapter.

et al., 2015). Epidemiological changes, combined with evolution in consumption patterns, changes in lifestyle, increasing spending and awareness among the consumers, have created a high and complex demand for inclusive, accessible, and affordable health care infrastructure and delivery. With the COVID-19 pandemic unleashing catastrophic consequences, the healthcare sector has become a key priority of the government (KPMG, 2020).

In India, about 3.5% of GDP is spent on healthcare and government's share is only 1% (Table 11.1). It roughly means that the government contribution is about 30% of total healthcare expenditure. Furthermore, only a small part of population is covered under health insurance and out of pocket expenditure on healthcare as high as 62.4% of the total healthcare expenditures (Table 11.2), against a global average of 18.12 (World Bank, 2021c). Looking at per capita figures, the per capita expenditure on healthcare in India in 2018 appears as very low, amounting to 275 USD at purchasing power parity, in comparison to a global average of 1467 USD PPP (World Bank, 2021b). Out of this amount, 199 USD PPP are financed through domestic private expenditure, either as prepaid amount to a voluntary health insurance schemes or as directly out-of-pocket expenses (World Bank, 2021c). Expenditure on medical device in 2015 amounted at only 3 USD per capita (Table 11.3). There is a significant disparity in the healthcare infrastructure across urban and rural areas, with heavy concentration of doctors and hospitals in urban areas, even though over 70% population lives in the rural areas (Table 11.4). At the same time, in 2011 India reported a 22.5% population living below the poverty line (World Bank, 2021d) – hence at least 307 million population who cannot afford private healthcare diagnostics and treatment and hence avoid seeking healthcare or delay it to the point of incurring catastrophic expenditures. This data clearly shows that a significant segment of the India population is in dire need for affordable, innovative solutions for healthcare diagnostics and treatment.

238 Anand Kumar Jaiswal and Federica Angeli

Table 11.1 Total Healthcare Expenditure as a % of GDP in 2018

Countries	Healthcare Expenditure as a % of GDP
India	3.54
Brazil	9.51
China	5.35
Germany	11.43
Japan	10.95
USA	16.89

Source: World Bank (World Bank, 2021a), Current health expenditure (% of GDP)

Table 11.2 Comparison of Healthcare Indicators in India and Other Countries

Countries	Beds Per 10000 Populations	Physicians Per 10000 Populations	Govt. Expenditure of Total Health Care Expenditure	Out of Pocket Expenditure
Global Average	27	14	58.80%	18.12%
India	7	7	30.00%	62.67%
Brazil	23	19	46.00%	27.54%
China	38	15	55.80%	35.75%
Germany	82	38	77.00%	12.65%
Japan	137	23	83.60%	12.75%
USA	29	25	48.30%	10.81%

Source: SKP (2017) Medical Device industry in India and World Bank (World Bank, 2020b)

Table 11.3 Per Capita Healthcare Expenditure, Medical Devices Expenditure and Income Comparison

Countries	Medical Devices Expenditure (2015)	Income – 2016/2017	Income 2020
Global average	47		
India	3	1862	3500
Brazil	28	10826	11730
China	178	6895	8330
Germany	313	45552	47200
Japan	221	47608	46200
USA	415	52195	54800

Source: SKP (2017). Medical Device industry in India. Figures are in USD per capita

Against this backdrop, the private sector can have a very important role in bridging the gap between growing healthcare needs and stalling government investments. This chapter illustrates the prominent case of General Electric (GE) and its decision to enter the Indian medical device market. In 2009, General Electric (GE) developed a new innovation strategy known as Healthymagination as part of which it committed to spend USD 6 billion in the next six years to develop affordable healthcare solutions. GE announced that that it would invest about USD 3 billion on research and development to bring out 100 Healthcare innovations for people living in different

Table 11.4 Rural-Urban Divide in Healthcare

Indicator	Rural Population	Urban Population
Hospital %	31	69
Hospital bed %	20	80
Doctors %	08	92
Doctors/100,000 people	05	50
Doctors Composition	Specialists (5–10%) General Practitioners (GPs) (MBBS) and RMPs (90–95%)	Specialists (50%) General Practitioners (GPs) (MBBS) and Consulting Physicians CPs (50%)

Source: CII-PwC Report, "India Pharma Inc.: Capitalising on India's Growth Potential," Pharma Summit 2010, November 27, 2010; Manoj Garg and Perin Ali, "India Pharma Sector – Delving Deeper," Edelweiss Securities Limited, April 26, 2011. Retrieved December 3, 2014, from www.scribd.com/doc/54137140/Pharma-Sector-Edel

parts of the world. Through these innovations, GE aimed to significantly reduce the cost of healthcare, improve quality and make healthcare universally accessible. The company planned to spend USD 2 billion on financing and USD 1 billion on technology and other areas. Among many products that GE developed and commercialized within its India strategy, this chapter particularly focuses on MAC 400, an electrocardiogram (ECG) machine. The MAC 400 is an innovative medical device which was unique owing to its small size and ultra-low cost, as it was offered at USD 1,000 and developed for rural markets in India. For its flexible design and low-price, the device is often showcased best exemplifying GE's success and unique Indian strategy. Though the device was originally developed for low-income countries, it is now selling also in the United States where it has brought an entirely new customer segment to the market. Importantly however, MAC 400 was only part of a much larger strategy implemented by GE to enter Indian healthcare, with a twofold aim to discover profitable opportunities whilst addressing the compelling healthcare affordability issue. MAC 400 was in fact only 1 of the 25 super value products developed by GE in India. LOGIQ A3 ultra sound device, Tejas XR 2000 X-Ray machine, Lullaby Phototherapy system and Discovery IQ PET CT scanners were some of the other super value products developed by the local team of the GE. This chapter illustrates GE's strategy in India and describes the multinational corporation's approach to business model innovation. We first outline the characteristics of Indian healthcare sector, we then consider GE's strategy to make healthcare affordable in India, by illustrating the case of MAC 400 – a breakthrough, innovative, portable ECG machine designed for rural areas. We subsequently offer a theoretical analysis of GE's strategy, and conclude with a theoretical framework of strategy evolution and its antecedents.

The Indian Healthcare Sector and Cardiovascular Device Market: An Overview

In the context of changing healthcare demand scenario in the country, India's health care sector has achieved a significant growth and is now one of the largest contributors to India's GDP and employment (IBEF, 2018). The industry was worth US$140 billion in 2016, with a projection to reach $372 billion in 2022 with a compounded annual growth rate (CAGR) of 16.28 % (the base year 2008) (Statista, 2021b). Based on nature and function, the healthcare industry is classified into four major categories – hospitals (specialized care provider), pharmaceuticals, medical equipment and diagnostics with the relative share of 77%, 14%, 6% and 3%, respectively in the year 2016 (Statista, 2021a).

As per World Health Organization (WHO), cardiovascular diseases (CVDs), also known as heart or heart-related diseases, cause a very large number of deaths worldwide and resulting in loss of about 17.9 million lives in each year. Globally, 30% of deaths are due to CVDs, and the cost of CVDs was estimated to be US$ 863 billion in 2010 and is expected to increase by 22% to $1044 billion by 2030 (Fior Markets, 2020). Out of all the death due to CVDs, 80% occur in the low- and middle-income countries. India shares the load by 14% of deaths due to CVDs, which also shows the high market potential for the CVDs devices in country (Prakash, 2020). The CVDs are the also leading cause of mortality among the NCDs in India. In India, the CVDs account for 26% of the death cases due to NCDs which constitute 60% of the total death cases (World Heart Federation, 2011).

The prevalence of CVDs in India was about 54.5 million in 2016. Moreover, one among the four deaths in India due to CVDs, with ischemic heart disease and heart stroke accounting for more than 80% of the burden of CVDs (Abdul-Aziz et al., 2019). In this context, with the accelerating growth of the elderly population and changing lifestyles, India is becoming an attractive market for pharmaceutical and medical devices for CVDs. Globally, the CVDs device market size stood at $49.90 billion in 2018 and is estimated to reach $82.20 billion by 2026 with a CAGR of 6.4% (Fortune Business Insights, 2020), whereas the Indian CVDs device market contributes to 1.7% of the world market with a year-on-year growth rate of 15% (Amritt, 2020).

The Indian cardiovascular device market is at the nascent stage with suboptimal penetration. Further, the Indian CVDs market is dominated by imported devices. Other factors that boost the growth of the CVDs device market, such as increasing R&D, growing cardiac health centres, at both public and private levels, and growing participation of domestic players which are competing with MNCs (Invest India, 2021; Research and Markets, 2018).

GE's Strategy to Make Healthcare Affordable

GE had the twin objectives behind this strategy to reduce cost of healthcare in the LMICs. The first objective was to penetrate the markets in the countries such as India where more than three-fourths of the population is characterized as bottom of the pyramid (BOP) population. In these markets GE's presence was confined to the premium segment of the market. The second objective was to pre-empt the competition from domestic companies in the markets who could eventually develop affordable healthcare products, given the market gaps and could start giving tough competition to GE in the high-income markets in the long term. GE realized that, in order to succeed in the next decade, it needs to develop low-cost quality products and then eventually sell them in high-income markets. A strong presence in the emerging markets was as seen a prerequisite to ensure success in the developed world (Immelt et al., 2009). However, GE also realized that to bring affordable healthcare devices to low-income markets, major changes in its current strategy for India, China and other LMICs were necessary.

Medical Device Innovation at the Base of the Pyramid   241

Need for Affordable Medical Devices

GE executives in India realize that medical device users and diagnostic centre are typically concerned not only about the total spending on the medical device but also about fixed costs such as electricity, rental, expenses on technical support staff. This is because they knew that eventually they could charge only a limited amount for each ECG or x-ray, as customers have affordability constraints and price competition is fierce.

In India, the financial rationale dominates decision making, especially in healthcare contexts. For example, decisions by consumers as well as medical equipment and device buyers are driven greatly by strong economic considerations. This is because consumers pay for healthcare out-of-pocket in most cases. Only a small part of the population is covered by health insurance. Hence, price sensitivity is a very important factor affecting purchasing decisions. In most high-income countries consumers do not directly pay for the medical treatment as they are covered by medical insurance schemes (insurance-based or Bismarckian systems, such as Germany or the Netherlands) or subsidized by the government (tax-based or Beveridge systems, such as Italy and the United Kingdom). Hospitals then charge the amount to insurance companies or to the government. Hence, people only indirectly bear the cost. India's position is quite unique in the sense that it has very low government contribution and second, it has very high underserved population. Given that the cost of healthcare is out of pocket expense, and hence the high degree of transparent pricing mechanism, there is need for cost-competitive products that can cater to the unmet needs of large segments of the population.

In India for India strategy

Like most multinational corporations (MNCs), GE initially followed a globalization-based approach towards emerging markets like India, hence it attempted to sell products designed and manufactured in the developed world to LMICs. This strategy was adopted with the aim of exploiting scale advantage and cost efficiency benefits. Subsequently, in order to better meet local needs in LMICs, GE and other MNCs started following a glocalization-based strategy. As part of this strategy, GE attempted to better respond to the needs of consumers in LMICs. Though, new product development, and research and development (R&D) activities were still held in the high-income countries, part of its manufacturing activities shifted to LMICs. This was also done to gain advantage of lower cost manufacturing in these countries. However, this approach has not helped GE much in understanding and responding to customers' needs in India and developing appropriate products and technology which can address local needs (Immelt et al., 2009; Knowledge@Wharton, 2012). V. Raja, former president and CEO of GE Healthcare-South Asia, notes,

> We realized that the biggest impediment was that we were selling what we were making [rather than] making what the customers here needed. It was clear that if we had to grow here we had to shift gears and align our products to the needs of the customers.

> (Knowledge@Wharton, 2010)

242 *Anand Kumar Jaiswal and Federica Angeli*

Therefore, in 2009 it decided to follow 'In India for India' strategy to stimulate local innovation. In this approach, the product development and all the R&D activities were shifted to India to better respond to local markets. The thinking behind this approach was that one cannot design cars in Detroit that need to be successful in India. GE felt that one cannot innovate for consumers of India, a major part of whom are the BOP population, when the entire business is centred around the top of the pyramid or the premium consumers. Ashish Shah, former General Manager, GE Healthcare's global technology, stated:

> *So far, innovations were geared toward the United States and Europe and artificially pushed into the Indian market. Today, we innovate for India in India, thinking in rupees and paise rather than dollars and cents.*
>
> (Chandran, 2010)

Selecting High Impact Areas

While deciding on which areas to focus on in the healthcare domain and the kind of innovation to develop, GE's leadership team decided to select Areas where it can create the largest impact. It decided to focus on areas such as infant care, maternal care, cancer, cardiac diseases and oncology. These diseases account for most mortality in India and most other places globally. For example, infant care was selected as the infant mortality rate is high in the country. In India, infant mortality rate (per 1,000 live births) was 28 in 2019 whereas in the US and China, it is 6 and 7, respectively (World Bank, 2020a). Similarly, the penetration of PET/CT scanner is exceptionally low in India in comparison to other countries. India had only 60 PET/CT scanner against 133 in China in 2012 (Rezende dos Reis et al., 2016). In most cases, cancers are detected only in advanced stages when it is not possible to treat them. Therefore, GE team decided to develop Discovery IQ, a low-cost PET CT scanner that can contribute to early detection of cancer and its management.

Developing a New Organizational Structure

GE in India has been following a traditional organizational structure and profit and loss (P&L) model like most MNCs. As part of this, all the functional teams including units responsible for product development and innovation were reporting loosely (or on a dotted line basis) to the country head but firmly (or on a bold line basis) to the functional heads globally. Country heads of most MNCs in LMICs are typically made responsible primarily for generating additional revenue for the organization. They are not often expected or held accountable for new product development or for bringing out innovations. Even if local subsidiaries like to develop new products and solutions for local markets, for that, they need to take approval from the global functional head or people at headquarter of MNC. This invariably is a very time-consuming and inefficient process. GE's Indian subsidiary contributed only about 2% of revenue GE's Healthcare revenue of US$17 billion in 2010. Often 'share of revenue' translates into 'share of mind' for the global functional heads in MNCs. Understanding unique needs of local consumers and Indian environment were far from a priority for them. Accordingly, the time and resource commitment by the headquarters for product development in LMICs is far lower.

Medical Device Innovation at the Base of the Pyramid 243

In 2010, GE completely flipped this organization structure for Indian operations. Local businesses were given complete authority and decision-making powers and also accountability for all strategic decisions such as where to invest at, how to grow the business and shape its strategy. For product development, it means all the decision making now lies with the local businesses without the need for regular approvals from the global headquarter. Guillermo Wille, Former Managing Director, John F Welch Technology Centre (JFWTC), noted

> We will treat India the same way as we treat any other business in the company. This is a big difference for us. Previously, countries were never treated like a business, a P&L.

(Forbes, 2009)

The thinking was that local management of various businesses of GE would decide what products they want and the local technology team would design and manufacture these products (Forbes, 2009).This approach gave a new impetus to the new product development at GE owing to three reasons. First Indian markets are extremely price-sensitive and this is equally true even for healthcare and medical device products. Second, Indian market is highly diverse, and the market landscape changes greatly when one moves from metropolitan cities to small towns to rural areas. Third, the market environment in India is very different from those of high-income countries, on factors such as lower government spending on healthcare and a large population of underserved and unserved segments.

Leveraging Parent's Technological Resources

The 'In India for India' strategy and new organizational structure led to all the decision making of product development being shifted locally. However, the local product development was greatly supported by the design team's access to worldwide technology and knowhow of GE. Local team could technically take anything they needed from the global portfolio of technology and knowledge of GE. The team had access to GE portfolio but they were also completely free not to take anything in case they felt there was no need for it. In some aspects, teams were unlearning traditional ways of innovation, whilst balancing learning from what is already known, developed and available. For example, in the case of the baby warmer which GE developed in India and is selling in market, the core of the product is the technology used in the heating element. Local team responsible for this product development decided to use the same basic material and technology in the low-cost $800 warmer for local markets which were used in its premium product offered at the $30,000.

Clean Slate Approach

The GE team knew that markets in LMICs are highly price sensitive. Serving these competitive settings successfully requires reducing the price point of significant levels, to make products affordable to consumers. The assumption was that if there is a clear and recognized market need – like cardiac or cancer diseases, a major health challenges in India and elsewhere – and an appropriate formula, products would be able to penetrate the market. People do need quality healthcare and unfortunately that is not

244 *Anand Kumar Jaiswal and Federica Angeli*

available to large segments of the population; therefore, medical devices such as ECG or X-ray machines would sell automatically once cost is reduced. Therefore, the challenge before the product development team was to reduce cost without compromising the clinical performance of the medical devices.

While developing affordable medical devices, the GE team initially adopted de-featuring as the main approach to reduce the cost. Under this strategy, the assumption was that there is a linear negative relationship between product performance – in terms of number and accuracy of the tasks the product can perform through its technological features – and price of the product. Hence, if we represent product performance on a vertical axis and price on a horizontal axis then we will get a straight line. At the lowest end of the line there are no features at zero price and at the top maximum possible features – delivering highest product performance – are offered at full or premium price. So as part of product development one needs to decide the price one wants to achieve and then remove the features of the product gradually to achieve the desired price level. For de-featuring purposes, the team looked at all the existing product features and parts in the device and screened for features which are not needed or machine parts which can be replaced with lower cost alternatives. For example, certain features like automatic operations of a device can be replaced with manual operations. Motorized controls can be substituted by crank motor shaft for adjusting tilt and height of device. Metal parts can be replaced with plastic ones. A bigger sized screen can be replaced with a smaller screen or an LED screen can be replaced by LCD screen. Instead of providing bigger wheels devices, one can have small size wheels and so on and so forth.

The team achieved significant cost reduction with this approach to the extent of 50–60%. However, despite this price reduction many of its super value products were still not selling well in the market. The team realized that this failure could be explained by two reasons. The first was that, despite 50–60% price reduction, these products were still not affordable or beyond the reach of consumers in most cases. Given the very low-income levels of targets patients, doctors and clinics could charge only a small amount. Therefore, they needed to develop products which are exceptionally cost competitive. To achieve dramatic cost reduction, the team realized that it needed to follow a 'clean slate' (*tabula rasa*) approach, as part of which product design and development process should start from zero. The team decided to go back and start from an in-depth understanding of what the actual customer needs are, while unlearning or forgetting completely about the products currently available in market. The problem needs to be defined in terms of what customers actually need, not based on what currently is made available to them or on what innovators and producers *assume* they might need. The GE India team realized that designing the products from scratch and using a lateral and completely innovative approach was an absolute necessity. This would only ensure that entirely new design and radically new product architecture are developed. They had complete freedom to question all the existing approaches and develop purely new mechanisms, processes and product designs.

GE executives also realized that the second reason for why the initial products developed using a defeaturing-based approach did not achieve the desired success was that they failed to create an impact in the market. In order to create an impact, they need to work on not only price reduction but several other factors. Multiple other factors make a product acceptable to consumers. The product works in a unique environment, of which various factors need to be taken into account while designing the

Medical Device Innovation at the Base of the Pyramid 245

product. The fit of the product to its physical and socio-cultural environment of use is crucial when serving BOP consumers. If a product fails to succeed in the market, as a design engineer, one cannot have the excuse later that it was used in a different environment.

In a rural environment, there are no specialist doctors and trained technicians. Instead, rural areas have medical staff or technicians with a much lower level of skills. Hence, ease of use of medical devices becomes a very important consideration. In this environment, users are often intimidated by seeing a complex medical device, as they struggle to understand how to effectively use it and maintain it.

The product reliability and service requirement is second factor to consider while designing the products. In these markets, at times the people who are procuring these devices are different from those who are using it. Like in public health centres, these devices might have been purchased through government tenders or in some cases donated by others. If these devices break down there is nobody available to repair them, with the result that a large number of dis-functional or non-operating devices might end up lying in the health centres. These may sometimes be even used as a bookcase or table or for purposes other than medical diagnosis and treatment. These devices are used in tier 2 and tier 3 towns which are not well served as service engineers do not easily visit these places. These places are also not well connected for service engineers to travel and provide support services. Hence, reliability needs to be built in the product. For example, voltage fluctuation is a major issue in rural areas. Commonly used devices are designed to work well in the voltage range of 210–250. However, the voltage fluctuation in these environments can be extremely high. Doctors need a device which can work with the voltage of as low as 80 or as high as 400. Machines with this range of tolerance are not normally designed or developed for users in large cities in LMICs and users in high-income countries. Further, in rural environments there is no electricity, or a regular supply of electricity is not available. Hence, the product design team realized that it needs to develop devices with battery backup, without which the machine cannot be operating most of the time during the day. V Raja, Former President and CEO GE Healthcare, noted,

> And for us, the products developed for sophisticated markets didn't work well in situations like erratic power supply, space constraints, heat and dust.
>
> (Mahanta, 2011)

The other dimension is about product packaging. The rural and semi-urban areas are often not well connected with good roads and lack basic infrastructure. It was observed that often, by the time these devices reach the endpoints which are health centres, they become dysfunctional due to lack of proper packaging which could withstand the poor conditions of the roads, poor connectivity and other infrastructural bottlenecks.

For rural environments one needs to develop products which require no consumables to the extent possible. If these devices are donated to health centres, often they have no provision plans to procure the consumables. Even for government-procured devices, purchasing consumables may not be an easy task as consumables may not be easily available in the local market. The team noticed that often devices have become non-operational due to lack of consumables. So, the challenge was to develop

246 *Anand Kumar Jaiswal and Federica Angeli*

products which do not need consumers so that they can continue operating without interruption.

The design team also realized that they needed to go beyond the traditional product development concept which looks at a new device development process from lab to manufacturing facility and then to their warehouse. In these environments they need to think from end to end. GE did not have any distribution network to serve these markets, so the challenge before them was to understand how exactly they can sell the product to a new set of users or how exactly they can manage the supply chain and distribution. They needed to decide how exactly they can provide after sales support. It was imperative for them to look at what all problems users would eventually encounter while using the product. These issues are not normally part of traditional product development approaches but become very silent and critical in the BOP market. It requires business process innovation; an entirely new distribution approach, a new service strategy, a new go-to-market strategy. The GE team did not have the option to limit themselves to only product design and product development; instead, it faced new challenges in sales, distribution and service support areas. They needed to re-envision their role and to provide an end-to-end solution in the market.

MAC 400: The Development of a Low-Cost Portable ECG

Given the very high death counts due to cardiac diseases in India, their diagnosis and treatment require screening patients using devices such as ECG machines. GE had premium ECG machines such as Mac 5000 and Mac 5500 which were offered to high-end hospitals in large cities (Figures 11.1–11.5). For instance, the price of Mac 5000 was about INR 200,000 while other high-end ECG machines were sold as high as INR 500,000 or more (Mahanta, 2011). These machines were simply unaffordable to general practitioners and small clinics in small towns and rural areas. Further, these machines were of significantly large size and have a complicated design. They required a cardiologist and a trained technician to use and interpret the output. As such, these machines were not suitable for the rural environment where it is hard to find specialist doctors or cardiologists. In these areas, general physicians are mostly responsible for early detection and treatment of cardiac diseases.

Project Beginnings

In 2007, the GE team commissioned a market research to investigate how much an average potential patient in India is willing to pay for an ECG. They also did research to find out the price which an average doctor or clinics providing ECG service to patients is willing to pay for a new device. The team found that a consumer could afford to pay $1 for ECG while service providers were willing to pay $700 for ECG device. The prevailing average price of the ECG machine in the Indian market was $2,000 (Forbes, 2009).

GE started the project to design a USD 1,000 US (40,000 INR) MAC 400 ECG machine in its John H Welch Technology Center (JHWTC) in Bangalore. This was the one-third the price of an imported equivalent ECG machine (Chandran, 2010). The aim was also to make this a small size, portable machine which can fit in in a backpack and therefore the physician can easily carry it with them to the rural settlements.

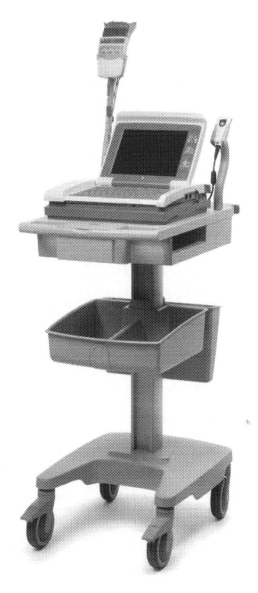

Figure 11.2 The MAC 5500 ECG.
Source: www.gehealthcare.in/products/diagnostic-ecg/mac-5500-hd

Mr Oswin Varghese was made the project head and there were 10 members in his team, most of whom were fresh graduates. This project was a somewhat unusual challenge for the design team, as so far GE teams in JHWTC worked on projects to develop premium-priced and higher-margin products. For them, cost was generally never a major issue while designing new products. These projects often experience cost overrun and this was eventually passed on to customers in the form of increase in the price. For the first time they were working on product development where

248 *Anand Kumar Jaiswal and Federica Angeli*

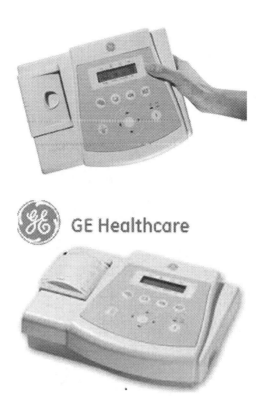

Figure 11.3 MAC 400 and MACi.

Source: www.medgadget.com/2008/06/mac_400_portable_ecg.html and www.indiamart.com/thebrightassociates/ge-mac-i-ecg-paper.html

the end price was already set, and was substantially lower in comparison to existing products. The project was full of challenges for the team, and from the beginning the team felt that somehow, they would eventually be successful in developing the product (Mahanta, 2011).

Ensuring High Quality and Clinical Efficacy

Even though it was important to reduce cost significantly to make ECGs affordable, the process of creating MAC 400 has been complex. Like other medical equipment, the product needed some form of corrective maintenance during its lifetime. However, the design teams aimed for the product to be operating all the time because they are used for medical treatment and saving lives or related decision-making processes. Further, in India these devices are used heavily or for longer hours given their low penetration in the market. The GE team encountered several of these constraints and carefully planned to deal with them in an environment where affordability requirements are very high.

GE design team faced twin challenges of reducing cost to $1,000 level and at the same time providing machine with very high quality and safety standards in line with

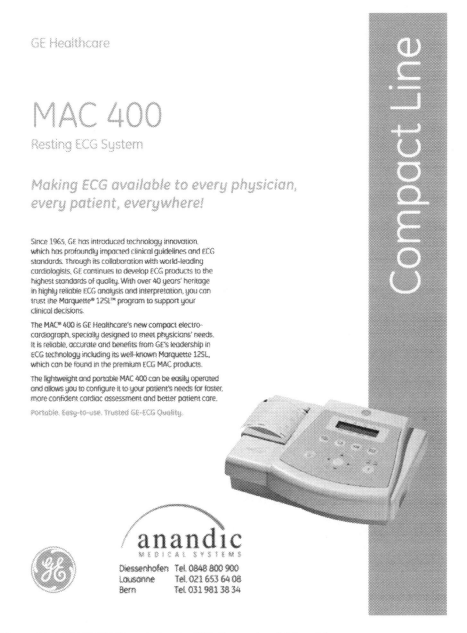

Figure 11.4 MAC 400 Description in GE's Promotional Material.
Source: www.anandic.com/bausteine.net/f/9631/

the strategy of GE to provide best quality products to its customer. Since the onset, the team decided to use Marquette, a patented sophisticated algorithm used in the existing premium ECG machines of GE. This was done to provide a high clinical performance to the users (Mahanta, 2011).

Portable. Easy-to-use.

- **One Touch Operation**
  for acquisition, analysis and printing, minimizes training needs.
- **Alphanumeric Display**
  for easy visualization of ECG setup information.
- **Ultra Portable**
  ECG device (with battery) of 1,300 Gms, for easy transport.
- **Long-lasting Battery**
  using Li-Ion platform, lasts for 100 ECGs in auto mode and recharges in less than 3 hours.
- **Reliable Printer Design**
  to last for many years of trouble-free operation.

- **Wide Paper Size**
  of 80 mm for clear visualization of ECG waveforms and reports.
- **Multiple ECG Modes**
  (Auto, Manual & Arrhythmia) to allow you to adapt to your specific patient needs.
- **Reliable Decision Support Software Package Options**
  such as Marquette 12SL Measurement & Marquette 12SL Interpretation are available to meet specific customer needs.

MAC 400 Supplies & Accessories
GE Healthcare offers a wide range of tested and approved quality accessories and consumables that are specifically designed to maintain the performance of the MAC 400.

Examples of ECG reports with Marquette 12SL analysis and interpretation program.
The interpretation program is optional.

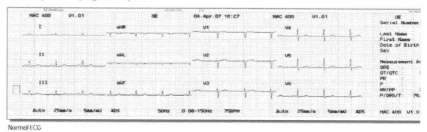

Normal ECG

Acute Inferior Wall Myocardial Infarction

Figure 11.5 MAC 400 Description in GE's promotional material.
Source: www.anandic.com/bausteine.net/f/9631/

Using off-the-Shelf Products

As per the standard "GE's way" of developing products, Verghese and his team initially planned to use internally designed and available components and parts of the machine available in-house. However, they soon realized that with this approach they would never be able to reduce the cost of ECG machine to a desired level. Furthermore, some of the product's parts currently used were not actually designed for typical

Medical Device Innovation at the Base of the Pyramid 251

rural environment. For instance, the printer used in high-end ECG machines requires a control environment consisting of air conditioning and dust-free setting. This was simply not possible in rural areas where MAC 400 was expected to be used. Additionally, printer cost was a major component of cost of ECG machines. Design team contemplated to design new components internally. However, this would result in the project needing a lot more time than originally planned as well as incurring extra cost associated with developing each component internally afresh.

After evaluating many different alternatives eventually, the design team decided to use the printer used for printing tickets on buses. These printers were robust in design as they were designed to work well in a dusty environment, even at high temperatures. The GE team also realized the need for making these machines battery-operated, to counteract the irregular supply of electricity – a major problem in rural areas. To provide battery backup, team decided to use batteries similar to the ones used in smartphones. In fact, the battery technology in smart phones is matured and affordable and therefore can easily be used in ECG machines with some modification in the design. A machine operated through a battery with three hours charge could deliver around 100 ECGs. Apart from the cost advantage of using these off-the-shelf products, their usage resulted in easy spare availability for the final product, ease of maintenance and high product reliability. Varghese noted:

> It's hard to tell engineers to stop designing. Just buy from somewhere and integrate. As mechanical engineers it was frustrating for team members. But then, it was a very different path we had chosen.
>
> (Mahanta, 2011)

Ease of Use

GE decided to provide one button ECG machine which is very easy to operate for a normal physician and semi-skilled operator. Initially, it provided two ECG product variants: one with and the other without interpretation of ECG output. The ECG machine costing a few thousand extra but equipped with an algorithm for interpretation of ECG output for diagnostic purposes was preferred by almost all the physicians. This was starkly different from the behaviour of cardiologists working in high end multi-speciality hospitals in cities, who instead preferred to have only the output delivered by the machine and leave the interpretation to their own reading and experience.

Distribution Challenges and Building Partnerships

The MAC 400 ECG product was targeted at physicians practicing in small towns and rural areas. GE soon realized that it is not easy to reach out to them. There are over 700,000 doctors in India if one includes doctors from traditional medicine systems like Ayurveda. There is no list of these doctors and there are no magazines which all of these doctors read. There is no single sales organization that has a connection with all these doctors. So, it was not easy to develop awareness of the product and to communicate that the new ECG machine is something that would be valuable to them. GE executives were also not sure on to provide training needed to use the machine. How to sell products to them? How to connect with them and how to provide post-sales service and technical support?

GE hence decided to leverage local partnerships. They partnered with pharmaceutical companies, as they have a large number of medical representatives or sales people who visit these doctors regularly. GE particularly approached pharmaceutical companies selling drugs that were dealing with either hypertension or diabetes. Doctors treating the patients having these diseases normally want to check for ECG once in a while. However, the GE team also realized that partnering with just pharma companies would not guarantee enough reach. For the financial sustainability of the model, they needed to scale up not just the product manufacturing but the whole eco-system, including supply chain, distribution, technical support and services. They also partnered with MART, a marketing research agency specializing in rural marketing. With the help of MART, GE executives visited doctors and clinics to better understand their needs and the environment in which they use ECG machines.

Developing MACi

After successfully developing Mac 400, in 2013 the GE team developed another ECG machine MACi at a 50% of cost of Mac 400 or $500. It was slightly lighter than MAC 400, with a weight of less than 1 kilo. Unlike MAC 400 which is a three-channel machine, MACi was a single channel machine. A single machine prints one ECG waveform or channel at a time. Three channel ECG machine print three ECG waveforms or channels simultaneously and thus saves time in completing full set of recording. It reduced cost of each ECG further to $0.20 (Chandran, 2010). MACi was designed to conduct 250 ECGs with a single battery charge of 3-hours (Business Standard, 2013).

The MAC 400 achieved worldwide success. By 2009, GE sold over 6,000 machines in more than 50 countries. Only 20% were sold in India. GE decided to manufacture this product in China give a great demand of the product there (Forbes, 2009). Later GE added new features to MAC 400 such as USB and Ethernet ports for enhanced computer connectivity and launched it as MAC 800 in developed countries, keeping in mind the special needs of consumers in these countries.

GE's India Strategy and the ECG Development:
A Theoretical Analysis

GE's innovation strategies in the Indian healthcare sector – as exemplified in improving diagnostics of cardiovascular diseases – provide a vivid illustration of base-of-pyramid practices and their evolution over time. GE's innovation strategies in India involve four key stages: defeaturing, clean slate approach, situated innovation and reserve innovation. We discuss in the following sections three dynamics of change between different phases, which allow for the development of the theoretical framework in Figure 11.6.

From Defeaturing to a Clean Slate Approach to Overcome Institutional Dualism

The initial approach adopted by GE in addressing the resource-constrained BOP market evidences a general naivete of many MNCs initially venturing in very low-income settings. GE soon realized that defeaturing – hence removing costly product features

Medical Device Innovation at the Base of the Pyramid 253

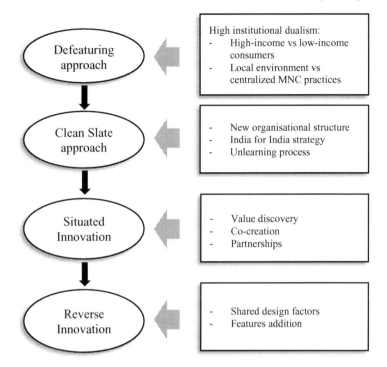

Figure 11.6 Theoretical Framework.

Note: The four stages in the strategy for local and reverse innovation are shown on the left side while factors contributing to the approach in each stage are shown in the boxes on right side.

to reduce the price point and meet affordability requirement of BOP consumers – would not be a successful business strategy. First, because it did not prove successful enough to lower costs to a significant level; second, and most importantly, because penetrating BOP market required a much wider and more profound innovation of both product and business model design. While affordability is an important aspect of BOP products, the availability, awareness and acceptability aspects of the product are of equal – if not higher – importance (Anderson & Markides, 2007; Angeli & Jaiswal, 2015). This is because of the deep institutional divide between innovators, who traditionally serve high-income consumer segment, and BOP customers, who are instead characterized by highly idiosyncratic and heterogeneous needs, lifestyle, spatial constraints, socio-cultural customs and beliefs, family dynamics, purchasing behaviour and priorities (Banerjee & Duflo, 2012; Černauskas et al., 2018; Rivera-Santos et al., 2012). For example, sophisticated, heavy ECG machines were suitable for specialised cardiologists mostly providing care to wealthy urban customers. These were not suitable options for rural physicians who needed instead sturdy, dust-resistant portable devices that could be easily transported across rural areas. Moreover, because the skill level of rural healthcare workforce is lower, it was important to equip these machines with fully interpreted output. MNCs' subsidiaries attempting to serve BOP markets face challenges of institutionalism dualism, namely the need to balance demands and isomorphism requirements by high-income and low-income market segments and by both local environments and the MNCs' centralized practices. These tensions can result in the MNCs' difficulty to deeply engage with BOP markets and fully adapt their offers to BOP needs, resulting in lack of flexibility and reduced competitiveness with respect to local companies (Angeli & Jaiswal, 2015). These considerations point to the need to *ecosystem* – rather than just product – innovation, which broadly reconsiders relationships with customers and suppliers to lower internal costs and price points while enhancing the acceptability of the product, the effectiveness of communication campaigns and the reach of distribution channels.

Considering the limitations of defeaturing, GE soon realized that it needs to adopt a clean slate – *tabula rasa* – approach. Traditional production and distribution processes are influenced by deeply rooted mindsets and cognitive frames that have evolved over time in adaptation with high-income markets. These, however, proved to be detrimental to serving BOP markets, which are instead so markedly different from both traditional customers and the lived experience of innovators. GE opted for a deliberate process of unlearning traditional practices, supported first and foremost by structural changes. GE soon recognized this challenges and decided to respond with an ' In India for India' strategy and changes in its organizational structure, which significantly strengthened the autonomy of local subsidiaries and marked the shift from a globalization/glocalization strategy to a strategy of local – situated – innovation (Immelt et al., 2009). We identify 'situated innovation' as not only developed locally, but also mindful of the socio-cultural and socio-economic context of the prospective innovation recipients. Focusing the attention on the India BOP market favoured the process of unlearning necessary to unleash a clean slate approach, hence to go back to the design board with no preconceived ideas about either the product design or the surrounding ecosystem.

From Glocalization to Situated Innovation

The situated innovation-based strategy pursued by GE India was facilitated by its subsidiary engaging in the process of 'value discovery', deemed highly salient to develop or deliver complex products/services in BOP markets. Value discovery is a business model dimension distinct from the traditional value proposition/creation/appropriation put forth by the mainstream business model literature (Angeli & Jaiswal, 2016). The 'value discovery' aspect precedes the formulation of the value proposition and points to a process of in-depth engagement between the innovating company or organizational representatives and the target communities and customers. This entails twofold, bilateral benefits. On the company side, this process of deep engagement allows for a full immersion in the users' realities and in-depth understanding of their needs, which catalyses the 'unlearning' process of existing ideas and provides important insights for developing innovations that are situated and embedded in the multifaceted aspects of the local context. On the customers' side, the value discovery aims at creating awareness of an existing need that might otherwise go undetected among the potential customers. For example, BOP patients – typically characterized by low health literacy and low health-seeking behaviour – might not be aware of health conditions that could be easily curable, such as cataracts, high blood pressure or diabetes (Angeli et al., 2018; Angeli & Jaiswal, 2016; Das et al., 2018). Physicians working in rural areas instead might be well aware of the challenges related to diagnosis and treatment of cardiovascular diseases in remote areas but might be less cognizant of potential solutions existing in the market at an affordable rate. Deep engagement with the target consumers allows for raising awareness of both an existing need and a related solution, therefore partially bridging the important divide and the typical reluctance shown by target communities towards even very simple solutions (e.g. Banerjee & Duflo, 2012). Moreover, the 'co-creation approach' allows for the MNC's legitimacy development in the target setting and leads to the formation of the users' sense of ownership towards the innovation, crucial to guarantee uptake and desired fit of the innovative product or service to the socio-cultural context. In promoting situated innovations, an important role was played by local partnerships, as effectively illustrated by GE's example. In order to penetrate the difficult BOP rural settings, with no unified marketing and promotion channels, GE partnered with pharmaceutical companies and an agency specialized in rural marketing. Local partnerships have proved crucial to the success of many BOP business model, as important funnels of legitimacy and trust from BOP communities.

Interestingly, GE's shift to an approach of local and frugal innovation strategy mirrors the evolution of BOP 1.0 to BOP 2.0. The initial BOP approaches were mostly focused on product innovation (rather than on ecosystem innovation) and viewed BOP communities as consumers of innovation rather than local partners, entrepreneurs, producers or distributors. As a consequence, initial BOP attempts failed to address the deeper causes of social exclusion and poverty, namely lack of local capacity, infrastructure and economic opportunities. BOP 2.0 drew attention on the importance to design business models that spur local development in a sustainable long-term way, through the involvement of local communities within the new products and services value-chain. Local consumers hence became partners, through long-lasting engagement and mutual dialogue.

Reverse Innovation to Unleash Economies of Scale

An interesting point in this study relates to GE's capacity to scale-up production and sales of its ECG machine, particularly by exporting it to other BOP contexts and to high-income markets. The possibilities to realize economies of scale is one of the mechanisms that BOP business models leverage to achieve financial sustainability in difficult, extremely low-income markets (Angeli & Jaiswal, 2016). However, economies of scale are often challenging to achieve. The BOP market cannot be considered a monolithic entity with similar needs and characteristics; instead, the BOP environments feature a multitude of highly idiosyncratic communities that are highly heterogeneous both across and within countries. Each rural village is virtually characterized by a unique spatial environment and socio-cultural makeup, which requires highly customized approaches and makes it difficult – depending on the nature of the product or service – to adopt standardized solutions (Angeli & Jaiswal, 2015; Kolk et al., 2014; Rivera-Santos et al., 2012). GE's success in achieving economies of scale can be explained by three main factors. First, the intended customers have high literacy levels and recognize the need that the product responds to, hence requiring low efforts on the firm's side to raise awareness among the target users. Targeting rural physicians significantly lowers the information asymmetry barriers as the need for technological solutions enabling ECG in rural areas is immediately clear to local healthcare workforce. The remaining challenges relate to innovation in product design, innovation to

256 Anand Kumar Jaiswal and Federica Angeli

scale up production and distribution, along with effective marketing choices. However, the penetration of the product is easier than for example, delivery of antenatal care to expectant mothers in BOP settings, or sanitation efforts through toilet installations, which instead requires highly customized models that are in line with the specificities of the local socio-cultural fabric, and important efforts to educate the population to enhance product acceptance (Angeli & Westra, 2018; Banerjee & Duflo, 2012).

The second factor is that rural settings around the globe share geographical, spatial and socio-cultural similarities, which require the need for low-maintenance, dust-resistant products, battery powered devices that can resist power outages, portable solutions that can be easily transported and fully automized so that the output can be read and understood by lower skilled personnel. By focusing on the shared factors, which allowed to respond to the differentiating characteristics of different rural settings, at the same time enabled GE to create a universal machine that could be marketed not only in India varied rural areas, but also around the world. This can be seen as a benefit of GE's situated innovation strategy, managing to achieve local adaptation with a global perspective (Gould & Grein, 2009). The third factor relates to GE's capability to achieve reverse innovation (Malodia et al., 2020), hence to introduce the product – initially conceived for low-income, BOP markets – in high-income markets. GE added new features in the devices developed in India and sold them in developed markets to make them suitable to environment existing in these countries. This enhanced their acceptability and in the process, increased margins as GE could price these products at a higher level. This success can be explained through GE's strong leverage of its international presence and reputation but also through its in-depth understanding of global markets. At the same time, it is clear that the clean slate approach and situated innovation strategy succeeded in realizing the disruptive innovation anticipated by Christensen (Christensen et al., 2015; Hart & Christensen, 2002), namely the possibility to entirely disrupt high-income market through low-cost innovations. Malodia et al. (2020) explain this remarkable achievement by considering how understanding consumers' needs and translate them scientifically is crucial to local and reverse innovation. In exporting such innovation and realizing a competitive edge, the authors also observe the relevance of geopolitical factors and the identification of latent needs in developing markets (Malodia et al., 2020). Reverse innovation has been much theorized as a potential outcome of BOP strategies, but not often seen.

Four phases of evolution in GE's strategy can be highlighted (Figure 11.6), with related antecedents: a defeaturing approach, determined by the entrenched and difficult to overcome MNC's institutional dualism; the clean slate approach, enabled by new organizational structure choices, the India for India strategy and the unlearning processes; a situated innovation strategy, facilitated by value discovery, co-creation approaches and partnerships; a reverse innovation strategy, supported by price premium, shared design factors and scale advantages.

Conclusion

This chapter discusses the various aspects of GE's strategy in India to reduce costs of medical devices and deliver high-quality inclusive healthcare. The combination of clean slate approaches and situated innovation strategies have uniquely led to reverse innovation and the realization of economy of scale. This led to a BOP model that successfully balances financial profit and social impact. This empirical study is of

Medical Device Innovation at the Base of the Pyramid   257

important managerial and theoretical value to further BOP research and practice aiming to spur sustainable development, particularly in a complex environment such as healthcare, to advance the progress of SDG3. Box 11.1 proposes discussion questions that are useful to further reflect on GE's experience in the Indian market.

Box 11.1   Discussion questions to stimulate reflections on GE's experience.

1   Discuss GE's strategy in India. Why did GE decide to develop low-cost medical devices in the Indian market?
2   Discuss the clean slate approach. Why was it necessary? What was the difference from defeaturing? Would this strategy be advisable to any product innovation process? Is this strategy suitable for tapping markets in developing countries?
3   Discuss the situated innovation strategy. Why was it necessary? What was the difference from glocalization? Would this strategy be advisable to any product innovation process?
4   Discuss the role of reverse innovation in GE's strategy. To what extent do you think reverse innovation could be pursued for other types of innovation? You can think about different products in different sectors and markets.
5   What are the possible advantages and disadvantages of reverse innovation? What MNCs like GE can do to maximize its potential?
6   Discuss the evolution of GE's strategy in India over time? What were the most salient factors which affected its strategy at each stage of evolution? Could GE's experience stimulate learning for other types of private organizations?

Acknowledgements

The authors are thankful to Suvendu Kumar Pratihari for the research assistance provided in developing some parts of the chapter. The first author is also thankful to his co-authors with whom he published his previous work on GE in the form of cases and articles listed below

*   Malodia, S., & Jaiswal, A. K. (2015). *GE in India: Changing healthcare*. Indian Institute of Management Ahmedabad case;
*   Jaiswal, A. K., & Malodia, S. (2018). *Discovery IQ by GE: Launching super value PET/CT scanner*. Indian Institute of Management Ahmedabad case;
*   Malodia, S., Gupta, S., & Jaiswal, A. K. (2020). Reverse innovation: A conceptual framework. *Journal of the Academy of Marketing Science*, 48, 1009–1029.

Note

1 This chapter is developed by Professor Anand Kumar Jaiswal, Indian Institute of Management, Ahmedabad, and Professor Federica Angeli, The York Management School, University of York. It is out of authors' ongoing research on GE's innovation strategies for healthcare. It is written based on primary information, author's previous published work and secondary sources.

References

Abdul-Aziz, A. A., Desikan, P., Prabhakaran, D., & Schroeder, L. F. (2019, April 1). Tackling the burden of cardiovascular diseases in India: The essential diagnostics list. *Circulation: Cardiovascular Quality and Outcomes*. Lippincott Williams and Wilkins. https://doi.org/10.1161/CIRCOUTCOMES.118.005195

Amritt. (2020). *Cardiovascular devices in India | medical device market in India |Amritt, Inc.* Retrieved June 7, 2021, from https://amritt.com/industries/medical-device-india/cardiovascular-devices-in-india/

Anderson, J., & Markides, C. (2007, August). Strategic innovation at the base of the pyramid *Sloan Management Review*, 49, 83–88. https://doi.org/10.1108/02756660710732611

Angeli, F., Ishwardat, S. T., Jaiswal, A. K., Capaldo, A., Angeli, F., Ishwardat, S. T., & Capaldo, A. (2018). Socio-cultural sustainability of private healthcare providers in an Indian slum setting: A bottom-of-the-pyramid perspective. *Sustainability*, 10(12), 4702. https://doi.org/10.3390/su10124702

Angeli, F., & Jaiswal, A. K. (2015). Competitive dynamics between MNCs and domestic companies at the base of the pyramid: An institutional perspective. *Long Range Planning*, 48(3), 182–199. https://doi.org/10.1016/j.lrp.2013.08.010

Angeli, F., & Jaiswal, A. K. (2016). Business model innovation for inclusive health care delivery at the bottom of the pyramid. *Organization and Environment*, 29(4), 486–507. https://doi.org/10.1177/1086026616647174

Angeli, F., & Westra, D. (2018). Delivering value in the healthcare sector through the lens of hybrid organizing. In R. Wilden, M. Garbuio, F. Angeli, & D. Mascia (Eds.), *Entrepreneurship in healthcare*. Routledge.

Banerjee, A. V., & Duflo, E. (2012). Poor economics. *Poor Economics*, 303. https://doi.org/10.1007/s13398-014-0173-7.2

Business Standard. (2013). GE healthcare launches low-cost portable ECG. *Business Standard News*. Retrieved June 1, 2021, from www.business-standard.com/article/companies/ge-healthcare-launches-low-cost-portable-ecg-109112400032_1.html

Černauskas, V., Angeli, F., Jaiswal, A. K., & Pavlova, M. (2018). Underlying determinants of health provider choice in urban slums: Results from a discrete choice experiment in Ahmedabad, India. *BMC Health Services Research*, 18(473).

Chandran, R. (2010). In India, for India: Medical device makers plug in. *Reuters*. Retrieved June 1, 2021, from www.reuters.com/article/us-india-healthcare-feature-idUSTRE6640F120100705

Christensen, C. M., Raynor, M. E., & McDonald, R. (2015). What is disruptive innovation. *Harvard Business Review*, 93(12), 44–53.

Das, M., Angeli, F., Krumeich, A. J. S. M., & Van Schayck, O. C. P. (2018). Patterns of illness disclosure among Indian slum dwellers: A qualitative study. *BMC International Health and Human Rights*, 18(3), 1–17. https://doi.org/10.1186/s12914-018-0142-x

Fior Markets. (2020). *Global cardiovascular devices market is expected to reach*. Retrieved June 1, 2021, from www.globenewswire.com/news-release/2020/06/23/2051737/0/en/Global-Cardiovascular-Devices-Market-is-Expected-to-Reach-USD-71-05-Billion-by-2027-Fior-Markets.html

Forbes. (2009). *Finger on the pulse, at last*. Retrieved June 1, 2021, from www.forbes.com/2009/12/09/forbes-india-ge-healthcare-jeff-immelt-john-flannery.html?sh=6603ba705b57

Fortune Business Insights. (2020). *Cardiovascular devices market size, share | global industry report 2026*. Retrieved June 1, 2021, from www.fortunebusinessinsights.com/cardiovascular-devices-market-102418

Gould, S. J., & Grein, A. F. (2009). Think glocally, act glocally: A culture-centric comment on Leung, Bhagat, Buchan, Erez and Gibson (2005). *Journal of International Business Studies*, 40(2), 237–254. https://doi.org/10.1057/palgrave.jibs.8400410

Hart, S., & Christensen, C. M. (2002). The great leap: Driving innovation from the base of the pyramid. *MIT Sloan Management Review*, 44(1), 51–56.

IBEF. (2018). *Healthcare industry in India, Indian healthcare sector services*. Retrieved October 14, 2018, from www.ibef.org/industry/healthcare-india.aspx

Immelt, J. R., Govindarajan, V., & Trimble, C. (2009). How GE is disrupting itself. *Harvard Business Review*, 87(10), 56–65. https://hbr.org/2009/10/how-ge-is-disrupting-itself

Invest India. (2021). *Medical device industry in India | investment in medical sector*. Retrieved June 1, 2021, from www.investindia.gov.in/sector/medical-devices

Knowledge@Wharton. (2010). *"Reverse innovation": GE makes India a lab for global markets – Knowledge@Wharton*. Retrieved June 1, 2021, from https://knowledge.wharton.upenn.edu/article/reverse-innovation-ge-makes-india-a-lab-for-global-markets/

Knowledge@Wharton. (2012). *Vijay Govindarajan: How reverse innovation can change the world*. Retrieved June 1, 2021, from https://knowledge.wharton.upenn.edu/article/vijay-govindarajan-how-reverse-innovation-can-change-the-world/

Kolk, A., Rivera-Santos, M., & Rufín, C. (2014). Reviewing a decade of research on the "base/bottom of the pyramid" (BOP) concept. *Business & Society*, 53(3), 338–377. https://doi.org/10.1177/0007650312474928

KPMG. (2020). *Catalysing the national infrastructure pipeline – KPMG India*. Retrieved June 1, 2021, from https://home.kpmg/in/en/home/insights/2020/08/catalysing-the-national-infrastructure-pipeline-project-india.html

Mahanta, V. (2011). How GE got out of the GE way to create the Nano of ECGs. *The Economic Times*. Retrieved June 1, 2021, from https://economictimes.indiatimes.com/how-ge-got-out-of-the-ge-way-to-create-the-nano-of-ecgs/articleshow/7673404.cms?utm_source=contentofinterest&utm_medium=text&utm_campaign=cppst

Malodia, S., Gupta, S., & Jaiswal, A. K. (2020). Reverse innovation: A conceptual framework. *Journal of the Academy of Marketing Science*, 48(5), 1009–1029. https://doi.org/10.1007/s11747-019-00703-4

NATHEALTH. (2018). *NATEV 2018: 5th annual event of NATHEALTH*. NATHEALTH.

Prakash, V. S. (2020). *Indian cardiovascular med tech space is still at a nascent stage*. Retrieved June 1, 2021, from www.biospectrumindia.com/interviews/71/15674/indian-cardiovascular-med-tech-space-is-still-at-a-nascent-stage.html

Research and Markets. (2018). *Indian cardiology market research and forecast, 2018–2023*. Retrieved June 1, 2021, from www.researchandmarkets.com/reports/4721079/indian-cardiology-market-research-and-forecast

Rezende dos Reis, S., Oliveira, T. de, Cavalcanti da Silva, L., Pinto, S., Marta de Souza, A., & Santos-Oliveira, R. (2016). PET radiopharmaceuticals and PET/CT technology: Comparative numbers of Brazil, India, Canada and Latin America. *Austin Journal of Nuclear Medicine and Radiotherapy*. www.austinpublishinggroup.com

Rivera-Santos, M., Rufín, C., & Kolk, A. (2012). Bridging the institutional divide: Partnerships in subsistence markets. *Journal of Business Research*, 65(12), 1721–1727. https://doi.org/10.1016/j.jbusres.2012.02.013

Sengupta, A., Angeli, F., Syamala, T. S., Dagnelie, P. C., & Schayck, C. P. V. (2015). Overweight and obesity prevalence among Indian women by place of residence and socio-economic status: Contrasting patterns from "underweight states" and "overweight states" of India. *Social Science and Medicine*, 138. https://doi.org/10.1016/j.socscimed.2015.06.004

SKP. (2017). *Medical device industry in India – the evolving landscape, opportunities and challenges*. www.skpgroup.com

Statista. (2019). *Life expectancy at birth in India from 2008 to 2018*. www.statista.com/statistics/271334/life-expectancy-in-india

Statista. (2021a). *India – health care industry distribution by sector 2016 | statista*. Retrieved June 1, 2021, from www.statista.com/statistics/912403/india-health-care-industry-distribution-by-sector/

Statista. (2021b). *India – healthcare sector size 2008–2022 | statista*. Retrieved June 1, 2021, from www.statista.com/statistics/701556/healthcare-sector-size-india/

United Nations. (2019). *World population prospects 2019 highlights*. https://population.un.org/wpp/Publications/Files/WPP2019_Highlights.pdf

World Bank. (2020a). *Indicators | data*. Retrieved May 25, 2020, from https://data.worldbank.org/indicator

World Bank. (2020b). *Out-of-pocket expenditure (% of current health expenditure) | data*. Retrieved June 28, 2020, from https://data.worldbank.org/indicator/SH.XPD.OOPC.CH.ZS

World Bank. (2021a). *Current health expenditure (% of GDP) | data*. Retrieved June 1, 2021, from https://data.worldbank.org/indicator/SH.XPD.CHEX.GD.ZS

World Bank. (2021b). *Current health expenditure per capita, PPP (current international $) | data*. Retrieved June 1, 2021, from https://data.worldbank.org/indicator/SH.XPD.CHEX.PP.CD

World Bank. (2021c). *Out-of-pocket expenditure (% of current health expenditure) | data*. Retrieved June 1, 2021, from https://data.worldbank.org/indicator/SH.XPD.OOPC.CH.ZS

World Bank. (2021d). *Poverty headcount ratio at $1.90 a day (2011 PPP) (% of population) | data*. Retrieved June 1, 2021, from https://data.worldbank.org/indicator/SI.POV.DDAY?end=2015&start=1981&view=chart

World Heart Federation. (2011). *Cardiovascular disease in India*. Retrieved June 1, 2021, from https://world-heart-federation.org/wp-content/uploads/2017/05/Cardiovascular_diseases_in_India.pdf

12 Moving Beyond Fragmented Traditions

Toward an Integrated View of Organizing for Sustainable Development

Ashley Metz, Federica Angeli and Jörg Raab

Situating Organizational Approaches in Context

Biological research tells us that the neural circuitry necessary for fish to climb out of the weedy Devonian swamps 375 million years ago and "overcome gravity" to walk on land existed before legs evolved to do the walking (Falkhingam, 2018; Jung et al., 2018). If today's organizational approaches to sustainability are the *tiktaalik*[1] walking us toward a wider, sustainable world, we may just have it backward: the legs are there, but the circuitry has not yet evolved. In other words, organizational structures have emerged, but we are not yet using them sufficiently – in part, we argue here, because organizations sit in a larger macro and micro context and views on their limits and roles have not yet settled and sufficiently been transformed.

In this book, we discussed many shapes and sizes of those possible *legs* – organizational approaches to addressing grand challenges using a variety of theoretical lenses to analyze current topics relevant to each approach. Chapters address organization-level approaches such as Corporate Responsibility (Chapter 1), hybrid organizing (Chapter 4) and nonprofit organizations (Chapter 5). We also cover blended financing tools (Chapter 7) that facilitate new organizational models. In other chapters, supra-organizational efforts including base of the pyramid strategies (Chapter 3) and inter-organizational networks (Chapter 6), demonstrate how narratives about doing business with the poor and doing business while adhering to high social and environmental standards are evolving and ideas about how different types of organizations can work together, each bringing their own skills and resources into efforts to address grand challenges. We also cover how progress toward grand challenges can be measured (Chapter 8). In the chapter on responsible innovation (Chapter 2), we discuss the role of structures and practices in how innovation processes can reflect responsible innovation dimensions, reflecting in part on the different levels at play in determining the responsibility of outcomes. Taken together, these chapters cover the current landscape of organizational efforts toward grand challenges.

The approaches discussed in these chapters also illustrate a snapshot of the current organizing environment, while attending to their dynamism. A common theme throughout the book was that of change; for example, change in how CSR is practiced, or forward-looking views on how responsible innovations could be more thoroughly embedded, how nonprofit approaches evolve and how BOP narratives morphed over time. Organizational approaches will continue to evolve, in relation to the macro and micro forces that influence them, and which they influence. Attending to the context,

DOI: 10.4324/9780429243165-13

This chapter has been made available under a CC-BY-NC 4.0 license.

and interrelations between levels may help us develop more sustainable *circuitry*, which itself can and arguably should continue to evolve. Given the continuation and exacerbation of global issues, organizations have not yet enabled systemic changes necessary to halt climate change, end global poverty and make serious progress on other grand challenges. What is the role of organizations in enabling more sustainable economies and societies? By placing the organizational approaches in context with macro and micro forces, we can sketch a view of the structures and behaviors that enable and constrain them (Figure 12.1). Doing so can help us illustrate some of the links and interconnectedness between these levels at which structures shape behavior, and action shapes structures, influence one another, and how different levels can help facilitate or hinder the organizational level. The figure illustrates various links between organizational approaches discussed in this book and the broader macro and micro environments. On the organizational level, corporate responsibility efforts, hybrid organizations, impact financing and nonprofit organizations are all locations where sustainability efforts are carried out or inhibited. These are influenced by and influence the macro and micro levels, respectively. For example, as discussed in Chapter 5 (Responsible Innovation), structures like legal forms can help embed responsible innovation dimensions (anticipation, reflexivity, inclusivity, responsiveness). Legal forms can also be understood as inhibitors that have, until relatively recently, only offered for-profit and non-profit options, while now the use of alternative options is growing.

The stylized illustration in Figure 12.1 starts with organizational efforts discussed in this book and offers examples for different levers and influences across levels, but it is naturally not exhaustive and simply illustrative. A macro and micro context illustrates the importance of understanding what organizations can and cannot do alone. While organizations and more recently organizational networks have thoroughly permeated modern societies (Perrow, 1991; Raab & Kenis, 2009) and have therefore become the primary sites in which behavior plays out, decisions are made and structures and changes are addressed or reified, they are also the recipients of macro-, meso- and supra-organizational forces. Organizations can play roles in changing macro level structures, such as by challenging norms in the case of some hybrid organizations (Haigh & Hoffman, 2014) or by pressuring governments and international organizations for clear standards and level playing fields toward more sustainable production and consumption (admittedly organizations often even do the opposite and lobby governments to loosen regulations). Yet, even if they want to, such organizations are not heroic saviors that can change the entire macro landscape single-handedly. In the end, it is the national governments and international organizations and regimes backed by them that need to set the incentives in terms of regulation, taxation and financial subsidies that for example will drive massive efforts and investments into innovations and new sustainable products. Interestingly, this micro-meso-macro framework ties in with a socio-ecological approach (Brofenbrenner, 1979; Mcleroy et al., 1988), which highlights the intersectional, micro-meso-macro interdependencies between individual, community, organizational, policy and environmental factors in explaining individual and systemic outcomes. The socio-ecological perspective is widely used in a variety of domains, to design of health promotion initiatives (Golden & Earp, 2012; Mcleroy et al., 1988), to explain seeking behavior of prenatal care (Sword, 1999), to study food choice in schools (Moore et al., 2013), to guide interventions tackling social inequality (Costanza, 2014) to inform domestic violence prevention (Centre for Disease Control and Prevention (CDC), 2020; World Health Organization, 2021) and

Moving Beyond Fragmented Traditions 263

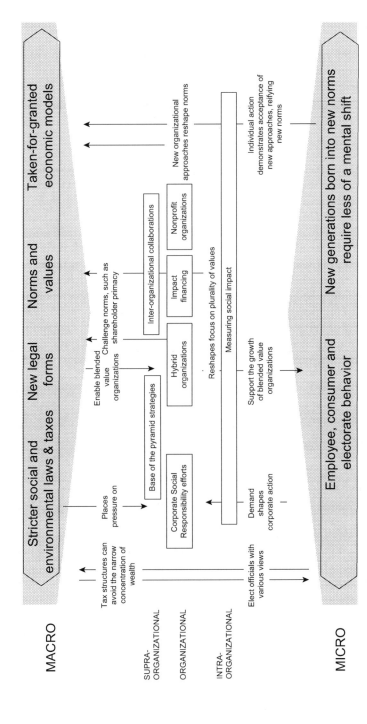

Figure 12.1 A stylized illustration of organizational responses to grand challenges in macro and micro contexts.

also to understand menstrual hygiene and health (UNICEF, 2019). Yet, its application within the organizational and management field is to date very limited.

Overall, changes to the macro level could instigate a much faster shift toward a sustainability transition, and toward addressing grand challenges. If ideas like 'planned economic contraction' or de-growth (Alexander, 2012; Latouche, 2010), and measuring country success by happiness or broader welfare indicators over GDP, caught on, organizations would have to innovate in response. Localizing taxes or changing tax codes in certain jurisdictions could redistribute wealth locally among communities near organizational offices, rather than concentrating wealth with few shareholders, first safeguarded by offshore accounts. Macro structures can indeed influence organizations in very drastic ways. In certain regions such as China, a state-organized capitalist system influences the speed at which organizations adopt changing norms, where other regions rely more on micro-level actions, such as consumer demand, as larger levers toward organizations, and may result in slower organizational changes.

Micro-level action is also a crucial component to organizational efforts to address grand challenges. Organizations depend on the behavior of employees, customers and voters who enable them to act in more sustainable ways, or who help elect legislators who reshape the macro environment. The values and makeup of the individual level is shaped differently by regional cultures and environments. Consumers and employees reaching the workforce today were born into a normative environment primarily in favor of sustainability and painfully aware of the challenges societies face (Capgemini, 2021; Haigh & Hoffman, 2012). For example, millennials place a higher value on healthy living, environmental and social justice and ecological sustainability than earlier generations, which manifests itself in the products they purchase, the companies they invest in, the movements they support, the companies in which they work and their broader lifestyles (Sogari et al., 2017). These are also known as Lifestyle of Health and Sustainability (LOHAS) consumer segment (Haigh & Hoffman, 2012; Pícha & Navrátil, 2019).

The relationship between various macro or micro actions and other actions on the same level can raise important questions. New norms and values influence the creation of new legal forms; but likewise new legal forms will influence norms and values at organizational and individual levels. What legal actions can governments or others take that can play an outsized role in shifting norms and values, and influencing meso- and micro-level action? Are actors on different levels working *hard enough* to facilitate a more sustainable world? And is academic work helping?

For those working in organizations, including social entrepreneurs who start or manage their own social purpose organizations, employees working in networks of organizations or on CSR projects, innovators, and other actors trying to improve social and environmental outcomes, attending to the macro and micro context is important. Doing so can help actors understand if and how macro structures inhibit or enable their efforts, as well as how structures inhibit or enable their social efforts to become taken-for-granted rather than novel. Further research is needed to better understand the links between levels and their relationship with social and environmental impact.

Analyzing organizations and their efforts to develop more sustainable economies and societies in their macro-micro context does not mean that we should let them off the hook. Many organizations already show that it is possible to make their activities more sustainable but others are still dragging their feet or take action to secure short-term rents and continue to externalize costs to the environment or the societies

Moving Beyond Fragmented Traditions

they operate in. Any transformative change manifests itself in and through organizations and requires great management efforts. The importance of organizational forms and practices can therefore not be overstated. But we also have to acknowledge that the macro and micro context organizations operate in enable but also constrain their strategies and actions.

Interconnectedness, Yet Lack of Integrated Focus on Solving Grand Challenges

This image of organizations in relation to macro and micro levels implicitly highlights interconnectedness between many academic disciplines and their traditional levels of analysis and sectoral purviews. Researchers of psychology, economics, public management, public policy, management and organizations, and others have investigated pieces of this puzzle. However, many independent theoretical streams have emerged and evolved separately without extensive interaction and overarching aggregation – and in particular, without common goals. On the organizational level, separate fields of public management and public policy, management and organization studies, as well as fragmented theoretical discussions within them, tend to operate as though the organizations under their respective microscopes operate in a vacuum and focus on best practices firmly rooted in one area. Integration between disparate theories has tended to focus on the intersections and overlaps between traditional sector boundaries and exchanges of ideas and methods across them.

Such work investigates the shifting and melting of strong sectoral boundaries. For example, work on how the social sector is becoming *business-like* (Maier et al., 2016), or the rationalization, professionalization (Hwang & Powell, 2009) and marketization (Eikenberry & Kluver, 2004) of organizations, including funding organizations and membership associations (Mair & Hehenberger, 2014) comes to mind in this regard. Scholars have unpacked how nonprofit organizations have adopted rhetoric, organizational practices and goals from business (Dart, 2004; Maier et al., 2016) imported through professionals (Hwang & Powell, 2009; Suarez, 2010) as well as resource providers (e.g. Rogers, 2011). Scholars concerned with rationalization investigate the effectiveness of business-like approaches (Maier et al., 2016; Suarez, 2010) and share the concern that idealism may be lost (Eikenberry & Kluver, 2004).

There is also a large body of work that takes the *business-like* turn for granted and studies the business practice of revenue generation and its interplay with the production of social value. Hybridity, discussed in this book, is understood as a permanent characteristic of the social sector (Brandsen et al., 2005). A large field of study has emerged to analyze social entrepreneurship (Mair & Marti, 2009; Peredo & McLean, 2006), also conceptualized as hybrid organizing (Battilana & Lee, 2014; Battilana et al., 2012). In this body of work, a central discussion is about the issues that arise from the co-existence of social and market goals such as governance issues and mission drift in dual-mission or hybrid enterprises (Ebrahim et al., 2014; Lee, 2014). Interestingly, in public management, the term 'hybrid organization' refers to organizations that blend ideal – possibly incommensurable – types of organizations from the traditionally distinction between public, private and third sector (Brandsen & Karré, 2011; Evers, 2005; Karré, 2020), whereas in the management literature, hybrid 'tends to refer to' organizations attaining to both social and financial goals (Lee & Battilana, 2013) – an example of separate research traditions and disciplinary fields that have evolved separately while investigating the same subject. Additionally, scholars study the use of mainstream market tools and organizational forms including impact investing (Brest & Born, 2013; e.g. Carroll & Shabana, 2010; Unruh et al., 2016) and the application of certifications, such as the B Corp certification or Fair trade (Bridge Ventures, 2015; Reinecke et al., 2012) as a means to enable for-profit businesses to gain reputational value for blurring their remit across sectors. These scholars are interested in how traditionally 'for-profit' organizations deliver social value in addition to economic value. This integration work has focused on intersections between sectors and thus hints at multi-level perspectives, but is largely focused on the organizational level, as is this book. The tendency for this work to essentially occupy itself with concerns about the shifting of traditionally profit-orientation in favor of a larger cornucopia of ways and degrees to which organizations can create social or environmental value, is useful. However, as a mental structure to guide us toward a more sustainable world on its own, it is at best, antiquated, and at worst myopic. Instead, we can appreciate today's forms and approaches for their efforts pulling and pushing across levels toward a sustainable future. This book chronicles main approaches, of relevance for students as well as academics, but is perhaps most fruitfully placed in a temporal perspective to call attention to the most important next areas of work – *making them all redundant*. We can shift our focus from what they are doing now, and their intersections, to the degree to which they are able to actually change the status quo; evaluating their successes on a grander scale.

From Organizations with Multiple Goals to Societies with Different Rules

Organizational approaches discussed in this book implicitly sit at the nexus between traditional sectors, but also the nexus *between current times and the future*. The specific organizational approaches discussed in this book are important *for now*, and organizational approaches in general, will continue to be important. What will be invented and implemented to make the transition to more sustainable economies and societies, will be done in and through organizations. Organizations therefore play crucial roles in enabling the transition to a sustainable world. They are the foot soldiers on the frontlines, where decisions are made that affect global supply chains, workers and the environment. Individually, they can raise questions about taken-for-granted ways of operating and collectively, they can stimulate greater change. However, organizations single handedly or collectively cannot pull the strings on the global economy without changes in norms and behavior which in turn shape organizations, and crucially, facilitation from governments. To consider organizational approaches *enough*, or to get extraordinarily excited about their ability to transform the planet, is to miss out on crucial details or mistakenly forget that all such organizations operate within a macro and micro context and are privy to such forces.

It is important to study the current moment in this dynamic evolution as major transitions need to take place in this decade, as well as to consider that it is, in fact, only a snapshot in time. Eventually, and arguably *hopefully*, the approaches discussed in this book will become extinct. It could be our goal that CSR, hybrid organizations and the like become so thoroughly taken for granted that we teach them only from a historical perspective, bones in the fossil record. What will it take for hybrid organizations to disappear, leaving equitable organizations in their place? How could we eliminate social entrepreneurs by reshaping our idea of 'entrepreneurs'? How can we as academics avoid a clingy love affair with the labels, catch phrases and theoretical concepts that define this era, but let them go when they are no longer needed, like the gills and scales of our ancestral waterborne years? The organizational legs toward a sustainable world are a first step. We must do all we can to rewire the neurons and eventually take a first breath in a different world.

Note

1 The tiktaalik was a fish-like organism that had wrist bones and is understood as a transitional link between fish and tetrapods.

References

Alexander, S. (2012). Planned economic contraction: The emerging case for degrowth. *Environmental Politics*, 21(3), 349–368. https://doi.org/10.1080/09644016.2012.671569

Battilana, J., & Lee, M. (2014). Advancing research on hybrid organizing – insights from the study of social enterprises. *Academy of Management Annals*, 8(1), 397–441. https://doi.org/10.1080/19416520.2014.893615

Battilana, J., Lee, M., Walker, J., & Dorsey, C. (2012, Summer). In search of the hybrid ideal. *Stanford Social Innovation Review*, 10(3), 51–55. http://ssir.org/articles/entry/in_search_of_the_hybrid_ideal

Brandsen, T., & Karré, P. M. (2011). Hybrid organizations: No cause for concern? *International Journal of Public Administration*, 34(13), 827–836. https://doi.org/10.1080/019006 92.2011.605090

Brandsen, T., van de Donk, W., & Putters, K. (2005). Griffins or chameleons? Hybridity as a permanent and inevitable characteristic of the third sector. *International Journal of Public Administration*, 28(9–10), 749–765. https://doi.org/10.1081/PAD-200067320

Brest, P., & Born, K. (2013). When can impact investing create real impact? With responses from Audrey Choi, Sterling K. Speirn, Alvaro Rodriguez Arregui & Michael Chu, Nancy E. Pfund, and Nick O'Donohoe. *Stanford Social Innovation Review*, 11(4), 22–31.

Bridge Ventures. (2015). *To B or not to B: An investor's guide to B corps.* Retrieved June 9, 2021, from www.bridgesfundmanagement.com/wp-content/uploads/2017/08/Bridges-To-B-or-Not-To-B-screen.pdf

Brofenbrenner, U. (1979). *The ecology of human development.* Harvard University Press.

Capgemini. (2021). *Generation green is leading the sustainability agenda.* Retrieved June 9, 2021, from www.capgemini.com/2020/08/generation-green-is-leading-the-sustainability-agenda/

Carroll, A. B., & Shabana, K. M. (2010, March 1). The business case for corporate social responsibility: A review of concepts, research and practice. *International Journal of Management Reviews.* John Wiley & Sons, Ltd. https://doi.org/10.1111/j.1468-2370.2009.00275.x

Centre for Disease Control and Prevention (CDC). (2020). *The social-ecological model: A framework for prevention \violence prevention\injury center\CDC.* Retrieved January 17, 2021, from www.cdc.gov/violenceprevention/publichealthissue/social-ecologicalmodel.html

Costanza, R. (2014). A theory of socio-ecological system change. *Journal of Bioeconomics*, 16(1), 39–44. https://doi.org/10.1007/s10818-013-9165-5

Dart, R. (2004). Being "business-like" in a nonprofit organization: A grounded and inductive typology. *Nonprofit and Voluntary Sector Quarterly*, 33(2), 290–310. https://doi.org/10.1177/0899764004263522

Ebrahim, A., Battilana, J., & Mair, J. (2014). The governance of social enterprises: Mission drift and accountability challenges in hybrid organizations. *Research in Organizational Behavior.* https://doi.org/10.1016/j.riob.2014.09.001

Eikenberry, A. M., & Kluver, J. D. (2004, March 1). The marketization of the nonprofit sector: Civil society at risk? *Public Administration Review*. John Wiley & Sons, Ltd. https://doi.org/10.1111/j.1540-6210.2004.00355.x

Evers, A. (2005). Mixed welfare systems and hybrid organizations: Changes in the governance and provision of social services. *International Journal of Public Administration*, 28(9–10), 737–748. https://doi.org/10.1081/PAD-200067318

Falkhingam, P. (2018). *"Walking" fish help scientists to understand how we left the ocean.* Retrieved June 9, 2021, from https://theconversation.com/walking-fish-help-scientists-to-understand-how-we-left-the-ocean-91411

Golden, S. D., & Earp, J. A. L. (2012). Social ecological approaches to individuals and their contexts: Twenty years of health education & behavior health promotion interventions. *Health Education and Behavior*, 39(3), 364–372. https://doi.org/10.1177/1090198111418634

Haigh, N., & Hoffman, A. J. (2012). Hybrid organizations: The next chapter of sustainable business. *Organizational Dynamics*, 41(2), 126–134. https://doi.org/10.1016/j.orgdyn.2012.01.006

Haigh, N., & Hoffman, A. J. (2014). The new heretics: Hybrid organizations and the challenges they present to corporate sustainability. *Organization and Environment*, 27(3), 223–241. https://doi.org/10.1177/1086026614545345

Hwang, H., & Powell, W. W. (2009). The rationalization of charity: The influences of professionalism in the nonprofit sector. *Administrative Science Quarterly*, 54(2), 268–298. https://doi.org/10.2189/asqu.2009.54.2.268

Jung, H., Baek, M., D'Elia, K. P., Boisvert, C., Currie, P. D., Tay, B. H., Venkatesh, B., Brown, S. M., Heguy, A., Schoppik, D., & Dasen, J. S. (2018). The ancient origins of neural substrates for land walking. *Cell*, 172(4), 667–682.e15. https://doi.org/10.1016/j.cell.2018.01.013

Karré, P. M. (2020). Hybrid organisations: Between state and market. In *Handbook on hybrid organisations*. Edward Elgar Publishing.

Latouche, S. (2010). Special issue: Growth, recession, or degrowth for sustainability and equity? *Journal of Cleaner Production*, 18(6), 519–522.

Lee, M. (2014). Mission and markets? The viability of hybrid social ventures. In *Academy of management proceedings* (Vol. 1, p. 13958). Academy of Management Briarcliff Manor.

Lee, M., & Battilana, J. (2013). How the zebra got its stripes: Imprinting of individuals and hybrid social ventures. *Harvard Business School Organizational Behavior Unit. . .*, 51. https://doi.org/10.2139/ssrn.2291686

Maier, F., Meyer, M., & Steinbereithner, M. (2016). Nonprofit organizations becoming business-like: A systematic review. *Nonprofit and Voluntary Sector Quarterly*, 45(1), 64–86. https://doi.org/10.1177/0899764014561796

Mair, J., & Hehenberger, L. (2014). Front-stage and backstage convening: The transition from opposition to mutualistic coexistence in organizational philanthropy. *Academy of Management Journal*, 57(4), 1174–1200. https://doi.org/10.5465/amj.2012.0305

Mair, J., & Marti, I. (2009). Entrepreneurship in and around institutional voids: A case study from Bangladesh. *Journal of Business Venturing*, 24(5), 419–435. https://doi.org/10.1016/j.jbusvent.2008.04.006

Mcleroy, K. R., Bibeau, D., Steckler, A., & Glanz, K. (1988). An ecological perspective on health promotion programs. *Health Education & Behavior*, 15(4), 351–377. https://doi.org/10.1177/109019818801500401

Moore, L., De Silva-Sanigorski, A., & Moore, S. N. (2013). A socio-ecological perspective on behavioural interventions to influence food choice in schools: Alternative, complementary or synergistic? *Public Health Nutrition*, 16(6), 1000–1005. https://doi.org/10.1017/S1368980012005605

Peredo, A. M., & McLean, M. (2006). Social entrepreneurship: A critical review of the concept. *Journal of World Business*, 41(1), 56–65. https://doi.org/10.1016/j.jwb.2005.10.007

Perrow, C. (1991). A society of organizations. *Theory and Society*, 20, 725–762.

Pícha, K., & Navrátil, J. (2019). The factors of lifestyle of health and sustainability influencing pro-environmental buying behaviour. *Journal of Cleaner Production, 234*, 233–241. https://doi.org/10.1016/j.jclepro.2019.06.072

Raab, J., & Kenis, P. (2009). Heading toward a society of networks: Empirical developments and theoretical challenges. *Journal of Management Inquiry, 18*(3), 198–210. https://doi.org/10.1177/1056492609337493

Reinecke, J., Manning, S., & von Hagen, O. (2012). The emergence of a standards market: Multiplicity of sustainability standards in the global coffee industry. *Organization Studies, 33*(5–6), 791–814. https://doi.org/10.1177/0170840612443629

Rogers, R. (2011). Why philanthro-policymaking matters. *Society, 48*, 376–381. https://doi.org/10.1007/s12115-011-9456-1

Sogari, G., Pucci, T., Aquilani, B., & Zanni, L. (2017). Millennial generation and environmental sustainability: The role of social media in the consumer purchasing behavior for wine. *Sustainability (Switzerland), 9*(10), 1911. https://doi.org/10.3390/su9101911

Suarez, D. F. (2010). Street credentials and management backgrounds: Careers of nonprofit executives in an evolving sector. *Nonprofit and Voluntary Sector Quarterly, 39*(4), 696–716. https://doi.org/10.1177/0899764009350370

Sword, W. (1999). A socio-ecological approach to understanding barriers to prenatal care for women of low income. *Journal of Advanced Nursing, 29*(5), 1170–1177. https://doi.org/10.1046/j.1365-2648.1999.00986.x

UNICEF. (2019). *Guidance on menstrual health and hygiene*. www.unicef.org/wash

Unruh, G., Kiron, D., Kruschwitz, N., Reeves, M., Rubel, H., & Zum Felde, A. M. (2016). Investing for a sustainable future: Investors care more about sustainability than many executives believe. *MIT Sloan Management Review, 57*(4).

World Health Organization. (2021). *WHO | the ecological framework*. Retrieved January 17, 2021, from www.who.int/violenceprevention/approach/ecology/en/

Index

Note: Page numbers in *italics* indicate a figure on the corresponding page.

ABI global 52, *53*
abstract management 107
accountability: external accountability, contributions 169; systems, development/ maintenance 99–100
accounting practices, impact 37
adaptable (responsible innovation principle) *32*
adaptation: belonging tensions model 89; goal, achievement 80; performing tensions iterative model 92; result 73
adaptation, organizing tensions iterative model 87
adaptive outcome attainment, process *83*
adaptive processes, iteration 91
additionality 144–145
advocacy NGOs, awareness (creation) 167
affordable medical devices (AMD) 235
African National Congress (ANC), reform promises 193–194
age decline, report 179
agreement, implementation 129
Alexander, Kelly 5, 9, 72, 190
American Research and Development Corporation 157
Angeli, Federica 1, 5, 6, 8, 10, 12, 46, 72, 99, 167, 235, 260
antenatal care: cross-sector collaboration 213–221; setup 213–214; delivery, complexity 213
anticipatory innovation process, facilitation 34
Aravind Eye Care: achievements 66; BOP strategy 46–47, 49, 66
Ashoka (social enterprise network) 167
Asia, economic development (impact) 117
asset owners, impact 147
asymmetric power dynamics 39
attribution, challenges 171

average topic share per topic, evolution *62*
Ayurveda systems 250

Barilla, participatory structures 36
Bartosch, Julia 4, 15
base of the pyramid (BOP): business approach 5; cross-section collaboration, context 231; literature 222; market penetration 252; medical device innovation 235; scientific studies, longitudinal text analysis 5
B Corp status 173
belief systems, sets 72
belonging tensions 94; adaptation 86, 88; model of adaptation 89
below market investments (concessionary investments) 154
below-market return investing 143
Benefit Corporation, legal form/investors 34–35
Best Alternative Charitable Option (BACO) 168
Beveridge systems 240
"Beyond the Business Case for Social Responsibility" (Kaplan) 20–21
bias, reflexive consideration 32
"big strategy," embracing 167
Bill and Melinda Gates Foundation, health impact 109, 118
binary thinking 108
biodiversity: loss 127; restoration 131
Biovison 119
Bismarckian systems 240
blended culture: emergence 229; importance 227
blended value 141–143
board-level stakeholder committees, prevalence 35–36
BOP 2.0 56, 61, 64
BOP 3.0 50, 64; network-based approach, advocacy 65

Index 271

bottom/base-of-the-pyramid business (BOP): approach, evolution 51; approach, invention/popularization 47; articles, publication number 55; average topic share per topic, evolution 62; BOP 2.0 56, 61, 64; BOP 3.0 50, 64; BOP 3.0, network-based approach (advocacy) 65; consumers, socio-economic outcomes (improvement) 48–49; data analysis 53–55; depletion 49; descriptive analyses 55–56; efforts, ethical rooting 63; enthusiasm 47; fortune 46; keyword combination (search database) 53; methods 52; narratives, chronological evolution 55; narratives, evolution (understanding) 46; policy/practice, lessons 65–66; practices, heterogeneity 66; PRISMA flow diagram 54; results/ discussion 55–63; search strategy 52; strategies, changes 64; strategy, success (examples) 46–47; study selection 52–53; systematic literature review/topic modeling analysis 46; theoretical background 48–51; theoretical/methodological contributions 63–64; top modeling analysis 56, 57–58, 59–61, 63
bottom of the pyramid (BOP) population, market penetration 239
bounded voluntariness 123
Brazil, Russia, India, China, and South Africa (BRICS) 235
Bretton Woods Institutions (BWIs), development obstruction removal (advocacy) 101
Broad Based Black Economic Empowerment (BBBEE) 194, 198; corporate incentivization 203; scorecard, improvement 199
business: cases, usage 20–21; mission, associations 90–91; modeling, profitability 64; profit increase, social responsibility 3; strategies 60–61; wordcloud 6, 59
business model sustainability 153

Cambridge Energy Alliance (CEA), organizational identity (shift) 88
capability development, focus 50
capital flow 145
carbon dioxide, impact 1–2
cardiovascular device market 238–239
cardiovascular diseases (CVDs), impact (WHO) 239
Caritas 119
Center of Development for Innovation (CDI) 223
Central African Republic (CAR), HRP cards (usage) 219

change: commitment, legal/moral justifications 21; pathways, intervention logic model 176
"Child Labour Due Diligence Law" (Netherlands) 23
child labour, issues 23
circular economy, building 120
civil society organizations (CSOs): political role 7; practices, transformative critiques 111
clean slate approach (tabula rasa approach) 242–245, 253
clean water, access (improvement) 171
Climate Action Network Europe 119
climate change, impact 127
co-create methodology 228
co-creation: approaches 228–229, 254; efforts 63; emphasis 227; practices, importance 231; process 214–216
cognition, translation process 86
cognitive rules, representation 75
cognitive schemata, adaptation 83
coherence, defining 149
co-investment, allowance 149–150
collaborative governance 119; regime 130
collaboratives 223
collateral, absence 154
commercial entrepreneurial ventures, challenges 202
commercial finance organizations 151
commercial markets 151
commercial value, defining 153
communities, wordcloud 60
community engagement projects 171
Community Healthcare Volunteers (CHVs) 215
Community Interest Company (CIC) 34
community level 130
companies, profit/public health priorities 16
compartmentalization, threat 83
competency-oriented motivations 122
compromise: emphasis 227; meaning 83; usage 229, 231
concessionary investments 154
conflict zones 212
connectivity, increase 117
control group, recruitment (feasibility) 178–179
controlled consumption, focus 175, 177
coordination, term (usage) 149–150
corporate actions, appropriateness 19
corporate fraud 23
corporate fraud/misconduct 23
corporate irresponsibility/misconduct, examples 22
corporate philanthropy, alternative 48
corporate policies/practices/outcomes 15

272 Index

corporate responsibility 15, 260; business cases, usage 20–21; concept 4; defining 19–20; development, CSR (link) 19; practice 23–26; question, handling (reasons) 15–17; research foci 20–23; role 24; stakeholder perspective 21–22; variability/contestedness, acknowledgment 20

Corporate Social Investment (CSI) 203; corporate responsibility development, link 19; spend (South Africa) 204

Corporate Social Responsibility (CSR) 15; adoption 24–25; adoption rate 25, 26; alternative 65–66; approaches 48; assumption 19; business case 21; concept, relevance (increase) 24–25; efforts, negation 33–34; link 19; practice, change 260–261; practices 24; reports, importance 24; spending 2023

corporate, wordcloud 4

corporate wrongdoing 22–23

corporations: focus 33; responsibilities, identification 17–19; role, political/ethical recognition 63; societal service 18; tax avoidance practices 22

corruption 23

Council of Europe Development Bank (CEB), social inclusion bond 155–156

COVID-19 pandemic 158, 236; burdens 235; inequalities 1; interconnections 2–3; societal goals 2

Covid outbreak, impact 16

Cox, Joshua 194–205

critical management studies (CMS) 100; attention, reason 103–105; challenges 101; concerns 108; learning 106–109; power asymmetries, focus 108–110; usage 99

cross-sector collaborations 119

cross-sector partnerships 116, 127; formation 223

crowdfunding 156

customer base, serving 91

data synthesis 79

Decent Work and Economic Growth 9

decoupling, meaning 85

definition practices *41*

de-identification 86, 88

de Jong, Ronald 222

deliberation 32

deliberative innovation process, facilitation 34

deliberative thinking 40

de-naturalization 107

design, wordcloud *60*

development assistance committee (DAC) countries, assistance 102

development banks/institutions 151

development impact bonds (DIBs) 156

development management 99; criticisms 105; NGOs, relationship 103–105; popularity 107; relations, inequality 108

development NGOs, rise 101–103

develop, wordcloud *7*

Discovery IQ PET CT scanners 238, 241

disenfranchised communities: MNC market opportunities 48, 63; socio-economic inequalities 63

displacement areas 212

diversity and inclusion advisory board, impact (Barilla) 36

diversity, business case 21

DLA procedure 56

d.light, achievements 50, 66

"doing well by doing good" 20

Doriot, Georges 157

double-entry bookkeeping 37

Doughnut Economics, concept 117–118

Dow Jones Sustainability Index 24

Du Mortier, Stephane 221

DuPont, Solae 47, 49

dynamic systems models, creation 79–80

EBSCO host 52, 53

ecological interdependencies 126–127

economic goals, primacy 33

economic value, examination 37

economies of scale, reverse innovation (usage) 254–255

ecosystem approach 146

"elements of value" 132

emergent culture, concept 227

empowerment: emphasis 61; freedom, equivalence 49–50

enabling actors, operation 151

engineered networks, defining 123

Enterprise and Supplier Development 203

Enterprise Development Intermediary 199

enterprises, social impact/financial return generation 147

entrepreneurial ventures 154; challenges 202

environmental mistreatment 33

environmental, social, and governance (ESG) criteria, noncompliance 157

environmental, social, and governance (ESG) data (Thomson Reuters) 24

environmental, social, and governance (ESG) investment, focus 142, 144

environmental sustainability discourse, integration 51

environmental topics, issues 23

equilibrium states, dynamism 76

equity crowdfunding, usage 156

equity investors, impact 150

Essilor International (mobile eye clinics) 47
ethical banks 151
ethics, topic (examination) 63
EU Programme for Employment and Social
    Innovation (EaSI) 141
European Anti-Poverty Network 119
European Federation for Street Children 119
European Federation of Food Banks 119
European Fund for Strategic Investments
    (EFSI) 141
European Investment Bank (EIB): Social
    Impact Accelerator 141; Social Impact
    Bond Co-investment Fund 141
European Social Survey 182
European Union, non-financial reporting
    directive 23
European Venture Philanthropy Association
    (EVPA), impact investing concept 142–143
Europe, impact investing (development
    barriers) 153–154
evidence-based medicine, usage 173
experiences, management 75
external accountability, contributions 169

face-to-face engagement 231
facilitative infrastructure 148
Fairphone, smartphone offering 31
filtering, role 86
finance first, impact first (distinction) 150
financial dependence, patterns
    (alteration) 201
financial instruments 154–157
financial models 156
financial return, generation 147
firm-stakeholder interactions, review 35–36
Fix Forward (FF) 9–10; challenges 199;
    contractor profile 195; discussion
    questions 207; economic impact
    highlights (2018) 196–197; funding,
    staged model 206; hybrid organization
    case 190; hybrid organizing, perspective
    201–202; institutional context 193–201;
    introduction 190–193; matric results 192;
    mission 195; South Africa, CSI spend
    204; South Africa, unemployment levels
    (education analysis) 193; sustainable
    development goals 191; sustainable
    funding dilemma 202–205; theoretical
    analysis 201–205; training, challenge 199;
    website photos 191, 198
flexibility, emphasis 227
for-profit logic 72
foundations 152
fragile settings: antenatal care, cross-sector
    collaboration (setup) 213–214; health,
    value co-creation 211
fragmented traditions 260

frames, semantic evolution 66
framing: theories, occurrence 64; work 65
freedom: empowerment, equivalence 49–50;
    promotion 175, 177
Freeman, Edward 21
Friedman, Milton 17–18
FTSE4Good Index 24
functional profiles, creation 129
Funding, staged model 206

G8 Social Impact Investing Taskforce
    (SIIT) 141
GAVI vaccine alliance/partnership 116, 118,
    123, 126
General Electric (GE) 237–238;
    achievements 66; clean slate approach
    242–245, 251–253; defeaturing
    251–253; design team, cost reduction
    challenges 247–248; ECG development
    11, 251–255; ECG machine, usage
    (ease) 250; economies of scale, reverse
    innovation (usage) 254–255; experience
    10–11; experience, questions (discussion)
    256; glocalization 253–254; healthcare
    affordability strategy 239–245; healthcare
    revenue 241; high impact areas, selection
    241; high quality/clinic efficacy, ensuring
    247–248; India strategy 235, 251–255;
    institutional dualism, overcoming
    251–253; MACi 247; MACi, development
    251; MAC project beginnings 245–247;
    medical devices, affordability 240; off-
    the-shelf products, usage 249–250;
    organizational structure, development
    241–242; parent technological resources
    (leveraging) 242; situated innovation
    253–254; sustainable development goals
    (SDGs) 236; theoretical framework
    251–255, 252; wordcloud 11
General Electric (GE) MAC 400 (low-cost
    portable ECG) 238; description (promo
    material) 248, 249; development 11,
    245–251; distribution challenges 250–251;
    partnerships, building 250–251
General Social Survey 182
genetic algorithms, usage 75
Germany, legal standards 22
Girei, Emanuela 6, 99
global development, NGO involvement
    (increase) 103
Global Entrepreneurship Monitor (GEM)
    report 193
Global Financial Crisis (2008) 194
Global Impact Investing Network (GIIN):
    financial instruments classification
    154–155; impact investing study 140, 144;
    R3 Coalition 159

274 *Index*

Global Impact Investing Rating System (GIIRS) 144
Global North: actors role, dominance 105; maternal mortality, contrast 212
Global Reporting Initiative (GRI) 124
Global South: divisions 104–105; economic decline 101; maternal mortality, contrast 212; NGOs, impact 111
governance: external structures, focus 40; impact 31–32; networks 119; principles 32; quality 175, 177, structures 33, 130
governmental infrastructure 148
governments 152
Grameen Bank 200
Grameen microfinance initiatives 50
"Grand Challenges" 118
grand dependency, problem 154
grassroots: aspirations 99; involvement, decrease 105
green bonds 155
greenhouse gas emissions, company responsibility 18
Greenpeace 119
greenwashing 23
guarantees 155
Guatemala, Covid outbreak (impact) 16

healthcare: affordability (GE strategy) 235; compounded annual growth rate (CAGR) 238–239; indicators (country comparison) 237; per capital healthcare expenditure, medical devices expenditure/income comparison 237; robotics, usage 4; rural-urban divide (India) 238; total healthcare expenditure, GDP percentage 237
health field officers (HFOs), quotes collection 219
Healthymagination 237
herding spaces, connections 86
heterogeneous ecosystems, components diversity 149
high net-worth individuals 152
high-risk cooperation problems 128
high-risk pregnancy (HRP): cards, collaboration 225; co-create process, visualization 220; co-creation approaches, emphasis 228–229; compromise/flexibility, pursuit 227–228; implications 229, 231; Referral Cards 10, 216–218; referral cards, tool description 216–218; referral tool, deployment 219; tool case 221; tool, outcome (testing/refining) 219, 221; trust formation/consolidation, theoretical analysis 221–229
high-risk pregnancy (HRP) referral tool 211; antenatal care, cross-sector collaboration

213–221; co-creation process 214–216; sustainable development goals (SDGs) 212
HIV/AIDS campaigns, issues 177
HO structures, discussion 201–202
human development 102
hybrid behaviour, instigation 90
hybrid entities, heterogeneity 153
hybridity, term (usage) 201
hybrid logic, achievement 90
hybrid organizations: adaptation, organizing tensions iterative model 87; adaptive challenges 76; adaptive outcome attainment 83; belonging tensions, adaptation 86, 88; challenges 72–73; data synthesis 79; functioning/development 74; learning (systematic literature review) 72–75; learning tensions, adaptation 80, 82–83; learning tensions iterative adaptive process model 84; literature clustering 80; literature results clustering 81; literature review results 77; logic tensions, types 81; management implications 91, 94; mapping tensions 93; methods 76–79; operations, transparency 94; organizational capability (OC) process 83; organizing tensions, adaptation 83, 85–86; performing tensions, adaptation 90–91; PRISMA flow diagram 77; results/discussion 79–80; search keywords 78; search strategy 78–79; social/commercial values, defining 153; tensions, adaptation 80–91

ideas/plans/issues, inclusive/deliberative (responsible innovation principle) 32
identity transformation 86
impact assessment, iterative characteristic 183
impact capital chain 147
impact investing 140; action orientation 157; actors, involvement 146–153; blended value 141–143; capital chain 147; capital providers 150–151; capital providers, description 151–152; concept (EVPA) 142–143; defining, ambiguity 8; definition, evolution 143–145; definitions, summary 145–146; development 148; development barriers 153–154; ecosystem 8, 148–150, 149; field, history/definition 141–145; GIIN study 140; mainstream investing, merger 159; organizational actors, relationship 153; phases 143–145; term, coining 141; trajectory 157–160
impact investment types, continuum 142
impact investors, recognition 142
impact research 168
impression management 169
improving actors, role 151

include/engage 32
inclusion 32
India, healthcare: cardiovascular device market 238–239; clean slate approach 242–245; high impact areas, selection 241; India for India strategy 240–241; indicators (country comparison) 237; rural-urban divide 238; sector, overview 238–239; sector, study 46–47; strategy 240–241
individual learning (organizational learning form) 75
information asymmetry, reduction 254–255
innovation: development 48; impact, assessment 35–36; issues, anticipation 40; organizational approach 39; problem definition, relationship 39–40; process 31; reverse innovation, achievement 255; situated innovation, identification 253; social/environmental impact reporting 37; types, expansion 32–33
Innovation Union Initiatives 140
innovator: responsibility, increase 40–41; wordcloud 5
institutional dualism, overcoming (GE) 251–253
institutionalization, meaning 129–130
institutional logics, divergence 90
institutional work 5
insurance-based systems 2340
integrated reporting (IR), International Integrated Reporting Council creation 38
intended/unintended consequences, anticipation (responsible innovation principle) 32
intentionality 144
interconnectedness 264–265
interdependent subproblems 117–118
inter-generational justice 51
Intergovernmental Panel on Climate Change (IPCC), oil/gas industry (impact) 19
intermediaries, impact 147
internal stakeholders, institutional compliance (perception) 85
international aid, alternative 48
International Committee of the Red Cross (ICRC) 118, 211, 213–221; co-creation process 214–216; health field officers (HFOs), quotes collection 219; HRP referral tool, deployment 219; images/photos 216–218; mission 215; partnership 10; tripartite cooperation, visualization 214
international development: managerialism, adoption 6; performance culture, impact 104
International Integrated Reporting Council: IR development 38; ISO26000 124

international NGOs (INGOs), pressure (increase) 104–105
intervention, complexity 174
intervention logic model 176
investments, exit strategies 160
investors, power shift 184
invest, wordcloud 9
iPhone, production (harm) 31
irresponsible innovation, transition 33–34
ISO26000 (International Integrated Reporting Council) 124

Jaiswal, Anand Kumar 10, 235
John F. Welch Technology Centre (JFWTC) 242, 245, 246
Joosse, Koen 10, 211

Kaplan, Sarah 20–21
key performance indicators (KPIs), usage 144
"Konzernverantwortung" (Switzerland) 22
Krlev, Gorgi 8, 167
Kumar, Arun 6, 99

Latent Dirichlet Allocation (LDA) model 47, 53
launching actors, role 151
learning: experiences management 75; failure, impact 76; literature, information 74; occurrence 75; resolution literature, theme 82–83; systematic literature review 72
learning tensions 77–78, 94; adaptation 80, 82–83; iterative adaptive process model 84
legal forms, impact 34–35, 41
legal person, limited liability/rights (privilege) 17
legitimacy oriented motivations 122
lending, usage 156
Le Slip Français, social/environmental goals 35
LGBTQ employees, Barilla (impact) 36
life expectancies 1
life-serving economy, profit maximization (impact) 18
Lifestyle of Health and Sustainability (LOHAS) 263
literature clustering 80
literature results clustering, types 81
literature review: results 77; systematic literature review 72–75
local health systems, disempowerment 110
logical framework analysis (LFA) 104
logic model 168, 174; complexity 175
logics, hybridization tendency 90
logic tensions: impact 6; types 81
LOGIQ A3 ultra sound device 238
longitudinal quantitative data, usage 181

276 *Index*

low-income markets, innovation
(development) 48
low-middle-income countries (LMICs) 211,
239, 240; machine tolerance 244; markets,
price sensitivity 242–243; MNC country
heads, responsibilities 241
low-profit limited liability company (L3C),
non-financial purposes 34–35
Lui, Patray 10, 211
Lullaby Phototherapy system 238

MAC 400 (low-cost portable ECG) 247;
description (GE promo material) 248, 249;
development 11, 245–251
MAC 5000 245
MAC 5500 ECG 245, 246
MACi 247; development 251
macro contexts 263; challenges,
organizational responses 262
management: orthodoxy, criticism 106–107;
principles, priority 103; pro-social values
90–91
managerial burden, increase 76
managerial imperatives, denaturalizing
107–108
managerialism: adoption 6; ideology, CMS
challenge 101
managerialization, consequences 104
mandated networks, voluntary networks
(distinction) 123–124
mapping tensions (hybrid organizations) 93
Marinov, Kristian 5, 72
market organizations, responsible innovation
33–34
market rate investments 154
markets, wordcloud 61
Martinez, Esperanza 222
MaxQDA, usage 55
measurement, monetization/challenges 172
mediating role 86
medical device: affordability 240; innovation
235
Mediterranean Renewable Energy Centre
125
mental map 75
mentorship, focus 197
Metz, Ashley 1, 4, 5, 8, 12, 31, 72, 140, 260
micro-activities 107
micro business 149
micro contexts 263; challenges,
organizational responses 262
microfinance 144; approach 48
microfinance institutions 152
micro-level action 263
micro-level negotiations 85–86
micro-meso-macro interdependencies
261, 263

micro-performances 107
micro-results 107
Millennium Development Goals 1
mission drift, threat 83
mission related investments (MRIs) 157
Mondragon Corporation 157
motivation, cognition translation 86
motivations/assumptions, reflective
(responsible innovation principle) 32
moving actors, role 151
MSCI Climate Change ESG Index 24
MSCI Emerging markets-China, addition 25
multi-actor initiatives 23
multinational corporations (MNCs)
52, 240; BOP efforts 59–60; failure
64; opportunities 48; prominence,
disappearance 56; role 56
multi-organizational systems, collaboration/
coordination requirement 120
multi-party governance systems, usage
123–124
multi-sector partnerships 116
multi-stakeholder collaborations, usage 211
multi-stakeholder partnerships (MSPs)
221–229; challenges/enablers 230;
organizational culture 226–227; questions,
discussion 232; social impact 222; trust
224–226; trust, co-evolution 226–227
multi-stakeholder (cross-sector) partnerships,
definitions 223
mutual commitment, focus 50
mutual value, concept 61

Narayana Health: achievements 66; BOP
strategy 46–47, 49
narratives 47, 54–55; organizational meta-
narratives 88; semantic evolution 66;
summary, appropriateness 79
National Environmental Policy Act, response
37
nation states, global agreements
(transformative changes) 3
negotiation: outcomes 85–86; phases/
commitment/execution, distinction 129
neoliberal reforms, development agenda
domination 101
Nespresso (Nestlé) sustainable supply chain
network 124, 125
net value, calculation 31
Network Administrative Organization
(NAO) network 125–126
network governance, adjustment 128
networks: development stage 129–130;
differentiation 124; evaluation,
complications 132; formation, link
132; governance, ideal modes 125;
organizational networks 116, 120–122;

problem, type 128–129; types 127–128; types, distinction/evolution 123–124; wordcloud 9

"new commons" school of thought 50

new social funding 140; field, history/definition 141–145

Nike, World Shoe project 47, 49

non-communicable diseases (NCDs), acceleration 235–236

non-conformity, disguising 127

non-financial models 156

Non-Governmental Organization (NGO) 99; advocacy 100; defining 100; "democratizers of development" 99; development management, relationship 103–105; development NGOs, rise 101–103; evolution *106*; involvement, increase 103; local NGOs, inclusion 51; management, impact 6; managerial imperatives, denaturalizing 107–108; managerialization, consequences 104; meanings/organizational forms, plurality 100; mission/legitimacy, voiding 109; operational autonomy, weakening 104; policy/practice, lessons 111–112; political role 7; power asymmetries, focus 108–110; scepticism 106–107; support 111; tensions, modelling *106*; wordcloud 7

Non-Government Development Organization (NGDO), focus 100

nonstakeholders, stakeholders (separation) 22

NPO legal entity 197–198

NPO sector 204

official development assistance (ODA) 102; financial flows *102*

oil/gas industry, alternative research financing 19

operational capacity, value delivery 167

operational strategy, complexity 175

operations, disruption 88

organic growth 149

organizational activities 179; examples, discovery (difficulty) 177; triggers 184

organizational approaches, situating 260

organizational capabilities (OCs) 80, 82–83; development, iterative enactment/feedback 83; process *83*

organizational culture 225–226; defining 225; holistic perspective 82

organizational forms, active tools 3–4

organizational goals, range 35

organizational identity, filtering/mediating rol 86

organizational innovation processes, re-orientation 37

organizational learning: forms 75–76; literature, development 73; requirements 75

organizational learning capabilities (OLCs) 82–83

organizational memory, importance 75–76

organizational meta-narratives 88

organizational networks 116, 118; discussion 132–134; evaluation process 130–132; existence, reason 120–122; function, process 126–130; governance 124–126

organizational participatory structures, impact 35–36

organizational practices, RI manifestation 33

organizational practices/structures, role 31

organizational processes, manipulation 74

organizational structure, development (GE) 241–242

organizational survival/success, learning (importance) 74

organizations: agentic capacity, mobilization 91; BOP strategies, change 64; challenges, reaction 73; collaborative arrangements 116; coping modes 85; fluctuations 74; goals, multiplicity 265–266; performance, measurement 178; problems, solutions 38–39; role, monitoring 128; rules/controls, constraints 75; theories 121–122

organized, wordcloud 7

organizing, new forms (challenges) 1

organizing tensions 78; adaptation 83, 85–86; iterative model of adaptation *87*

organizing, wordcloud *10*

Orientalist, term (usage) 108

output-based aid (OBA), usage 107

outputs, focus 171

overarching stories 88

Overseas Development Assistance (ODA) 194

paradoxes, defining 76

participatory development 102

participatory structures: impact 35–36, *41*; role 36

partnership: expectations, management 229; institutionalization 129; rhetoric 104–105; wordcloud *11*

"partnership for the goals" 118

"Pay for Success" 156

payments-by-results (PbR) 107, 156

performance: culture, impact 104; management 169

performing tensions 78, 943; adaptation 90–91; iterative model of adaptation *92*

PET/CT scanner, market penetration 2431

philanthropic foundations, development actors (partnership) 109–110

philanthropic investing 143

philantrocapitalism 109

Philips Experience Design (PED) 118, 211, 213–221; co-create methodology 228;

278 *Index*

mission *215*; partnership 10; tripartite cooperation, visualization *214*
Philips Foundation (PF) 118, 211, 213–221; mission *215*; partnership 10; tripartite cooperation, visualization 214
Pohlmann, Paul 18
positive value spillover 201–202
post-conflict zones 212
post-development 102
postnatal care, delivery (complexity) 213
poverty: alleviation 50, 52; eradication 109
power asymmetries 122; focus 108–110
powerlessness, underdevelopment (equivalence) 49–50
pragmatic idealists 150
preferential procurement 203
Pre-post comparison 179
pre-post quantitative testing 184
Primary Health Care (PHC) resource centre 219
PRISMA flow diagram *54, 77*
PRISMA guidelines 76–77
private donors, development financial flows (evolution) *110*
private investors 152
problem conceptualization 38–40, *41*
problem definition: innovations, relationship 39–40; shift 40
process evaluation, usage 180
Procter & Gamble, water purification powder 47
product, wordcloud *11*
profit maximization 17–18
program related investments (PRIs) 157
project cycle management 104
Public Benefit Organisation 199
public investors, private investors (contrast) 150–151
public private partnerships 119
public-private partnerships, impact 131

Quakers, investment/value alignment 141
qualitative data collection/analysis, importance 184
qualitative methods, usefulness 181
quantitative data: generation 180–181; longitudinal quantitative data, usage 181
quantitative method, usage 180

Raab, Jörg 1, 4, 9, 12, 15, 116, 190, 260
Raja, V. 2344
Rana Plaza disaster 22
Rathert, Nikolas 4, 31
rationalization process 158
realist evaluation 173, 184
Red Cross Kenya, operation 219, 229
reflective innovation process, facilitation 34

reflexivity 32, 40
Reid, Grant 18
Renewable Energy and Energy Efficiency Partnership (REEEP) 125
Resource Based Theory of the Firm 121
resource oriented motivations 122
Response, Recovery, and Resilience Investment Coalition (R3 Coalition) (GIIN) 159
responsibility, defining (difficulty) 18
responsible innovation (RI) 31; dimensions 37; dimensions (integration), innovation (enabling) *41*; discussion 40–41; governance structures 34–36; legal forms, impact 34–35; manifestation 33; organizational practices 36–40; participatory structures 35–36; principles *32*; principles, application 32–33; principles, embedding 38; problem conceptualization 38–40; shift 33–34; social accounting 37–38
responsive (responsible innovation principle) *32*
responsive innovation process, facilitation 34
responsiveness 32
return on investment (ROI), seeking 145
reverse innovation, achievement 255
rights-based development 102
rights, promotion 175, 177
Rocchi, Simona 10, 211
Rockefeller Foundation, impact investing origination 140, 141
Roundtable on Sustainable Palm Oil 23

SAB Miller: achievements 66; local economic support 50
Salvation Army 119
sanitation, access (improvement) 171
Saraswati Cristin, Stephanie 10, 211
scaling: difficulties, threat 83; rapidity 149
scepticism 106–107
SC Johnson, home-cleaning services 47
search keywords *78*
search strategy 78–79
second-order framing 64
Sectoral Education and Training Authorities (SETAs) 200–201
selective coupling 85
self-declared goals, achievement 133
self-determination, commitment 6
Sen, Amartya 49
sensemaking: importance 86; process 88
sequential interdependencies 120
serendipitous networks, defining 123
shared value 20
shareholders: responsibility 17–18; value, primacy 33

Simanis, Erik 66
Simputer 49
situated innovation, identification 253
SMMEs, financial independence 197
social accounting 37–38, *41*
social bonds 155–156
Social Business, concept 170
social businesses 34
Social Business Initiative (SBI) 140–141
social change, NGO Focus 103–104
social context, importance 179–180
social-ecological networks 119; impact 123
social-ecological system, coordination
    capacity 131
social enterprises (SE) 200–201; emergence
    194; Fix Forward 194; income level,
    generation (problem) 154; logic tensions,
    impact 6; revenue generation, importance
    202; running 94
social entrepreneurship 48
social/environmental outcomes, accounting
    (requirements) 183
social finance 143–144
social impact: appreciation 184; assessment
    strategy, formation 173–183; attribution,
    challenges 171; creation 144; data types
    172–173; generation 147; intervention
    logic model *176*; interventions, complexity
    (differences) *177*; logic model *174*;
    measurement 170; outputs, focus 171;
    research designs, types 172–173; scope/
    measures, defining 177–178
Social Impact Accelerator (EIB) 141
social impact bonds (SIBs) 144, 156
social impact evaluation 167; fascination
    169–170
social impact, measurement: data types
    180–181; design, control group (usage)
    178–179; design, pre-post comparison
    179; design, realist approach 180; design,
    selection 178–180; design, transformation
    process focus 179–180; goal, complexity/
    clarification 174–177; malpractice/
    consequences 170–173; measures, refining
    181–182; monetization/challenges 172;
    pre-testing 182–183; study, execution
    182–183; theory/practice, implications
    183–184
social imprinting 88
social inclusion bond (CEB) 155–156
social innovations: impact, reduction 36;
    need, growth 34
social investment funds 155
Social Investment Package (SIP) 141
social justice, commitment 6
social lending, usage 156
socially acceptable messages, crafting 65

Socially Responsible Investment (SRI) 144;
    exclusions 142; role 141
social network theory 121
social return on investment (SROI) 167, 170;
    ex ante-ex post observation 172–173;
    methodology, usage 145; reports, analysis
    172; review 172–173; seeking 145; studies,
    analysis 170; systematic review 172–173
social sanction, defining 17
social service provision, user-oriented
    evaluation 182
social stock exchanges 152
social transformation logic 111
social value: creation 201; creation,
    requirements 76; defining 153
social venture capital funds, usage 149
social, wordcloud 9
societies: public health emergencies 2; rules,
    differences 265–266
socio-economic disparities, impact 1
socio-economic inequalities, reduction 63
Solae (DuPont) 47, 49
South Africa: children, performance
    (problems) 192; Corporate Social
    Investment (CSI) spend *204*; GEM
    report 193; Sectoral Education and
    Training Authorities (SETAs) 200–201;
    unemployment levels, education analysis
    193
South America, economic development
    (impact) 117
stakeholders: approach 21; corporate
    responsibility perspective 21–22;
    engagement 35–326; group, focus (shift)
    39; internal stakeholders, institutional
    compliance (perception) 85; mobililization
    220; multi-stakeholder partnerships
    221–229; multi-stakeholder (cross-sector)
    partnerships, definitions 223; needs,
    response 34; nonstakeholders, separation
    22; relationships, network 147; sub-
    interpretations 22; well-being, increase 23
STATA 14.0, usage 53–54
state-led development practices,
    disillusionment 101–102
Strategic Management (Freeman) 21
strategic management, stakeholder approach
    21
sub-problems, interdependencies 128–129
success factors 127
Sultany, Zahra 10, 211
"Super Wicked Problems" 117–118, 127
sustainability: business case 21; change,
    urgency 16; partnerships 128–129; trend,
    leveraging 143
sustainability issues 127; awareness, growth
    116–117

280 *Index*

sustainable circuity, development 261
sustainable development 52; organizational
  networks 116; organizing, integrated
  view 260
sustainable development goals (SDGs)
  191, 211, 212, 236; connections 4;
  development, measurement 107; problems
  7–8; public-private partnerships,
  impact 131
Sustainable Development Goals Quality
  Education 9
symbolic recomposition 94

tailored financing 144
tax avoidance practices, political dispute 22
tax-based systems 2340
technological resources, leveraging 242
Tejas XR 2000 X-Ray machine 238
TEMPORG, selective coupling 85
tensions: adaptation 80–91; resolution
  literature, theme 82–83; types 80, 94
tertiary emissions 18
The Energy and Resources Institute
  (TERI) 125
"theory of change" 174
Thompson's typology, usage 120
topic modeling 52; usage 65; value,
  appreciation 54–55
topic modeling analysis 46, 56, *57–58,*
  59–61, 63; wordcloud *59–61*
topics, user-inputted number 56
Toschi, Laura 8, 140
total healthcare expenditure, GDP percentage
  237
Tracking Universal Health Coverage report
  213
traditional birth attendants (TBAs) 212, 215,
  219
"tragedy of the commons," avoidance 121
training, challenge 199
transactional infrastructure 148
transaction costs, minimization 121
Transaction Cost Theory 121
tri-dimensional space: axes, topics/words
  (presence) 56; translation 53
tripartite cooperation 231; missions,
  overview *215;* visualization *214*
triple-bottom-line visibility (3BL) 157
trust: building, literature 221–222;
  co-evolution 226–227; density 126;
  evolution 229–230; expression 223–224;
  formation/consolidation, theoretical
  analysis 221–229
trusted-based relationships 50

underdevelopment, powerlessness
  (equivalence) 49–50
UNICEF 118, 192
Unilever, shampoo distribution 49
United Nations Global Compact (UNGC) 23,
  24, 124; adoption rate 25
United Nations Sustainable Development
  Framework 2
United Nations Sustainable Development
  Goals 2, 15, 117, 190; "Partnerships for
  the Goals" 133
US Community Reinvestment Act 157
user-oriented evaluation 182

validate, wordcloud 59
"valid causal inference," arrival 181
value co-creation: multi-stakeholder
  collaborations, usage 211; multi-
  stakeholder partnerships 221–229; process
  231
value creation, concept 145
value generation 141–142
value spillover 202
Varghese, Oswin 246, 249
venture capital (VC) industry, investment
  practices (comparison) 150
venture philanthropy 144
Venture Philanthropy, concept 170
ViaVia Café 82–83
visualization techniques, usage 65
Volkswagen emissions scandal 22
voluntary networks, mandated networks
  (distinction) 123–124

water purification powder (P&G) 47
Web of Science 52, *53,* 78–79
Wille, Guillermo 242
Wirecard accounting scandal 22–23
within-community power dynamics 51
women, empowerment 177
wordclouds *4–11;* derivation 55; production
  54–55
working, *a priori* proof (nonnecessity) 82
Work Integration Social Enterprises
  (WISEs) 79
World Bank 119, 211
World Economic Forum 167
World Health Organization (WHO) 119,
  211; CVDs, impact 239
World Shoe project (Nike) 47, 49
World Values Survey 182
World Wildlife Fund (WWF) 119

Yunus, Muhammad 159

Printed in the United States
by Baker & Taylor Publisher Services